Shared Intimacies

Also by Lonnie Barbach

Shared
Intimacies

WOMEN'S SEXUAL
EXPERIENCES

Lonnie Barbach, Ph.D.
and Linda Levine, A.C.S.W.

ANCHOR PRESS/DOUBLEDAY
GARDEN CITY, NEW YORK

To all of the women in our families past and present who nourished us with their love.

To Alberto Villoldo, my husband, my lover, and my dearest friend.

To Robert Kutler, who believed in me and L.B. and helped make this book a reality.

L.L.

Contents

Contents

Acknowledgments

This was a time-consuming and sometimes difficult collaboration that grew out of a long-standing personal and professional relationship. Although we drew on our combined skills as sex educators, therapists, and interviewers, we also wish to acknowledge our separate contributions: Linda for conceiving the idea for the book and Lonnie for having the experience and skills to materialize it.

Shared Intimacies could never have been written without the help and support of our many friends and colleagues. We are indebted to Paul Fargis for his guidance on the initial stages of the book and to Loretta Barrett, our editor at Anchor Press, for her enthusiasm and expertise. Our agent, Rhoda Weyr, for her ongoing caring and support. Alan Margolis and Mark Glasser were invaluable in providing us with the necessary medical information.

The typing requirements for this manuscript were enormous. All of the interviews had to be transcribed and the manuscript itself required numerous retypings. We would have been lost without Kathy Adams, Joan Delaney, and Sharon Bauman-Leach, who carried out the major typing responsibilities, and Laurel Wensel, Carmel Densley, and Angela Tillin, whom we could count on in times of emergency.

x   *Acknowledgements*

We also appreciated our friends and colleagues who arranged interviews, provided technical information, and gave of their time and energy at various stages of the manuscript:

Rosalind Andrews, Elaine Blank, Jane Browning, Cheryl Chisholm, Norma Davidoff, Pat Deloreme, Ken Dychtwald, Caroline Fromm, David Geisinger, Rita Martin, Barry McCarthy, Jeanne Mitchler-Fiks, Beverly Richmond, and Kathy Tyler Scott.

Finally, we are indebted to all of the women who were willing to share with us the pleasure and sometimes the pain of their intimate sexual relationships. There would have been no book without them.

Introduction

"I'm very sensual. So one of my most favorite things to do with my partner is to give and get a complete body massage prior to having sex," said thirty-five-year-old Sharon, a teacher who is divorced and living alone. "My partner and I lie on the floor, on a blanket or sheet thrown over a soft rug. The lights are off except for a candle. I like to have music playing softly in the background. Oftentimes, before I start the massage, I will use flowers from a vase on the floor to caress my partner's body. Sometimes I might use a silk scarf instead of flowers. Then I start with the body massage. I use olive oil because it absorbs so beautifully into the skin, and my personal preference is to add rose water to the olive oil. I pour a little of the massage oil into my hand and then hold it over the candle to warm the oil. This massage oil goes on so beautifully that I can give a very sensual massage without very much physical effort. I love the silky, slick feeling I get when our oiled bodies touch. By the time we have made love, we don't even need to take a shower because the olive oil has absorbed into our skin. If we use a sheet on the floor, then all I need to do the next morning is to pick up the sheet and throw it into the washing machine—no mess to clean up."

Until recently, there has been little opportunity for this explicit sexual sharing to take place in our culture. Although it is possible to ask your aunt Mary about her unique recipe for chocolate chip cookies, it is not permissible to obtain the same specific information on her favorite lovemaking techniques. And if problems occur with a recipe or with child rearing, or if an appliance breaks down, we are able to telephone a neighbor, a friend, or a professional to assist us. But when we have a problem with our sexual life, we frequently keep it all to ourselves and do not worry about it until the problem grows into a crisis. By the time we seek professional help, it is seen as a last resort and we feel like a total failure if that step is necessary.

We, as psychotherapists specializing in female sexual problems, are particularly aware of this cultural syndrome. Over the years, we have learned much about the factors involved in women's enjoyment of their sexuality through running preorgasmic women's groups, therapy groups designed to assist women who are not yet orgasmic. Much of this information was imparted in the book *For Yourself: The Fulfillment of Female Sexuality*, by Lonnie Barbach. Yet intuitively we knew there was still much more to be learned—little tidbits that could add fun and enjoyment to a sexual relationship.

This book has evolved from our accumulated experience in running educational and therapy workshops for women. During this process, we began to realize how much information women attending these programs had to share with each other and how unusual it was for this exchange of information to be taking place in our culture. Many women participated in the workshops out of curiosity, out of an interest in improving and enriching their sexual relationships. Others came with questions or problems they had been unable to resolve. Some worried that their need for clitoral stimulation was excessive, some didn't feel that they experienced orgasm quickly enough, and others felt uncomfortable that their children might walk into the room in the middle of sex. Often, the group provided them, for the first time in their lives, with the opportunity to talk to other women explicitly about sexuality and sexual problems. The workshops provided a forum to solve problems that had been bothering some women for years, simply because the necessary knowledge and information was available within the group.

We realized that if this much information could be shared in a two-hour program with a small group of women, a plethora of ideas could result from interviewing a large number of women from different backgrounds, of different ages, and with different relationship experiences. Making this information available in book form would enable us to reach many more women than would ever be possible through running workshops.

Another part of our excitement was the realization that we could assist in removing the cultural barriers to a free exchange of information concerning female sexuality. Both men and women are often not aware of the range of sexual preferences and practices among women. Society has placed men in the role of sexual teachers; most women learn about sexuality from their first male partners. Even lesbians often have their first sexual experiences with men. Armed only with information gleaned from books and peers, a man is burdened with the role of orchestrating the sexual act, initiating the various sexual activities, and satisfying both his partner and himself. He is expected to carry out this task without any input from women, who are considered to be too pure, and therefore too inexperienced, to have any sexual ideas of their own. Women learn whether they are good lovers, whether their responses are normal or abnormal, and which lovemaking techniques are appropriate from their male partner's response and approval. And if the woman's early partner's style differs from her own, she is left feeling inadequate or abnormal. She might find herself wondering why rapid thrusting does not turn her on or why sex in the missionary position leaves her unsatisfied. She may feel it takes her too long because he comes more quickly or that her genitals are dirty because he dislikes oral sex. What a difference it would have made if she could have exchanged information with other women; if she could have used other women as resources for questions, for role models, and for new ideas. This would also relieve the pressure on men to be omniscient, to be the teachers, the initiators. If women were more knowledgeable, more assertive, and more creative sexually, then the flow of communication could be more equal in relationships between men and women. We felt that writing a book like *Shared Intimacies* would contribute to the evolutionary process of freeing communication among women, and hence, between men and women. The prospect was exciting to us and we enthusiastically began our interviews.

In general, we interviewed women who felt good about their sexuality since we did not want the book to be one of dysfunction, but one of celebration of what we do well as sexual women, what we enjoy, and what we have resolved sexually. Not that everything about the sex life of the women we interviewed was perfect; each had areas she was working on and did not feel entirely good about, but each had struggled successfully in other areas. For example, one woman had a number of very innovative ways for keeping her sexual relationship active despite the presence of children, but was totally unable to communicate her sexual preferences to her husband. Women who believed that sexuality should not be talked about so openly, or who were currently inactive sexually, or who were very uncomfortable or unhappy in their sexual relationships either refused to be interviewed, canceled the appointment at the last minute or, when interviewed, provided very little useful information that would enable other women to feel more confident or competent sexually. Hence, we did not include much from those interviews. We concentrated on positive experiences and creative solutions to problems.

Consequently, this book is not designed as a statistical study of a random sample of women to enumerate the number of women who have tried oral sex, participated in group sex, or had premarital intercourse. The fact that we were limited to women who were willing to discuss intimate aspects of their sexuality with a complete stranger automatically biased our sample considerably. We have no information from the perspective of women who feel sexuality is too private a matter to be discussed in an interview.

Instead, *Shared Intimacies* is a compilation of helpful hints and solutions devised by women to deal with the day-to-day problems that affect the sexuality of most people. It is a compilation of the sexual attitudes, activities, and feelings of 120 different women. It

is a potpourri of ideas on how to keep a long-term sexual relationship alive and interesting, how to communicate about sex, how
to creatively minimize the negative effect of work and children
upon one's sex life. It poses solutions for normal difficulties encountered by most women in terms of dealing with pregnancy, the maturing process, and various physical ailments or disabilities that interfere with "sex as usual" and necessitate a change in sexual
activities. It contains models for those of us who are embarking on
our own evolution as females and as sexual beings.

In the beginning, we found our interviewees by two methods:
asking our friends and offering sign-up sheets at the end of our
workshops. After these initial contacts, the women we interviewed
supplied us with from one to ten other names of friends because
they were so excited about the forthcoming book that they felt certain their friends would want to participate. Most did, and we
ended up with far too many names to follow up on all the women
who expressed interest. In one case, a woman who signed up at the
end of one of our workshops telephoned a number of weeks later
asking, "How come you haven't called me? Today is my birthday,
I'm sixty-one years old, and I have a lot to tell you about sex." We
even interviewed one mother-daughter team: an interview with
one woman got her thinking a lot about her mother, at which
point she said, "Gee, I wonder if my mother would like to be interviewed." In our usual manner, strict confidentiality was maintained regarding the information given by the fifty-five-year-old
daughter and her seventy-nine-year-old mother.

Some potential interviewees popped up most unexpectedly. We
called a typist at a typing service which transcribed some of our
tapes, and she requested to be interviewed for the book. In addition, we met women from a church group in a rural town in California who were so enthusiastic about the book that we ended up
interviewing nine women, including the minister's wife.

As we started interviewing, we found there were tremendous
differences sexually among the women we interviewed. There was
no way to tell from a woman's educational background, from the
way she dressed, from her personality, her job, or the way she
walked what she was going to be like sexually. A well dressed, so-

phisticated, verbal woman might have a varied sex life and have no difficulty discussing her sexual exploits, or she might just as easily be ill at ease discussing sex, or have a very rigid and patterned sexual relationship.

There were women throughout the country who talked freely about the importance of their sexual lives, and similarly, there were women everywhere who were uncomfortable discussing the subject. Women from Indiana or Alabama presented as much interesting information as women from California. Unfortunately, we did not obtain a sufficiently large sample to ascertain the percentage of women who were comfortable discussing sexuality versus those who were not in any given area. This was not our purpose in writing the book. However, we did notice differences in style of presentation. Whereas women in Birmingham were just as interested privately in exploring their sexuality as women interviewed in San Francisco, they were often more hesitant about publicly discussing it with other people in their area because the general atmosphere was less permissive.

Consequently, there may have been more conservative women in Atlanta or in a rural town in California than in Washington, D.C., but there were women everywhere who were exploring and experimenting sexually just as there were women in San Francisco who were too uncomfortable talking about sex to be interviewed. A range existed both in small towns and in large cities, in the East, West, South, and North.

The women we interviewed came from a variety of backgrounds (see table on p. xxi); however, they were largely middle- and upper-income, career-oriented women who were either currently active in their work or temporarily discontinuing work to raise a family. The majority of women were heterosexual, some were lesbian, a few were bisexual and related equally to both men and women. We combined these women throughout the book despite their age, marital status, or sexual orientation, in order to show the spectrum of female sexual expression.

The women we interviewed were not only highly educated and articulate but were also interested in discussing sexuality to learn more about it for themselves, even if they were slightly uncomfortable in doing so. In this sense, our sample is comprised of a unique group of women who considered an exchange of specific personal details of lovemaking techniques and their feelings about them, an important dialogue to be established.

Initially some women hesitated to be interviewed because they felt that they had few original or creative sexual experiences to contribute. However, as the interviews proceeded, we found that almost every woman had some innovative sexual experience or idea to share. Some were embarrassed, like Susan, a thirty-six-year-old part-time airline employee, part-time housewife, married for fifteen years with two children, who when asked specifically what made sexual experiences good for her replied, "When I think about a good sexual experience, I feel a nice glow but there isn't anything in particular that I think about. I know there must be. But for some reason, I don't want to say it. I guess it's hard to talk about what pleases me."

To be sure, some interviews were more awkward than others, but the women generally became more relaxed and more willing to share intimate material as the interviews progressed. Our agreement in every interview was that a woman could freely refuse to answer any question without further inquiry. We would merely move on to the next category if there was any discomfort.

For the most part, the women were exceedingly frank in their interviews—so much so that when some women received copies of the excerpts of their transcripts, which we sent out to ensure their confidentiality, they were quite shocked to see their words in black and white. Although they recognized the words used as their own, they were amazed at how candid they had actually been during the interview.

Consequently, although women were surprisingly open about divulging the details of their lovemaking to us, they were often uncomfortable having certain specific sexual experiences going under even their assumed name. Many times they had shared with us a story or incident that they had never told anyone before and were quite anxious to ensure their complete anonymity. Even though all of the women who are quoted have been given pseudonyms, they were concerned that a friend or a past or present lover might recognize one of their stories in the book and in guessing their identity, would break the code. To protect these women and to ensure that they would not be connected to a particular experience, we created a fictitious woman, Ms. X, who doesn't exist at all in reality, but represents a true story told by a woman who is a little too embarrassed to let anybody recognize it as belonging to her.

Since we took only those instances in which women felt good about their sexuality or had found inventive ways of solving a problem, it might appear that none of the women we interviewed were having any difficulties they were unable to overcome and that everyone except you, dear reader, is swinging from the chandeliers in terms of her sex life. This, of course, is far from the truth, which we as sex therapists know only all too well. There are far too many couples for whom sexuality is too onerous a subject to even mention because of their feeling of helplessness in dealing with their problems.

We ended up interviewing some of these women as well. Some felt that talking to us about sex would be a good experience for them. Others just sought a sympathetic ear. Many of these interviews turned out to be more therapy sessions than information-gathering ones. One woman had serious sexual difficulties due to severe communication and relationship problems. Another's spouse's depression resulted in a lack of sexual activity for a period of over ten years. Another woman had recently entered into a marriage with a man who was unable to obtain an erection and who was unwilling to talk about it. And there were more. In these cases, we attempted to offer as much information, expertise, and resources as we were aware of, but generally could do little more than sympathize with the woman's pain. However, since we are writing a book about creative ideas and solutions to problems, the most painful parts of these interviews, due to the unresolved nature of the problems, are not included in this book.

With the exception of editing out duplicate responses and problems without solutions, we have tried to accurately portray the range of behaviors, activities, interests, and desires of the women interviewed. The more women we interviewed, the more voluminous the material became, since every woman was unique and had something different to contribute. We finally stopped the interviews when we realized we would never run out of useful information and we had already collected more material than we could handle.

We have tried not to make judgments about whether activities and experiences are good or bad or right or wrong. Some of the things women have disclosed, such as the smoking of marijuana, are not legal, but we have included them in order to report those activities that people engage in, the things they enjoy sexually, that turn them on and do not seem to cause any harm, either to themselves or to their partners. Some of the women's explicit language may be startling. But we felt it important to convey the women's stories in their own words to better represent the range of differences among women.

You may read about an incident of a particular woman and think, "My goodness, how could she say that?" or, "How could the authors of this book include such an experience?" We are not saying that we necessarily agree with everything we have included, in terms of our own sexual preferences, but we are saying that they are activities that people participate in and find pleasurable. Since we are all unique sexually, what works for one person is not necessarily applicable to another.

This brings us to our purpose in writing this book. One need we hope the book serves is to answer a question which is asked more frequently than any other: "How do you keep a long-term monogamous relationship from becoming boring sexually?" For this purpose *Shared Intimacies* can be used as a resource, either to be read independently with the forethought of trying out some new ideas, or as a game, possibly by randomly picking a page in Chapter 3 and trying out the activity described. Another aim is to provide information and solutions which have worked for women who have encountered a particular sexual problem in their lives. There were, by the way, very few women who did not feel that they had had some sexual problem at some time in their lives which they had successfully overcome.

Shared Intimacies can be used to improve sexual communication in several different ways. The words some women have used to initiate sex or communicate sexual preferences can be practiced in fantasy to see if they "fit," and, once rehearsed successfully, could be practiced with a partner. Also, both partners could read their own copy of the book, underlining the sections which communicate their own interests or needs, and then the copies could be exchanged as an introduction to talking about it, or instead of talking about it.

Shared Intimacies also provides information which can prepare women for experiences that they have not yet had. It could provide a woman who has never been pregnant with some understanding of what other women have experienced sexually during their pregnancy. It might give women a better idea about planning for changes which may result from parenthood in regard to their sexuality and enable parents to provide better information than the infamous Kotex pamphlet. Women in their twenties and thirties frequently ask about what kinds of physiological changes they can expect to experience during and after menopause. Again, the experiences of the women interviewed can provide some sense of the range of responses among women of this age and what factors appear to be responsible for minimizing adverse effects.

Our major intention, however, is to provide the kinds of information and sense of personal sharing which is not yet widely available in the culture in an effort to contribute to the evolutionary process of women owning and enjoying their sexuality. It cannot fully replace direct personal sharing, but it can provide intimate information and models for handling sexuality more comfortably and with greater satisfaction.

We hope to give women permission to try some sexual activities that they have always wondered about or wanted to try, but felt no respectable woman would consider doing. Our sample of upstanding American women indicates that a whole range of sexual activities are enjoyed, depending on the taste and sexual styles and preferences of the people involved. We would not expect that all of the sexual experiences mentioned in the book would appeal to any one person, but the variety provides a range to choose from. And some women or men may never wish to actually engage in *any* of the activities mentioned, but may enjoy including them in their repertoire of sexual fantasies.

But, most importantly, we hope that the material in the book will convey the *excitement* that is generated when women share their sexual feelings and secrets! The women we interviewed conveyed a joyous feeling of celebration, of real accomplishment, as they related their sexual experiences, thoughts, and feelings—sometimes for the first time. For the women we interviewed, sex was an important and fulfilling part of their lives. Sex provided some with exciting adventures, others with a sense of diversion and fun, but for most sex offered a special and intimate way of expressing their love. The women we interviewed chose to participate in the creation of a new level of communication and sexual enjoyment for both men and women. Their hope, as well as our own, is that in sharing their sexual experiences with us, they will add richness, diversity, and joy to yours.

DEMOGRAPHIC DATA

Number of Women Interviewed: 120

AGES		GEOGRAPHIC AREA	
Under 20	2	East Coast	46
20–29	19	South	13
30–39	64	Midwest	14
40–49	16	West	47
50–59	3		
60–69	12		
70 and up	4		

RACE		SEXUAL ORIENTATION	
Caucasian	109	Heterosexual	96
Third World	11	Heterosexual with some experiences with women	8
		Bisexual	2
		Lesbian	6
		Lesbian with some experiences with men	8

WOMEN CURRENTLY MARRIED OR LIVING WITH PARTNER: 71

NUMBER OF YEARS TOGETHER

Under a year	4
1–10 years	50
11–20 years	8
21–30 years	4
31 years and over	5

CHILDREN*	MARRIED OR LIVING TOGETHER	SINGLE MOTHER
Pregnant or child under 1	11	0
Children ages 1–11	26	11
Children 12 and older living at home	12	3
Children grown	13	9

	LIVING WITH A PARTNER	LIVING ALONE
NO CHILDREN	20	28

* Eleven women have children in two age groups and are counted twice.
One woman has children in three age groups and is counted three times.
One divorced lesbian's husband has custody of their children, ages eleven and
fourteen, and is counted as having no children.

OCCUPATION

Accountants	2
Administrators/supervisors	7
Airline personnel	2
Artists/craftswomen	7
Businesswomen	6
Clergywomen	1
Educators/teachers	19
Housewives/mothers	7
Lawyers	2
Mental health professionals	22
Office personnel	7
Physical health professionals	10
Researcher	3
Retired	5
Saleswomen	4
Students	9
Writers/editors	7

1

Qualities of Good Sex

Many people consider exciting sex to be the hallmark of a *new* relationship and experience a diminishing enjoyment and interest as time goes by. This, however, need not be the case, as indicated by Tara after forty-two years of marriage:

It's like anything else that you enjoy and do over and over again. It doesn't get boring any more than the sunset is boring. The sun goes down every day and yet every day it's different.

What makes sex continually enjoyable and interesting for one person and boring or a chore for another? Much of it has to do with knowing which qualities are important in creating a good sexual experience. However, given the historical repression of sexuality in women in this culture, many women simply do not know how to go about creating good sex for themselves.

The culture dictates that women should not talk about sexuality. This is obviously a topic they need not concern themselves with since men are considered the experts on sex and a woman need only wait for the right man and a good sexual relationship will automatically result. The myth goes something like this. Find Mr. Right and you will live happily ever after (both in and out of bed). Women are then placed in the position of learning about sex from their partner(s). Since each man has his own unique sexual style, the sexual style(s) the woman learns are the result of the partner(s) she chooses. If she has sex with only one partner, that is the style she is familiar with.

Women can't really talk with men other than their partners about the ways they like to make love for fear they will appear to be coming on to them. So how can a woman learn about ways of making love that might appeal to her? Theoretically, she could talk with other women; but, practically speaking, this is not easy to do. Because of the personal nature of the subject, it is often difficult to find another woman who is willing to talk about sex explicitly. Initiating the conversation can be quite awkward and uncomfortable. How do you begin such a conversation? How will the friend respond? Will the talk interfere with the friendship? Will she misinterpret the conversation as a sexual overture?

If a woman feels good about her sexuality, she might hesitate to talk with other women for fear her friends will find their experiences mundane in comparison to hers. In this society, women are not generally brought up to compete; it's not quite feminine to be better than others. If she doesn't feel good about her sexuality, she might fear that she will find out that her sexual experiences are a part of the Dark Ages and that she is missing out on what it appears everyone else is enjoying. Many women do not share information out of a need to protect their partners. An explicit discussion, they fear, might expose their partners as being inadequate.

Society just does not give women the same permission to discuss sexuality as it does to discuss other topics. If we cooked a great chicken in a *special* wine sauce for our spouse or lover, we would think nothing of describing the taste, the ingredients, the way the table was set, and the special little touches we used. But we seldom talk about our sexual relationships in that same candid way.

Given the fact that women in this culture have been taught not to talk about sex, you may feel awkward reading certain portions of this book. You may feel you are peeking into the private experiences of women and forget that these women have been willing to share this information with you in an effort not only to open the subject of sexuality for others but also to learn more about themselves.

Another reaction you may have while reading this is that the women we interviewed are very different from you. You may think that if they were able to discuss these topics in detail, they must be loose or promiscuous. However, many women reported that they had never had such an explicit and detailed conversation about sex before the interview and said something like "I've never told anybody this" or "I can't believe I'm saying this." A seventeen-year-old woman who had been having sex for only six months said at one point in the interview: "I feel so strange talking this way. These are things you are just not supposed to talk about." In several instances, when we informed the women that the interview would take about two hours, they said not to plan on such a long time, because they didn't think they had that much to tell us. At the end of two hours, however, the interview was often unfinished and another appointment had to be scheduled. For many women, this was the first opportunity they had ever had to talk about sex so openly.

Women were also curious about the reactions of other women. What had they disclosed? Were their preferences and responses similar to or significantly different from their own?

The first question we asked women was to describe the qualities that, for them, make for a good sexual experience. This question was often not an easy one to answer. Many women simply had never thought about it before. To help them crystallize their ideas, we had them recall those sexual experiences that stood out in their minds and then see which qualities those experiences held in common.

Frequently, the exact nature of a particular quality or why a particular quality was chosen did not become explicit until the end of the interview, when a more complete understanding of the total woman and her sexual relationship(s) could be ascertained. Then the parts began to fit together, like the pieces of a complex puzzle.

At the beginning of the interview, Mary, a forty-eight-year-old artist with four children who was recently divorced from a twenty-seven-year marriage, related the following:

Well, ten years down the road in a marriage and there are a couple of kids, life is very busy, and there isn't a heck of a lot of romance. I mean, you're busy with everyday kind of life stuff. Sure, there's the feeling that sex is an enjoyable experience on both our parts, but above and beyond that, there is something about it which makes me feel special. I'm trying to think of what that is . . . somehow the attention is focused on me as a person and as an important person. It has to do with the surroundings, the setting, change in the time of day, like after lunch is great . . . or something that gives it a special quality. It isn't like a performance . . . like before you go to sleep at night or before you get out of bed in the morning. It's a break in the routine and there's something special about it.

By the end of the two-hour interview, she said:

I guess what makes it important is that making love takes me out of the housewife role. I feel more equal . . . more like going out on a date, that kind of thing. You know, after you've been in a marriage for that long, there's the feeling of being part of the furniture. So anything that breaks it makes it special. When we go out for dinner, I don't want to talk about children, money, in-laws; talking about those things makes me feel like part of the furniture. What was really important was what I was doing, things he was doing . . . more intellectual stuff.

At the conclusion of the interview, it became clear that certain occasions countered her usual view of herself as only a mother/housewife and the resulting enhanced feelings of self-worth led to more enjoyable sex.

What was most interesting was that no one quality stood out as *the* answer for all women. Rather, a range of qualities evolved from the 120 interviews. Each woman's idea of what was important in a good sexual experience reflected her own uniqueness. Every woman's approach to the world is different and each has her own individual idea as to which factors are necessary for a satisfying life. Consequently, it is only natural that each woman would define the conditions necessary for a good sexual experience differently.

In general, relationship factors, such as love for the partner and the comfort, familiarity, and security of an intimate relationship, were considered most important by the majority of the women we talked with. Next came concerns the women had about themselves: their sense of personal desirability and feeling of self-confidence made a significant impact on their enjoyment of a sexual experience. Qualities such as playfulness, illicitness, variety, and sufficient time were also mentioned, but were generally considered to be of lesser importance.

Darielle, who at the age of twenty-seven had been married three years, covered the whole gamut of factors important in good sex for her:

There are several things that stand out as critical to having a good, satisfying, and fun time when I have sex. One of the most important things is for the atmosphere to be very relaxed and friendly. I really don't like to be hurried or for there to be things that bug either of us. It's also important to spend enough time with the person. Having enough time is really essential to being able to move into a sense of intimacy you can then match with your bodies. Whenever either of us is trying too hard, it is just never very satisfying. I believe that a real easygoing, casual, "let-whatever-happens-happen" attitude guarantees me a much nicer time than a real effort at sex. It's nice to have sex when I'm free enough to make my fantasy life available so that some of the fantasies can be shared or acted out. To be able to engage that whole playful part of my mind and integrate it with sex is an important dimension.

Sometimes, the qualities chosen were more a reflection of the woman's situation at that particular moment, not something that would necessarily remain true throughout her life. For example, there are some women who had been married for a long time and had never been sexually involved with any other partner. Once divorced or widowed, many went through a period of exploring their sexuality and did not want any real commitments. Their focus was more on variety: experiences with new sexual partners and new sexual activities, and feeling comfortable in these situations as well as being more assertive sexually. They had already experienced a committed relationship and were currently uninterested in developing this kind of relationship again; whereas women who had been single for a long time and had experienced a variety of partners were often more interested in developing the communication and closeness involved in a long-term relationship. Women who had been involved with the same partner for a period of time were frequently interested in deepening the relationship and possibly gaining greater comfort with areas such as nudity or with exploring their partner's body without shame. Others who already felt comfortable in these circumstances might be more interested in trying something different, something they might not have been ready to try two or three years earlier, or at an earlier time in that particular relationship. Women in their sixties and seventies tended to value different aspects of sex than they had valued when they were in their thirties. So the factors that a woman perceived as important in good sex depended upon her current life situation.

At one point in the interview we asked women to describe their best sexual experience. Each woman had at least one sexual experience which was so special that it would remain a fond memory for the rest of her life. These experiences were also reminders about particular qualities that had been important during a specific period in her life, which might or might not have remained important.

At this point, you might be wondering why we even bothered trying to ascertain the qualities that make sex good. Wouldn't it be better to maintain the mystery and never think about or analyze sex? This is certainly the message we get from the culture. Somehow we have gotten the idea that to analyze sex is to take away the thrill; that true spontaneity is at the heart of good sex. But we have found that for most women this is not the case. Not knowing which qualities make for enjoyable sex often leaves a woman with some wonderful memories of sexual experiences, but also with many others that stand out only because they were so uncomfortable or disappointing. And she seems to have no way to predetermine which will occur.

It is important to understand the qualities that make up a good sexual experience because each person's conditions for good sex are so unique. Unfortunately, most of us have never really taken the time to think about or analyze what separates a good sexual experience from a mediocre one. However, once these conditions can be articulated, the woman has the ability to create them, no longer leaving good sex to chance, but making it available whenever she chooses to make the necessary effort. For example, an intellectual dinner beforehand, sex in a different bed, a bath together, or a fight to clear the existing strain on the relationship might make all the difference between a special sexual event and a routine or even negative one.

Cortney, at age thirty-one, was just beginning to determine the elements necessary for good sex for herself:

I never had an orgasm within eight years of marriage and I didn't even realize it until books about sex started coming out. I was kind of ignorant as to what I was supposed to get out of sex. Sex became something that I did because I thought I was supposed to. After I got divorced, it was like every sexual experience that I went through was new and each time I got something new out of it. It was exciting and satisfying at first, but what I've learned about myself during the past four years is that caring about somebody and loving somebody is more important. That's when I can really enjoy sex. I've always had this wall that I couldn't break down because I was afraid of being disapproved of. I felt I had to do everything right like the books said I was supposed to. I was always supposed to have an orgasm, so I just faked it because I didn't want my partners to be disappointed. Now I've discovered that when I really care about somebody and really love somebody, I'm able to get into it and all that head stuff just goes away. It's the trust built up with this person that's in my life now, the compassion, the complete honesty in everything and that total acceptance that makes the difference.

Before or after you read this section, you might want to determine for yourself those qualities that go into making a sexual experience a good one for you. A good way to do this is to pick out three or four good sexual experiences that stand out in your memory. Then, go back over each of these, one by one, very slowly. How did the sexual encounter begin? What were the kinds of things you were doing even before you considered sex? Did you wake up that morning together? How were you feeling about your partner? Had you been particularly close during the day? Had you just met? Did you spend a leisurely dinner together or had you spent the evening talking about things of particular importance?

How was sex actually initiated and who made the first move? Where were you and what was the setting like? What proceeded next? What was the actual lovemaking like? What activities occurred? Was your partner treating you roughly or gently? How did the lovemaking come to an end? What occurred afterward?

As you go over the three or four experiences, note any similarities. These similarities may represent the qualities of importance to you. The rest of this chapter contains the qualities and experiences that accounted for good sex for the women we interviewed. We are not trying to come up with a magic key for all women, because there is no one magic key. It is very clear that, depending upon the woman, different qualities are important. As you read this, you might want to consider which aspects are relevant to your own sexual relationship(s) and which are totally irrelevant. This analysis can make you more aware of your needs. Awareness, in turn, will help you control your sexual encounters so that more of them prove satisfactory, if you choose to act on the awareness.

Women frequently mentioned more than one factor as critical to a good sexual experience. One woman combined the need to be accepted by her partner with the need for variety in terms of places to have sex and sexual positions used. Another woman talked briefly about the importance of her partner's acceptance of her, but then went on to her own feelings of needing to be turned on before she engaged in sex.

THE RELATIONSHIP

The quality that was expressed most frequently was the importance of the relationship. Women talked about the security, comfort, and sharing that took place in the emotional relationship as being necessary prerequisites for good sex. For example, fifty-nine-year-old Ann telephoned back a few days after our interview to say that she had forgotten the most important thing about a good sexual experience for her, "You must be in love with your partner," she said. "That's the most important thing."

Sarah (twenty-nine, married) explains how an intimate relationship enhances the sexual experience for her:

I find that, for me, what makes a sexual experience very high in quality is having been with the person long enough to be able to share with each other the things I like about sex and the things I don't like, areas of the body I like having touched and areas of the body I prefer not having touched. It is important to have some sort of emotional commitment to each other so it becomes a more emotional experience rather than a strictly genitally focused experience. In the past, first sexual encounters were not very positive for me because we both needed time to get more in rhythm with each other. The quality of our sex was very much improved when we got past the initial brunt of getting to know each other's bodies and what pleased each other.

Becky, a twenty-one-year-old, single, legislative researcher, also feels that sex within the context of an intimate relationship provides her with her best sexual experiences:

The most important thing is the sharing and the attention we give each other. I need to have a person who's very aware of my feelings, who's going to be in tune with me emotionally and physically, somebody who, first and foremost, I want to wake up in bed with the next morning. If it's not an ongoing kind of sharing, then I don't feel that secure. If it's just going to be a one-night stand, I don't want to be part of that. I've been in enough of them to know there's a feeling of dissatisfaction that's too overwhelming and just not worth it for me.

The necessity for closeness, caring, and affection was described by a number of women.

For example, Roberta, thirty-five years old, felt:

The most important factors in a good sexual relationship are emotional closeness, mutual caring, sensuality, and tenderness. Of all of these I think emotional closeness is the most important, because if there are feelings lacking or if there is anger brewing in the background, I can't experience a very close relationship. The true essence of lovemaking is a real emotional closeness.

Of course, it is not always possible to completely eliminate the anger arising from the differences and dissatisfactions that naturally crop up in an ongoing relationship. As a matter of fact, some women mentioned that their highest sexual experiences occurred after an intense argument or fight. Emotions are already aroused to a high pitch and intimacy is created by the vulnerability of sharing painful or difficult feelings.

Rebecca, thirty-two, married five years, explains her perceptions of this:

I realized recently that sex is often best after an argument or a fight. I think it may have something to do with your physiological arousal and the energy that comes with emotions, like hatred or anger, that can be transformed into a powerful sexual experience. That has been true for me, especially once we've made up. There have been occasions where I've been the one who's been mainly pissed off and he's come over and put the moves on me and, even though I'm still angry, I respond and get into it. Sometimes, I think the making up and having sex is a way to say I love you, I didn't mean to hurt you.

The sharing of important feelings can also result in an unusually good sexual experience, as it did for thirty-seven-year-old Kathryn, a real estate agent married for sixteen years:

One night I was very upset because a very emotional experience was coming up in the next few days. I was going to visit my father's grave. I'd never known my father. I had traced him down and found out where he was buried. And I was just . . . I really had funny feelings. I was not very in touch with myself at the time. I remember I was with this man . . . we were feeling very, very close, and we talked and I cried some and he was really there for me. He wasn't trying to solve my problems or anything, he was just somebody who was there for me. It evolved into a very big sex experience. I don't think it had anything to do with technique or physical attraction—it was just coming out of a real in-depth communication.

An emotional bond or feeling of connection was mentioned frequently as the most important factor in good sex. For most women, this deep feeling of knowing the other person, of feeling totally relaxed together without the usual game playing, developed over a period of time as the couple grew closer together. However, some women reported that under rare circumstances such a bond seemed to occur at the outset of a relationship, and sometimes could be present even with a one-night stand. Theresa (thirty, lesbian, living alone) described how feeling this connection frees her up sexually:

I can let go and be who I am when I feel totally accepted by my partner. Then I can loosen up—let go of my defenses. I don't have to censor my feelings. I don't have to censor anything because there is that bond, there's that acceptance of what's happening . . . and of me.

The importance of communication or of being attuned to each other was described in a number of ways. Two years into her second marriage, Elaine believes:

The relationship is what has always mattered to me. I never went to bed just to be going to bed or because he was "Joe Blow." It had to be with a person who had some depth and warmth. I didn't have to be in love necessarily, but we had to be able to communicate well. For me, good sex comes from good communication.

Suzanne describes a ballet type of experience in which the familiarity with another's body and knowing how to please one another enhances the sexual pleasure:

I was married for ten years and then got divorced. A few years later I got into a relationship with this man and we had really incredible sex together. When we made love it was like our bodies were orchestrated; it was almost like a dance and the more we did it the more there was a precision in it that was like being on a cloud, like being nowhere else in the world. We knew what excited and turned us on and how to give to each other. Then the whole thing would just culminate in the most incredible explosion of orgasms . . . it was just totally magnificent. The best way I can think of it is this total orchestration of our bodies blending as one. It was something that didn't happen right away, it's something we developed. Our first sexual experiences were very exciting because we did blend together real well, but then as we spent more time together it just heightened and increased.

For many, their ability and their partner's ability to be both active and passive was very important in the lovemaking, as evidenced by Sally:

To me, good sex means being able to give and also being able to take. When I'm with a man who doesn't like to take, who's unwilling to just lie back and let me give to him, a man who needs to be in charge all the time, I lose interest. It may sound strange, but I feel somewhat unacknowledged. At first that's a real turn-on, but if there's no reversal, I end up feeling left out.

Women talk about a special state of being unself-conscious, and a willingness to give up control that they find supremely important in terms of their enjoyment of the sexual experience. Harriet, age thirty-four:

For me, the major thing is losing myself in my sensual experiences. That's what makes them terrific. Being oblivious to pretty much everything else besides my actual physical and emotional experience. Not noticing whether the room is hot or cold, whether it's raining outside or not, not being much in touch with whether there's music on or the baby's crying, or how much noise I'm making—real unself-consciousness.

Betty, a sixty-five-year-old divorcee, describes those situations which cause her to be self-conscious rather than unself-conscious and how a partner hinders or helps with that:

I'll tell you what does me in: if I get any sense of somebody waiting for me to come, then I get worried about whether his arms are tired and I start worrying and all my feelings get cut off. I feel watched. If the man sees my orgasm as his goal, if his own performance is tied in with satisfying me, if he needs to prove that he can do it, that really gets in the way. I don't believe in simultaneous orgasm—I don't have to come before he does, and if a man has two good hands, I don't need his penis in order to orgasm. I get aroused by his arousal and I would rather that he just forget me and go ahead at his own pace. What I want from sex is to feel good as a woman, to feel desired. If that's clear in the process, that is enough. It's not that important whether or not I have an orgasm. I just need to feel wanted.

A few women mentioned that although relationship factors were important to their sexual enjoyment, the security gained by an ongoing meaningful relationship could be offset by the excitement of a sexual relationship with someone who is unknown and with whom there are no strings attached. These women tended to prefer one extreme or the other: secure sex or the "zipless fuck." It is interesting to note, however, that no woman mentioned the "fantasy fuck" as being the one sexual experience continually sought after.

It was always mentioned in comparison to a secure sexual relationship.

Diane, a thirty-two-year-old unattached lesbian, reports:

Those experiences I find most satisfactory can be divided into two categories. The first would be recreational, lustful encounters, with no strings attached, where both people really enjoy it. With these situations I feel less restricted about what meaning there is to the relationship. I don't have to worry about any other part of the relationship except for the sexual part. The other one is being involved with somebody for a long time and the closeness that goes along with that. The sex is often not as exciting, but there is much more of a feeling of security.

Paula, thirty-two and single, finds:

Once it seems like the relationship is going to last for a while, I'm more open to experimenting. I feel more secure so I'm relaxed and more apt to try new things. When I relax, I enjoy sex a lot more. It's really difficult for me to be at ease with somebody who I think is going to disappear tomorrow. On the other hand, I've had an occasional good experience under circumstances like on a vacation or if somebody just sort of breezes into town. Then I don't feel there's any risk. I can be completely without any defenses because I know it won't develop into anything.

Twenty-year-old Sylvia describes the "zipless fuck" element and how it was heightened by her fear of being caught:

I had been up in New York on some business. It was my last afternoon in New York and I was on my way back to the city from Long Island. This guy who sat down across from me on the train just came over and said something to me like, "Do you want to read this newspaper?" I said, "God, what a typical pickup line!" He said, "Well, I *am* trying to pick you up." I said, "How do you know I'm not married or taken?" and he said, "I don't care, I think you're beautiful." That was a nice way to start things out, so we spent some time talking and laughing together on the train. When we got into the city, he had to deliver a package to some office building so he said, "Why don't you come with me?" He knew my train back wasn't due for a while. I said, "All right!" since I really had nothing else to do. First, we went out and had a drink and then sat and talked in Central Park for a while. Then we went to deliver this package. After we delivered it, we were near the elevator and saw an empty room. It looked like they were in the middle of remodeling it. He said, "Gads, what a shame we can't go in there and make love." And I said, real snotty like, "Well, I've got news for you. I'm not going to make love with you anyway." And he said, "Well, okay!" The elevator was taking a long time, so he said, "Let's take the stairs." When we got in the stairway and the door closed, he turned around and kind of attacked me! That was such a turn-on! I just loved it! It was so passionate. I think he thought that we were still going to make love, but instead I went down on him. We both still had all our clothes on and he just had his pants unzipped. It was absolutely outrageous because we kept hearing people walk by in the hall. It was great and then after that, he went down on me. We took turns leaning against the door, so if anyone tried to get in, at least we'd have some warning. Nobody came up and down the steps the whole time. The exciting part was knowing that people were there, just through the wall, and that they could've come in at any moment and we'd have been discovered.

INTERNAL FEELINGS

Some of the women felt that their enjoyment of sex had less to do with how they felt about their partner than with their feelings about themselves as desirable and competent women. When they felt good about themselves, they enjoyed sex.

Anna, married for three years after being divorced, confesses:

If I feel really good about myself, everything seems to fit and sex is really special. If I don't, the quality just isn't there. I think my partner responds to that feeling I have coming from within me. If I feel good about myself in other areas, that manifests itself outwardly in my sexuality. If I feel good about myself, I'm going to feel like being caressed. I'm going to take the time to have those special caresses and kisses and nibbles. If I don't feel good about myself, if I have gained five pounds or seven pounds and it is in the wrong place, which it always seems to be, or if I'm tired or feel "yukky" all over, I won't be able to relax enough to let the quality prevail.

Many women mentioned that feeling good about themselves also influenced how turned on they felt prior to beginning the sexual encounter. Other women felt that their hormonal cycle, degree of relaxation, or appreciation of their partner affected their initial level of desire. They all agreed, however, that when they started off feeling turned on, the experience was qualitatively better.

Aruna, a thirty-three-year-old housewife:

I have to actively want to make love; when I do, I'm the aggressor and I really enjoy that. Sometimes this happens because I'm feeling very appreciative and very loving toward him all day. Then my feelings build up and I really want to make love.

Recognition of this internal desire for sex, as well as its opposite, can be of paramount importance, as indicated by Judith, a forty-year-old bisexual librarian with two teen-age children, married for eight years to her second husband, Nathan:

The biggest factor for me is where my mind's at. If I'm clear that sex is what I want and I'm turned on, then it's almost always a good experience. In my first marriage, I didn't realize that if I didn't want sex or didn't feel turned on, I could say so. I'm not saying I just laid there and let somebody do it to me, but I had big conflicts about saying no and they carried over into sex. So naturally, I was angry a lot of the time because I was so conflicted. I would be interested if all of the right things were done, but I wasn't bringing a "this is what I want, I'm looking forward to it" attitude to the sexuality. And I've learned over the years that if I'm not turned on or I'm uninterested, it's best for me to not go ahead with it. Otherwise it will just be a mediocre experience. What makes it good for me is the attitude and interest I bring to it. What makes it spectacular is when what I bring to it and what the other person brings to it match so well that it sort of goes on its own.

Edith, a sixty-six-year-old housewife with grown children, who has been married for thirty-seven years to a retired professor, talks about how important the reciprocal nature of the relationship is:

What has made sex special for me is a feeling, a sort of ebullience of life, that I can share sexually with my partner. It wouldn't necessarily be precipitated by any terrific experience like doing something new or taking a trip, it would just be the way I'm feeling. It would be an internal thing, but it would have to be reciprocated, though. So it would be inner-generated by each of us and then shared.

This responsiveness on the part of the partner was also mentioned by Allison, thirty-five, divorced:

It's really important for me to make love with someone who makes me feel attractive, who makes me feel like I'm exciting him—that no matter what I do it's wonderful. Part of it is from comments about how I look or saying things like "Jesus, you turn me on," or "I love fucking you." I don't have to do anything other than just be myself, and that's wonderful. The other important factor is if he's good. Good means that he can go forever, that he doesn't come fast, that he can hold off coming and just really stay there and fuck and stop and fuck again.

THE PARTNER

Spontaneous, physical attraction was mentioned by some women as being an integral part of their good sexual experiences. After thirty-six years of marriage, Ann, fifty-nine, can still say:

My husband is the best lover I've ever known. One of the reasons I married him was that he was so exciting to me. I think initially it was chemistry, and it has continued. That's not to say that we don't have the problems that I think are indigenous to married life, but we have been sustained by that initial excitement, which we have always been able to recapture.

Alexandra, a thirty-two-year-old divorced therapist who lives alone, says:

The attraction and sexual tension were there from the beginning. We had highly charged sexual encounters from the start and soon developed a kind of joyfulness and ease you usually can't have the first time you sleep with somebody, at least I usually can't. There was no need to manufacture anything. We were both so sure about our attractiveness to each other that there was a real sense of security.

The importance of sharing common interests was a repeated theme as most women wanted the sexual relationship to be built on something more than just chemistry. Tricia, age sixty-seven, a salesperson, married for nine years to her second husband, Bert, a salesman:

The important thing is that the man that I'm with and I have something in common besides sex, for instance, liking the same kinds of books, the same kinds of movies or theater, just a sharing of other things. Then it's very easy.

Women mentioned other qualities in their partners which affected their sexual relationships positively or negatively. A partner's openness and lack of inhibition were important to some. Sonya, (forty, separated two years) found she responded negatively if her partner was inhibited and not able to be open sexually:

I basically enjoy having sex, but I'm somewhat inhibited when my partner's inhibited. I sort of follow, rather than take the lead. The partners I'm most inhibited with are the ones who are stiff and awkward and uncomfortable with sex in some way. The more spontaneous they are and able to express their sexuality and not be inhibited, the more I'm able to respond.

Connie, age twenty-six, widowed four years, believes:

The sexual experiences that were the most satisfying to me emotionally were with people who weren't afraid to be open with their sexual feelings. They were with people I never would have had a long-term relationship with, but I enjoyed them because they allowed themselves to be totally with me; they didn't try to mask or disguise themselves in any way. I've had very good relationships with men who weren't particularly skilled or experienced sexually, but had the confidence and trust to be themselves. Some guys can come on really macho, and say, "Let's do this and let's do that" and they've got great skill, but because they're not giving anything other than performance, it's not satisfying.

The partner's caring nature, gentleness, and enthusiasm were mentioned by others. Judy enthusiastically describes her husband of two years:

He is such a loving and gentle human being. It has been that way since the very beginning. I was totally taken with him the first time we made love. He wasn't a particularly great lover, but he went into it with such gusto, such a feeling of being thrilled about it—you could see it all over him. He was not the best lover I have ever had, by any means. But there was a look on his face and a whole thing about his attitude that really sucked me in. Over the years he has become a much better lover mechanically, but he has never changed his attitude: he is very gentle and loving and sex means a great deal to him. With him it's not just something to do and get over with.

Many women mentioned their partner's technique as well as his attitude as being particularly important. Rosemary, thirty-six, divorced four years:

The first thing that's important is that the man cares, that he wants to please me and is interested in my being satisfied sexually. The second thing is technique—that he knows about a woman's body. Someone who knows where and how to touch me and asks me what I like or I don't like. Someone who isn't uptight about me being aggressive and taking the initiative in sex. Someone with whom I can openly say, "I want to do this or I don't want to do that," and that's fine with him.

TIME

A significant number of women focused on qualities of the sexual interaction itself rather than any physical or emotional qualities of her own, her partner, or their relationship. The factor mentioned most often as being of prime importance in a good sexual experience was time. Having ample time, which afforded a slow, leisurely pace to the lovemaking, was mentioned over and over again.

Alice (thirty-eight, single):

Having enough time so I don't feel hurried or rushed through it, so we can touch and talk is important to me.

Connie talks about the importance of a slow buildup:

I always enjoy and rely on a gradual buildup. I like that "ceremony" in the beginning; it sort of marks it as something important. I don't hold a lot of value for a real quickie, unless it's like the third time of the night. But a buildup can be anything—it can be making dinner, going out to the theater, going out for a long drive—that in itself can be foreplay. The buildup is more exciting to me than just lying naked in bed and saying "Let's do it."

Meg, a thirty-six-year-old college professor, married six years and the mother of a two-year-old daughter, talks about the importance of time during the act of lovemaking:

The most important aspect in having what I call good sex is taking the time to enjoy each other. I like to caress and be caressed for a long time. Then it feels like being together in more than a sexual way. I feel aware and really in touch with my partner. I like to have my whole body touched, not just my cunt and breasts. My toes are just as important as my nipples, or my hair. Then I feel whole. I feel appreciated and turned on. I like the feeling that the whole world has stopped and nothing else is going on except what is going on between us.

In contrast, Helen turns lack of time into a best sexual encounter:

One time, the man I was living with had to attend this business function, and he kept procrastinating because he really didn't want to go. Yet it was important so he didn't want to be late either. About five minutes before we were ready to leave, he said, "Come on, if we're going to do this, we've got to go now." And suddenly I began to feel very sexy and I said, "Uh-uh, I'm not going. I want a quickie right now." I thought he would have a heart attack! He said, "What are you talking about?" I said, "I'm not going." So we jumped into bed for a grand total of, at the most, five minutes. I got very excited very quickly. Maybe because I knew we had to be somewhere in a few minutes. And the rest of the night was so much fun. We kept looking at each other and grinning, knowing that we had just had this little encounter. After that, we would have a quickie every now and then if we were going somewhere we didn't want to go, or if we were running late. It would help us get through some of those long business dinners and parties.

PLAYFULNESS

Sex as a form of fun or play was also described by many women as important to a good sexual experience. The element of playfulness is often in direct opposition to the cultural messages that many women and their parents received: sex is for procreation and not for enjoyment. We are not taught that sex can be erotic and intense *and* fun. An understanding of the significance of playfulness in good sexual encounters often took years to evolve, as in the case of forty-year-old Judith.

The older I've gotten, the more it's become apparent that sex is just some kind of grown-up play and whenever I can play I can develop it into a sexual experience. If I'm feeling playful, relaxed, having a good time, then that's the time I'm most likely to expand it into something sexual.

Ruby (thirty-nine, married eighteen years) believes:

The one quality that all good sex should have is the quality of play. You and your partner need to be able to laugh together in all walks of life, not just in bed. Laughter's orgasmic anyway, so if you can laugh and have fun and play while you're making love, you're bound to have a good time.

Thirty-five-year-old Sally, mother of two teen-age sons, married sixteen years and a psychotherapist, illustrates how play resulted in one of her best sexual experiences:

One of my best sexual experiences started out as a whipped-cream fight. I was in the kitchen putting some whipped cream on a pie. Dan pinched my ass as he walked by. I got pissed and squirted him with the whipped cream from the can. He grabbed the can and retaliated. Our clothes seemed like they were getting in the way at this point, so we took them off and just used our hands to throw whipped cream at each other. Although we were still laughing, it also started to feel very sensual. We went in the living room, lay down in front of the fireplace, and started eating the whipped cream off of each other. Naturally, it ended up in some very intense sex. What was really nice about this experience was that it happened in the middle of the day and that it was really a fun experience. We did a lot of laughing and giggling, and I learned that it was okay to laugh and have fun and really enjoy each other during sex.

Jacqueline, a thirty-three-year-old entrepreneur, divorced two years after a ten-year marriage, recalls how one lover in particular helped her to appreciate the quality of playfulness through his creative, spontaneous approach to sex:

Once I had a lover who was always coming up with some wonderful, creative ideas of how to spend an afternoon or an evening, because they were so much fun and so unexpected. Like the time I came home from work and he greeted me at the door, took my purse and my papers, and lured me off into bed. After making love he decided we needed a bubble bath so he ran the bath water and poured the bubble bath. I gratefully sank into a tub of warm bubbles but he disappeared. You have to get the picture. I'm sitting there in this nice, beautiful, warm bubble bath all by myself wondering where he went and in he comes. There he is naked except for a little white waist apron and a hard on and a tray with a whole chicken dinner on it! We were going to eat chicken dinner in the bathtub! He served me my plate and I was giggling the whole time. Of course, I'd never been served dinner in the bathtub before. And he went and got his plate and we sat there and ate chicken amongst the bubbles, in the bathtub. It was wonderful!

VARIETY

Variety, innovation, and surprise were found to enhance sexual relationships. Many women achieved this variety by being open to having sex at different times, in different places, and by using different positions. Ann, at age fifty-nine, states:

We were always open to new experiences: we did all kinds of different things. We had sex in all different kinds of places. We always sought new ways of pleasuring each other.

Monique, thirty-two, married nine years:

I try very hard to initiate or ask to have sex in a variety of ways so we don't get locked into a stale routine. Sometimes I ask for sex when I know it's not possible, just to stimulate him and to get a rise out of it myself. Once we were driving down the parkway and I took his penis, and said, "Let's fuck!" knowing very well that he couldn't in the middle of the parkway. I try not to fall into an unexciting "routine" approach.

Two years into her second marriage, Elaine describes how she maintains sexual variety:

I like sex anytime. If my husband came home right now and the kids weren't around, that's what we would do, if we were both in the mood. I do not like set patterns. I like things to be different. So we try to keep some variety by not using the same position every time. We do it standing, sitting, lying on the table—different positions for different moods. If we did it one way last time, then we try and think of a new way the next time. We use different candles, different rooms of the house, or different pieces of furniture. My daughter has a water bed so if she's not around we use that, or our bed, or the couch in the living room, or our Roman tub.

Susan, a thirty-six-year-old part-time airline employee, has been married fifteen years to Paul, a salesman, and has two children. She experiences variety in a quieter way:

Our sexual interactions tend to be the same because we both know what the other one likes. There is, however, usually something different each time, just enough that each time is a little different. That makes it interesting. I don't think either one of us knows how it is going to be different before it happens. It's not that we do things that we have never done before, but we do different things than we did the last time. It just happens and then I think, oh, yeah, I forgot about doing it like that.

The element of surprise was sometimes linked with the need for variety. Jackie found that allowing her partner to take charge added variety and enhanced the sexual experience:

What really appeals to me is the surprise element in sex. It is always exciting to me to be totally out of control, which occurs when my part-ner takes control over what happens. I love not knowing what will be coming next, and each time having it different. And my partner loves variety, which makes it great. He's in charge and I don't initiate any-thing; and it almost doesn't matter what he does. I mean, I have a basic trust that he's not going to hurt me and that he's not going to do any-thing he knows I don't like particularly, but he directs. For me, that's the one thing that can't be boring because I never know what is going to happen next.

Paula (thirty-two, single, and a potter) describes how she created an element of surprise that ended up in great sex:

We had been having an argument about spontaneity. I said, to be spontaneous, the person who's introducing a spontaneous act has to almost not be spontaneous. You have to set everything up because that's the only way that something's going to come off being spontaneous. To prove my point, I went and set up an elaborate "fantasy night." I have this fantasy of being a gypsy and so I first found an affordable Middle Eastern restaurant with the right kind of atmosphere. Then I got a card and I wrote, "Your presence is required, be prepared to be kidnapped. Meet me at this place. This is your secret lover." So I invited him to meet me anonymously for dinner. I mean, this was the guy I was living with, so he kind of knew who it was. Then I spent a day running around looking for a black garter belt and dark stockings. I was able to find dark blue. And I went home and put the garter belt and stockings on without underpants. I was feeling really sexual at that point. I was on! We met at the restaurant and about halfway through supper I said, "You know, I don't have any underwear on under this!" He got really interested! We were sitting there just mooning at each other over dinner. We went home and made love. The whole experience seemed to bring out other things in him. He sort of opened up and was a lot more experimental that evening, and it was really nice. I don't know if he ever conceded that I had been right about being spontaneous, but that experience was one of the best in our whole relationship.

The excitement produced from the possibility of being caught heightened the sexual experiences for some women. Many felt this recaptured the intense sexual feelings felt during their adolescent and young adult days when sex was illicit.

Mary Lou, thirty-one and married ten years:

My best sexual experiences are when I know there are other people around and there's even a slight chance of getting caught. I really get turned on then. Sometimes we make love in the living room in front of the fireplace. The living room has a sliding glass door and I always make sure the curtains are closed. If someone is in the house, I try to be really quiet. I'll try to do everything I can to make sure they don't hear. I'll even move to the floor if the bed is squeaking. Yet sex is always better then even though I'm sure no one ever hears us or sees us.

Fran, thirty-two and single, describes how she carried out her enjoyment of illicitness in a most daring manner:

Making love by the ocean has a real primeval feeling for me. I can remember once in Honolulu, there was a pier that goes out quite a ways and underneath it is a small area that two people can barely fit in. I liked to go there around sunset. Once I went there with a boy friend of mine. To my surprise, he began making love to me. There we were, with all this concrete around and the waves crashing around us and drenching us. We could hear people shouting and children playing above us, and the fact that at any moment someone might discover us or the police might arrest us just added to the excitement. This was one of the few times I have ever been able to have an orgasm strictly through intercourse, and it was one of the most incredible orgasms I've ever had.

COSMIC SEX

On another level, women talk about an altered state of consciousness that, when it exists in their lovemaking, makes the experience particularly good. Some of these experiences have a spiritual, if not a religious, sense about them.

Justine, a thirty-one-year-old artist, divorced and living with her female lover, Ellen, describes her experience of sex and orgasm this way:

It was a total orgasmic experience, not just a genital one. I felt like I was going out of my head—like I expanded out of my body. There is no terminology to talk about this. You're in a special place, like behind a sacred door. It's like going through the door and out someplace else. It's a shifting from the genitals up. It feels like the energy goes out through the top of my head. . . . beautiful sensations and colors. What I do is to get into my head, without being totally conscious, but not in the form of thoughts. There is a blurring or an expanding and I keep going further and further out. I feel like I have to have this experience or sex is just not worth it. And if we're not having a power struggle we can get to that place together. The way we do it is by doing it at the same time, by doing "sixty-nine." It took a long time just to get the mechanics down so we could both be receptive and active at the same time. Then I can tie into the energy in the room, in the universe and in everything. I feel completely connected to her and yet it is completely anonymous energy. I had the flash once that she was every lover I ever had and ever will have.

Christine, a forty-one-year-old teacher, after nineteen years of marriage and three children, finds a religious approach of paramount importance in sex:

I think the most important thing is a Christian or God-oriented relationship which binds you together. We both have a very strong faith and believe we not only have a relationship between ourselves, but it's also a relationship with Christ. He's there, too. He's part of whatever we do together and so we're not only responsible to each other, but also responsible to Christ, I mean as far as my feelings are concerned. Say I'm having negative feelings about my husband or something. And that, in a way, is how I turn myself around. I know that a Christian relationship is a loving thing. That thought is always subconsciously with me and that helps to straighten out my own feelings. It helps me to accept my husband as he is and to feel more sexual toward him. So it isn't just the two of us, it's the three of us.

Sage describes an egoless state that occurs with good sex:

Once I took LSD and experienced a kind of egolessness during sex. It was the same dissolution of ego that happens sometimes when I smoke dope and am no longer aware of myself and my boundaries. Then I am very much in an altered state. It's only after I come back that I realize I have been elsewhere other than in my own self-definition. This quality of absolute dissolution of boundaries has nothing to do with orgasms. It has to do with touch and some kind of electrical magnetic thing that happens, which is in the contact of skin to skin.

Sage goes on to describe a specific cosmic experience that occurred one night:

I had gone to a women's retreat with a new lover. The retreat was on the headlands over the Pacific. A group of women had built a pyramid for themselves and their friends to do workshops in. The pyramid was a magnificent space, three stories high with wonderful wall hangings. It had a very splendid, magical effect on me, especially when I went up into the apex and sat and looked at the ocean.

My lover and I had had a terrible fight about something or other, and she went to sleep in her van. I went to sleep in the apex of the pyramid, which is just a platform for meditation. In the middle of the night, when I was asleep, she came to the pyramid and climbed up to the apex. The moon was coming through the windows, giving her an almost ghostly aura. She seemed transformed to me—almost unrecognizable. I remember her being silhouetted against the moon. She had her bib overalls on and she very slowly undid the clasps and got undressed in a very rhythmic and transformed way. She seemed to draw power from the moon and the pyramid and used it to make love to me. It was very powerful. I remember feeling as if I was being carried somewhere out of time and out of space. The power of it was indescribable, of being taken away, removed. The orgasm was sort of wrenched from me, and I had nothing whatsoever to do with it. . . . I felt almost disembodied. It was a very memorable, unearthly experience as far as lovemaking is concerned.

FIRSTS

The quality of being the "first" was mentioned by some women as creating a particularly good sexual experience. A person's first experience with anything—a plane trip, skiing, visiting a foreign country—often remains a special event provided the experience was good.

However, most women's first experiences with intercourse are often not particularly good ones. Due to their lack of knowledge, they may not be aware of what is needed to make the experience a satisfying one. In addition, women often look forward to their first intercourse experience with unrealistically high expectations, especially if their preintercourse experiences of caressing and petting have been sexually exciting. They may expect intercourse to be more fun, more arousing and exciting, and are often disappointed when the "real thing" does not measure up to the fantasized image.

Lorraine's experience, however, was different from the norm. A twenty-seven-year-old single counselor for disabled people, Lorraine, disabled with cerebral palsy herself, shares how her partner made her first sexual experience one of her best:

I was attracted to this man and thought it was mutual so I asked him to go to bed with me and he said okay. But I said, "I have to tell you something. This is my first time." And he said, "That's okay, it will be something special." Actually, in some ways, it was the best sexual experience I've ever had and I feel very grateful for that. Not many people have had that kind of experience.

We started by undressing each other and the first thing that he did was to take off my shoes and rub my feet. This moved me very much. It was an affirmation of my whole body being okay and my feet and legs weren't excluded. Then he kissed the scars on my legs and said, "I love scars and I love stretch marks." I couldn't believe it. How did I find this person? Gradually we proceeded to touch each other and fondle each other. It turned out that he really liked oral sex and I found out I liked it too. It was my first experience with oral sex and we got into that for a while. He kept trying different positions with me. I said, "Wait a minute, I can't do that. I can't get my legs apart enough for that. That hurts. Let's try it another way." So we tried it other ways. We tried lots of different positions. He ended up finally penetrating me from the rear with me on my hands and knees and that was okay. Later on we used another position where I was on my back with my legs up but resting on his shoulders. We tried sideways too. It was really exciting and the whole experience left me feeling good about myself as a sexual woman.

First orgasms, like first intercourse experiences, represent a hallmark in a woman's sexual growth.

Louise, thirty-nine, two years into her second marriage said:

The one best sexual experience that comes to mind happened after Dick and I were reunited after having been separated for a month and a half. Prior to that I believed I was orgasmic. I used to have a lot of tingling and good feelings during sex and then felt quiet afterward, which I thought was the resolution phase of an orgasm. Anyway, that afternoon we began lovemaking in our somewhat established way, taking a bath together, giggling and playing with one another, caressing each other's sexual areas, rubbing each other with soap, finally getting out of the bathtub and moving into the bedroom. So there he began kissing me on the face, on my mouth, my neck, my breasts, licking me all over around my stomach area down to my clit, until it was really a good feeling. I was aware again of the familiar tingling sensation. Then all of a sudden I thought, "Something else is happening." What he had done was to insert his finger into my anus and I was beginning to get a different kind of feeling and started thinking "What's happening to me?" I was scared but I thought, "Wait a minute now, I don't need to be afraid of this." He was gently massaging my anus and licking me at the same time. Suddenly I remember arching my back and I thought, "Oh, my God, I think I'm going to do a backbend. No, that's not possible," and then feeling a tremendous ripple of orgasm. It was like I had charley horses in my legs, and then that ripple effect. He just stayed with it. Then I thought, "He's got to stop touching me." It was that feeling of "don't touch me anymore." I can remember just settling down on the bed and he stayed there with me but slowed down his caressing. I remember feeling stunned. I said, "I don't think I've ever had that feeling before." He said, "Well, at one point you hollered 'Don't stop, don't stop.'" I didn't even remember saying that.

So we talked about that, and felt really close for the rest of the afternoon. It wasn't until about several months later that I could deal with my sadness, that I was thirty-three years old and had not been orgasmic up until that day. That was a kind of sad time for me, and at the same time very happy.

Sylvia, a twenty-year-old student, living alone, excitedly described her first memorable sexual encounter, which occurred just two months after her first sexual experience:

I had known this guy for about two years or so but I'd never spoken to him for more than five minutes. I had theater tickets but my boy friend was sick so I asked this guy to go. We went to the theater together and really enjoyed it. Afterward we went out to eat and the place he chose was very close to where he lives; in fact it was three doors away. I told him I was very self-conscious about being close to where he lived and I wanted to know if that was intentional on his part. He said he chose that restaurant because he liked the place but if it worked out that we went back to his place afterward, that was fine too. So it was up to me at that point. I was very uncomfortable. I started to tell him about where I was coming from, that I had been a virgin until the last two months. Before that I had been a cockteaser and had been having oral sex a lot. He told me he was getting very turned on by the whole discussion. We paid the bill, got up and walked outside. Halfway between his car and his apartment, I said, "Why don't you decide what to do?" He said, "Well, all right, let's go to my apartment." I said "All right!"

At his apartment I sat down on the couch and he put on some sensual music. At this point, I felt sort of awkward, like here comes step number one—the kiss—and step number two—the touch. He started leaning over to kiss me and I thought, "Oh, God, now here it comes for sure," but when he kissed me, all of those feelings went away. It was just very natural and nice. He picked me up and carried me into the bedroom. This was my fantasy come true—I had never done that before.

I didn't let him enter me right away, which wasn't what he'd been used to. He's thirty and at this point in his life he was more used to just "wham, bam, get in and fuck and have your orgasm." But I didn't let it be that way because I think what's more important in sex, or just as important, is what happens before and after.

So I touched him a lot all over and made him just receive, rather than him constantly wanting to please or to give to me. First, he was lying on his back and I was just touching him very gently all over his body with my hands—very gently though, like my fingertips were gliding all over his body and playing with his penis, not like a quick hand job, you know, just touching and running my fingers through his hair and touching his face, which I find very sensual. I also turned him over and touched him all over his back and massaged him a little bit, and ran my tongue all over his body, and he was just so high from it! I mean, he was absolutely, like "Oh my God, I can't believe this, oh this is so wonderful, oh wow," and because he was so turned on I got really turned on from that, too. During that whole time he didn't want to just receive, he wanted to touch me and he wanted to play with me. I just wanted him to receive and enjoy that for a change, I knew my time would come. So I just ran my hair up and down his body, and since it was lighter than my fingertips, it really gave him tingles. Then I touched him with my breast down on his penis and on his face and he kept telling me what a tit man he was and that turned me on too.

After he played with me a little bit—I didn't want him to play with me a lot, because I didn't want the turn-on of him receiving to go away —I was ready to be entered and I told him that. This was absolutely my picture of making love, the rhythm was right and the desire to please each other was right.

I was on top of him and he was on the bottom and then he was on top and I was on the bottom, and oh, yes, I forgot to tell you this before. He did this thing I absolutely never heard of or even read in a book or anything—you know how when you fall asleep together you roll over on your side and put your arm around your partner; well, we made love like that. Instead of coming in from the front he came inside of me from the back; he was behind me with his arms on my breast and he went into the—you know, the regular hole, not the anus, which was absolutely a trip to me. I never knew that was possible and that was like such a turn-on because that's how I masturbate, in that position. I mean, like that freaked me out. That's how we reached orgasm together. After that I was just so blown away and he was too, especially me being so new at it.

Suzanne, a thirty-seven-year-old bisexual businesswoman who is divorced and lives alone, shared her first experience of making love to a woman:

The first experience I had with another woman came after I became aware that I was open to relating to women sexually. I had never known that or even fantasized it before. I would go to the movies and all of a sudden I found that I was just as attracted to the women as to the men.

Soon after, I had lunch with a bisexual woman. I told her I was really impressed by the fact that she felt comfortable relating to both women and men. She ended up giving me pointers such as: when you meet a woman you're attracted to, be sure that you tell her, and see if she's interested in relating sexually. Women have a way of being passive, so she said to be more assertive if I thought she could handle it. At the end of the lunch I said, "Well I think I'm going to practice what you preached. I find that I'm attracted to you and I'd like to spend some more time with you. Are you interested?" She said yes, so we started dating.

She eventually became my first woman lover. She was rather reticent at first because she didn't want to be my first woman lover since some women may freak out the first time and that didn't appeal to her. I was fairly persistent, though, in my caring for her, but I dropped the subject of sex. One day we had something to eat and were listening to music and she became assertive and said, "I'd like to make love to you but I'd like you to feel comfortable so at any time along the way stop me if it's not feeling comfortable for you."

Well, I was excited and scared at the same time because in my head I knew I wanted to have this experience and I felt a great deal of love for her, but how do you make love to a woman? Would I enjoy eating a woman or would I enjoy kissing a woman deeply on the lips? It was a taboo that I had grown up with and my body wanted it, but my mind said I might not enjoy it. So I finally said okay since she said we could stop anywhere along the line, and I just relaxed with it. I'll never forget that first experience of unhooking a woman's bra, I don't know why it was so profound but that was just a memory that will last with me. I unhooked her bra and she kind of led the way and I mirrored the things she did. We had about two hours of making love again and again and it was such a high experience. The mirror image of making love to someone of the same sex was unique and fascinating. Also feeling the sensation of excitement, love, lust, sex, emotion, and beauty all intertwined was just the heights for me. I found that the experiences I thought might turn me off didn't. I loved eating her, I loved holding her breasts, I loved holding her close and I loved whatever she did to me. When she left I was just exhausted and exhilarated at the same time.

Sixty-year-old Jesse, a divorced artist, tells a story that illustrates that it is never too late to experience a first:

Once there was this beautiful, strong, big man who had no awareness of the unspoken graciousness of his personality. He saw himself as a hulking, big bruiser. When it came to having sexual experiences with this person, who happened to be a sculptor and had a great sense of form and rhythm that came out of his work, the request came almost nonverbally . . . and yes, we both wanted it. It was interesting that I forgot my age as we undressed. I was sixty and he was thirty-five. I had had only three sexual partners since my separation and, of course, only one during my marriage, but this partner introduced me to a whole new way of relating sexually. He had big rough hands as he was an automobile mechanic as well as a sculptor. He had great physical strength and could easily lift me. We found that we moved in unison with no spoken agreement. It was kind of flowing from one position to the next, which really was delightful and amazing.

This was our first intercourse and, much to my astonishment, we had simultaneous orgasms. I mentioned that I thought this was very rare and he laughed and said, "Well, we'll have to give that Kinsey guy a call and tell him we broke the record," and then he asked after a brief respite, "How about another go?" "Fine," I said. So he said, "Would you like it from the back?" I had never had anal sexual intercourse before, so I said, "I don't know, but I'd like to try it." So I was introduced to this kind of intercourse and found it a very different experience that I wouldn't necessarily like to repeat because it was not that comfortable, but at the same time it was satisfying sexually. The discomfort was a strange kind of sweet/sour experience. Our movements throughout were so light and so beautiful and mutual that I couldn't help but think of a ballet. I had read this somewhere before and had thought, "Oh, that's such a romanticized concept," but it really wasn't.

What to make of it all—quiet sex, gymnastic sex, sensual and leisurely sex, sex as communication, sex as validation of self, sex as communication with the cosmos? One thing appears to be true. Once each woman can articulate the qualities important for good sex through recalling those experiences which were particularly good for her, she can then create the sexual environment necessary to make future experiences truly good ones.

Through reading this chapter you may have become more aware of those qualities that distinguish your good sexual experiences from your usual ones. The next step is to find ways to implement these qualities. If you have been raised in typically female fashion, you may feel that you do nothing to prepare for a sexual experience. You may feel that that role belongs to your partner. However, if you think about it carefully, you may become aware of certain things that you do unconsciously, that are almost second nature to you, such as wearing perfume, taking a bath before sex, or cleaning up your room in anticipation of lovemaking. Or perhaps you take charge in a more direct way by lighting candles, undressing your partner as dinner ends, or leaving a note with your intentions clearly stated. The next chapter is about setting the scene for enjoyable sex, and even if you don't think you do anything in this department and don't really care to, you may be interested in learning what works for other women.

2

Setting the Scene

Certain subtle or not-so-subtle nuances make a sexual encounter special, unique, or memorable. These ideas are not necessarily implemented every time sex occurs, but are used to add variety and to enhance a sexual relationship, particularly a long-term relationship.

Going through this chapter is similar to visiting department stores at Christmastime, when the shelves are bulging with toys, games, and puzzles. As you walk down the aisle, your eyes may fall on familiar items, such as pickup sticks, dominoes, and checkers. You might come across Chinese checkers for example, and find yourself thinking, "Chinese checkers! I outgrew that years ago." Some of the ideas might bore you. And others might just seem outrageous. Take Pet Rocks, for example: everyone might be buying them up like crazy while you stand there in disbelief and wonder what the appeal is. You might feel more comfortable tucking some ideas away for a future time, like a certain item that might not be appropriate for Christmas, but could be saved for another special occasion, such as a birthday or an anniversary. Theoretically, you could try out all of the ideas (if you had the time and energy), but we expect most people to test some of them out while passing others by.

FEELING TURNED ON

A necessary prerequisite to engaging in any sexual activity is feeling turned on. Unless a woman is aroused or has enough libido to be intrigued with the possibility of sex, the encounter is unlikely to be a fulfilling one. On occasion, this is not true and good sex can evolve out of what seems like total lack of interest; however, this outcome is rather rare.

A number of things seem to account for a woman's being in a sexual frame of mind. Many women we interviewed started out with the idea that being turned on had something to do with their physiology. Some days they were turned on, while on others they were not. Some felt that their level of sexual interest was connected to their menstrual cycle. Stress also frequently affected a woman's sexual desire, as did work pressure and concern about health or the welfare of family members.

Sometimes women felt that there was nothing they could do about their level of sexual interest—"When you're hot, you're hot, and when you're not, you're not"—while under other circumstances they felt there were things they could do to revive their sexual interest. For example, taking time to relax or going to a movie or a party might take their minds off their busy lives or worries, at least for a short time.

Some women found that there were specific things they could do which would guarantee raising their level of sexual interest. As with going out to eat when you are not particularly hungry, it is possible to whet your appetite by picking a restaurant carefully. You might select one with a cozy candlelit environment where there are fragrant flowers on the tables and the smell of garlic greets you at the door. The same can be true of developing an interest in sex. Although you might have had a long hard day, you may find that your desire grows if you read some erotica, think about a past sexual experience that turned you on, or create a sensual atmosphere with candles and music.

Creating the mood by doing something specifically aimed at arousing you runs counter to the way many women have been traditionally reared to approach sex. Our culture teaches us that it is the man who is supposed to turn us on. Our role is to wait around looking pretty, and his job is to set the atmosphere and whisper sweet nothings in our ears. Many women do not realize that the power to turn themselves on lies in their own hands. Some women argued that their best sex always occurred spontaneously. However, most of those women, once they thought about it, realized that many of their best sexual experiences took place when the situation was premeditated, when they actually took the time to set the scene and create a special experience. One woman always cleaned up her bedroom before having sex. Although she felt it might be a neurotic thing to do, she found that a messy bedroom detracted from the experience. Another woman took the phone off the hook or took other precautions to make certain that nothing would interfere with their enjoyment. This does not mean that sex late at night for five or fifteen minutes is inferior sex and should be avoided, but when a special sexual experience is desired, it is possible to create one.

It seems clear that being interested in sex has more to do with a variety of feelings evolving over a period of time, rather than those occurring just at the particular moment when sex is available. Feelings about themselves and their partners, as well as feelings generated by their interaction together, was what enabled most women and their partners to feel turned on sexually. Consciously generating a sense of anticipation was mentioned by a number of women as a particularly good way of turning themselves on. This level of anticipation often developed over a couple of hours and sometimes over a day or two. Kathryn (thirty-seven, married sixteen years) describes two ways she and her partner would slowly lead up to sex:

We had different ways of leading up to sex, none of which was, as I recall, planned. One time we were together watching TV. It was like it just happened; the TV was on and we were playing with each other's feet and spending a lot of time just working up from there. About halfway through the program we weren't watching the program as much, and by the end of the program we weren't watching TV at all! Another time at dinner, he put a note under my plate that said, "Are you doing anything special after you finish your dessert?" That was great, because all through the meal I kept thinking about what was to come!

Thirty-four-year-old Harriet, married ten years, uses the idea of a sex party as a creative turn-on to rejuvenate her sex life with her husband:

We usually make an appointment with each other for a sex party, either days in advance or sometimes on the spur of the moment. Wanting a "sex party" usually comes out of feeling we've been distracted by our work, our child, our friends, or all the other things that go on in our lives so that our sex life is less interesting than at other times. Then we say, "Let's have a sex party."

Having a sex party means doing whatever strikes our fancy that turns each of us on. We can have a sex party at night or during the day, but we need at least several hours. Sometimes we get stoned and sometimes we don't.

Let me give you an example: We might start by going out to dinner someplace we like that serves nice food, but not too heavy, and has lots of atmosphere. During dinner we talk to each other about all the titillating things we're going to do to each other later on. Then we'll look in the paper and find a dirty movie, and go to it. Neither of us gets real turned on by the movie, but it's a subliminal thing . . . we touch each other a lot on the way home and talk about the movie, and by the time we get home we're feeling passionate. Then we might take a hot tub,* or build a fire and massage each other, depending on how turned on we've gotten. Sometimes we just rush in and rip our clothes off and do it. Other times we sort of neck and pet for a while. Then maybe if we've planned it ahead, and I've put on my sexy underwear before we went out, I'll have Tom lie down on the bed and I'll do a strip for him. By the time I'm done, we're usually pretty excited and we make love. We spend a lot of time on love play before we actually have intercourse. I usually have a bunch of orgasms first and then when we have intercourse I usually come again. And that's a sex party!

Many women talked about how important it is to keep this sense of anticipation going during the early part of their lovemaking.

---

* A special tub of hot water designed so that four or more people can sit in it comfortably.

They feel that when they prolong the initial sexual contact, a more exciting and satisfying experience is likely to result. As the old saying goes: "Making love is like a Chinese box: half of the interest is in opening it up."

Sonya (forty, separated):

Oh, I know something that's fun. I enjoy undressing a man and having him undress me. And making that a slow process where I savor each step. I would probably start in a standing position. Maybe I'm undoing the buttons on his cuffs and then unbuttoning his shirt slowly, meanwhile kissing his neck and hugging and embracing him. He might be taking my blouse off at the same time, and then when both of our tops are off, we embrace and feel each other's chest and that's very erotic. At that point, we'd probably sit down on the bed, and I might take off his shoes and his socks. Then, we'd spend a little time kissing and caressing each other before I took off his belt and he took off my pants. Taking off my hose would be a whole other step. And sometimes it's fun to leave on my panties and for him to leave on his shorts for a little while. Every step of the way has to be exciting enough to add to the whole process. It's like having sex that's forbidden.

Some women found that being partially clothed was more of a turn-on than being nude.

Sylvia, twenty, single:

A big turn-on has been when one or both of us still have some form of clothing on; like my bra on but unsnapped or his shirt on and halfway unbuttoned. Nudity can become boring, while having even one piece of clothing on is really exciting.

Prolonged initial contact by telling stories and sometimes acting them out was also described by a couple of women. For example, Penelope (forty-six, married) shared the following:

We turn each other on by telling erotic stories; we even draw pictures to illustrate them and then we act them out. For example, once I went into the bathroom and got into the tub, and just like in the porno story I had told him, he came in and peed on me, which was a highly erotic experience. I didn't know how aroused I'd be by that, but the idea of doing something "bad" got me turned on.

With her first husband, Penelope found an unusual way of keeping their sexual excitement level high:

Sex with Peter was always very exciting and we found the way to maintain that was to keep the frequency down. We had sex no more than once a week and then we'd have it for about three hours!

Alexandra (thirty-two, divorced) gives an example of how her partner increases the sexual tension by playing hard-to-get:

Sometimes we'll be reading in bed and I'll get turned on and I'll start touching him, but he'll just keep right on reading and won't move. I'm getting more and more turned on and this guy will not move —and it kills me! He knows what he is doing because we talked about it, as I'd wondered if he was just being passive or absorbed or preoccupied, or if I was just getting turned on and he wasn't. He said no, that he knew what he was doing. He was just letting me go crazy. And then eventually he would relinquish this lofty role and we would get together. It would be wonderful because by that time I would be so turned on I would be ready to come.

Alexandra found that when she was not initially in the mood, incorporating fantasy with some physical self-stimulation was a way to get herself warmed up for a sexual encounter:

If I'm going to have sex and I'm not feeling particularly excited, I might stimulate myself a little bit, so that by the time I get to the bed I'm a little bit on the way, as opposed to being ungracious about it. It helps me get into the mood much quicker. Touching my nipples while fantasizing, or just doing anything to get myself up for it works.

Bernice (sixty-seven, housewife, married to Alan, an architect, for forty-two years) occasionally reads erotica during the day when her husband is not home:

Pornography is not a bad stimulant—it keeps my mind open to sex. My husband will come in with a *Penthouse* or *Playboy*, and I'll read it. In the early days of our marriage, the *Thousand and One Nights*, the Burton edition, was the thing. That was stimulating to both of us!

The fun of setting up the scene can be an important sexual turn-on. The ways women set the stage so that they feel turned on sexually will be described in more detail in the next chapter. However, Judith, age forty, married eight years, goes into a delicious description of how she makes sure the situation is set up in a way that is especially erotic for her:

I have a wonderful time, although it's taken me years to get to the point where I can do things like this. I drag out my sexy nighties. . . . I'll get candles, incense, a joint, make the bed, and straighten up the room—I don't want to have fabulous sex in a messy bedroom! I almost always want to take a hot bath. I want to be clean, to feel smooth. We have a fireplace in the dining room, so sometimes we'll make a fire in the fireplace, spread the pillows out, and go get whatever it is we want to eat and drink. A lot of times we get into the bath together. . . . Sometimes massage is involved, not usually a long-term massage, but something that starts out that way. Part of having sex for me is being able to relax enough to enjoy it. The hot bath, massage, and sensual stuff helps to start untangling all those knots so I can let go and have a really sexy experience. Also, I turn off the telephone because the telephone is constantly ringing. It took some sex education courses for me to be comfortable enough to admit that I wanted to do all that stuff. I used to feel embarrassed, but the more I've done it and found out that I usually got what I wanted, the easier it's been.

CLEANLINESS

Probably more than any other single factor, women mentioned the importance of cleanliness in leading to an enjoyable time in bed. Women felt more comfortable if they were clean; they certainly felt more comfortable about oral sex if they were clean, and they often felt more turned on to their partner if he had taken a shower immediately before making love.

It is not surprising that women feel this way. Cleanliness is endemic to our culture. There are hundreds of different underarm deodorants, aftershave colognes, perfumes, scented soaps, and talcum powders. Advertising in the media convinces us that the only good smell is an artificial fragrance or no smell at all. "Clean is sexy," repeats the Noxzema commercial and vaginal douches and sprays have been hyped to make us feel bad about any natural odor our genitals might give off.

While growing up, women are often given the strong message that we are dirty "down there." We had to wipe ourselves with scented toilet paper, and many of us had to use two washcloths—a separate one for our genitals, because that area might contaminate the rest of our body.

Alexandra (thirty-two, divorced):

Cleanliness is very important to me. Sometimes if I don't have time for a shower and I want oral sex, I might go to the bathroom and wash my genitals with soap and water. I like to take a shower before sex, not after. I like the way I smell and feel after making love. I love getting up in the morning knowing I've had sex and even smelling it on my body and then just going to work. But I like to take a shower when I get home because I like to get rid of the day's sweat.

Christine (forty-one, married nineteen years):

I like him to be clean. He knows that it's a real turn-on for me, so he'll jump in the shower.

A few women felt differently about the need to be superclean to enjoy sex, as typified by thirty-two-year-old René:

I don't feel it's necessary for me to shower every time I have sex. There are some times when I feel dirty, especially with the sticky summertime air, and I just feel more rejuvenated if I take a shower. But unless I have some physiological problems like vaginal discharge or reeking armpits, I don't feel any necessity for taking a shower or sponging off prior to sleeping with somebody. I also rarely take a shower after I've slept with someone. I guess I don't see sex as dirtying in any sense so that I don't feel any need to wash to clean myself before or to wash to divest myself of it afterward. I just never made that link.

Some women even find that natural bodily odors enhance their sexual arousal. They find the smell of their partner's skin just as enticing as the smells of soaps or colognes. As twenty-eight-year-old Claire, a television director who has been married for five years to Alex, an attorney, recalled:

Once we were on a wonderful camping trip in the mountains. At the end of a full day of hiking, we broke camp and cooked dinner. Afterward, we were sitting around the fire under the stars. We just became very excited with each other and had sex. We were absolutely filthy and smelly dirty, but it was a very exciting experience.

Sally, thirty-five years old and married for sixteen years, adds:

I love the popping noises that our bodies make when we really are wet from sweating. Maybe I'm weird, but I love getting sweaty; I even love the smell.

Bathing and showering was not always used only as a way to get clean, but also as a "sensual appetizer."

Morgan (forty-two, married nine years):

It is really relaxing for me to take a shower accompanied by music or candlelight with or without my partner. When I'm really tense and tired, it's extremely soothing. All my bathrooms have candles in them, and they're usually big Dansk candles, not thin little tapers. So there's enough light to see by, but it's not like a bright overhead light.

Tara, a sixty-three-year-old housewife with five grown children, married to Herb, a businessman, says:

Sometimes we take a shower together and play with each other in the shower. Other times, we take separate showers, and I get into bed feeling very young and seductive, lying there nude, imagining how excited he is going to be because I'm powdered and oiled, and then I'm really ready to make love.

One woman mentioned that she had a massage head on her shower and found the pulsing water very exciting. Another woman talking about her special brand of soap and its novel effect said:

Dr. Bronner's Castile soap is terrific for turning me on. It is strong soap so you can't use too much of it. But if you dilute it and rub it around your genitals, it'll tingle long after you've rinsed and dried off.

Since cleanliness was such an important aspect of being comfortable and therefore being able to enjoy sex more, we asked women for suggestions about how they had dealt with this issue. Some women suggested wearing tampons or panty liners during the day or the evening before sex to absorb lubrication and prevent the buildup of vaginal odor.

Sage (thirty-five, lesbian) found a way to honor her need for cleanliness yet not let it destroy the spontaneity with her partner:

I have a washcloth by the bed so I don't have to get up and wash my cunt if I'm uptight about somebody smelling me. Once or twice I've gotten up to wash and the person would say, "Oh, don't be ridiculous. Don't get up." Now I have my washcloth there and I still can take care of my need for cleanliness but not disrupt the mood.

Some of these women were turned off by morning breath, either their partners' or their own. Again, a number of creative helpful hints were given:

Iris:

I really hate morning breath, so my husband and I keep a bottle of Binaca [breath freshener] next to the bed, and when we want to have sex in the morning, we playfully begin by spritzing each other's mouths before kissing.

Judith:

I get up in the morning, go to the bathroom, and brush my teeth if there's a possibility I might have sex afterward, because I can't stand it otherwise.

Sage:

It is really important to me to have something to eat or drink by the bed, like an orange, mineral water or tea left over from the night before, so I can make love in the morning without having to get up and brush my teeth. I don't like to have that nasty taste in my mouth and just start kissing somebody.

Some physical attributes, in addition to cleanliness, were mentioned by a few women as important in the turn-on process: "I never wear curlers to bed. I always try to keep my nails done, my legs shaved, and all those little things, so that I'm pleasant to jump in bed with."

But cleanly shaven legs was not a turn-on for all women. Alice, a thirty-eight-year-old teacher who is single, said:

I just decided this winter that I was not going to shave my legs; my lover was very appreciative of this. He said my hair felt very soft and sexy on his legs. It seemed to enhance the whole sexual feeling when we were together so I've decided not to shave my legs at least during the winter.

Ruby (thirty-nine, married eighteen years) added:

I've grown the hair under my arms; it's very soft, eliminates the irritation of shaving, and has a curious charm for my husband. I've heard other men say they enjoy underarm hair, but I haven't had the opportunity to test the breadth of its appeal.

Ruby also talked about her special tattoo that had been an enhancement to her and her husband's arousal:

We have enjoyed my small heart-shaped tattoo. It's located on the side of my hip, just above the panty line, which keeps it covered except in private situations.

PLACE

Where she made love was discussed by virtually every woman interviewed. Women found that making love in a variety of places was a real turn-on. This included different rooms and different pieces of furniture in their home as well as outdoors and in just about every conceivable moving vehicle!

Making love outdoors was especially erotic for some women. Women talked about making love in the woods, at the beach, in their back yard, anywhere where there was some privacy.

Cortney, age thirty-one and divorced, remembers:

One time my husband and I made love in our back yard. Our house is in a group of homes all clustered together. We have some privacy but you can still look over the fence. This time, none of our neighbors were home. It was a hot summer day, so we just went out and lay in the yard and made love.

Connie (twenty-six, widowed four years):

I grew up in the country and the first time I ever made love was in the grass, so my associations with that are really very pleasant. I didn't do that again until last summer when I went back to Texas and saw one of my favorite lovers of all time. He said, "What do you want to do?" and I said, "I want to go out to the lake." So we went out on the rocks and the sun was blazing hot and we climbed down the rocks to the water. First we took off all our clothes and jumped in the water, then we got back on the rocks until the sun went down and it was a little more private. Finally, we made love and had our last swim way out in the dark.

One woman said that the sun turned her on and making love anywhere in the sunlight made it enjoyable for her. Another was turned on by the cold. Living in a snowy mountainous area, she claimed that all you had to do was "put your parka down and have some fun." Still another woman talked about being comfortable making love outside with the aid of a sleeping bag.

Diane (thirty-two, teacher, lesbian):

Making love in a sleeping bag is really neat. You feel like you're in a cocoon when you're both in one sleeping bag. It's really cozy because it's warm and you're so close together.

Moving vehicles seemed to add a sense of danger or excitement to the lovemaking experience. All types of boats were popular, ranging from rowboats to fancy powerboats and sailboats.

Nell (thirty-six, married eight months):

We were in a rowboat in the delta and the boat was just bobbing along. We put down the anchor and made love sitting up in the boat. We were in a teeny little channel but another boat could have come along at any moment. I don't know if they would have noticed what was happening but I thought, "This is not like me, in a boat in the middle of the day; what must I be thinking?"

We've heard of the Mile-High Club, an underground organization of those people who have made love while in an airplane, but we had never met a real person who had done it before. Three of the women we interviewed said that they had.

Suzanne (thirty-seven, bisexual, living alone):

We wanted to try making love on an airplane and we did it. We made love on the way to Las Vegas in the bathroom of a 747. We both went into the bathroom, one at a time. He's six one and I'm only five two, so I sat on the sink. Then I was about the right level for where his penis would be. He entered me that way. It was very exciting. We just barely got done in time so that we could get in our seats for landing, because Las Vegas is a short trip.

The other two women mentioned that their partner sat on the airplane lavatory seat and that they sat on top of him.

Making love in a car, moving or parked, was not at all uncommon. Iris, thirty-two, single, living with lover:

Once while my partner was driving, I unzipped his fly and began playing with his penis. I could tell he was enjoying it, so I changed my position and starting sucking him. There was plenty of room to be comfortable. At first, he wanted me to stop. He was really getting turned on but I refused to and he really started getting into it. He was worried about getting into an accident when he came, so he moved into the slow lane and came without getting us killed or anything. It was a lot more fun than watching the freeway signs!

On another occasion he returned the favor and while he was driving he was fingering me. He is really talented: even with his eyes on the road he brought me to orgasm. I think I was turned on more than usual because of the added vibration of the car and the fact that we were on vacation.

Even the lack of privacy traveling on a bus did not stop one woman. Fifty-nine-year-old Ann, who has been married thirty-six years, recalls the following:

I remember about two years before we were married, we were on a bus and it was Christmas Eve. We put a coat over us and played with each other to orgasm. When I think about it now, I think "My God," but then it felt very right. We came from a generation where sex was illicit, so the illicitness was important—we knew we were getting away with it. That was a turn-on.

Places that were inside, yet not at home, were also described. Alexandra spoke of one of her escapades:

Most of my fun sex has been based on fantasy and a sense of danger. We had sex in my office—in a psychiatric clinic—which is the most dangerous place for me to have sex, particularly since my partner had such a high shrill laugh when he came; it was just the most dangerous thing I could do and we did it all the time.

Gail, age thirty-five, a lesbian and a writer who is divorced and now lives with her lover, recalled:

Once I was in a movie theater watching *The Last Picture Show* and was amazed to find that I was getting turned on. In the movie, an older woman and a young man were having a relationship and they were in bed together. I didn't think it was very good sex, but there was something about it that really turned me on. I found my hand was gravitating toward my crotch and I had a very short conversation with myself about whether or not I would do it! Then I looked around and there weren't a lot of people in the theater and it was very dark; so I put my coat over my lap and ever so quietly played with myself until I came. After being married for five years, I had learned how to masturbate very quietly! Acting on my impulse and doing something so very outrageous was really a turn-on!

Motels were mentioned by a number of women as a guaranteed turn-on. Thirty-five-year-old Allison, who is divorced and living with her boy friend, says:

When we go to a nice motel with crisp new sheets, it's a new room to me and a different feel to the bed, so I always want to fuck. It would be a completely wasted evening if we were in a really lovely motel and we didn't have sex.

Some cities, such as San Francisco, have special hot-tub centers with private rooms you can rent where you can be as sensual and sexual as you like—for an hour.

Judith (forty, bisexual, married eight years):

One of my biggest turn-ons is getting greased up and having the other person greased up too. I mostly indulge in that at the hot tubs since I can't stand the thought of having my sheets totally destroyed. The hot-tub places are just fabulous. They have a bed with a sheet on it and they provide you with towels. You can bring your own oils and creams, soak in your private hot tub, do whatever you want and it's ultra-sex! You're all slippery against each other and it's just incredibly erotic.

By and large, however, people have sex at home, and generally in the bedroom. As one woman said, "We always make love in bed. Things may start in another room, but they always end up in bed." This is, in large part, the result not only of convenience but of the ways we learned about sex. Since sex is something personal and private, most of us have never witnessed our parents interacting sexually. It was something that occurred behind closed doors. To deviate from sex in the bedroom for some people represents the radical, or even the perverted.

Having sex in the bedroom late at night and early in the morning can also be a way for some women who are not comfortable with their sexuality to avoid facing the fact that they are being sexual. They can make love in the dark late at night just before falling off to sleep, or in the early morning before they are fully awake. It removes the necessity to initiate sex in an overt way and hence can be viewed more as a marital duty than as something which might conflict with a puritanical upbringing.

More important, bedroom sex is convenient. It allows sex to take a natural place in our daily functioning. It enables those who are busy to enjoy sexual encounters without adding the burden of having to plan for sex. Routine sex can be the meat and potatoes of a sexual relationship. It is often a gentle and effortless way to communicate caring or to say, "I love you." However, some women find that straight meat and potatoes can become so routinized that it becomes boring. Many of the women we interviewed mentioned the need for variety to periodically enhance their lovemaking. One woman suggested sleeping in a different bed as a way of adding spice to her sexual relationship with her husband:

I love to sleep in one bed and make love in another. It makes sex more exciting and a little different.

Some people liked to make love in different rooms, or on the floor.

Heather, a thirty-five-year-old mother of a two-year-old daughter, says:

I enjoy having sex on the spur of the moment, on the kitchen floor, on the living-room floor, or kind of hiding from the baby by running downstairs and closing the door and having sex quickly—trying to get away with it, almost the way you would if your parents were in the room.

Another woman who is referred to here simply as Ms. X, the name we use when women shared something they were too embarrassed to have us print even under a pseudonym, recalls the following:

I remember we were in the middle of having sex and all of a sudden he said, "Do you mind if we move to the sink?" I said, "You must be out of your mind. What are you doing?" but he was already picking me up. I said, "You can't do this!" He said, "You'll like this, you'll see. If you don't I'll stop." And he sat me down in the bathroom sink. He carried me in there with his penis still in me, but I don't think it stayed in all the time. Anyway, he somehow got me in a position that gave him the angle and pressure he wanted and we had sex there. I remember that I felt a little self-conscious, but it also was really arousing, maybe because it was so different. I guess that's what made him such a good lover—I never knew what he would do next.

Samantha, a thirty-five-year-old hospital administrator, and divorced mother of an eight-year-old son, shares the following "ritual" that added variety to her lovemaking:

When I was married we used to christen every new piece of furniture by having sex on it. It was great fun. I'd always throw a sheet over it so I wouldn't worry about how I was going to get the stains out.

Rose, thirty-six years old, found a way to use one of her favorite antiques to enrich her sex life:

I have a lovely antique oak rocking chair without arms in my bedroom. Everyone comments on how sweet it is, which always makes me smile because I know that it's been the vehicle for many sexy evenings. After some arousing foreplay, my lover sits on the chair. I sit on his lap literally, with his penis inside me, and then we just rock away.

A few women recommended using the bathroom not only as a way to get clean or turned on initially, but as a place to have a sensual, romantic evening:

Taking baths together can be so sensual. I have a lover who will sit on the side of the bathtub and make love to me when I take a bath.

Another woman confided:

I like to take a bath with my lover and make it a really sensual experience. We usually pour a warm bath, sometimes using bath oil or bubble bath, and then light some candles for atmosphere. Sometimes we bring in some wine and just soak in the tub and talk and then kiss and caress each other. The trick to staying warm in the bath has to do with positioning. Either he sits at one end of the tub while I sit at the other with our legs entwined or sometimes I lie back on top of him between his spread legs.

DRUGS AS A SEXUAL STIMULANT

Many women discussed the use of mind-altering substances as a way to enhance all of the five senses. Alcohol, marijuana, cocaine, psychedelic mushrooms, and amyl nitrate were mentioned in connection with sexual experiences. In regard to these substances, Raisin, a thirty-one-year-old lawyer, who is a lesbian and lives next door to her lover, Rosie, made an astute observation:

There's a very fine line between what is sexually enhancing and what allows people to tune out and not take responsibility, and I think those things are different for everyone. In other words, I think certain people use dope to really avoid an experience and other people use it to enhance an experience.

It is interesting that although we interviewed a rather wide range of women, very few of them used alcohol to enhance sex, while a surprisingly high percentage had at some time made love after smoking marijuana. Most did not use pot in any regular fashion, but occasionally found that it enhanced sex, much in the same way their parents had used alcohol—as a way of relaxing and feeling less inhibited.

Forty-year-old Sonya, microbiologist, separated, says:

Smoking marijuana is definitely an enhancement. I use just enough to set the mood. Too much marijuana makes me too mellow.

Thirty-eight-year-old Elaine's most unusual sexual experience resulted from having taken a psychedelic drug for the first time:

I did take a psychedelic drug once that a lover had given to me. As a matter of fact, he was a physician, which made me feel safe because I had never been into drugs at all. But I wanted to experience what my kids are being exposed to and I thought I might as well do it while I was unattached since I was separated at the time. So this physician and I took some psilocybin together. It was a very interesting experience, particularly the sexual part. By the time we had sex, which was about two hours later, his penis seemed gigantic to me. Sex with his giant penis gave me the most wonderful feelings I've ever had. When he penetrated me it felt like his penis went all the way up to my throat. The music from the radio was magnificent. I could hear every single instrument clearly. But the physical contact with his lips, his warm body, and his giant penis was the main thing.

CREATING A SENSUAL ENVIRONMENT

For those occasions when sex occurs passionately on the spur of the moment, when the two of you decide to feel naughty in the car on a long trip, or have the luxury of hours in a motel room in a distant city or country, the excitement of the moment creates a sexual ambience of its own. However, for most women with nine-to-five jobs, married twelve years with 2.2 children, special attention must be paid to details.

Although intimacy is often deepened by the familiarity and comfort of a long-term monogamous relationship, the same familiarity and comfort of making love with one partner without any new influences can also result in routinized sex. Women in monogamous relationships often require an external catalyst to replace the excitement generally provided by a new lover.

Since the man is supposed to be the one to orchestrate the sex act, a new partner can provide a new style, a new approach, new activities. Without different partners to provide fresh input, women are often at a loss as to how to innovate and create that variety.

Creating a sensual environment that excites all the senses can take minutes or days and can make all the difference in the world. Some of the ideas the women shared with us dealt with the ways they used their senses to turn themselves on, to keep themselves turned on, and to turn their partners on as well.

Sharon (thirty-five, single, living alone) says it so beautifully:

What I do is to keep a very special, beautiful sheet that I can put down over a soft rug on the floor before we make love. I like to make love on the floor because I'm very muscular and a lot of my body is involved in the orgasm. Then I dim the lights and light a candle and bring whatever objects we are going to use in making love next to the sheet. The whole thing feels kind of magical, like suddenly we have created a very special, beautiful, sensual atmosphere in that space.

VISUAL

Special lighting seemed to create a warm, romantic atmosphere for most women. Candles, oil lamps, and fireplaces were mentioned over and over again.

Morgan (forty-two, married nine years):

We happen to be extremely lucky because we have a fireplace in our bedroom and in the wintertime we light it up with these marvelous little three-hour logs that you can buy in the supermarket and lie in our bed making love. We both think our bed is the most marvelous, fantastic bed in existence and it would become part of a custody battle if we ever got divorced.

Iris (thirty-two, single):

If you happen to live in the city and you have a streetlight outside your bedroom window, turn all the lights off and open up the draperies and let the streetlight shine in. It gives the room a softer, more quietly beautiful light. Sometimes just for variety we use black light, which throws a purply dark haze over the room.

Mirrors

Many women designed an exciting atmosphere for lovemaking using other paraphernalia. Some fancied mirrors positioned specifically for watching themselves making love. Sometimes the women arrange the mirrors.

Rosemary (thirty-six, divorced):

In my old apartment I had mirror tiles all over my walls so I could watch him while he was eating me or he could watch while I was eating him. Sometimes when I was on top, I'd be facing the mirror and I could see myself fucking him, which was a real turn-on.

Sometimes their partners arranged the mirrors.

Judy (thirty-one, married two years):

My husband likes mirrors because he likes to watch. He likes to arrange the scene, so he does all that stuff. I let him do his thing, joyously. I love it.

Clothing

Certain types of attire appear to enhance the sexual experience for some. Nightgowns were a favorite, particularly slinky ones or antique ones.

Edith, age sixty-six, married forty-two years:

A nightgown is a much easier garment for initiating physical contact. I always have attractive ones, both for myself and because my husband likes them too.

Some women preferred garments of a more explicitly sexual nature.

Harriet (thirty-four, married ten years):

The outfit I like the most is crotchless panties, a lacy hardly-there bra, a real frilly garter belt, and black net stockings.

Penelope (forty-six, married):

I have a silk "teddy" that only goes down to my thighs and has a snap crotch. It's got spaghetti straps and a lace top, and it feels really sensual to have silk next to you. I also use silk stockings and garter belts.

Nonsexual clothing can be very sexual, as one woman confided:

My husband and I used to have this ritual that we both enjoyed because it was a little kinky. Whenever I bought a new pair of shoes, I always wore them to bed to break them in. My husband used to like it if I would wear the shoes and slowly strip in front of him until I had only the shoes on. Then I kind of pranced around. I felt like I looked sexy walking around with high heels without anything else on. Then we would end up making love and I'd keep the shoes on all night.

Lacy underwear and crotchless panties were said to be found in specialty shops or by mail-ordering through Sensory Research, Eve's Garden, or Frederick's of Hollywood. Black corsets or waist cinchers are available in five-and-ten-cent stores. Antique underwear and interesting costumes were hunted down by devotees for a song at flea markets.

Actually most of us purchase even our street clothing for its sensual appeal—for example, lacy blouses, dresses made of soft and clinging material, or tight jeans. Just wearing this clothing can in itself be stimulating. Thirty-six-year-old Rose describes how she used certain articles for a very personal sex show:

I have a beautiful silk shawl that is quite large and has long fringe on it. When I wear it out in the evening, the fringe reaches down to my knees. My lover always smiles at me whenever he sees me wear it out because he also remembers the nights I have used it to do what we call the "shawl dance." On those occasions, I dim the lights and put on some Moroccan music that I bought on a trip there and come out wrapped in nothing but my shawl. Then I halfway close my eyes and pretend to be an exotic Eastern dancer and just move to the music and do a slow sensual dance by moving the shawl up and down my body and in between my legs. It's kind of a teasing strip dance that turns both of us on.

Getting dressed up this way is not easy for everyone. Christine (forty-one, married nineteen years) tells us about a delightful, but somewhat embarrassing experience:

Sharon and I are teachers at a nursery school and we were trying to think of doing something special for our husbands on Valentine's Day. The children were making these little red paper hearts. We decided to take these hearts home and paste them on our nipples and "down there" as a surprise. I did it and waited under the covers to greet my husband when he arrived home. It was a great success, but I was so embarrassed. And of course, he loved it and talked about it for hours. If I could do more of those things without feeling so embarrassed . . . but it's hard.

AUDITORY

Although some women mentioned that listening to music distracted them from what they were experiencing sexually, most women felt that music was a definite enhancement.

Cortney, thirty-one:

I really like having music in the bedroom. My boy friend has a really sexy house. He's got a stereo upstairs and two speakers in his bedroom too, so we can switch it off downstairs and have it playing in the bedroom. It's really neat—it gets you into that sexy frame of mind.

The women's taste in music varied considerably from ballet and classical music through country and western to hard rock. Some found that music helped stimulate their fantasies:

I'm a rock music fan and I find that having some of my favorite rock music on when I'm having sex is really a turn-on. The strong underlying beat is really sensual to me. When I concentrate on the music and let my body move to the music, I feel more sexual. I can also get into fantasies using some of my favorite female rock stars as heroines because I see them as being very sexual women. Ordinarily I have a hard time giving myself permission to be an openly sexual woman, but since I admire these rock stars who seem to feel okay about their sexuality, I can allow myself to act as I think they might. Sometimes I can be more "outrageous" with my partner because in my mind I'm really Janis Joplin.

Finally, women mentioned that music also provides a shield from noises made during lovemaking, especially when there were other people nearby. Harriet, age thirty-four, married ten years:

It's real nice for us to have music, especially if anyone else is in the house. Then we hear the music and we're not so concerned about whether anyone else hears us. That's what we do to be comfortable if somebody's staying here.

KINESTHETIC

It is necessary to create not only a sensual atmosphere, but one that takes care of your creature comforts as well. Being uncomfortable, particularly being cold, is a real drawback to a good sexual experience. Women found the following ways to create a comfortable environment.

Cortney (thirty-one, living with boy friend):

I really do like a water bed. It allows me to be so much more comfortable with somebody. I can have my arm underneath him and not get pinned down. I found that we could cuddle so much better. I also found with the water bed that my back and knees don't hurt like they do sometimes when I've been making love for a long time because everything sort of gives with you—and, most important, it's warm. But if I don't have a water bed, taking the time to turn the thermostat up or to build a fire in the fireplace can make all the difference.

Raisin (thirty-one, lesbian, living next door to her lover):

We take a hot tub first. What happens in a hot tub is that your body absorbs a lot of heat. Then we usually start a fire in the fireplace and get the house very hot so that we can keep off all our clothes and it's not uncomfortable—that way we can stay nude and still be comfortable.

Bev, age thirty, living with boy friend:

When it's cold, it helps to put an electric blanket on the floor or on the bed under the sheet. This keeps the bed warm and makes lovemaking in the cold more comfortable. A heat lamp is also good for the cold. It's not very expensive and we keep it hooked up over the bed. Not only does it warm up the whole bed, but it throws off a lovely red light as well.

Edith (sixty-six, married thirty-seven years):

My husband never liked my cold feet, so I would use a hot-water bottle to warm my feet first. I can remember him drawing away, they used to be so icy, because my circulation in my feet wasn't good. Taking a hot bath before I go to bed warms me up too.

Different sensual materials were incorporated into the lovemaking to enhance tactile feelings.

Sage (thirty-five, lesbian, living alone):

When I undress somebody and there's a particular part of her clothes that's very sensual, I just rub it on her skin for a while with different kinds of pressures. I rub it around her genitals and between us as part of the sensual experience.

Kathryn describes the way a particularly sensual lover used to incorporate silky material into their lovemaking:

He started out first with satin sheets and then he got pieces of satin and other kinds of soft, silky material. He'd put it across himself and across me, then I'd play with his penis using my hand. The material over his penis changed the way it felt for him and for me, too. The pieces, I guess, were about two yards long and of different thicknesses. Sometimes we put really thick satin over me with the smooth side next to my body, then he played with my nipples, real hard but it didn't hurt. It felt really different, really erotic.

Samantha, thirty-five, divorced, hospital administrator, found some offbeat uses for an ordinary household item:

I bought a handmade duster made of ostrich feathers as a Christmas gift, but I think I'm going to keep it myself because there's so much you can do with it besides dusting furniture! It feels so soft and sensual when I lightly run it over my body. I love to use it when I'm masturbating and I've also gotten into using it with my lover. I put it over his penis and swirl it around and it drives him crazy!

Other women suggested using rabbit-skin mittens and a rabbit blanket for a soft teasing touch.

Oils

Women described using oils not only when extra lubrication was necessary, but also for heightening the tactile sensations of a massage. Different oils or lubricants were named: baby oil, Nivea cream, mineral oil, Albolene, Kama Sutra Massage Oil, and plain saliva.

Cortney described an unusual sexual experience for her in which musk oil played an integral part:

There is this kind of oil which comes in different flavors. You just kind of rub them all over your body and it's really nice. I think the time we gave each other massages with musk oil was the time we went to bed with two other people—another couple. We were all high and we had this musk oil all over us, and everyone was all greasy and it was kind of neat. It was something I never thought I'd do, but the people we were with were my friends and we were like a family.

We all massaged each other together and then we made love separately. We were all on this giant king-sized water bed, but we had our own little private areas where different things were going on and that made it a really special experience for me.

TASTE

The sense of smell is intimately tied to one's sense of taste. Lickables or flavored oils were found to enhance three of the five senses: touch, taste, and smell. Suzanne (thirty-seven, bisexual, living alone since divorced):

I've used flavored oils that you can put on a man's cock or a woman's vagina. It comes in cherry flavor and strawberry flavor and actually tastes quite good.

Certain foods enhanced the sexual scene. Joan (thirty-one, married nine years):

Certain kinds of food, such as avocadoes, black olives, strawberries, grapes, and wine, are really erotic. We don't feed each other, but what is erotic for me is when he prepares it. I really like all that thought for me. Just eating it together is erotic because of the textures and the taste of those foods.

Penelope, age forty-six, married ten years:

When we go on long trips, I'll pack a "sex kit" to take along. I take a cooler in which there are Bloody Marys, beer, Coca-Cola, melon balls, cold seedless grapes, a whole bunch of different things like that, and good dope. Sometimes I'll also include nylons to tie each other up, my vibrator, and some Albolene cream. That's about all. Maybe some costumes, too.

Another woman, under the pseudonym of Ms. X, shared how she used the promise of a special meal to create a uniquely erotic evening for herself and her lover:

One night I had a date coming over for dinner and I just didn't feel like cooking. So I got into one of my most sexy-looking lounging gowns and I carefully arranged a place setting without a plate on the couch.

When he arrived at the apartment, the lights were low and I greeted him at the door looking really sexy. He asked, "What's for dinner?" I casually took his hand and led him over to the couch, sat down between the knife and fork, pulled back my gown, and said, "Me!"

That was three years ago and just recently he called me from Texas, where he had moved, to let me know that he often still thinks about me, and that that had been the most exciting evening he had ever had.

Ariel's best sexual experience indicates yet another sensual activity that can result from creatively employing food—real food in this case—olives:

My best sexual experience was with a guy named Drew, about eight years ago. I had just moved to New York and was staying at the Barbizon. His name was given to me by my ex-boy friend. I had been getting phone numbers from everybody because I didn't know anyone in New York, and he just happened to be the first person I called. He came to pick me up to go out to dinner and we just—you know—drooled at each other and he took me back to his apartment. His apartment was built into a cliff in the part of New Jersey which looks across the Hudson River at the New York skyline. It was just this glorious place! We didn't sleep together that first night because I wasn't going for that, that was just not my thing at the time, but when I got back to the hotel, I cursed myself for being a crazy person. Needless to say, the next time we saw each other, we did, and I practically moved in for the next three months.

In those days, we both had very flexible work hours. Drew used to call me up and tell me that he was sitting down on Wall Street with a huge hard on and could I meet him at the Port Authority bus terminal. We would meet at the bus terminal and go back to his house and fuck all afternoon. My favorite, favorite, favorite memory—and this got to be sort of a habit—was the way he would eat olives out of me—that's one of my all-time great, great memories.

Let me explain about the olives. Drew used to eat olives while we were watching the news and waiting for dinner to start. He was the first person who had ever gone down on me, which I adored of course, and he took to pushing the olives up my vagina and then spending time with his tongue getting them out again—that was the whole thing. I'd be laughing and giggling and acting silly for fear the olives would be lost up in me and I would have to go to the doctor and have them retrieved or something, but that never happened. He would just push the olives up with his tongue and then try to get them back again and the great joke was, "that's the only way to eat olives!"

Good sex, like a good meal, requires preparation. A meal which is quickly thrown together can provide sustenance and satisfaction, but lacks the specialness of one which has had attention paid to the details. The setting and the way the meal is served are as important as the skill with which it is cooked. The preparation involved in setting the table attractively, with flowers, intimate lighting, and soft music, adds to the anticipation, creating a magic all its own.

Now that we have addressed the preparation in anticipation of the meal to follow and savored an innovative way to serve olives, we will continue past the hors d'oeuvre on to the main course.

3

Gourmet Lovemaking

Gourmet sex is similar to gourmet cooking. The most renowned gourmet cooks are those who have the sensitivity to appreciate all the nuances that go into creating a sublime culinary experience. The subtle nuances that require forethought and planning often separate a tasty meal from one that is exquisite down to the last detail. Not only is the table set with impeccable care, but all the details are carefully considered, such as the colors, textures, and tastes of the different foods, as well as the selection of complementary wines.

Gourmet sex requires not only deliberate preparation, but oftentimes special accessories. It is not unusual for the gourmet cook to collect particular cookbooks or kitchen accouterments that may not be used frequently but are seen as indispensable for a truly superb sauce. When not in use, these items occupy drawer space or can be attractively displayed on the walls. Accouterments for gourmet sex such as vibrators might be hidden away in drawers, while sensual and attractive fur rugs could be displayed prominently on the walls. As with cooks who have their culinary preferences (French, Italian, or Chinese cuisine), gourmet sex enthusiasts find some indulgences pleasurable, others boring or uninteresting. And we would not expect even the most superb chef to have experience preparing every possible dish.

Finally, even the best of gourmet cooks would not want to go to the trouble of preparing an elaborate meal every night. It would simply require too much energy and time. Nightly gourmet meals, like nightly gourmet sex, would soon become tedious and might even be experienced as a burden rather than a treat.

Women often get plaudits for being good cooks, but creating gourmet sex does not evoke similar reviews. It is difficult to describe in detail the fabulous sexual scene created the night before in the same way you would explain to a friend how the rack of lamb was prepared. Praise and reinforcement comes either from your partner or from yourself. We hope this chapter will add to this process of reinforcing and encouraging you in your creation of gourmet sex.

As a part of the interview we asked women to share the special techniques, intercourse positions, and accouterments they used to enhance their sexual relationships. Almost every woman initially said she really had nothing special to offer. The assumption was that a "really sexual woman" is someone who uses bizarre and unusual sexual techniques to enhance her sexuality. In reality we found that each woman had at least one special way of keeping her sexual relationship alive and interesting. Often, however, the women were so focused on what they could not do that they failed to appreciate the creativity and novelty of the special techniques they already used. Since they carried out these techniques so naturally, they did not realize that these might be interesting and innovative to someone else.

Our biggest problem with this chapter was what to leave out. We had such a plethora of ideas that it felt almost overwhelming. So it is important to remember in reading this chapter that the ideas contained within are a composite of suggestions from 120 women, not one woman's private recipe collection. It contains each woman's favorite and special recipes for enjoyable sex. The suggestions come under different headings. Instead of fish dishes and pastas, we have included the special ways women like to be touched, the different sexual techniques they employ, and their special intercourse positions, as well as a variety of sexual accouterments and fantasy games.

TOUCH

Touch is a major form of communication. A reassuring hand on our shoulder or a hug when we feel low is one way to express our feelings. Different types of physical touching while making love can similarly produce differing emotional and physical reactions. The types of touch—rough, gentle, tickling, scratching, teasing—and the areas that respond positively to being touched in particular ways reflected each woman's individuality. More specifically, all the women we interviewed agreed that, except under unusual circumstances, spending a lot of time on kissing, touching, or caressing was an essential part of their lovemaking experience.

Sylvia (twenty, single) describes the gentle kind of touching she likes to give and receive:

Gentleness and the prolonging of foreplay seems to be what works for me. I start anywhere with my hands, my hair, my fingertips, and touch very gently all over his body. I do it for as long as I can possibly hold out—until it seems like one of us will go crazy. I love touching him this way because the pleasure it gives him is so arousing to me. When he does it to me, it feels so tingling, so warm, and comforting. To me, it's a kind of all-encompassing feeling. You just get lost in it. It's like intercourse without intercourse.

At thirty-seven, Suzanne prefers a more forceful touch:

I enjoy having pressure on my wrists. It's funny, because I don't like to wear a wristwatch or a tight bracelet, but in lovemaking I like somebody to just hold both wrists down or just one. The pressure from that seems to go all the way through my body down to my clit. I also like to feel pressure on my teeth during kissing. It may sound strange, but this male lover I had would press his fingers against my upper teeth and the sensations would go right through my body. Even just rubbing my head real hard or yanking on my hair a little will send vibrations all the way down my body.

Anna, after three years of marriage to her second husband, describes her sexual buttons and how she likes them pushed:

There are certain touch points that are sexual buttons I like to have pushed, like kissing the back of my knees and the nape of my neck. It's really sensual when someone licks my fingers—just brushes his lips over my fingertips—really light touches all over my skin, especially the back of my knees. What it feels like is a whipped-cream waterfall. You end up in a pool of big bubbles and you ride on top of one bubble and it explodes, and then you go into another and then it explodes, and then another.

Alexandra and other women mentioned that, among other areas, the small of the back was particularly sensitive:

I learned from Rick that I had these very delicate hairs on my lower back just where my ass is—where my rump comes to an end and my lower back begins. When he kisses them very lightly, it sends shivers up and down my spine—an incredible feeling. Also, I enjoy very subtle, light touching on my back, and I love toe sucking and finger sucking . . . between my fingers particularly. I really get passionate when my hands are stimulated.

Rosemary, a thirty-six-year-old divorcee, describes how she likes to be kissed, particularly on her breasts:

I'm lying on some nice clean sheets and he starts off by kissing me all over: first on the lips and then moving down my body and kissing my breasts, and I really like him touching my armpits very lightly. I'm very sensitive there and I love that, so while he's touching my armpits with his fingers, he also plays with my nipples with his mouth. He tugs at them with his lips and that's very arousing to me. And then he moves on down and kisses my stomach and my inner thighs. I like that to be very slow and then there's some suspense to it because I don't know exactly when he's going to stop all this kissing around and get down to business. He doesn't touch my genital area at all for a while because he's kissing me all over. Maybe he'll suck my toes or go down my leg licking me with his tongue. His tongue is caressing me all over my body. Then after maybe an hour of that he starts kissing me around the vagina and touching me very softly, kissing my lips and clitoris and putting his tongue inside me as far as it will go. Then he might kiss my breasts some more and I get very, very aroused from all this!

Other women described their breasts as being particularly sensitive. However, some women's breasts responded to gentle touch while others liked a more forceful approach. For example, thirty-three-year-old Aruna said, "When I feel very passionate, I like my tits to be pulled hard, but I don't like my nipples touched too much."

Clearly, for many women, stimulation of other areas proved to be at least as arousing as direct genital stimulation, particularly initially. However, this type of touching, or foreplay, did not always have to be seen as a prelude to intercourse.

Monique (thirty-two, married nine years) had an enlightening point of view:

A new thing we've started doing is making love without screwing. It's given us, particularly me, a tremendous feeling of freedom and excitement, knowing that I have the option to caress and be caressed without having to have intercourse and without having to have an orgasm. The whole idea of foreplay is one that I've always found very troubling. I don't like the word foreplay because it sounds like you're doing something in order to get ready to have something else happen. When Brent is touching my breasts, I can't stand the idea that just because my breasts are touched, it means I have to get ready to have an orgasm. I like the idea of just having him touch my breasts or my stroking his penis, or hugging and kissing and talking for a little while, and half an hour later maybe we'll decide to have intercourse and maybe not. What is so erotic as well as comforting to me is the notion that lovemaking can just be a mutual pleasuring and need not be genitalized.

It is important to realize that even if a particular type of touching or thrusting is incredibly arousing initially, it may after a period of time become irritating or cause a numbing of the sensation in that area. This is of concern to women because often they request a particular type of touching which they initially find arousing and worry that something is wrong with them when they no longer find it pleasurable. Sometimes this causes them to hesitate to ask for a particular touch again for fear that the feelings will disappear. It is important to know that this is a normal response to any continuous, unchanging form of stimulation. The nerve endings in the area being stimulated will accommodate to the feelings, much as someone who lives over a noisy boulevard no longer notices every time a truck or bus goes by. Physical sexual stimulation works the same way. Consequently, a break in the routine will refresh the sensors in that area and increase the perception of the sensations. Stopping the stimulation for a moment, changing the tempo by slowing it down or speeding it up, or changing the site of the stimulation if the sexual feelings which were once exciting have died down, all help to increase and enhance awareness and sensitivity to touch.

ORAL SEX

A large majority of the women we interviewed had experienced oral sex, both fellatio and cunnilingus. Most considered oral sex, particularly cunnilingus, one of their most special and enjoyable sexual activities.

Heather (thirty-five, married three years):

I guess oral sex is so nice because my husband really works at it. He knows how to use his tongue; he tongues me in all the right places, on my clitoris and my lips. I especially like when he even sucks on my clitoris a little bit, but not too hard because if it's too much, it hurts. He puts his finger up my anus as well, when his tongue is inside me and that's nice, too.

Theresa (age thirty, lesbian):

I really, really, really like oral sex with tongue or lips or nibbles with teeth, but mostly with tongue and lips and kissing and sucking my clitoris or my vagina. While my partner is going down on me orally, I enjoy playing with my breasts and particularly my nipples. I find that when I squeeze my nipples at the same time, it increases the pleasure and the sensations of oral sex.

As with cunnilingus, most of the women enjoyed fellatio. They enjoyed the experience of turning their partner on, the sensualness of the texture and taste of the penis in their mouth, and for many the sense of power and control they felt was a turn-on in itself.

Rosemary (thirty-six, mental health administrator, divorced, living alone), describes her technique in exquisite detail:

Being licked all over is a real turn-on for my boy friend. He loves to have his balls and anal area licked and kissed and for me to stick my tongue in his anus. He likes it when I almost adore it, and he can see that I really enjoy doing it. He is particularly sensitive on the underside of his penis on down to the balls and all around the anus. He also likes me to put my finger inside his anus. I put Vaseline on my middle finger and I stick it all the way in, while I'm licking his balls. Then I move on to the penis while I've still got my finger in his anus and I'm sucking and putting his penis all the way in my mouth. He reaches a climax pretty quickly this way so it's a real turn-on for him and for me too.

I use the "butterfly stroke," where I flick my tongue up and down the length of the penis and back and forth over the area under the corona. And I do a lot of tantalizing even before I get to the penis, like caressing the sensitive area on the upper thigh, near the crease. I go round and round that whole area with my fingers or my tongue. I do all that stroking early on and continue it until he *really* wants me to caress his penis. I did the same thing when I was a teacher—I never told until they really wanted to hear it.

There were some women who disliked cunnilingus, fellatio, or both. In general, their discomfort with cunnilingus was related to concerns about cleanliness, fears that they would not taste good or smell good, and consequently would offend their partner. Women who liked oral sex generally had a clear idea about how they liked it done. Most tended to be turned off when their partner handled them roughly by sucking too hard or by biting them. Many enjoyed direct sucking of their clitoris while others found this to be uncomfortable and preferred the surrounding areas to be massaged with their partner's tongue or lips.

Those who did not enjoy fellatio generally had an aversion to receiving their partner's ejaculation in their mouth. Consequently, some women would stop fellatio at the point of ejaculation and move on to intercourse or some other type of touching.

Paula, thirty-two, describes her experience in overcoming her discomfort with fellatio and cunnilingus, as well:

As I've gotten more comfortable with my body and having other people explore it, the thing I find that brings me to a higher level of excitement is cunnilingus. It's really enjoyable to have a guy manipulate my clitoris with his tongue. It's gentler than a finger, and once I got over my embarrassment about having somebody's mouth down in that area, the feelings I got out of it were wonderful. In fact, I find that cunnilingus really helps the whole sexual experience. Now I'm able to perform the same sort of act on men. It took me a while to be able to get over my dislike for the taste of semen. At first, it was gagging me, kind of like drinking beer, but eventually I got comfortable with it. Oral sex freed me up from simply "lying parallel on the bed." It makes me more active and brings a little bit of humor into sex because some of the positions we have to get into when we're trying to mutually satisfy each other get us all tangled up. If I can relax about it and move around the bed more freely as opposed to the traditional way of making love, it introduces a little lightheartedness into the act and makes it much more enjoyable.

Alexandra suggested this helpful hint in relation to a common problem occurring with fellatio:

The hair on my head is thick and long and gets in my way, especially if I'm sucking him. It's just impossible. I always keep a rubber band by the bed so I can pull my hair back in a ponytail.

Simultaneous fellatio and cunnilingus or "sixty-nine," as with everything else, was disliked by some and enjoyed by others. Ruby (thirty-nine, married eighteen years):

To me, just the mere fact of getting to the point of making love orally means there's something special going on between us. There is a real trust involved in the sixty-nine position and that feeling of trust enhances the love. It enhances my response to my partner, and whether or not I climax in that position or move on to something else, I think the whole experience has been greater for both of us.

Sally (thirty-five, married sixteen years):

I really like oral sex—both ways—when my partner goes down on me and when I go down on him. Sometimes we go down on each other at the same time, but I usually prefer one at a time. Otherwise, there's too much going on. I feel like I'm going to miss out on something, especially since I love oral sex when I'm the recipient. I love the feelings. I feel really tingly and excited like I'm going to burst open any minute. I like to try to stay at the edge. I actually try not to have an orgasm for a long time, then when it happens, it's really intense.

When it's my turn to go down on my partner, I love to put his penis in my mouth, massage it and take it out, and watch to see how he is reacting. I can feel when he is getting ready to come, then I stop and start all over again. I love seeing his excitement. That's tremendously exciting for me. I can have an orgasm just by doing that.

POSITIONS

There was an unlimited variety of intercourse positions engaged in by the women we talked with. Some felt that using different positions was a major way of spicing up their sex life, whereas others really preferred one or two positions, which they engaged in most of the time, and used other activities to provide the variety they sought.

Monique (thirty-two, married nine years):

When we start making love, we usually start in a conventional way, meaning that we'll be touching each other in an understandable sequence where we both know what's going to happen next. I think it's important for both of us to try to be creative and to take off from that routine and change the mood, the tempo, and the positions. Sometimes we'll assume different positions, meaning that I'll be on top, or we'll be side to side, or I'll have my legs hanging over the edge of the bed, or we'll be on the floor. There are a variety of positions that we use to keep the excitement up.

The missionary position, with the woman on the bottom and the partner on top facing her was not only used by most of the women interviewed, but also preferred by a large majority of them.

Harriet, thirty-four, still prefers the missionary position after ten years of marriage to her cotherapist partner, Tom:

The missionary position is exciting for me because I really like his body weight on me. Even if his body weight is not on me, I can put my legs up in a way that insertion is really deep. Sometimes my legs are up and sometimes I'll put one leg down and the other up. That's to facilitate being stimulated in a particular place in my vagina. I have real definite places in my vagina that are real turn-ons for me and they bring me orgasms. If "six o'clock" is down by my perineum and "twelve o'clock" is closest to my clitoris, then the parts of my vagina that are most sensitive are at "six o'clock" and "four o'clock." "Ten o'clock" and "twelve o'clock" are good, too, but they're not as reliable as six and four o'clock.

Claudia (thirty-two, lesbian, living alone):

I like the position where we are both stimulating each other's clitoris by rubbing against each other. I've always done that face to face and we both get off at the same time. It's really terrific.

Tara (sixty-three, married forty-two years):

The missionary position is the nicest. There is something about the coziness, it's a cuddly kind of thing.

Rose (thirty-six, single) found a technique that turned the old missionary position into a very special event:

I will never forget a wonderful technique that one lover used during intercourse. After some lovely extended foreplay, he first entered me when I was on my back on the bed. He was positioned between my legs and had his hands on either side of me and used them as levers to raise and lower his body. He would alternately kiss, lick, and nibble different parts of my face, neck, and breasts until I was quite aroused. Then he would quickly raise himself higher and suddenly thrust into me. The shock and suddenness of it felt like a sword being thrust into my vagina. He would thrust away for only a few seconds, then slowly withdraw. At the same time he would begin caressing me again until I was at a fever pitch and almost begging him to enter me. Again, without any warning he would thrust back into me and repeat this process for the longest time until both he and I were so excited that we both climaxed in a series of thrustings.

Women had other preferences in positions. Susan, thirty-six, married:

There are certain positions that I initiate. I like being on top of him. That gives me more freedom of movement. I also like the way the hair on his chest feels against my breasts. So I manage to always get in that position at one time or another during the lovemaking.

Mary Lou, thirty-one, married for ten years, prefers the side position:

I like being embraced, and when we're both on our sides, then we can embrace each other.

Rear entry was second in popularity to the missionary position and could be achieved in a number of ways.

Harriet, thirty-four, married:

I like to be fucked from behind. I'm on my hands and knees and he's behind me on his knees. He's also either stroking my clitoris or he has my breast cupped and is pressing it so I'm getting additional stimulation while we're having intercourse, and I really like that a lot. In this position his penis hits a special part of my vagina much more powerfully and consistently. We also both have more freedom of movement and I like that.

Claudia, thirty-two, lesbian and living alone:

I like being on my stomach and having someone on top of me, having her hand on my clitoris and me reaching around, doing what I can to stimulate her at the same time. She's also getting off by rubbing herself on my rear end.

Billy, forty-three, married:

I prefer the intercourse position of him entering me from the back when I'm on my side. When he enters me from the back, his penis seems to reach an area that normally isn't reached when I'm lying on my back. Sometimes I give myself additional clitoral stimulation with my hand if it's necessary.

Rosemary (thirty-six, divorced four years):

I like the position where I'm leaning over the bed, and he's behind me and pulling me toward him. I'm bent over at the waist with my face down on the bed and my feet on the floor and I'm pressing against the bed. He enters me from behind. Then he can grab me around my hips, and I can rest my head on the bed while he pulls me back and forth toward him.

Anna, a twenty-eight-year-old educator's wife, describes some other possible positions:

He's on top while I'm on my back and my legs are curled up around his neck. I like this position because the penetration is really deep and he's able to move well. I can feel the pressure points in different areas inside me if he moves to the left or to the right. Another good one is when he's sitting on top of me and he turns all the way around to where his head is between my legs. Then he's able to lick my ankles and pay attention to the back of my knees.

Women favored certain intercourse positions because they provided more clitoral stimulation than others. The amount of clitoral stimulation seemed to be determined by the anatomical fit of the woman and her partner. Those positions which allowed for direct stimulation of the clitoris by their partner's pubic bone or which provided sufficient space for manual stimulation were often preferred.

Alexandra, thirty-two, divorced and living alone:

I need a position where I have a lot of freedom of movement, and one where my clitoris is easily accessible to the man. I like to be on my side because then it's very easy for me to come when someone manually stimulates my clitoris.

Thirty-five-year-old Allison, not being quite so dextrous, found a pillow helped solve the problem of reaching her clitoris:

I really like deep thrusting and also I like to touch my clitoris when I'm having intercourse so I can come. That's the way I come. And in order to make my clitoris more available and also to enhance the deep thrusting, I always put a pillow underneath my rear end while we're fucking and he holds my thighs down.

Squeezing the vaginal muscles during intercourse was a technique used by some of the women to enhance sexual pleasure.

Ariel, age thirty-three and separated, used this technique for her own arousal as well as to bring her partner to orgasm:

Something I have learned to do is to use my vaginal muscles to hold and release my partner's penis and establish my own rhythm. I do that when I feel like giving somebody a thrill, because it kind of blows their minds if they're not expecting it, or if I'm just tired and want somebody to hurry up and come.

A few of the women offered some helpful hints, ways they found to ameliorate some of the discomforts of intercourse caused by lack of lubrication. K-Y jelly, Nivea, coconut oil, or Albolene, were recommended when there was insufficient vaginal lubrication. Using lubrication on the clitoris was also suggested by a few women. For whatever reasons—differences in nerve sensitivity, individual preference, or sensation thresholds—women were different in their need for or ability to tolerate intensity or pressure in clitoral stimulation. Women who were very sensitive often found that additional lubrication enabled them to tolerate direct pressure on their clitoris.

Lubricants were also recommended for manually stimulating a partner. One woman made the following suggestion: "When one of us isn't in the mood, we'll stimulate each other using Albolene cream, because it's lighter than Vaseline and we don't like K-Y jelly because it disappears too fast."

ANAL SEX

We were surprised at the number of women who had tried anal intercourse at one time or another. In Kinsey's study during the 1940s, the number of women who had tried anal sex was negligible. Hunt's study in the 1970s found that one sixth of the women under twenty-five had tried anal intercourse and that 6 per cent had used it occasionally during the preceding year.* We found that approximately 10 per cent of the women we talked with spontaneously mentioned anal sex in answer to our question on what sexual positions they used or if they had any experiences they would call unusual. As one woman remarked, "We've even gotten into anal sex a little bit, and I never, never thought I would do that."

Women talked about certain conditions that made anal sex possible and pleasurable, such as being particularly loose or relaxed,

* Morton Hunt, *Sexual Behavior in the 1970's*. New York: Playboy Press, 1974, p. 167.

feeling especially erotic, or proceeding at a very slow, delicate pace. One woman started having anal sex because frequent vaginal infections often left her vagina too tender for vaginal intercourse. During these periods, anal intercourse provided her with a regular sexual outlet.

Alexandra, (thirty-two, divorced two years):

Craig and I felt abnormal about anal fucking as much as we did. We felt we were secretly perverted and we were absolutely delighted by the idea. In the book *The Joy of Sex* by Alex Comfort, it said that most people try anal sex once in their life just to try it and get it over with and here we were liking it and loving it, so we really felt peculiar.

Sufficient lubrication preceding anal play was described many times as being very important. Contraceptive jelly, baby oil, Vaseline, and Albolene cream were all suggested for preparing the anus for anal play or anal intercourse.

Allison (thirty-five-year-old administrator, divorced two years and living with boy friend) gave good instructions for initiating anal sex:

Anal intercourse is an important and enjoyable part of my sex life. I know that many women find it too painful to contemplate, but I was lucky because my partner helped to initiate me in such a way that it was not a traumatic and painful experience. I'd like to share what I learned from him and from the experience. Two key factors are that the woman should be completely relaxed and her partner should initiate penetration very slowly, always responding to the woman's directions about whether to stop or proceed. The penis should be well lubricated. Some people use K-Y jelly, but I like to use lubrication from my vagina. For me it was helpful to have vaginal stimulation from my partner before anal sex—to take my mind off the anxiety. Friends of mine say that they like to have an orgasm in foreplay beforehand to be completely relaxed for the anal insertion. When your partner does start the insertion, he must again respond to your directions. Another important factor to remember is never to have vaginal intercourse after anal intercourse. The fecal matter from the anus could start an infection in the vagina. So I make my partner wash his penis before we have vaginal intercourse after anal intercourse. If your partner gets carried away and does penetrate your vagina after anal intercourse, just get up and wash out your vagina with your fingers using soap and water or by douching.

One woman found that mental preparation helped her enjoy anal sex:

Anal sex usually starts in kind of a doggy position with him between my legs and with me down flat on my stomach. When he's entering me, I just try to breathe with his thrustings. Mentally, I try to see if I can interpret the feeling as one of pleasure. All of a sudden there is a barrier that I pass, and it isn't a physical barrier, it's an emotional barrier. Then I open up and it feels real good. But a few conditions have to be right for me to get into anal sex. I have to feel like I've had my fill of vaginal stimulation and I can't have anything in my lower bowel.

Other positions can be used for anal sex. One woman mentioned the missionary position with her knees bent as being a good one; on the side in the spoon position was also suggested; another said, "I kneel over the bed with my knees against my chest on the bed," and one woman used a vibrator to accompany anal sex.

Forty-eight-year-old Sara, who is a teacher and writer, has used a unique position for anal intercourse in her twenty-six-year marriage to Sam, a college professor:

My favorite position for anal intercourse is where I'm on top straddling my partner, who's lying on his back. My weight is on my hands, which are next to his arms or shoulders. His penis is well lubricated either with lubrication or vaginal secretions. Then I move my hips toward his shoulders so that the angle of his penis is about 45 degrees and can easily be inserted into my anus. I lower myself slowly onto his penis, allowing it to penetrate as far as is comfortable. Then I can move my body back and forth along his penis to suit my own pleasure. I also like having my breasts fondled and nipples sucked at the same time. What I like most about this position is the control I have and the fact that I'm facing my partner and able to have so much contact with him.

SELF-STIMULATION WITH A PARTNER

Several women said that one of their most powerful sexual experiences was being able to masturbate in front of their partners. As sex therapists, we have also found this to be true of many women. Masturbation for many of us has been associated with words like dirty, shameful or at the very least, private; so masturbating in front of another person can feel like an overwhelming step. It can, however, be a very positive one. It can be a learning experience for your partner in terms of what you like and need sexually to achieve orgasm and at the same time it can be a turn-on for the other person. Being able to pleasure yourself in front of your partner can involve so much trust, understanding, and support that it can be a very intimate experience. Beverly, (thirty-six, married nine years) tells how difficult this was for her, but how powerful she felt afterward:

For me, the one big thing that I've worked on in the last few years is being able to masturbate in front of my partner, which I never could do before. It was one more step in claiming my sexuality, in feeling good about my body, about orgasm, and about sex and sharing that with my partner. Masturbating in front of him is so intimate, it's a real letting go, it's a real sense of freedom and that makes it exciting.

First I talked about it with Mark, my husband. I was telling him how uncomfortable I was about doing it in front of him, even though he knew that I masturbated and I knew that he masturbated. It just was nothing that we had ever shared with each other before. We talked about my fears. They were some more vestiges of all those negative messages about masturbation, how perverse it is and how afraid I was of how awful I would look. I'd never seen how I looked when I masturbated. Then, one night after we'd had sex, I told him that I still had a need to have more orgasms. I felt as if I could have unlimited orgasms. In the past, we would always rely on intercourse or sometimes mutual masturbation, but this time I thought, "I'm going to try it, I'm going to try masturbating to orgasm in front of my partner." I didn't say that in words, I just started, and he put his hand over my hand while I was masturbating myself and I came. It was so exciting, it was such a thrill that we just hugged each other. It was like we really made it that time. It was so freeing and liberating that we went on to make love again. That night I had five orgasms! That was the first time I had ever had five orgasms. I just thought my body was something super! I thought I could do anything with this body. I even walked differently. Getting over this thing about one-orgasm-was-enough was a big thing for me. You know, I had the idea that that's enough pleasure, don't have more, don't give yourself too much. It was a big thing for me to get over that.

Iris, a thirty-two-year-old writer, describes how she masturbated for the first time with the man she lived with:

I read about masturbating in front of your partner and I told Jake about it. His answer surprised me because I was kind of uptight about it, but he said, "That's a great idea, when do you want to do it?" "Next time," I said, because it made me nervous. Then one day I was feeling adventurous and decided we would do it that night. It was really fun. I turned on some music and began with a whole striptease. As he was sitting there watching me, I stripped to the music until I had no clothes on. I began to feel awkward, but I think these feelings just added to the sexual tension I was feeling. Then I lay down and began to masturbate and was fairly turned on. I was also feeling like I was onstage with him watching me. Then he did the most wonderful thing. He got up and went into the bathroom and came back with some toilet paper! At first I had no idea of what he was doing, but then it dawned on me. He started masturbating too. I had never seen a man masturbate before and it was so interesting that I almost forgot about myself. He had an orgasm and it was fascinating. Then he continued to watch me until I came.

By the way, after that one experience of watching me masturbate, his techniques of stimulating my clitoris improved by 1000 per cent.

A number of women talked about masturbating, either in front of their partner or at the same time as their partner, not only as a way to receive sufficient clitoral stimulation, but also as a turn-on in its own right. They found that using masturbation as a tease heightened sexual feelings for both themselves and their partners.

Penelope (forty-six, married ten years):

I often masturbate myself in front of my husband, Harold. It tantalizes him when I don't let him participate and I get off on the fact that he's getting hot watching me.

Monique:

When we're going out at night, sometimes I won't wear any under-wear and I'll just wear this black, lacy garter belt, and on the way to a party, in the car, I'll start masturbating myself and my husband has to keep driving. I've made up the rules that he must keep driving and he can't touch me. It makes me excited and also it drives him crazy.

TALKING

In addition to different sexual positions and different types of physical stimulation, some women mentioned that talking during sex could be a real enhancement to their lovemaking. The kind of talking women preferred covered a wide range. At one end of the spectrum was Iris:

I'm a real romantic. I love to have sweet nothings whispered in my ears when I'm making love. Nothing really nasty or anything like that, but I just like to hear how good he feels being inside me and how pretty I look and stuff like that. The best thing, though, and Jake just discovered this himself, is just as I'm about to climax he'll tell me he loves me and that makes me feel so good and so close to him. It really intensifies my experience.

Rosemary (thirty-six, divorced) prefers just the opposite.

I like it when he talks dirty to me in a rough, physical way. You know, when he says, "I want to fuck you," or "I'm going to put my cock in you." That's a real turn-on for me.

EROTICA

Talking dirty sometimes took the form of telling erotic stories as a way of building arousal. Or sometimes a woman would read erotica alone or with her partner as a way to warm up. Take thirty-four-year-old Harriet, married for ten years for example:

Mostly we read out of *Penthouse* magazine. They have letters that people send in, most of which I don't believe, but some are a real turn-on! We also have some old, incredible stuff that we got at a bookstore years ago. They're porno books supposedly written by a Ph.D. They're obviously not, but who cares? They really turn us on!

In addition to reading erotica, many of the women we interviewed had seen erotic films at least one time in their lives. As therapists, we are well aware that seeing the right erotic movie can sometimes help a couple who have been feeling asexual or sexually bored to feel more turned on.

Some of the women did not like going into an adult movie theater, but enjoyed the movies themselves. A few handled this by purchasing their own projector and films.

One woman who owned her own erotic film had a creative way of sharing that film with her lovers:

Here's how the evening usually goes: First I set the 16-millimeter projector up in my cozy bedroom on a night table next to the bed. The shades are drawn and a number of candles are lit and placed around the room. My honey and I have taken a shower together and smoked a little dope. We kiss and caress each other as we remove each other's robes and get into bed. Then I start the film.

At first his attention is absorbed in the film, especially since it takes place in a French brothel. Needless to say, the "young ladies" in the film are all absolutely beautiful and into all manner of sex, particularly licking, sucking, and eating their partner and/or partners. While he's turning on to the film, I'm turning him on by starting leisurely at his toes with my mouth and tongue and working slowly up to his balls and penis. Poor guy! He struggles with wanting to concentrate on the film but not wanting me to stop. I'm also extremely turned on at this point, so we spend the rest of the time making love, as the film continues.

Others, like Bev, a thirty-year-old therapist who lives with her boy friend, took advantage of nearby motels:

I like porno movies, at least some of them. We've gone twice to a porno motel where they have closed-circuit TV with grade Z porno movies. Some of the motels have hourly rates, afternoon rates, or nightly rates. Most of the movies are dreadful, but that's not the point. The movies play as long as you want to watch them and some are arousing. The motels have vibrating beds and everything. It's terrible pornography but still the cumulative effect of it is a real turn-on. Even with the two of us, who are big voyeurs, it is only something we can do once every year or so—otherwise we'd really OD on it.

Although many of the women we interviewed enjoyed erotic books and films and found them arousing, some were turned off by their male orientation.

Penelope, who at forty-six has been married ten years to her third husband, Harold, a physician, solved this problem by making her own home movies:

We record ourselves sometimes and make an audiotape of our screws. We also have a video recorder and we have filmed ourselves with the camera and then played the tape back on our television. Then we watch it and fuck along with it.

FOOD

We have mentioned how women used certain foods to enhance the sexual atmosphere but foods were also used by some as an integral part of the lovemaking. However, the following kinds of experiences occurred only rarely and then as a special innovation for the sake of variety.

Billy, forty-three, a craftsperson, married twenty-six years with three children, finds a unique way to sip wine:

I really enjoy using wine and putting it on my body. My husband will pour the wine on my nipples and then gently lick it off, but I wouldn't want to do that every night.

Whipped cream, jam, honey, and chocolate syrup were put on the genitals and then licked off. Suzanne (thirty-seven, bisexual, divorced) found a way around the fattening aspects of such foods:

I'm on a diet so I use diet whipped cream and put it on a man's cock and lick it off. Sometimes I also use diet jelly or jam, which is good, too.

Alexandra:

Once someone covered me with those little red-hots, shaped like hearts, on Valentine's day, and ate them off my body.

And of course, ice cubes. Thirty-one-year-old Cortney, a secretary who is divorced and the mother of a six-year-old son, describes the time she and boy friend Chuck used ice cubes:

Oh, one time we used ice cubes. Those little cocktail ice cubes. We just put them up inside of me and then had intercourse. It was difficult because the heat from your body melts the ice cubes and it was kind of hard to get them up there before they'd melt. It was funny and we were laughing most of the time, but it was also a nice feeling, too.

VIBRATORS

Vibrators were the sexual aids most frequently mentioned by the women we interviewed. Many women had tried a vibrator at one point or another. Some enjoyed the vibrator and continued to use it frequently; others enjoyed it only occasionally. Many women tried it once or twice and then abandoned it because it was too awkward to use, too noisy, too intense, or too unnatural:

I have a vibrator that I use by myself or with my husband. Sometimes I like it but not often because it's too fast. I'd like to experiment with some other ones to see what they're like, but with this one, I come like crazy, but it doesn't feel that good. It just feels wired and too fast.

I have tried a vibrator and I like it. It does feel good, but somehow, I don't feel right about it. Probably because it seems artificial to me and that seems wrong.

Through continued experimentation some women learned to enjoy the vibrator even though they may not have liked it initially.

Ann (fifty-nine, married thirty-six years) recalled her first experience with a vibrator:

Steve used the vibrator first. The first time he used it he gave me an orgasm in about three seconds, and I was scared shitless of it. I didn't want to use it for a long time. I told him I didn't like it. It just wasn't me. It felt like a kind of reflex mechanical reaction. But he continued to bring it out and we used it differently—slower and not directly on the clitoris, and it got more stimulating and easier for me. Sometimes we use it up to the point of orgasm and sometimes I go off on it. I use it on him around his anus and around his glans, which he likes. I'm not sure how often we use it, but it's often enough, and we usually think of using it at the same time.

There are many different kinds of vibrators and many different ways to use them.†

Suzanne enthusiastically showed us her collection of vibrators:

† See Chapter 4 for descriptions of different types of vibrators.

I have a wide assortment of vibrators. One I particularly like is a penis-shaped vibrator that rotates around rather than up and down. It looks like a Santa Claus with a little polar bear on it. The polar bear part hits your clit and at the same time you've got the Santa Claus part inside of you. I also have these egg-shaped vibrating balls that you can put inside yourself. You insert them and then turn them on and they vibrate; I use them when I'm by myself or when I'm with somebody making love.

Samantha (thirty-five, divorced):

I have used a vibrator by myself, but recently I've used a hand massager with my present lover. It fits over my hand with straps, so that my hand is massaging and touching the other person. He uses it all over my body, but when he massages my clitoris it just about drives me crazy. I love it. There is nothing better as far as I'm concerned.

Heather (thirty-five, married three years):

My vibrator is shaped like a penis. We use it as part of foreplay or when we're having intercourse, especially if he's coming from the rear. Then he can just roll it around on my clitoris and it's very enjoyable there. In foreplay, we use it on my clitoris or actually insert it in my vagina with baby oil. While he's using the vibrator, he can be playing with my breasts or stroking me somewhere. A lot of times he'll be putting the vibrator in my vagina and stroking his penis at the same time.

Some women are embarrassed about integrating a vibrator into the lovemaking experience with their partner because they feel their partner will be offended. Since we did not interview any men, we do not know how males respond to vibrators. But we imagine Theresa is describing similar feelings in her response to her female partner's suggestion to use a vibrator:

Both the vibrator and the dildo were totally new things for me. My partner was talking about how this vibrator was her best friend. At first I was real jealous of it. It was like "I can't give you an orgasm like it can." We went round and round about that and I used to laugh and joke about it, but there were real feelings behind it. We talked about it many times and I said, "I know it's not rational to feel that I'm no better than a vibrator." It's funny because the first couple of months I wasn't into it, I wouldn't even try it and then once I tried the vibrator, it was great. I'm so glad she told me about it. Now every once in a while, it's reversed and Betty will say, "Oh, so you'd rather make love with it than me."

Some women have discovered ways to use the vibrator so that their partner is receiving as much stimulation as they are. These women report that their partners really enjoy the vibrator, too.

Rosemary (thirty-six, divorced):

We use a light, plastic penis-shaped vibrator. I use it on him most of the time. I put it under his penis at the point right between his penis and his balls, or right under the balls. We have a smaller one and sometimes I put that in his anus.

Sarah (twenty-nine, married two years):

The latest thing that we've gotten into is the vibrator. We find that not using the vibrator too often makes it more exciting when we do decide to use it. Sometimes we tease each other with it by using all the attachments on different parts of our bodies. That's very sensual. Then I go for the "joy button." The joy button is the attachment that's used for clitoral stimulation; however, it's also extremely stimulating to the penis and in fact I have had my husband ejaculate numerous times by just touching the joy button to his penis, right under the head of the penis. I move it around a little bit and then sort of concentrate right at the glans, under the head of his penis by the ridge. Since we've never used any other devices or props in our sexual relationship, we found the vibrator to be very exciting.

A lesbian couple used it this way: "Both of us lie on either side of the vibrator and press it against us. That way we both manage to get some vibrations."

A few women suggested keeping the vibrator plugged in at all times by the side of the bed so that it would be available whenever they wanted to use it. One woman generously suggested having two vibrators; one for herself and one in the guest room on the nightstand near the bed—a nice touch of hospitality.

DILDOS

A dildo is any phallus-shaped object that can be safely inserted in the vagina or anus. Only a small number of women we interviewed had ever used dildos, but those who did expressed great pleasure in using them. Vegetables were popular as dildos.

Heather (thirty-five, married three years):

Using a cucumber as a dildo was an idea we got from one of our erotic films and it works pretty well. First you wash it and put some baby oil on it to lubricate it, and then you just insert the cucumber in your vagina and move it around the way you like it. We use it as part of foreplay. It seems kind of funny, but it works really well.

Women also used zucchini and carrots. Some women made their own dildos, or borrowed or bought those made by friends.

Theresa loved her dildo, but had an interesting reaction about having her feelings appear in print:

My feminist stuff is coming out—I don't even want you to write about a dildo in this book. I'm not really saying don't, but part of me is saying don't because of course what's going to happen is that all heterosexuals who read this are going to say lesbians use dildos and the reason they use dildos is because they are trying to re-create the heterosexual intercourse. That's not true. I do it because it feels good. It feels good to have something in my vagina, something going in and out of my vagina and stimulating that tissue.

BODY PAINTING

Decorating one another's body was mentioned by a couple of women as being particularly enjoyable on those nights when passion is not high, but the desire for fun and intimacy are.

Iris (thirty-two, divorced and living with boy friend Jake):

One night Jake and I had decided to devote the evening to being alone and being "intimate." We specifically did not want to limit or inhibit ourselves by feeling that that would necessarily mean intercourse. As it turned out, that evening we weren't really feeling that passionate. So we started out just giving each other massages in front of the fireplace; then we were feeling warm and relaxed and a little playful. Jake grabbed a magic marker from his desk and started making designs around my mons area. Not to be outdone, I grabbed a few myself and turned his penis into a beautiful hanging purple flower. We laughed and laughed and ended up drawing all over each other's bodies. Body paints that turn into bubble bath in the shower have since become a substitute for magic markers.

FANTASY

Not all women fantasize, but many feel fantasy is an important part of their sexual encounters. The way these women used their fantasies varied. The large majority of women never shared their fantasies with a partner, but kept them as their own personal, secret turn-ons.

Rosemary (thirty-six, divorced):

I sometimes fantasize while I'm having intercourse. For example, if I'm particularly attracted to somebody that I've met, I'll start thinking about him and fantasize that I'm fucking him while I'm having intercourse with someone else.

Some women purposely did not talk about their fantasies, either because they found them too personal or embarrassing, or because they felt guilty about them.

Diane (thirty-two, lesbian):

It's really hard for me to talk about my fantasies, particularly because I have fantasies while I'm making love and I feel guilty about that.

Some women shared their fantasies verbally with their partner, but had no desire to act them out.

Monique (thirty-two, married nine years):

We often joke about our fantasies because mine are often so different from his. He usually has the same fantasy. His fantasy, 90 per cent of the time, is of having another female in the room. My fantasies can be having a team of men, or another female, or being on a beach. I find that I can share my fantasies with him when they aren't threatening to his sense of manhood. It's difficult to share fantasies about other men without his getting threatened, but I can share fantasies about other women, since he has shared his about having sex with two women. The only problem is that I often feel just because you share fantasies, does that mean you have to act on it? Then I feel pressure, and we have to talk about it so that I'm reassured that that's not the case.

The whole idea of creating fantasies, like games, to be play-acted together, was new for most of the women interviewed. However, the women who did create and act out fantasies with their partners felt that it greatly enhanced their sexual experiences and made them very special. One common fantasy theme was recreating a first meeting.

Allison, age thirty-five:

Once we were traveling out of the country and we decided to act out a fantasy of mine. I went down to the hotel bookstore and Murray came down and acted as if we were strangers and picked me up. We just started talking, asking each other our names and where we were from. Then he invited me back to the room and it was as if we hardly knew each other and were having sex for the first time.

Thirty-four-year-old Florence, a businesswoman, has been living with her lover, Kate, a lawyer, for the past two years and related the following fantasy where each person played a character other than herself:

Kate and I wanted to go to a porno drive-in but we got there late and were unable to get in. On the way home, we decided to act out our own fantasy, to make up our own film, so to speak. The script we decided on was as follows: we were two businesswomen at a conference who were getting more and more turned on to each other as the conference progressed. By some set of circumstances we ended up staying in the same room together at night. So after the aborted attempt to get into the drive-in, we, as these fantasy women, came back to the room—our bedroom—and one of us smoked a joint and the other had a drink.

It was weird because when we walked in the door, we felt like these other people. We sat on the couch and talked, and I don't remember if we had much of a dialogue. I don't think we did. I think it was mostly expressions, visual, eye contact and that sort of thing. And we went to bed and put on our pajamas, which we don't wear ordinarily. We crawled into bed and we lay there for a long time with no conversation and found ourselves getting closer and closer and then touching. I put my arm around her and we lay like that for a long time, feeling very, very close. Then it became obvious to both of us, these two new people, that there was an interest and a desire to continue from that point on. We undressed each other and explored each other's bodies and the whole time it was nonverbal, there was no verbal communication. We made love to each other, I don't remember the specific events, but we kissed and held each other and got into oral-genital sex and held each other afterward. Then we just went to sleep. The next morning, we were back to ourselves.

Bev (thirty, living with a male lover):

Once we were in Chicago having dinner and we noticed that the restaurant seemed to be full of call girls. They were the most diverse bunch of people I've ever seen and it was a very peculiar restaurant. Without any clue beforehand, Jim asked me how much I charged. For a second, I didn't know what he meant and then I caught on. I played the call girl and he played my john for the next three or four hours over dinner. I did a whole number about what I charged and the kinds of things I would do for certain fees. We continued the roles until the middle of the night until sex was over. As soon as we came, we both went back to being who we were again.

Not everyone is turned on by the call-girl image. Rosemary (thirty-six, divorced four years) acts out a more innocent fantasy:

We fantasize that I'm a Girl Scout who comes to the door selling cookies. I'm very innocent-looking with long socks, a short skirt and a sweet-looking blouse on. He opens the door. Since he's a very kind man, he invites me in and offers to buy some cookies from me. Then he sits beside me and puts his arm around me. He is very sweet and we talk. Then we end up going to bed with each other.

A fantasy scene can be created verbally rather than acted out. Connie (age twenty-six, widowed) created an environment of new and different places without ever leaving home:

I said to a man I had just started seeing, "Why don't we play this fantasy game? Let's pretend to take a trip. Where would you like to go?" and he said, "Okay, let's go to Italy. Let's have a Porsche with a beautiful cashmere blanket in the back seat." We both went on describing what the roads were like, what the hills were like, where we would stop to eat, what the bread was like and the wine. He started telling me about how we went to this little inn and we were the only two peo-

ple there. We had the fireplace all to ourselves and we had the cashmere blanket and sat in front of the fireplace. We ended up snowed
in for a weekend and then he gave this vivid description of everything
that happened, including a wonderful sex scene, and afterward we
made love for the first time.

Fantasies that surfaced most frequently were variations on the
theme of being dominant and submissive. Sometimes these included forms of bondage or spanking. Often, various costumes or
paraphernalia were utilized to set the scene or make the fantasy
more realistic.

Many of the women were turned on either by being helpless
and having their partner "force" them to submit sexually, or by the
reverse, where they were the ones in power. The following are rep-
resentative of this kind of fantasy.

Anna (twenty-eight, married for three years):

I'm really turned on by the following sexual fantasy: Some man just
really wants at me and he's going to get me, even if that means ripping
the clothes right off me. So sometimes I put on an old T-shirt and let
my husband go at it, rip it up or whatever, or vice versa. When we do
this, it feels like we're almost consumed by our desire.

Ariel (thirty-four, separated):

My favorite fantasy is of the man being helpless; therefore, the success of my fantasy relies on some external thing happening like my
partner's being on the phone, at which point I love to seduce him. I
may start out using my hands on his penis or doing a mouth job. Then
I might get on top. This is so arousing to me but it's important that he
stay on the phone so I'm really in control.

Actual bondage was far and away the most popular acted-out
fantasy. Almost every woman who played out her fantasies had
tried bondage at one time or another. Bondage ranged from simple
"tie and tease" described by the following woman:

I enjoy playing tie and tease every once in a while. It is kind of like
the old sadomasochistic stuff, but it seems benign enough to me. One
person is willing to let himself be tied up with thread, just plain thread
that you could easily break whenever you wanted to. The person's

hands and feet are tied and then a blindfold is put across their eyes. The other person then teases them with a variety of objects and parts of their own body, like their breasts or their mouth, as well as with foods and perfumes and feathers.

. . . to light sadomasochism, as described by Allison:

One of my sexual fantasies that I always wanted to live out was having some sadomasochistic sexual experiences. Although I didn't want to be whipped and permanently damaged, I did want to feel that my partner was controlling the sex and that his control came in the form of physical demands, by either hitting me, tying me up, handcuffing me, or mild beatings. My lover at the time was also into that so it was great! It made our sex so intense and arousing. I eventually outgrew that fantasy, but I really enjoyed it when I was going through it.

Pain is sometimes an integral part of a masochistic fantasy. Suzanne (thirty-seven, bisexual, living alone):

I have this leather fly swatter that I got as a gift and I use in lovemaking. I got into sexually enjoying being swatted on the ass, but it can't be too hard and it can't be too soft. If just a certain amount of pressure is applied, like somebody slapping me on the ass, I'm able to have orgasms. I'm a little bit less into that now, but there are times that I still find it enjoyable.

Women today are actively raising their consciousness. They are breaking old stereotypes about how women ought to be and are developing their more "masculine" side, the side that is rational, competent, and assertive, both in and out of bed. Consequently, women are often horrified when masochistic fantasies of being forced to submit sexually are found to be arousing by other women or even themselves. A group of feminist therapists we worked with felt that rape fantasies were sexist and that no feminist worth her salt should be turned on by such fantasies.

However, what women enjoy in fantasy and what they actually find arousing in reality are two very different things. Many women enjoy being raped in fantasy, but would be devastated if the act were perpetrated on them in real life. The fantasies we find arousing have a great deal to do with our culture and the sexual images we had during our adolescent years. Adolescence was, physiologically, a time of highly charged sexual energy, but a period when culturally, socially, and morally it was "wrong" to feel that way. The only way we could legitimately feel turned on sexually was if we were forced to submit. Otherwise, the expectation was that we would suppress our sexual feelings to prevent them from getting out of control. Also, as with Allison, the types of sexual fantasies that turn us on frequently change during the course of our lives. One theme might be a highly charged turn-on over a particular period in our lives and then wane in interest and intensity as other themes and images catch our attention.

Unlike the psychoanalyst's theories, our sexual fantasies do not necessarily "tell" something about our inner wishes. Enjoying fantasies of submission are not necessarily signs of a masochistic personality. As a matter of fact, we often find that women who can truly enjoy those fantasies are women who feel sufficiently stable and secure to know that in real life they are not masochistic at all.

Alexandra (thirty-two, divorced):

Barry and I had some sadomasochistic fantasies which were never played out in any way that was dangerous, just fun. It was definitely on a fantasy level. It was comfortable for us to act it out in bed; it would have been uncomfortable out of bed. I don't like to play the masochistic role nor do I like a man to play being dominant over me in any aspect of my life, but in bed it was just fine because it was so obviously a game.

We played it out by having him hold down my arms while I tried to fight against him as though I wanted to put my arms around him but he wouldn't let me. It was like being tied up. There was a lot of sexy talk about what he was going to do to me one day, like tie me up and do all these things to me and drive me crazy. That was while he was inside of me and it just heightened things. He would just tease me and drive me nuts by not letting me have it right away so I had to beg for it. The begging was very exciting, because that is absolutely not the way I really am.

Tying someone up can be done with scarves, silk ties, handcuffs, ropes, stockings, clothing, or bed covers. Ms. X:

The man that I was living with at the time introduced me to a very gentle, fun type of S-M. I had a big brass bed and sometimes we would take turns tying each other up to the bed. I would save my stockings that had runs in them and we would use them to tie each other up. We would have very clear ground rules. If the person who was being tied up wanted the other person to stop for any reason, all they had to say was "stop" and it would end. And we never hurt each other. The object was to tease each other, to stimulate each other until the other person was just begging to come. The ground rule was that you just had to *beg* for intercourse. One night, it was his turn to be tied up. That night for some reason, I decided to combine it with another thing he liked, which was for me to dress up as a whore. I had these outrageously high heels, silk stockings, and a black garter belt. I had one of these black bras that push your boobs to the middle, and for some reason I just got really outrageous. You have to picture the scene to understand why. I'm feeling like I'm just this incredible whore, and I've got this guy tied up and spreadeagled on the bed, and I can do anything I want to him. So, for a while, I kind of just pranced around, and every once in a while, I'd come over and touch him or I'd kiss him. Then I'd do this incredible oral sex thing on him and each time I'd bring him to the point of almost coming, then I'd stop. And he knew the ground rules were that he could say stop anytime and I'd just untie him. But it was like he was hooked on it. It was like he couldn't wait to see what was coming next, yet he really wanted to come and he couldn't stand it.

And finally—I don't know what possessed me, but I got so much into the person that I was playing, I was no longer myself. I was just "fucking outrageous." So, I got up on the bed and sat up on the pillow next to his head, and started touching myself and playing with myself. I thought he would go crazy! Then for some reason, I decided, "This isn't enough. I'm going to really drive him nuts." So I got up and sat on his chest and continued masturbating; and his face was close enough to see everything and smell everything and he was almost able to reach out, but not close enough. And I came. On his chest. Almost in his face. And that's when he yelled, "STOP!"

Although a few of the women felt that playing bondage developed trust in their relationship, some felt it important to establish rules ahead of time for self-protection.

Judith (forty, bisexual, married eight years) discusses both:

I found out a lot about trusting myself and trusting Nathan by playing bondage. He didn't have as many problems being tied up as I did.

I had real reservations and was very frightened. I learned that he wouldn't do any more than what I wanted, but it was important for me to establish rules. If I'm tied up and I'm freaking out behind it, part of what I want to be able to do is say "no, no," or, "*Stop*," but not really mean it. You need to build in a safeguard and just saying "*No*" is not safe any longer, so what we did is use a word that you would not ordinarily say—"chrysanthemum," for instance—something that is way off. It's whatever word we choose for the time. It's a word that means "I'm serious—stop. I don't want to go any further." But we don't have to use it very often.

Initiating this kind of role-playing with a new partner is difficult for many women. Suzanne describes a subtle way to introduce bondage:

I wouldn't do it with just anybody—I think it would freak a lot of women out. The last time I did it, I just brought out a scarf and laid it down beside me. We were watching the fire in the fireplace and I said, "Has anyone ever tied you up?" and she said no but that she'd like to try it. I said, "I don't have ropes, but we can just use my scarf." Sometimes I'll just ask if they have ever tried bondage before and then continue depending on their reaction.

Fantasy can be used as a substitute for reality, particularly when it is not possible to enact the desired activity in real life.

Samantha (thirty-five, divorced) describes how she and her lover use fantasies to make love when they are physically separated:

Because we can't live together right now and are often separated, we masturbate together on the telephone, which is just out of sight! We talk to each other late in the evening because both of us are very busy during the day and sometimes we'll be on the phone almost all night talking each other into coming. We talk about what we've done sexually with each other in the past and how good it felt; we talk about what we've done with other people that we've liked. He tells me about various things women have done to him and it's a real turn-on to just imagine it while I'm masturbating. That way, I can have several orgasms in one conversation. He usually has one and then we become more intimate and feel closer.

It's not like masturbating alone; that's a whole different thing, but it's sort of like sharing something very intimate with someone that you care about. It's not as good as the real thing, but it's pretty damn good.

ORGASM

All of the foregoing games, props, and techniques can create a break from the general routine and add fun and excitement to a sexual relationship. They do not, however, necessarily increase the woman's sexual responsiveness. Many women have concerns about orgasm. The majority of the women we spoke with felt that orgasm was important and they tried to maximize the likelihood of its occurring. In the process, they discovered some useful techniques.

Allison (thirty-five, divorced two years) devised ways to stimulate her own clitoris in almost any position:

The most important breakthrough in my sex life was when I learned it was all right for me to touch my own clitoris during intercourse. Since I've started doing that, I almost always have orgasms, and I have come to believe that this is just the way I am and that there's nothing wrong with it. Because I believe that, my partners have accepted it without any difficulty. Sometimes during intercourse I need more lubrication on my clitoris; otherwise, stimulating myself would be painful so I just put some saliva from my mouth on my hand and there's no problem. Now I feel entirely different about myself. I feel that I'm a very orgasmic woman, very sensual and a great lover. And I can orgasm in almost any position.

We discovered that it was even possible for disabled women and women who had very little genital sensation to experience orgasm. Lydia, a twenty-one-year-old spinal-cord-injured quadriplegic, informed us:

No matter what kind of orgasm I have, I usually experience a rise in my temperature and my whole body becomes really warm. But with genital-type orgasms, I have a rippling sensation throughout my abdomen. Nongenital orgasms are not so localized in my genitals. I'm more aware of the sensation throughout my whole body and I'm not so genitally centered since my accident. Now I respond more to total body touching as well as fantasizing.

Some women felt that orgasm was secondary and considered the closeness, touching, and caring of the lovemaking the most important factors. Billie (fifty-four, married):

Sometimes, just being close and being loved is all that I really need. It feels so nice just to be cuddled, and I always feel loved when we are together sexually.

Just as women's need for an orgasm differs, their experience of orgasm differs as well. Some came quickly, others needed more time. Some had a series of orgasms culminating in one "tremendous" orgasm; others had one orgasm and felt no desire to have another. Some thought simultaneous orgasms were a myth, or were unimportant; others sought the experience and had them often. The following woman offered a detailed account of how she and her partner orchestrate simultaneous orgasms.

Bev (thirty, living with a man):

We spend a lot of time getting very close to the point of orgasm and just staying up there as long as possible. It's like there is a kind of agreement between the two of us that we're not going to come for a while. It's very intense. The closer I get to orgasm, the slower I move, and the feeling keeps getting thinner and thinner as I get closer to coming. I think what happens with me is that there is almost a split in my awareness. I do something with my body while I keep my mind at this level of tension. I can't allow any more tension to develop or I'll go over. I have to watch it very carefully. And if I start to go over, it is probably too late. So it's a matter of letting my partner know just when I'm getting too close so we can kind of cool out or do something different for a while or just stop for a few minutes. During this period I don't pay attention to what's happening with him because I'm really focused on myself, but we'll cue each other in on our individual arousal levels. If I stay at that high level for a long time, then it is very easy to come at the same time with my partner because we've both been ready for so long that it doesn't take much to go over the edge. And when one of us starts coming, we take the other one with us.

Another woman shared a preference that enhances orgasm for her. Mary (forty-eight, recently divorced):

I usually experience just one orgasm. Also, I don't know if it is an idiosyncrasy or what, but when I'm about to have an orgasm, if there isn't either fingers or a penis in my vagina, it hurts because there is nothing there to grab on to. So I always ask him if he's sucking or tonguing me and I'm about to come, to put his fingers in my vagina, too.

AFTERWARD

It was clear that sex did not end after the orgasm for most women. They found ways of making the time afterward an integral part of their lovemaking. Fran (thirty-two, single, flight attendant, living with a roommate):

Sometimes, after sex, I feel energetic and particularly close to my partner. He may be ready to doze off, but I'm still interested in pleasuring him. In these instances, I'll go to the bathroom and bring a nice warm washcloth back to the bedroom to wash off my lover's penis. Then I'll massage him with a towel or talcum powder. Sometimes he's so relaxed that he falls asleep, but that doesn't bother me. I just enjoy the closeness and I enjoy giving to him.

One woman who did not have a regular sexual partner found a way to have the feelings linger for days afterward. Sage (thirty-five, lesbian, living alone):

I don't change the sheets for a while, a week or so after I've had a really loving experience in my bed. You see, I do a lot of my writing in bed, and the marvelous smells allow me to have a rerun of the experience. It is a wonderful prop for me because I keep reliving flashes of it with the smells. I change sheets before anyone new comes, but I will stay in the old sheets for a while. I think this is a really good tip for people who are alone, and don't have regular partners, but have these wonderful experiences from time to time.

A number of women had helpful hints that they had developed to take the muss and fuss out of making love. Keeping tissues or wipettes on the nightstand was a common solution. Elaine (thirty-eight, married for two years) suggested keeping a towel neatly folded under her pillow. She also recommended diapers for those women with babies who wish to be discreet:

The things that we used over the years were diapers, which are handy for people with babies. It's the most accessible thing and no matter where you are when you have babies around, you have a diaper. We also did a lot of visiting relatives, sleeping on their couches and stuff. It was the place to sleep when we were on vacation. And nobody ever thinks about a diaper being out of place in your suitcase when you have small children.

One woman kept the wash rag or hand towel between her legs all night to absorb the moisture and then put a tampon in for a couple of hours in the morning if she was still dripping. Another woman suggested a minipad for the same purpose. Two other creative suggestions were made for women who are concerned about the messiness of having sex during their period especially when they are flowing heavily:

I wear my diaphragm during my period when I'm having intercourse. That way the blood stays up under the diaphragm and doesn't make a mess. Another way I can always have intercourse during my period is to use a towel underneath me to make sure that I don't get the sheets all bloody. This tends to make me feel much more relaxed about having sex because I'm not afraid of getting blood all over the place.

MOST UNUSUAL SEXUAL EXPERIENCES

We waited until the end of the interview before we asked women for their most unusual sexual experiences. During the course of the interview, women were usually slowly establishing a rapport with us by revealing small pieces of information. The general result was that the interview grew more personal and intimate as it progressed. In this way, the women could check out our reactions and establish a sense of safety before disclosing further intimacies.

Women recounting their most unusual sexual experiences represented the female version of locker-room talk. Sometimes we were shocked together, or we would laugh together, but often it was just an opportunity for some lusty communication, something that we, as women, had often not had the chance to experience.

There are very few times that women have the opportunity to talk about their sexual exploits. Whereas retelling sexual adven-

tures connotes prestige and status for men, women in similar circumstances might be considered sluts, hussies, or floozies.
Women in this society are not supposed to flaunt their sexuality.
They are expected to be demure and discreet. Somehow, women
are not supposed to have the same sexual interest, the same desires,
the same titillating excitement that men are expected to enjoy.
These feelings and activities are forbidden, and even if experienced cannot be shared with anyone else.

Imagine overhearing a man tell his friend about how he went
out to a bar the night before and saw this attractive woman. He
finally managed to meet her, bought her a couple of drinks, sat
down and had a pleasant conversation. After that, he left with her,
helped her into his automobile, and went back to his apartment,
where they made love. We would consider this a real conquest.
According to the culture, the man would have done everything
right. Now, imagine overhearing this story all over again, but this
time with a woman describing the same set of events. She goes into
a bar looking for an interesting man. She sees an attractive man
across the room and manages to meet him; they sit down together,
talk and have a drink, after which she invites him back to her
place and seduces him.

The exact same story elicits acclaim when told by one person
and disdain when told by the other. Even if she were seducing him
while he was thinking that he was seducing her, he could brag to
his friends about the experience, whereas she could not be open
about it. She could not really say, "You won't believe what I did
last night. I met this adorable man and he was fantastic in bed."
The man is always the seducer and the woman is the one being se-
duced. The process is acceptable only if he initiates it and she goes
along with it. For a woman to seek out sexual experiences, to or-
ganize them, to take part in them fully and joyfully, not because
her partner has set them up but because she wants to, is a new
trend in women's enjoyment of their own sexuality.

Although many women are participating more actively and creatively in sex, this is by no means the norm. It is the beginning of
women feeling free enough to be able to enter what has been considered male territory. Consequently, some of the women we

talked with felt that they had never experienced anything that they could call an unusual sexual event. They believed that they had only participated in conventional sex and that none of their experiences had been out of the ordinary. Others, however, were able to talk about unusual sexual experiences with the awareness that they were an equal partner in it.

Unusual sexual experiences ran the gamut. What was the norm for one woman was unusual for another and vice versa. Much of what was considered unusual for some women has been discussed in other sections of this book. For example, acting out various sexual fantasies was considered exotic by some; others considered sex outdoors or in a movie theater or at work to be unusually daring. The experiences saved for this section were those which were fairly universally considered to be unusual. Therefore, you may find some of the following tales shocking or unbelievable. However, they are all true and were found enjoyable by the women describing them.

One theme that was repeated by a few women was the *déjà vu* experience. These were sexual experiences with someone out of the past. In some cases the two had been lovers in the past, while in others they had never been lovers, but had had a very intimate relationship.

Sage, a thirty-two-year-old therapist who lives alone, describes her feelings when she went to bed with a man after relating only to women for ten years, and then, in another situation, her experience of making love with someone she had not been sexually involved with for years:

The most unusual experience was when I went to bed with a man after not being with one for ten years. Since I'm a lesbian, it was very strange to be with a man again. I just wanted to see what it was like. I hadn't slept with a man since I was about twenty-two or twenty-four. What was striking was not the penis at all, because I liked to do a lot of penetration with women. What was so strange was the texture differences—the hair, the skin coarseness, no softness. It struck me as very bizarre, although mechanically it was pleasing. It just sort of struck me as very, very unfamiliar.

The other time I remember finding things very strange was when an old lover whom I hadn't even seen in a number of years and I went to bed. That was sort of a déjà vu experience. But yet it was sort of new, too. It felt like time had collapsed. It felt old and new at the same time. It was very odd. The smells, all the things from the past were the same. I hadn't experienced those in five years and yet it was the same.

Some of the best déjà vu experiences, however, included the forbidden. Veronica, thirty-one, a business executive, after separating from her husband, impulsively called an old flame whom she has not had contact with for twelve years:

After seeing a movie that reminded me of the sixties I decided very spontaneously to contact my first lover, William. We had been college freshmen together and we had not seen nor talked to each other in twelve years. At that time, we were talking about getting married, except that I was also in love with someone else and I couldn't make up my mind between them. I finally chose the other guy for reasons that made sense to me at the time. That had been a mistake, since our marriage had ended in divorce, but that wasn't really why I wanted to call William. At this point, it was mostly out of curiosity.

In those days I was a virgin and felt very strongly about saving myself for my husband, so William and I would have these long, drawn-out necking and petting sessions where we would almost be dying from wanting to really make love. We'd always talk about it, but would ultimately decide to wait.

I knew where William's family lived so I looked up their number. His father answered and said William was in town visiting, but was out at the moment. I left my name and said to tell him that an old friend was trying to get in touch with him. William returned my call that evening and asked if he could come over in about twenty minutes and I said sure. I was really apprehensive because I couldn't imagine what it would be like to see him, but I cleaned up the house in a hurry. While I was frantically cleaning, I thought, "I bet he's bald and weighs three hundred pounds." I had no idea what he would look like when I opened the door. And was I ever surprised! He was beautiful! Gorgeous!

It was a little strained at first, but then we sat around and talked about our old college relationship and what it had meant to each of us. He told me he felt I had been playing games with him then and we talked that out. We ended up feeling totally comfortable with each other and decided to go to bed. It was the strangest experience. It was like going back in time and finally consummating our old relationship. I felt like I was seventeen years old again. I went through flashbacks of wondering, am I going to go all the way or not? Even our sex play leading up to intercourse was exactly the way I remembered it. Then we finally had intercourse. It was extremely good for me, just terrific! I couldn't believe how comfortable it was, when it could have been so embarrassing and awful. It was a strange, wonderful encounter that has nothing to do with the future. I don't even know if we'll see each other again, but it doesn't matter. It just felt like something was finished, completed, between us.

A number of women had sexual experiences of a voyeuristic or exhibitionistic nature. In our culture we are not supposed to watch someone else being sexual, must less be watched ourselves. Since heightened sexuality often comes from engaging in the forbidden, like almost being caught having sex or turning someone else on by having them see our sexual excitement, we were not surprised that women prized these experiences.

Suzanne (thirty-seven, bisexual, divorced) confided:

We went down to a health spa where you take saunas, go on special diets, and sit in the sun. There was a treehouse there. I'll never forget this. We climbed this treehouse; it was real rickety and we made love on the top of the treehouse. People were passing down below us but didn't know we were there. The sun was shining real bright and it was beautiful to be up so high in the treetops. It was also risky, because if people looked up, they would be able to see us up there and that made it a real scary and yet much more exciting experience.

A number of women reported unusual experiences of a voyeuristic nature. Viewing others to create sexual arousal is usually considered perverted; for example, Peeping Toms. However, watching or listening to others being sexual provided the tension and excitement for creating a memorable sexual event for a few women we interviewed.

Iris:

I was up in Big Sur once with my friend Paula. We both had sleeping bags and were sleeping on the floor of a friend's very small cabin consisting of only one big room. Our friend's girl friend had returned to town from a trip. We felt funny about staying there, but we really had nowhere else to go. Paula and I went to sleep in our sleeping bags on the floor and they went to sleep in the bed. I was having a hard time falling asleep and after a while, I noticed that the couple had started making love. There was just enough moonlight for me to see what they were doing. I had never watched anyone making love before and I got really turned on. Just watching was one of the most stimulating experiences I have ever had. I was so turned on that I started masturbating. I must have been really involved with what they were doing, because when they came, I came too. After that, the guy's girl friend came up to me and asked if I wanted to join them, but even though I wanted to, I was too self-conscious to do that—mostly because I was afraid of what Paula would think if she woke up and saw the three of us together fucking on the bed.

In the following situation, the event was unusual because it did not just occur once, but was repeated a number of times.

Ms. X:

I had a very bizarre experience which I became addicted to for a very long time. I once made a phone call to a friend and got the wrong number. There was a man on the other end of the phone and he began to masturbate. It was very obvious he was masturbating and he got me very turned on so I ended up listening and masturbating too. He never knew my phone number. He never knew who I was. It was like something out of a book. That relationship with him went on for about two years. When I was in the mood I would call him. He used to get me so turned on over the phone that I would swear that I would never do this again. But I would call him again and I would say, "Hi," and then he would do this whole routine. He gave me a name—my name was "Candy." He would tell me that all I had to do was call and his cock would get hard. He would also tell me exactly what he was doing as he masturbated. It was incredible. When I got married, I stopped calling him. I never even told him why, I just stopped calling.

Without doubt, the most popular unusual or forbidden sexual experience was sex with more than one other person. Although these experiences were not common, a number of women had, at some time, experienced a sexual encounter with two men, a man and a woman, or a group of people. And there was no way we could predict, from the woman's appearance or personality, if she had ever had this kind of sexual experience.

Group sex or *ménage à trois* was not something that any of the women had participated in frequently. They had generally engaged in that type of activity once or at the most a couple of times but those experiences stood out in their minds. Group sex created a situation where it was possible to watch as well as be watched with a sense of safety. It combined the forbidden qualities of voyeurism and exhibitionism with a heightened level of stimulation resulting from two or more mouths, four or more hands, and possibly an extra penis.

Roberta (thirty-five, divorced, with a ten-year-old daughter):

Two summers ago, I had sex with two men in a king-sized bed, and that was a fantastic experience. I was—how can I say this?—approached from both ends; I was on my side and one man was behind me and the other in front of me. The two men involved said it was really strange to have their genitals touching each other as they were entering me. One was in my anus and one was in my vagina, and they said it was a really weird feeling. But it was just an ecstatic experience for me. It was one of the high points in my sexual life.

The way it happened was that we were going to the beach. I was with my boy friend and a mutual friend of ours who didn't have a date. We'd been jokingly talking about group sex up till then. That evening we smoked some dope and were all very relaxed. My boy friend and I went into the other room and then he was the one who suggested that the other guy come in, so we just fooled around and it was a really nice experience.

Some of these group sex experiences took place while the woman was away on vacation. Iris (thirty-two, living with a man):

Once I was traveling and staying with these two men in their house in Paris. It was early evening and we were wrapped up in this blanket lying on the floor listening to music and talking. Soon I noticed that one man was stroking my body under the blanket. It felt good, but I can remember worrying about what the other guy might think. Then the other one began stroking my leg. And I thought, "What am I going to do? They are both coming on to me and neither is aware of what the other is doing." I wondered how I was going to get out of it, but decided to just relax and see what happened. Apparently they had been involved with the same woman together before because neither of them seemed surprised when their hands met as they were rubbing me. Once I realized they both knew what was happening, I felt better. They weren't comfortable doing things with each other sexually, so I had all their attention. Slowly, the blanket began sliding down from my body as they became more active. Jean-Paul undressed me while Frederick began kissing me where my clothes had been removed. I remember that one of them began eating me, I don't remember which one, while the other played with my breasts. After a very long time of touching and kissing, Jean-Paul began to have intercourse with me. Frederick never did, but contented himself with my sucking him at that point. All of us had orgasms and then Frederick went into his bedroom after staying and cuddling for a while and Jean-Paul slept with me. It was one of the most gentle, sensual, and wonderful sexual experiences I've ever had.

Sometimes the group sexual experience was more than a casual fling with an unknown person. The following two women had deep emotional relationships with both people they were sexually relating to.

Judith (forty, bisexual, married, children away at school) used sexuality as a way of comforting a friend and deepening their friendship:

My husband and I experimented a lot sexually in the beginning of our relationship. Now neither of us seeks out a third person to add to our sexual relationship, although occasionally the circumstances all fit and we include a third person. This happened just a couple of months ago. An old friend of ours, Mel, whom I have known for about fifteen years, who lives back East, was out here visiting. He's been a very good friend of mine for a long time. Last fall, his oldest son died in an accident and he was devastated by that. He hadn't been able to talk to anybody about it. He came out here in January, about four months later, and for some reason, he wanted to talk to us about his son. So we spent one whole evening going over what had happened, trying to help him sort out his feelings. My son has been having a lot of problems too, so I was very involved in this conversation. All of us were trying to look at how we related to our children, how responsible we are for what happens to them, that kind of thing. So it was a very intense four-hour discussion and at the end, we felt so close that it seemed very artificial not to have any physical contact. At one point in the discussion I had massaged my friend's shoulders, but it wasn't a sexual experience at all. By the time we finished talking, it was midnight and I was exhausted, so we ended it and Mel went to the guest room and Nathan and I went to our bedroom. Nathan and I looked at each other and said, "Do you think Mel would be offended if we invited him to come sleep with us?" It was apparent that Mel was very fragmented from what had happened. So we invited him and said specifically, "This isn't a sexual invitation," It could turn out that way, but it wasn't said like "Do you want to fuck?" What we said was, "We wondered whether you would like some physical comfort and closeness." He's a straight man, so we thought we would give him the option of being near me instead of Nathan, but he opted to get in the middle, which I thought was very unusual. He's a fifty-five-year-old man and has never had any experience with other men as far as I know. However, what evolved sexually during the evening was at Mel's initiation. The three of us had sex. It wasn't fantastic sex. It wasn't like we went on all night, or like I had twenty orgasms, it wasn't anything like that. What happened was that the sex became the expression of the love and caring we had shared all night. The whole experience was beyond anything I have had happen to me sexually in a long, long time. It was unique and very beautiful. I don't know that that would ever be repeated again.

In this excerpt, Suzanne (thirty-seven, bisexual, divorced) was able to have a sexual experience with her male lover and her female lover at the same time. The intensity of the experience appeared to result in the necessity of giving up one of them:

After a month or so, we did a three-way. Here was the man whom I loved most in the world and here was the woman whom I loved most in the world and we were going to all make love together. I was both scared and excited. First we went to dinner together to see how everybody liked each other because they had not known each other that long. We went to a restaurant and the vibes were good and everybody said okay, let's try it. We came up here and we made love and that was my first three-way experience in my life. I was sexually and emotionally turned on to both these people in a very real way, in a very deep way. However, it was not the same experience for all of us. For me it was magnificent, for Carol it was quite good, but Franklin felt a lot of jealousy seeing Carol and me relate sexually. He felt jealous of our relationship and that kind of thing tinged our relationship for the next several months till we got to a point where he gave me an ultimatum. He said that he wanted to live with me, possibly marry me, but definitely live with me and be in a monogamous relationship with me. I thought it over for a while and I said, "I can't accept this ultimatum, I'm just opening up to women. I really don't want my life to be monogamous, and although I love you very deeply, I can't abide by what you're offering." He said, "Okay, I really can't see you anymore," and he left town. I have never seen or heard from him since.

The ultimate favorite fantasy of many people is not just to have sex with two people, but to take part in an orgy, to be able to make love to as many people as they desire during the course of the evening. The people who reported having such an experience had attended an event organized specifically for the purpose of providing the opportunity for group sex. It was not something that occurred on the spur of the moment. Judith (forty, bisexual) enjoyed her experience with group sex, although she also felt it was no big deal:

The first time I had group sex, I ended up having sex with nine people that night. I've never done it before or since. On some level, I wanted to prove that I could do that if I wanted to.

Louise (thirty-six, widowed) found it to be a more exciting experience:

I went to this group for swingers with a male friend of mine with whom I was not sexually involved, but you have to go as a couple. I had told him that I was feeling I wanted to do something different because, before my marriage, I hadn't had any sexual experience. I thought now I can do anything I want and he suggested I try this.

The club we went to is for couples, most of whom seem to be married. Every few weeks they meet at a motel and rent a large room where you can dance or sit and talk and drink. They also have several rooms that couples or groups can go to. In addition, they have one room that everybody can go to all at once, but you have to go into the large group room with your partner.

Tom agreed that if I wanted to do something really different, that would be the thing. I was nervous because for me that was a wild thing to be doing. At the same time it was also very exciting for me to be doing something absolutely crazy that would shock anyone who knew me. So we went. When I got there, I was really afraid somebody would approach me and I wouldn't know what to do. After we'd been there a couple of hours talking to people, I started worrying instead that maybe *nobody* would approach me and *nothing* would happen, but finally two other couples we had been talking with asked Tom and me to join them. The other five all wanted to do it and even though I was uneasy, I said okay. So we went upstairs to the room and as soon as we got in the room everybody took their clothes off. I had never taken my clothes off in front of a group of people before, but I felt more uncomfortable being the only one dressed, so I took them off.

There were two beds in the room and the guy that I had come with and the other two women went off to one bed and the two guys got into the other bed with me. My one really big sexual fantasy had always been having sex with two men at the same time, and just realizing I was going to have the chance to actually experience it was quite something. Both of them started touching me at the same time and then one guy said, "I'll take one half and you take the other half." They were doing all kinds of things to me at once, you know, and just having so many hands and mouths at the same time was terrific. I didn't end up having super orgasms, because I think I wasn't totally relaxed in the situation. I also had some apprehension because these were people who did this a lot, and I wondered what I was expected to do. The two men were just great. They said to tell them exactly what feels good and they would do it. So I told them things and they did it, both of them at the same time, and then first I had intercourse with one while the other was kissing me and touching me and then with the other and it was just super. A total orgy.

I didn't know these people's names, they didn't know mine. In fact, nobody shared anything about themselves, so there was nothing except sex—the experience was purely sexual. For me that experience clarified what I like about sex: It is the relationship that is the important part of sex for me and even really great physical sexual experiences aren't the peak if it doesn't happen in the context of a meaningful relationship.

By this time, after having exhibitionism, voyeurism, and group sex as input, you may find yourself feeling overwhelmed, your head spinning from all of the possible ways you might enhance or enlarge your sexual repertoire. You may have found that you were only able to read short portions of this chapter before you had to stop and let your head clear. Or maybe you read intently through this entire section without putting the book down for a moment, in excited anticipation of the next innovation.

In either case, you may find yourself ready for a change of pace. Rather than being a potpourri of sexual ideas, the following chapters focus on separate areas of sexuality or sexual functioning that affect most people's lives. The first of those areas and the subject of the next chapter is masturbation.

Although it is important to learn which qualities and preparations are necessary for enjoyable sex, most of us would be lost if we were not also comfortable with and knowledgeable about our bodies sexually. Each of us is sexually unique. We have different areas of sensitivity which require different types of touching for sexual satisfaction to result. Much of this is physiologically based. Therefore, it is imperative that we have intimate knowledge of, acceptance of, and mastery over our own bodies so that we can share this with our partners. Although learning about our sexual uniqueness can happen in the context of an intimate relationship, for most of us, masturbation is the most direct, uncomplicated, and pleasurable way to do it.

4

Solo Eroticism

Masturbation is still one of the most difficult sexual topics for women to talk about. Even though most of the women we interviewed were socially sophisticated, well-educated, working women, we found that we obtained fewer data on this subject than any other. Either masturbation was an unimportant part of their lives, or it was not easy to talk about because it touched off too many uncomfortable feelings. The antiquated cultural messages—masturbation is shameful or dirty and nice girls do not touch themselves—remain deeply embedded in the consciousness of American women, as is shown in the following excerpt by Dolly (age sixty-four):

I never masturbated until I was fifty-five years old, or maybe even older. Although I can't remember being told as a child not to touch myself down there, I felt it was wrong for me to touch my body; that masturbation was just a no-no and very shameful. All my life I thought it was shameful to touch myself and that only a man was supposed to touch my body.

Many feelings women have about masturbation are the result of antiquated ideas. Although few people still believe that masturbation causes warts or hair on one's palms, many believe that it causes illness, either physical or mental. Many more think masturbation will interfere with their sexual responsiveness with a man, to the extent that some women who are orgasmic through masturbation, but not with their partner, secretly blame their years of masturbation for their lack of orgasm during intercourse. Long-lasting negative feelings about masturbation can result either when women are raised with puritanical religious beliefs that deem masturbation a sin, or when no information about masturbation has been received at all. Theresa (age thirty):

I was raised a Catholic and never even heard the word "masturbation" while I was growing up. I didn't masturbate until I was twenty-five. I didn't even know what a clitoris was until I was in my early twenties.

Another myth that women, as well as men, believe is that obtaining sexual satisfaction by yourself will create excessive narcissism. The fear is that a woman will become so wrapped up in her own sexuality that she will no longer desire sex with others. It is interesting that most men have masturbated ever since childhood, yet rarely find that they choose masturbation over sex with a partner they care about. Although masturbation can be enjoyable and satisfying for both men and women, and although it has some benefits all its own, it cannot offer some of the dimensions that sex with a partner does—such as physical warmth and contact and a sense of emotional closeness.

Another common fear is that if a woman masturbates she will turn to other women as opposed to men for her sexual satisfaction. This belief evolves from the fact that orgasms through masturbation are often more intense and hence more satisfying than orgasms experienced by other forms of stimulation. Therefore, some people suspect that lovemaking with another woman would produce similar results because of the expectation that another woman would know exactly what to do. However, in masturbation, the intensity can be maintained simply because the woman is completely in control and hence can instantaneously change the stimulation to meet her needs at any given moment—and this control is unavailable to another person, male or female. For the same reasons, men can also experience more intense orgasms with masturbation and yet men don't—by and large—turn to other men for sexual satisfaction because of this.

The negative effects of our social scripting, which stereotypes men as the sexual beings and women as the pure, chaste, and asexual ones, affects men and women alike. This cultural definition, we believe, creates considerable anxiety for women about masturbation. In other partner-related forms of sexuality, women can at least feel that they are merely responding to their partner's initiative, to the male sex drive; that she herself is not really doing it. In masturbation, however, she must take responsibility for her own sexual appetite. No one is making her do it nor is anyone doing it to her. If she masturbates, she has to reconcile that action with the cultural definition of being pure, chaste, and asexual. Since this is impossible to do, many women fear that enjoying masturbation might lead to becoming oversexed. These often unconscious fears exist on deep emotional levels regardless of a woman's social background. Consequently, the conflict between being sexual and pure often results in the woman's attempt to fight off her sexual urges. But suppressing these feelings frequently only makes the woman more aware of them.

Some women who have been able during adolescence to successfully suppress their natural sexual drive often later find that they have warded off their sexual feelings to such an extent that they experience considerable difficulty learning to turn themselves on again. They may then find themselves unresponsive with sexual partners without knowing why.

All of this is not to say that masturbation is a necessity, and that all women *should* masturbate in order to experience a fulfilling sexual life, but to emphasize that it can be a positive, enjoyable experience.

In fact, we found that most of the women we interviewed who did masturbate and who were also involved in serious relationships with partners considered masturbation a useful, but relatively unimportant, aspect of their sexual lives. Their main sexual focus was on their relationship, rather than on themselves.

Others, however, particularly those who were not relating to a regular sexual partner, tended to be more focused on self-sexuality. Masturbation provided these women with other options. If the sexual relationship was not going well, instead of feeling deprived or finding a partner outside the relationship, they could fill the gap with masturbation. For women who were not in a sexual relationship, masturbation afforded sexual release without the complications of picking up a partner solely for sexual purposes. For this reason, a number of single women who are orgasmic during intercourse join preorgasmic women's groups* in order to learn how to masturbate to orgasm.

MASTURBATION AND ORGASM

Masturbation is also a good way for women to determine the types of stimulation they find most satisfying and most likely to lead to orgasm. This self-awareness is especially important since each woman's orgasmic pattern is unique. Orgasms are often a concern of women because they either do not have them or do not have them often enough, or because they are not certain that what they experience are orgasms. Sometimes it is difficult to identify a mild orgasm because the experience does not meet one's expectations of what an orgasm is "supposed" to feel like.

Orgasms vary in number, quality, and intensity. They can range in intensity from a very gentle release to an intense feeling accompanied by distinct contractions if the vaginal opening, spasms of the hands and feet, and/or arching of the back. Some women have one mild orgasm, others have a few in succession, some have one intense orgasm, others have a few mild orgasms followed by an intense one or some other combination. And the experience of orgasm in terms of quality, number, and intensity can change over time.

It is also possible for a woman consciously to intensify her orgasmic response. Two techniques are useful in helping to intensify orgasm. One is to exercise the pubococcygeal (PC) muscle, the muscle that surrounds the vaginal opening and frequently contracts with orgasm. Dr. Kegel developed a series of exercises that

* Preorgasmic women's groups are educational/therapy groups designed to aid women who have difficulty in experiencing orgasm.

strengthen the PC muscle and that for many women increase both the sensitivity of that area to stimulation and the intensity of the contractions at the point of orgasm.† The exercises are simple and can be practiced fairly effortlessly. The PC muscle is the one you squeeze when you are urinating and wish to stop the flow of urine. Squeezing this muscle and holding it for three seconds before releasing it is the first exercise. Ten, or fifteen squeezes of three seconds each should be done in succession. The second exercise consists of squeezing and releasing the PC muscle as rapidly as possible ten or fifteen times in succession. Both these exercises can be practiced three or more times each day.

Another technique for intensifying orgasm is what we call the teasing technique. It consists of having the woman masturbate almost to the point of orgasm, at which time she stops the stimulation or reduces the intensity of the stimulation to prevent the orgasm from occurring. She then builds up the intensity once again and again decreases the stimulation just before the point of orgasm. Building and lowering the stimulation three or four times before allowing the orgasm to take place often intensifies the response.

Women are often confused by the terms clitoral and vaginal orgasm. In fact, an orgasm is a pelvic-area response, and oftentimes a full-body response. If an orgasm occurs through fantasy with no genital stimulation it is not a fantasized orgasm; neither is an orgasm that results from nipple stimulation a breast orgasm. Therefore, a clitoral orgasm is not the result of stimulating the clitoris, any more than a vaginal orgasm results from stimulating the vagina. An orgasm is an orgasm. The site of the stimulation that is most likely to lead to orgasm depends upon the unique sensitivities of the individual.

For most women the area of stimulation that is most sensitive and most likely to lead to orgasm is the clitoris. According to Shere Hite, 70 per cent of women require some form of clitoral stimulation in order to reach orgasm.‡

Some women respond to hard and direct stimulation of the clito-

† A. H. Kegel, "Sexual Functions of the Pubococcygens Muscle," *Western Journal of Surgery*, 60, 10(1952):521–24.
‡ *The Hite Report* (New York: Macmillan, 1976).

ris, while others prefer soft or indirect stimulation of this area. Often, during intercourse, the clitoris is being indirectly stimulated by the male partner's pubic bone or stimulated as the result of the penis moving in and out of the vagina. This is why some women find that they can have orgasms in some intercourse positions and not in others, or only with certain partners. In some positions they are receiving sufficient clitoral stimulation from the partner's pubic bone or from the angle of the penis, while this does not occur in other positions. Or the unique anatomy of the woman and one partner may fit together in a way that supplies her with sufficient clitoral stimulation, whereas the fit is different with another partner.

In terms of masturbation, some women prefer to start off with gentle stroking of the clitoris or of the inner lips or whole mons area and to stroke the clitoris more directly and with greater intensity as the genital area engorges with blood and they become more aroused. Other women prefer to begin and end with hard direct clitoral stimulation. Still others find direct clitoral stimulation uncomfortable at any point in the arousal process. The use of oil—olive oil, vegetable oil, baby oil, or Albolene—can be very useful in making clitoral stimulation less uncomfortable and more pleasurable for women whose genitals are particularly sensitive.

If this is the first time you have confronted the subject of masturbation, you may find reading this chapter makes you feel very uncomfortable. You may find it difficult to believe that some women have learned to enjoy masturbation, that they consider it an important part of their sexuality.

To many of you, reading this chapter will feel like voyeurism. You may experience feelings similar to those expressed by a woman after seeing an educational film of a woman masturbating:

Somehow, for me to do the same thing is okay, but to watch her doing it—I mean, if she wants to do it behind a door without me watching, that's fine, but to be watching her do it and see her exploring everything . . . I hate to use the word, but it was almost "dirty."

Another woman cried after seeing the same film. When asked why she was crying, she replied that it was so sad that she was in her fifties and had to come to a preorgasmic workshop to find out how women masturbate. She felt badly that she lived in a society that considered masturbation so dirty. Her reaction to the film was that there was nothing dirty about it at all; it was really beautiful.

The women we spoke with who masturbated had learned to do so at different points in their lives and were catalyzed by various forces. Although some began as the result of attending a workshop, reading books, or seeing a sex therapist, the majority of women we interviewed discovered masturbation on their own. Many learned at a very young age, such as the following woman:

When I masturbated as a child, I thought I had invented it. I thought it was something kids knew about, not grown-ups.

Others, such as Lorraine (age twenty-seven), discovered it during adolescence or afterward:

I taught myself how to masturbate when I was a teen-ager and it happened almost naturally. One night after my parents were asleep, I was just curious and started touching myself a lot—just touching my body all over. That felt so good that I just kept doing it. One night I got out a mirror and started looking at myself. Before I knew it, I started touching my lips and my clitoris and masturbating to orgasm. So I started spending all this time masturbating. Over time, I found that I was multiorgasmic. I probably spend a lot less time masturbating now than I did during the first couple of years after I learned to masturbate. I found when I was in college, if I lay down to read a book—forget it! After about half an hour, I'd be masturbating.

Some women learned about masturbation from their partner. Joan (thirty-one, married nine years):

I never knew that women masturbated until I was in my twenties. I remember that it was a shock to find out that women masturbated. I had a lover who talked to me about masturbation. He said that he did it and wondered why I didn't, and to me the whole idea was really surprising. At that time, I couldn't imagine myself doing it or even being interested in doing it, but the more I thought about it the more I wanted to, and eventually I started dreaming about masturbating and started having orgasms while I was dreaming. Finally, I decided I would try it. The first time I was hesitant about doing it, but later as I got better at it, I really started to enjoy it a lot. In some ways, I have stronger sexual feelings masturbating than any other time, probably because it feels so safe and I have so much control.

PURPOSES OF MASTURBATION

Masturbation served a number of purposes and had different meanings for those we interviewed who masturbated. For some, it was strictly a physical release. Their bodies dictated the need for sexual release and masturbation solved the dilemma. Billy (forty-three, married twenty-six years):

I just respond to the physical feelings I have. I really think that it's something more physical going on with my body than mental. I can remember waking up one morning with the sense of wanting or needing sex. This was just before my period and all I did was wake up and turn over and I had already climaxed. So I didn't think it had anything to do with me mentally, but rather with what was going on with me physically.

Many women thought masturbation was good for relieving tension. When they were tense because of a problem, frustrated with another person or family member, or even bored with a current project, masturbation provided momentary relief. As one woman said, "Sometimes I'll use it to relieve tension: if I'm stuck on something I'll just masturbate and then I'll be able to go back to work again."

Many women recommended masturbation for the relief of menstrual cramps and minor aches and pains. Elaine, thirty-eight, a registered nurse, and mother of three teen-agers, married two years to her second husband Philip, a building contractor, said:

I don't like to use any aspirin or medication if I can help it. So normally I use sex as my outlet for relieving any aches or pains. However, when I was in periods where I wasn't having intercourse, I'd rely on masturbation to take care of all my aches and pains.

Most of the women we interviewed found their desire for masturbation dropped significantly when they became involved in a sexual relationship. These women generally used masturbation when there was no partner available to tide them over during lean times. Some of them, however, did not find this release completely satisfactory in meeting their sexual needs. For example, thirty-four-year-old Ariel, who has been separated for a year from her husband and lives with her four-year-old daughter, feels:

Masturbation is great if I have a buildup of sexual frustration, which I have these days since I haven't had a lover for a long time. However, there's a point where I'm frustrated, but not enough so that masturbation will be that satisfying. There's also an opposite point which I have reached many times in the last couple of years where what I really want is somebody's arms around me or somebody's weight on me, so masturbation doesn't work then either. I would still come if I masturbated, but it's just not the same, it's not as satisfying, so I usually decide to wait until I meet someone I want to have sex with. I guess what I'm saying really is that sometimes I enjoy masturbating and sometimes I don't.

A smaller group of women, as typified by thirty-two-year-old Alexandra, who is divorced, found that their masturbation activity increased, rather than decreased, during periods of frequent sex with a partner:

There are times when I'm not turned on sexually and I am not having sex, and I don't mind those times at all. If I am having good sex with somebody and it's pretty consistent, I seem to stay turned on pretty much all the time. Once my body is sexually awakened, it doesn't go back to sleep very easily. So even if I've had a really wonderful sexual experience the night before, I'll still be turned on the next day and then I might masturbate.

Many women felt being able to be sexual by themselves, without a partner present, had a number of other benefits. Roberta, who is a physical therapist, claimed that masturbation toned her muscles:

Masturbation tones your body for intercourse with a partner. It tones all the muscles that hold your abdominal organs in place. I can tell the difference when I've been having orgasm either through masturbation or through lovemaking. My abdominal muscles feel tight like I've been to the gym and worked out.

For some women, masturbation allowed them a freedom that they did not feel when they were with a partner. With masturbation, they felt no pressure to please anyone but themselves. The following two women share their views on the advantages of masturbation.

Cortney (thirty-one, living with boy friend):

One of the reasons I always enjoyed masturbation so much is because I'm the only one involved. I don't have to please anybody else. My main problem has been being open sexually with somebody, being able to be honest and not be embarrassed, but when I'm by myself, I don't have to ask anybody for anything or talk to anybody. I can go into my own little routine, and think about whatever I want to think about. I can even get into a sexual fantasy if I want to.

Alice (thirty-eight, single):

When I masturbate, I know exactly where the sensitive points are on my body. I know exactly how much pressure to exert and I can tell exactly where I'm going. There's never any question as to whether I can achieve orgasm. It's just a matter of how long I want to prolong it, whether I want to come then, or whether I want to hold off for a while. If I want to hold off, I do something else, like look at a book, and then I can come back to it later and still have my orgasm. I have total control over myself because I know my body so well.

Another good thing about masturbation is that I feel freer and less inhibited about trying more wild and daring things than I've been able to with a partner.

As sex therapists, we have advocated masturbation as a method of teaching women about their own sexual responsiveness and as a way to experience their first orgasm. With masturbation a woman does not have to worry if she looks unattractive, a fear of many women when they first experience orgasm; she does not have to concern herself with her partner's satisfaction or opinion of her competence as a lover. She is also able to apply the stimulation exactly the way she likes it—making it harder, softer, or moving the location a quarter of an inch to the left or right because she has instantaneous feedback from her body. She does not need to communicate these preferences moment by moment so that her partner can stimulate her correctly.

Jacqueline (age thirty-three) first learned how to be orgasmic through masturbation after her divorce:

Even after being married for almost ten years, I still felt like I was a virgin, probably because I had never had an orgasm. I didn't even know what an orgasm was. Anyway, I met someone who became a good friend and we started having sex. He would talk about the fact that I had never come. One day he decided that I had to do something about the fact that I was not having orgasms, so he bought me a battery-operated vibrator. At the time I was living in a group house and although I had my own room, people were always coming in and out because you had to go through my room to get to the laundry room. However, on Saturdays no one was usually around. I used to have more fun playing with that vibrator! I would start in the morning. I would play with the vibrator, have an orgasm, get dressed, go do my work, and an hour later go play with my vibrator again and have another orgasm. I would do this all day long as long as nobody was home. I kept wearing down the batteries all the time. Finally, my friend bought me a plug-in vibrator so I wouldn't have to worry about batteries.

Jane's reaction to learning about masturbation is not unique. Many women, once they have learned to have orgasms, find themselves masturbating frequently. Having discovered a brand-new feeling, they masturbate repeatedly at first not only because of the enjoyment and release they get, but also to be certain they will not lose this newfound ability. There is also the desire, as with any new ability, to experiment and become more proficient at it.

However, for many women, the major attraction of masturbation is that it is a vehicle to express their love for themselves. This is not generally a part of the male concept of masturbation, as evidenced by the terms men use, such as "whacking off," "beating your meat," and "jerking off." This concept of self-love is also new for most women: it brings up pejorative connotations of narcissism and egotism. In our culture, being socialized as a "good" woman means foremost being a nurturer. We are trained far better in serving and loving others than we are in nurturing and loving ourselves. Being good to ourselves is only beginning to be viewed as a valuable concept.

One of the interesting outcomes of the preorgasmic groups in which women are required to find time for masturbation is that they leave the groups feeling that they deserve more for themselves, especially more pleasure—sexually and in many other ways. They say that the time they were required to spend on themselves sexually was very important in elevating their sense of self-worth. Although they found it initially difficult to take the time (perhaps because they were anxious about it), they found that the more they were able to do so, the more comfortable they felt with masturbation, especially once they were able to experience orgasm. After the group ended, many women would still reserve special private time for themselves in which they might or might not masturbate. They had come to realize that it was important to take whatever time was necessary for them to value themselves physically, emotionally, and sexually, since the three are intertwined. The following women share how important it is for them to take pleasure in their bodies sexually and how masturbation plays a role in this.

April (forty-two, teacher, divorced):

My sex life before I was married was rather limited. I didn't marry until I was twenty-five and before that, as a young teen-ager and later as a young adult, I used to "neck" with my boy friends. We never went "all the way," and I certainly never masturbated. Years later, after I was married and divorced, I decided that it was important to me to learn to love my body. I had felt pleasure before about my body when I was dancing or swimming or playing tennis but I wasn't aware of how really neat it was to appreciate my own body sexually, so I began to gently make love to myself. For the first couple of years after my divorce, the times I masturbated were total glorifications of my body. At that time I wasn't having any sexual experiences with other males because I needed some time to learn to love myself, and taking care of myself by masturbating was an important part of that.

Roberta (thirty-five, divorced):

I started masturbating when I was six years old and my own daughter has been masturbating since she's been about eighteen months old. The first time my mother caught me, I didn't even know what I was doing. My mother said, "Don't do that." She didn't say why or anything, and I always had this feeling that it was a no-no. Now, as an adult, I feel that masturbation is a way of being good to yourself, a way of loving yourself, and feeling you're an okay person. That a feeling of release you get from masturbation is almost like a meditation, because it gets you into a place that is yours exclusively. It's a very important part of my life. I can really tell where I'm at, whether I'm depressed or happy, by how many times a week I masturbate. I may go for weeks or even months without masturbating, but when I realize that, then I know I'm really not feeling very good about myself and I start masturbating. I might do it three nights in a row or in the afternoon and again at night because it feels so good and it's a way of giving myself pleasure. I don't think that intercourse is a substitute for masturbation because masturbation is giving to yourself exclusively since you don't have to worry about your partner.

You may find it surprising at first that a woman would put the same energy into preparations for making love to herself as she would in making love with a partner. However, many of the women we interviewed who felt that masturbation was an expression of self-love took the same time and trouble to prepare for making love to themselves as they would if they were going out on a date with a very special person. Jesse, a sixty-year-old artist, who is divorced after a thirty-year marriage, explains her philosophy of why she feels it's important to adequately prepare for self-stimulation:

If you want to make masturbation something very pleasurable, and not just something to satisfy you or a substitute for the "real thing," you need to learn how to be as interesting for yourself as you would expect a partner to be. You need to do the same kind of things you would do to create an inviting environment with a partner, like playing soft music, taking your time, and trying new and different ways of stimulating yourself. You need to learn to relax with it instead of making it a very agitated, desperate way to feel sexually satisfied. Then it can be great, great fun.

THE SETTING

The following women share more specific information about how they enhance their masturbation experiences by setting the scene, much as they did when they planned to make love to a partner.

Joan (thirty-one, married nine years):

It's especially nice if I use some props, like scented candles, lotions, or body oil. I like the slippery feeling I get when I use a lubricant like K-Y jelly on my genitals, and I've also used a mirror to watch myself while I'm masturbating.

Judith (forty, married):

The setting itself is important. I like to masturbate in odd places. I haven't done it much lately, but I went through a phase where I masturbated in different places, like in the woods. There was something about the whole setting, the sun, trees, the water, that was very beautiful. I had been hiking, so I was out a ways in the woods. I was kind of far from the hiking trail, but I could still see the trail. I didn't think anybody could see me very clearly, and if they did, I didn't think they could figure out what I was doing. But I was willing to take all these risks, because it was so much fun. The other one I remember was in a partly constructed house that belonged to some friends of mine in a nearby resort area. I went upstairs in the bedroom when no one was around and masturbated and was very turned on.

The considerable range of ways that women use masturbation was expressed well by Morgan (forty-two, married):

Masturbation is something that really can't be hurried, so you have to know that you've got plenty of time and not try to sandwich it in between other things. I read a description once that said masturbation is everything from a quick fuck to making love to yourself and I think that's pretty accurate. I like it best when I'm making love to myself. I like to take enough time, and make sure I have everything I want: oil, the vibrator, an attachment for my vibrator that's shaped like a penis, and sometimes candlelight and music. I like to take time to stroke myself all over so all of me feels good, rather than just diving into the genital areas and going to work on that; then it's a sensuous as well as sexual experience. I also like a quick self-fuck when I'm really feeling excited about something I've read or something that's happened. It's short, quick, nice, pleasant, but it's different.

POSITIONS

Many women learned to masturbate as children and continue to use the position they first discovered throughout the rest of their lives. For example, they might have been lying in their crib and rubbed against the sheet and discovered it felt good. One woman talked about how swinging from the jungle gym created a certain tension and pleasant sensation, which made physical education her favorite activity at school. Some remembered the pleasant feeling they had as children rocking back and forth on chairs, so they just kept repeating it. It wasn't that these feelings were tied to sex, or even necessarily to orgasm, but that they enjoyed the pleasurable sensations. Sometimes the positions discovered during childhood masturbation are very different from positions used during partner sex. Although the women are able to have orgasms in the positions they have used since childhood in a matter of minutes, they often have difficulty or require a longer period of time to achieve orgasm in other positions with their partner. In a sense, these women have taught themselves to respond to one type of stimulation. Often, responding orgasmically in different positions, even with masturbation, requires practice. Other women prefer to experiment with masturbation and to use as many positions as possible, just as they might experiment with different intercourse positions with a partner. Some of these positions are found to be better than others for providing sufficient clitoral stimulation, sufficient vaginal stimulation, sufficient buildup of muscle tension, or a feeling of security and safety depending upon the unique needs of each woman. The following are some of the positions used during masturbation.

Morgan (forty-two, married):

I like to use different positions at different times, just as I do in lovemaking, so there's no one particular position that works best. Sometimes I like the sensation of lying on my stomach with my legs spread out—that has a feeling of helplessness that I like. Sometimes I like lying on my back with my legs bent and spread out. Sometimes I like to use that same position with some pillows under me. It varies.

A woman from a preorgasmic group discovered:

I have found that during both masturbation and sex, I can have an orgasm more easily if I put my feet up against the wall and press against it. I think it's because it provides me with more muscle tension, which I need in order to experience orgasm.

Women mentioned a few special positions which would intensify the experience of orgasm. For example, Rose suggested:

I teach yoga and I know that energy circuits in the body are important. Consequently, I've done some experimentation and I've found that if I masturbate sitting up with the soles of my feet flush against one another, I complete an energy circuit so that the energy can flow from my genitals through one leg and back up the other. This position intensifies the feelings of sexual arousal and orgasm for me.

DILDOS

Many women, when they masturbate, only give themselves clitoral stimulation. Others mentioned that they miss the feeling of fullness that occurs when something is inside their vagina or that they require vaginal stimulation to reach orgasm. In these cases, women used phallus-shaped objects or dildos inside their vaginas to recreate that sensation. The objects ranged from those fashioned specifically for sexual purposes to bottles, tampons, candles, and vegetables. A woman's choice depended, in part, on her feelings about using something artificial or organic. For example, some women were uncomfortable using the plastic handle of a toothbrush or hairbrush, but enjoyed using a vegetable of some kind. One of our sexual therapy groups roared with laughter as one woman related the story of how it took her fifteen minutes to pick out the zucchini that was exactly the right size and shape she wanted. She ended by saying that it is not often that one gets such a choice!

The following women share how they use dildos to enhance their masturbation experience.

Iris (thirty-two and living with boy friend):

In fifteen years of masturbating, I've always used a super tampon and placed a pillow between my legs to have something to move against. I use a tampon because I can move it against the full length of my clitoris, with part of it outside and part inside. When I'm fucking and have my legs apart, there is a lot of sexual tension built up by having something for my thighs to grab and grip against. So I put a pillow between my legs when I masturbate to create more tension.

Elaine (thirty-eight, married):

I use my diaphragm to masturbate with because it seems to work as close to a penis as anything I could find. I use my hands initially to stimulate myself and then I pull the diaphragm in and out of my vagina. The rim of the diaphragm gives me a sensation of fullness in the opening that I like.

Sherry (twenty-eight, office manager, lesbian and living with her lover for the past nine years):

I hold my dildo tightly between my lips and move it up and down in such a way that it actually massages my clitoris until I come. I also fantasize that somebody else is doing it to me.

Allison (thirty-five, divorced):

I wish I had a dildo but I can't bring myself to go to one of those porno stores and buy one, so I use the handle of a spatula. I always wash the handle very carefully before I use it. Sometimes I'll put a little cream on it, to make sure it's not rough, and then when I'm finished I always wash it off carefully with soap and water.

MIRRORS

A number of women mentioned that watching themselves in the mirror while masturbating was both very arousing and educational.

Suzanne (thirty-seven, bisexual, divorced):

I've used a mirror that has a magnifier to examine my genitals real carefully and that has been a turn-on. I enjoy seeing myself magnified and exploring all my different parts and watching the color changes as I get aroused.

Alice (thirty-eight, single):

One time during masturbation I decided to look in a mirror and I found watching my genital area engorge very exciting to me. While I was lying there nearing orgasm, the fantasy that went through my mind was that my genital area kept getting more and more engorged and kept actually getting larger and larger as it continued to engorge. I always had the idea that my genital area was very small and not capable of having much stimulation so when I looked at it in the mirror and found that it was very engorged, the image stayed in my mind. My orgasm was great probably because of my fantasy. I guess in my mind the larger the genital area became, the more there was to be stimulated and the more sexual enjoyment I'd get.

PHYSICAL STIMULATION

Women were quite creative about using different objects to create the physical stimulation. Some women basically used their hands—either their fingers, their palms, or the sides of their hands—to stimulate their vulva and clitoris. The following women described how they achieve the physical stimulation necessary to achieve orgasm when they masturbate.

Morgan (forty-two, married):

I need very direct clitoral stimulation to achieve orgasm. When I first start to masturbate there's a certain amount of indirect stimulation around the clitoris, but what really does it for me is using oils or some kind of lubricant on my finger or vibrator and rubbing in a circular motion directly on my clitoris.

Gaye (thirty-three, married):

I've been masturbating for a long time, probably since I was twelve or thirteen. I masturbate on my stomach with both hands between my legs, one on top of the other cupped over my clitoris. I move my hands in a circular motion and it's so effective that it doesn't take long at all. It has absolutely nothing to do with my vagina. I use fantasies if I'm real tired or anxious and it's not working, but otherwise I don't even need to fantasize.

Other women used towels or pillows to provide the stimulation.

Heather (thirty-five, married):

What I usually do is get a towel or something like that and lie on my stomach on my bed. I put the towel up to my clitoris with my legs apart and slightly bent with my knees on the bed and I rock back and forth. I've been doing that since I was thirteen and I still masturbate that way.

Some women use nothing to stimulate themselves directly, but instead use muscular pressure created by squeezing their legs, and especially their thighs, together. Thirty-two-year-old Monique, a graduate student, married nine years and the mother of a five-year-old boy and a four-month-old girl, learned a new way of masturbating from being in a female sexuality group:

There was a woman in the group who was so embarrassed because she said she never achieved an orgasm by masturbating manually, but she's done it another way. The whole group said, "Well, how do you do it?" She got down on the floor, although she was very chagrined and embarrassed, and showed us how she masturbates. She gets in a doglike position and crosses her legs and rubs her thighs together. Everybody was so intrigued we decided to end the session early so we could go home and try out this new technique. I found it to be very exciting. It's a whole new approach to masturbation because you don't use your hands, you just use your thighs.

VIBRATORS

Many women enjoy using a vibrator when they masturbate. Some of these women enjoy incorporating the vibrator into their lovemaking with a partner (see Chapter 3, pp. 80–82). Others are worried about using the vibrator for fear they will become addicted to it.

This fear is based on the fact that the vibrator offers more intense stimulation than can be duplicated by any human hand, mouth, or penis. Women who become accustomed to the effortless arousal guaranteed by the vibrator often become discouraged when trying to masturbate manually. Manual stimulation is more time-consuming and requires a greater effort to focus on the more subtle physical stimulation or on the mental fantasies that accompany that stimulation. Women who are able to accept the fact that non-mechanical stimulation requires more time before reaching orgasm and take this factor into account, rarely experience any problems with the vibrator.

There are two major varieties of vibrators: one is battery-operated and the other plugs into an electrical outlet. Battery-operated vibrators are usually made of plastic and are phallus shaped. They come in three sizes which range from quite small, about the size of a short, stubby cigar, to very large, approximately the size of an ordinary flashlight. These vibrators are generally used externally to stimulate the clitoris and the area around the clitoris, but can also be used as a dildo in the vagina or the anus for additional stimulation.

Electric vibrators are generally stronger than the battery-operated ones. They come in various sizes and shapes and range from producing very mild to very intense stimulation. Some varieties of electric vibrators, like the Prelude vibrator, are designed specifically for clitoral stimulation, and have a high and a low speed. Electric vibrators are used by applying the vibrating area onto the clitoris and/or surrounding areas. Another type of electric vibrator is the Swedish massager, which fits on the back of the hand. This massager causes the hand and fingers to vibrate as they massage the body directly. Vibrators or massagers can usually be purchased in the small appliance section of most department stores or can be ordered by mail.*

Thirty-year-old Theresa, a psychologist and a lesbian who lives alone, finds using a vibrator exciting and a different physical experience than masturbating with her hand:

A vibrator is something new in my life and it has made masturbation more exciting for me, more alive. With the vibrator I feel sexual excitement as opposed to sensuality. I have a wonderful vibrator called Prelude 2. The vibrator has revolutionized masturbation for me. My hand doesn't get tired and the sensual sensations feel like they're happening on the inside of me. I don't know how else to explain it. It's a different physical experience from other sex.

Some women used two vibrators simultaneously. Roberta (thirty-five, divorced):

The best masturbatory experience that I've had was using two vibrators at one time, using the Prelude 3 on my clitoris and a penis-

---

* Sensory Research Corporation, 2424 Morris Avenue, Union, New Jersey 07083, and Eve's Garden, 119 West Fifty-seventh Street, New York, New York 10019.

shaped battery-operated vibrator in my vagina. I fantasized that I was at the mercy of these machines and this feeling of helplessness intensified the buildup. I also kept postponing the orgasm, which really heightened it. When I finally did come, it was very intense.

WATER

Another popular way of masturbating is with water. Women who preferred the medium of water found that the jets from a hot tub, the spigot on their bathtub, or the Water Pik Shower Massager, could be used equally well on their genitals as on the rest of their body.

Cortney (thirty-one, divorced):

I really enjoy masturbating with my Water Pik Shower Massager. It has different settings for different water pressures and I can fix it so it hits me right on my clitoris. I really enjoy that! I often go in the shower and stay there for half an hour. Sometimes after my boy friend and I have intercourse, he'll be through and watching football and I'll be lying there going crazy. I just go in and take a shower and have a good time with myself and then crawl back in bed and read a magazine!

Jackie, a forty-one-year-old businesswoman who lives with her boy friend and their one-year-old child, uses the water from the faucet in her bathtub to masturbate:

My bathtub is perfect for masturbation. The faucet sticks out at the end of the tub and I scoot my rear end under the faucet so my clitoris is directly under the stream of water. In this position, I'm leaning back on an angle resting on my elbows, with my legs lifted up and pressed against the wall. I like the water to be a comfortably warm temperature. The stream of water directly on my clitoris feels so good, like a million tiny fingers massaging me. I've never had any difficulty having an orgasm this way.

MENTAL AROUSAL

Appropriate physical stimulation was just one of the important components of a good masturbation experience; the other was mental arousal. With masturbation, women had none of the usual arousal cues provided by their partners and had to manufacture these feelings on their own. This meant that it was terribly important for the women to be able to focus on sexual thoughts and feelings and to block out all other thoughts. Many women did find this a difficult task, but had found ways to help themselves concentrate. Some would read erotic books or look at erotic pictures or fantasize. Others found that certain types of music helped block out extraneous sounds or thoughts. Even a constant drone, as from a fan or hair dryer, helped them pay closer attention to the feelings they were experiencing in their bodies by blocking out other sounds.

Many women have no trouble coming when they focus on their physical feelings or when they recreate the feelings they have with a partner. Some have visual fantasies. Fantasies have received a lot of attention over the last five years, particularly with books like those by Nancy Friday. In the past women would have rarely admitted that they had sexual fantasies. Nice girls did not do that. Thank goodness for the research† which shows the wide range of women's fantasies and maintains that these fantasies do not necessarily carry implications about mental stability.

Now the pendulum has swung so far in the other direction that we, as sexual therapists, often see women who worry because they *don't* have fantasies. It seems that the media have just created another standard of sexuality for women, another "should"—women "should" be able to have sexual fantasies, with the result that many who do not fantasize often feel inadequate. Basically, no one method of mental arousal is better than any other, and what works for one person may not work for another. What is important is to find the method that works best for you. The fantasies women in our sample used covered a broad range of topics from the mundane to the extraordinary.

Monique (thirty-two, married):

I always used to feel that my fantasies were never as good as other women's and that I was very inhibited sexually. I remember the first

† E. Barbara Hariton and Jerome L. Singer, "Women's Fantasies During Marital Intercourse: Normative and Theoretical Implications," *Journal of Consulting and Clinical Psychology*, 42, 3(1974):313–22.

time I read Nancy Friday's book *My Secret Garden,* and I was absolutely appalled and terribly envious of the women who entertained those wild, wild fantasies. I always felt that my fantasies were so ordinary. This is one of the hardest struggles that I've had, feeling good about myself, feeling that whatever turns me on is okay.

Jane (forty-five, counselor, divorced, and mother of sons, thirteen and fifteen):

I used to think I was weird because all of my contemporaries, including my best friend, used to fantasize while having sex with their husbands. I never did. But I've used a fantasy since then to masturbate, and it's been very helpful. I either fantasize myself with somebody I have enjoyed being with before or use fantasy to get into some things I was afraid to get into in reality, like violent sex, or sex as an animalistic experience.

Most of the women's fantasies reflected possible situations and possible lovers or memorable past experiences.

Samantha (thirty-five, divorced):

I enjoy masturbating sitting in a warm tub with bubbles. As I'm beginning to fantasize, I start to touch myself. My fantasies are usually about having sex with somebody either real or imagined where I have control. Sometimes it's having the things done to me in the order and way I want them done, right up to orgasm. My fantasies are usually that somebody else is making love to me. I have some real experiences that I like to fit into my fantasies, like an experience with a lover that really turned me on. My fantasies range from relaxing ones, like being in the woods with the sun coming through the trees and having fantastic lovemaking, an esthetic kind of experience, to really wanton abandon, like someone having oral sex with me in the office.

Alice (thirty-eight, single):

One masturbation experience started out by looking at a fashion magazine where the models were wearing very revealing bikinis. I started imagining myself with one of those bikinis on and then imagined a man coming up and fondling me. I closed my eyes and touched that same point on my breasts. Then I fantasized that he touched a different part and then I touched that part, too. In this way, I slowly got very excited to the point where I thought I couldn't get any more excited, but somehow still did until I achieved orgasm. The orgasm seemed to last for a very long time.

It was interesting that some of the women's fantasies had very little to do with actual sex, but rather employed images that reflected the kinesthetic sensations.

Joan (thirty-one, married nine years) has a wide repertoire of fantasies; some are sexual and some are kinesthetic:

I like to fantasize when I masturbate and sometimes it's a very sexual fantasy and sometimes it's completely removed from sex. Some fantasies are "people fantasies," like being involved with men or women sexually, or more nurturing fantasies of someone taking care of me or holding me. Other fantasies are nature fantasies, like being a whale or a porpoise moving through the water. The image of going way down under dark, blue-green water with the different temperatures and the different sounds of being deep underwater is very powerful to me. I have another water fantasy of a flowing river where I'm a leaf on the water moving very fast down this river. I'm floating on my back and I'm part of the river, not just in it. It's hard to explain in words, but there's a lot of power for me in just the force of the movement in these fantasies and I start feeling that power inside of me. It's like a string's tied to my clitoris and someone is pulling me rapidly through the water or the air by that point. Of course, I'm making the power, no one's pulling me, but my whole body's just sort of flowing back from that point and following it.

Sometimes fantasies took the form of imagining the physiological changes of the genitals during the process of arousal and orgasm. Sharon (thirty-five, single) has found that this way of masturbating gives her more control over her body:

What I do is visualize the actual physiological changes that are going on in my body as I become more and more aroused. I'm trying to master the physical inside of me that's involved in an orgasm and it seems to work. For example, as I'm stroking my outer lips and clitoris with my hand, I'm imagining all the changes that are taking place inside my vagina—the walls opening up, the sweating processes, but most importantly for me, the area around my uterus and cervix. I imagine my uterus to be like a ball or a sun and just as I start my contractions that will lead to orgasm, I imagine my uterus moving up and down, vibrating, and, as it does, sending out sensations all around it. It seems to increase all the sensations that I feel deep inside of me. I become more aware of where sensations are or aren't and I'm able to enhance them at will. I found that over time this method has increased my knowledge of my body in such a way that I'm more orgasmic with myself and, therefore, more orgasmic with my partner.

Another woman, Sarah (twenty-nine, married) uses graphic fantasies of a penis to intensify her orgasms:

The most powerful fantasies for me are the graphic, visual fantasies of watching either myself or my partner masturbate to orgasm. Visualizing the hardness of the penis, the slipperiness of the penis with its "pre-turn-on" discharge, and then actually seeing the progression in my mind as the male gets more turned on and moves his penis in a faster and faster way until he finally ejaculates is the fantasy I use to have my own very explosive orgasm.

EROTICA

Erotica are used rather than fantasy by many women in order to supply the mental component for arousal.

Samantha (thirty-five, divorced):

I use erotic novels that some people might call "garbage books" to turn me on. I like to read descriptions of techniques and that kind of thing. It really enhances masturbation for me.

The type of erotica found arousing differed from woman to woman. Some liked flowery Victorian novels, others preferred those more explicit descriptions filled with four-letter words. Judy (thirty-one, married):

When I was younger I used to like to read dirty books when I masturbated, the raunchier the better. I had a girl friend who had them and passed them on to me. I was too embarrassed to buy one myself.

Many women found pictures of nude bodies—men, women, or both—a tremendous turn-on. Joan (thirty-one, married):

Another prop for me in masturbating is pictures of naked men and women. I liked the picture stories of couples they used in *Viva* magazine. I loved those. They were very erotic to me. Another prop we sometimes both use as a couple is movies. We don't see them real often, but movies like *Emanuelle* are very arousing for both of us.

The following woman, Louise (thirty-nine, married two years, second marriage) created her own erotica quite spontaneously:

Once I was tape-recording a letter to my lover, who lived in another city. I was sharing my memories of the last time we had made love and the longer I talked about it, the more excited I became. I started to think, "Oh, wouldn't it be nice to have him here," but then I thought, "No, he's not here so don't get so aroused!" Then it occurred to me that I could stimulate and satisfy myself by using what I was picturing in my head. It was easier to do this because I was away on vacation in this lovely room, so I didn't have any interruptions. So I began to rub myself and to tell him on the tape what I was doing and what I was experiencing. I felt gleeful knowing that he was going to be listening to this later and I was imagining how it was going to affect him. I remember giggling about that, but not letting it interfere with my getting into my own body. I was describing to him what I was doing. I was also totally engrossed in the feelings and sensations I was having, so much so that I didn't even remember what I said when I had an orgasm. Later, I played that part over and it was incredible because my voice had changed and I didn't remember saying some of those things. It was a lovely, lovely experience. It was like giving someone a running commentary of what was happening to me as I masturbated to orgasm. The end of the story is that the tape came to his office as usual, and he started to play it there. He told me he was playing it and all of a sudden he decided to stop. He said, number one, he was getting excited, and, number two, my voice had changed and then he knew he had to turn it off!

Whether you employ fantasy or erotica or just concentrate on the physical feelings to enhance your masturbation, self-stimulation remains essentially a solitary experience with all of the advantages as well as the disadvantages that that implies. Masturbation enables us to grow confident and comfortable in our sexuality while at the same time providing us with some good sexual experiences. However, most of us, during the course of our lives, choose to reach out and share our sexuality with another person. Then good communication skills become essential if we want to have our experiences with a partner that equal or surpass the sexual experiences we enjoy alone. After all, sex is in itself a very basic yet very special form of communication. Consequently, our next chapter forms the nexus between sexual self-knowledge and satisfying sex with a partner.

5

Letting Your Partner Know

A predominant myth in our culture is that sex should just happen naturally and spontaneously if it's right—if it's meant to be. The corollary to this myth is: If you are in love with someone, all you have to do is jump into bed and the sex will be perfect. Therefore, most people believe that if it's really love, you don't need to talk about sex, it just magically takes care of itself.

If sex isn't perfect from the beginning, if certain problems exist or if the sex is not as satisfying as they would like, some women jump to the conclusion that maybe it's because they're not really in love, instead of seeing it as a possible communication problem. Kelly (a thirty-six-year-old counselor who has been divorced five years, and is the mother of three children, ages ten to fourteen), explains how this cultural myth affected her:

Sex was a problem for me in my marriage as well as afterward because of my negative attitudes and feelings about sexuality. I bought into the myth that you don't need to talk about sex. If it's right, if it's really love, it will just go smoothly and everybody will know what they like and enjoy. It didn't take a whole lot to dispel that myth because it didn't work that way. I knew what physical things were sexually pleasurable, but my partner didn't automatically know them, even if he was trying to be sensitive and concerned about me. So I learned to tentatively get past my tongue-tiedness at first just by making little statements about what felt good or what didn't feel right. I learned to be able to tell a sexual partner that I liked to be aroused very slowly, that he would need to be patient with that or neither one of us would get to where we were physically enjoying ourselves—or he might, but I wouldn't. I began to explain that certain kinds of touches in the genital area, on certain parts of my body, felt good and others didn't. I discovered that it was easier to tell him about it afterward because by then I would be feeling more comfortable and closer to him, so it was easier to say things like, "When we do this again, it would be nice if you touched my breasts more, because that's very sensual and arousing to me." With practice, it became easier and easier to communicate.

Mind reading is a corollary to this myth. If our partners really love us, then they should be considerate and sensitive enough to read our minds. As sex therapists, we see many couples who get into trouble because they equate love and hence sensitivity and consideration with mind reading. They don't realize that mind reading is not always as easy as it appears, especially when both people are doing it.

Take, for example, the problem of the following couple who were very committed to making their marriage work. In their loving attempt at being considerate, the following would occur: Glenda would interpret something that Dick did in the evening to mean that he was interested in sex. Even though she was not feeling very sexual, she wanted to please him, so she would try to get herself in the mood by lighting a fire and putting on a sexy negligee. Dick, who wasn't conscious of sending sexual signals, would notice Glenda's activity and think, "Oh, Glenda must want sex. Therefore, I'd better get into the mood for it." As their sex would progress, each one would wonder why the other was not more enthusiastic. After all, he/she was the one who was interested in it in the first place. This is the way disappointment—and even anger—can result from noncommunication. If they hadn't been trying to mind-read, they might both have been happier reading a book.

We do not put the same expectations on other areas of interrelating that we put on sex. We would not consider decorating a house together without inquiring whether our partner liked a particular shade of blue or yellow. We would consider it quite natural to be told that our partner liked spaghetti sauce with a little more garlic. Yet we don't consider it normal to discuss similar nuances when it comes to sex. The truth is that the same rules that apply to communication about child-rearing, money, and division of labor apply to communication about sexual preferences, attitudes, and feelings.

Too often, rather than trying to communicate feelings, people get caught up in trying to prove that they are right and the other person is wrong. This approach is doomed to failure because even if one person "wins" the right/wrong battle, the other will find some way to retaliate.

Many people expect that in a good relationship there is never any anger, never any disagreement. However, anger and disagreement are as normal as joy and consensus. It is virtually impossible for two different people who grew up in two separate families with two different value systems to have identical views about everything all the time.

Once we can assume that differences are normal, we must realize that it is absolutely necessary to communicate our desires and preferences to one another. In fact, more problems arise when one person assumes he or she knows what the other is thinking or feeling and then acts on that assumption. Making assumptions stems from the belief that if my partner really loved me, he/she would know what I want or what I mean. Once this myth can be released, it becomes possible to ask the other person directly, thereby doing away with confusion and misunderstanding.

One way to clarify communication is to use "I" statements. That is, rather than saying "you" ("You didn't kiss me this morning"), use the word "I" ("I felt unloved [or unlovable] when you didn't kiss me this morning"). Since the importance of communication is to convey the feeling behind the act, it helps others to understand how we feel about something when we state it that way. When we begin a sentence with "you" as in "you never" or "you didn't" the other person immediately feels attacked and expends their energy trying to defend themselves rather than concentrating on trying to hear how *we* felt in that situation. Each person tries to be right by making the other one wrong. In the above example, it is possible for the one person to have *felt* unloved without the other person's intending to give that message. He or she may have just been pre-occupied. And, frequently, validating the other person's feelings rather than providing an apology or a solution is all that is sought after.

In terms of sexual communication, the same rules apply. "I like it when you softly stroke my neck" or "I feel like a sex object when you immediately grab for my crotch" is more likely to communicate the message than "You always rub me too hard" or "You treat me like a sex object." Whereas "I" statements tend to get the desired response, "you" statements frequently generate a fight.

Another helpful hint for communicating positively is to try to be particularly careful, when a fight is beginning, to understand exactly what you are starting to fight about. Otherwise, you may only recall the name-calling and the petty complaints, most of which may have nothing whatsoever to do with the initial argument. One way to do this is to slow the action down by having each person repeat exactly what it is that he or she understood the other person to be saying before jumping into their own offense or defense. That way, each person has the chance to confirm that the message sent was the intended message, or to offer appropriate corrections.

Many women have additional difficulty communicating about sex because of the cultural role scripting. The idea that women are the chaste and pure ones goes along with the cultural belief that the man is the authority on sex. Dolly (sixty-four, divorced):

One of the things I liked was having my breasts fondled. This was something I had to ask for specifically with my ex-husband and it was very hard for me to do. I felt the man was supposed to know what would satisfy me so I rarely made any requests. I guess I felt embarrassed or ashamed to ask for anything specific.

Since women are supposed to be chaste, pure, and therefore not sexual, how could they possibly have any information to communicate? If we have preferences, it must mean that we have had sexual experiences with other partners, a disparaging comment on our purity. After all, every sexual experience should be our first. Since women should not have such base desires, there should be no sexual preferences to communicate. Even though we would like to think that this is an outdated view, many women still don't feel good about enjoying sex. Even if we have grown beyond this rigid scripting and have chosen partners who appreciate a woman who is openly sexual, oftentimes old negative sexual messages surface to interfere with our enjoyment of sex.

Sylvia (twenty, single) for example, felt embarrassed about taking pleasure sexually:

I'm very open and hardly very modest when it comes to sex, but I still feel embarrassed about receiving pleasure, perhaps because I feel I'm not worthy of all this pleasure or of being with this guy because he's too gorgeous or whatever.

Alexandra (thirty-two, divorced), although comfortable with giving, found it hard to be the recipient of sexual pleasure:

After we slept together a number of times, he was concerned that I was a "giver" and that I wasn't as good a "taker." For example, I didn't let him eat me as much as he wanted because I felt that I wasn't giving to him at the same time. But he didn't necessarily want that, he wanted me to be passive sometimes and just receive. He asked if I was uncomfortable being entirely a recipient, and I agreed I was. I wanted sex to be mutual, because then I would feel less exposed. It turned out to be really easy for me to talk to him about that because of his attitude and who he is. He knows a lot about women, about sex and his own body; because he loves sex and I love sex with him, it was just no problem.

The idea that women as well as men can enjoy sex may be an attitude that is finally gaining acceptance. However, the idea that women can be assertive and ask for what they want sexually is not as acceptable. Many people still feel that it isn't quite feminine to be so direct. As seventeen-year-old Joey, a student who lives with her parents, said:

I'm just beginning to learn to communicate. I didn't communicate before except to say "That feels good," and if it didn't feel good, I didn't say anything. I didn't want to keep "bitching" in bed.

Many of us are afraid to bring up the subject of what we like sexually with our partner. We fear that if we give men feedback, we run the risk of being labeled a ballbuster or a bitch. Such women are often considered domineering or aggressive, negative terms for women who are willing to make their desires known. A "good" woman takes what is offered to her. Anything special that comes her way should be appreciated, but certainly not expected.

In addition, women fear that giving a male partner sexual information about themselves might suggest that he is inadequate as a man and crush his ego. Many women fear they will lose their partner if they start telling him what their sexual preferences are. They may think that he doesn't really want the information or they may be afraid to rock the boat. However, Cortney (thirty-one) expresses a different attitude which seems to serve her well:

I am very direct with the person and say how I feel about what they're doing. I keep it short and simple because any long explanations or long statements are, to me, disruptive during sex. For me, intercourse is not the time to be talking about what my attitudes or philosophies about sex are. I would say, however, "Put your hand here," or I would give directions. I believe my attitude is what helps me to communicate with men about sex, because I feel good about sex. I like sex, I enjoy it, and according to my standards, that's okay, no matter what some other people may think. I feel that sex is a feminine and healthy part of my life. It's not sluttish or nasty and I get a lot of reinforcement from men who appreciate a woman being open and talking matter-of-factly about sex, instead of being very coy or indirect and not letting a man know what she likes and what she doesn't.

However, some people feel that if they have to ask for something they want, it's not as good as if they did not have to ask. They're afraid that if their partner responds by giving it to them, it was done only because they asked for it, not because their partner really wanted to. They want their partner to think of it on their own. Somehow, a positive response to the request is not a sufficient demonstration of caring. Gaye, a thirty-three-year-old college instructor who has been married eleven years and is the mother of a boy, two, and a girl, eight, represents this all too common point of view:

I'd prefer it if my husband would put his arms around me and hold me when we're making love, but I can't ask him to do that. I have a funny quirk—if there's something I really want, I can't ask for it because if I do, it ruins the pleasure of having it. I've been this way all my life.

What a bind this places both us and our partners in. It's like going on a treasure hunt without any clues.

Another obstacle to talking about sexual preferences is the fear of rejection. Many women fear that if they go out on a limb and ask for what they want, their partner may be unwilling to accommodate. If the partner says no, the woman is concerned she will end up feeling rejected.

It is unfortunate that some people confuse a refusal to participate in a certain activity—sexual or otherwise—as a personal rejection. Suzanne (thirty-seven, bisexual, divorced) felt just the opposite and finds that her attitude helps her to get more out of sex:

The more I realize how important it is, the quicker I am about saying what pleases me and what doesn't. And I find I get more out of sex. I have to force myself to be open and to realize that it's not a put-down to tell somebody I don't like their tongue in my ear—it's just something that doesn't turn me on. Some people go into ecstasy over it, but it doesn't do anything for me. I have to be very honest right away.

Anytime we ask for what we want, we risk not getting it, but the more we ask, the higher the percentage of times we are likely to have our needs met. A therapist we know is fond of saying, "If I don't get turned down three times a day, I haven't asked for enough." She believes that the more you ask for, the more you get, even if you get turned down from time to time.

Negotiation cannot begin until we can state our needs and preferences. Otherwise, neither person knows where the other stands. For example, take a couple who is going out to dinner together. Let's say he asks her, "Where would you like to go?" Even though he would prefer going to a Chinese restaurant, he is not going to mention it first, in case she doesn't want to eat Chinese food. She answers, "I don't care, whatever you'd like," even though she would prefer Italian food. They might go back and forth like this for a while, neither wanting to risk stating his preference first. Soon anxiety mounts and even a fight can result. Things could have been so much easier if he had initially said, "I'd like Chinese food, how does that sound to you?" She might say, "Gee, I'd really prefer Italian food." At least they then have a point from which to negotiate. He might then say, "Italian food would be fine some other night, but I really don't feel like it tonight. She might respond, "Okay, Chinese food was my second choice anyway." Or they might decide to have neither and compromise on seafood.

Some of you reading this chapter may be wondering why we are spending so much time talking about women's difficulties communicating about sex. Communication may not be a problem area for you at all: talking about sex preferences may come easily for you. Or you may find that you never have to talk about sex; that for you, sex has magically taken care of itself. This was certainly true of a few of the women we interviewed, such as Billie (fifty-four, married):

It was never a problem to teach him what I liked. We clicked right away from the very beginning. There wasn't a problem with my first husband either. I just probably assumed that all men did it that way.

One woman felt little need to communicate because she pretty much liked everything and if she didn't, she would merely initiate the activities she preferred. Sage (thirty-five, lesbian, living alone):

I really don't do much about letting a partner know what I like or don't like because it's not an issue. Although I prefer some people's style of lovemaking over others, I don't think there is anybody who does anything I don't like. I mean I like it all. I like soft touching; I like hard touching; I like alternate hard and soft touching. If people are not into making love well with me, then I'll be more the initiator and take that role.

Most women, however, struggle for a number of years with learning to communicate. In fact, we were surprised at the large number of women we interviewed who still had considerable difficulty talking about sex. And these were women who were sexually innovative and who had in general, a fair degree of sexual comfort. Many of them mentioned that although they could talk easily with their partner about other subjects, communicating specifically and directly to their partner about sex was a problem. Susan (thirty-six, married fifteen years) boasted about the good communication she generally had with her husband, but when it came to asking him do oral sex, she realized that she had a problem:

I am usually the first one to initiate oral sex by sucking him. I like oral sex and he does too and we both know the other one likes it. Yet I have not found a good way to let him know I want him to go down on me. He has to initiate that. If I do it to him first, sometimes he follows, but not always. So I have no good way to say, "Now it's my turn."

It was not only women who had difficulty with communication, many partners did also. Monique (thirty-two, married) confides:

Communication is probably the toughest area for both of us. How do we each ask for what we want, or say no when we don't want to do something? I've had a real struggle in my marriage trying to help him talk to me about sex. He feels that sex is something that is very private, and much better when it's mysterious. But the other side is, how can he get what he wants if he doesn't tell me? So we've spent a lot of time in the last nine years working on being able to talk to each other. He has more anxiety than I do in this area, so I have to be very careful. I feel that his ego is more fragile in terms of his sexual identity. Sometimes when I'm abrupt or demanding, I can just see his body tighten up and, rather than getting into a fight, which has often happened in the past, I try to rephrase what I want, to say it in a little more delicate way. For example, oftentimes he'll be doing something that's painful, like stimulating my clitoris in a certain way and it just hurts and I feel either he's doing it on purpose or he's not being sensitive enough. I can immediately get angry and resentful and just want to yell at him, "You insensitive bastard, why can't you do it right?" I know if I say that, the entire experience will be ruined, so I have to swallow my rage and say, "Hey, that hurts, could you do it a little more softly please?" or take his hand and say, "I appreciate your doing that, but this way would feel a little better." I can't be demanding without taking his feelings into consideration. This is one of the hardest things about an ongoing sexual relationship.

Often, women don't communicate about sex because we haven't had any practice talking about sexual topics. We have learned to talk about a whole host of other subjects—food, religion, politics, children, fashion—but we never had any models who taught us how to talk about sex. Not only did most of us never talk about it with our parents, but also few have really discussed sexual issues with friends in any detail. So, in a sense, we never learned a language for discussing sex. Some of us do not even have a sexual vocabulary. We have grown up using certain words to designate various body parts, such as weiner, snatch, wee-wee, or ca-ca, but as adults these words are no longer adequate. Many of us actually developed the sexual vocabulary we use today when we were adolescents and have never bothered to update or reevaluate it. This is important to do because in relationships we often find that the same word will mean different things to different people. Sexual words in particular often have a variety of meanings or charges associated with them. While one woman may feel comfortable using the word "cock," her partner might be offended by that. Or if he uses the word "pussy," which might be a real turn-on for him, she might get upset and think he is being disrespectful.

Some words or phrases that the women we interviewed used might not fit your personality. You might feel cheap, or prissy, or prim, using certain words, whereas others would be more fitting. In the end, it is up to each woman and her partner to find words that fit them both. Consequently, you might first want to rehearse using some of the phrases in this chapter in front of a mirror to see if they fit before trying them out with a partner.

Many of the women we interviewed were embarrassed to give us specific phrases that they used to communicate with their partners. The following women, however, did feel comfortable sharing that information.

Darielle (twenty-seven, married three years):

For the most part, I use pretty direct communication during our lovemaking. I just tell him directly in a kind of whisper or ask him to please do that or please do this, or if something's uncomfortable, I just tell him to be careful, that that's hurting a bit.

Roberta (thirty-five, divorced):

I communicate verbally by saying "Oh, that feels good," or "That's too hard" or "Not there, higher up" or "lower down."

Samantha (thirty-five, divorced):

I'm very straightforward and open about saying what I want. I say, for example, "I want to suck your dick; I want you to suck me; I like the way you fuck." I tell him things like "You fuck as good as I thought you would," or I tell him how good he makes me feel by saying, "You make me feel that my fucking is okay." We talk a lot about sex, usually while we're making love to each other. Whenever he's doing something I like, I tell him so I can reinforce it.

I tell him something feels good or that something doesn't feel as good, and ask him what feels good for him, or even demonstrate the various kinds of touches that turn me on. That works better than just hoping he'll begin to understand.

We use a pretty professional kind of vocabulary, except that he calls his penis his "pete," but I call my vagina "my vagina." I talk about my clitoris, talk about the head of his penis, so we're very graphic about the parts of our bodies. If he's masturbating me in a way that doesn't feel as good, I might show him what I would prefer with my own hand or direct his hand in a way that feels better to me.

Most women struggled with finding a way to communicate without hurting their partner's feelings. As sex therapists, one suggestion we offer is to practice communicating by reversing the situation. If you're afraid to tell your partner something because you think it might be hurtful, imagine how you would want your partner to tell you the very same thing. Is there a way it could be said so you wouldn't feel hurt, or only minimally hurt? Women we interviewed came up with many ways of communicating that were most likely to produce good results. The method most often used was that of communicating positive information as frequently as possible. Judy (thirty-one, married to David, a rabbi) has carried that philosophy one step further:

The best helpful hint is to be positive. The greatest thing you can ever say to a man, even if it is not true, is that he is the biggest, most fantastic, most fabulous lover in the whole world. If you constantly remind him of it in one way or another, he will be. It's really true. It was a trick I had to play on myself in the beginning of our relationship, but now he really is a fabulous lover!

Suzanne, a thirty-seven-year-old businesswoman who is bisexual, says:

I start with the positive things that I enjoyed. For example, I'd say, "I really liked the way you licked my clit. The way you used your tongue on it was really good. I hope we'll do more of that." I might say, "I also enjoyed having your fingers in my vagina and I know we didn't do that very much, but you could do that a little bit more." Then I'd ask, "What kinds of things did you really like? Are there things I did that weren't a real turn-on to you?"

There's a woman I'm seeing now who likes to kiss a certain way. I didn't know that first she likes my tongue in her mouth and then she likes to put her tongue in my mouth. We couldn't work it out until she told me that really turns her on. It was neat to be able to talk about it and work it out.

The need to reinforce positive lovemaking techniques was noted particularly by women in committed long-term relationships. Whenever their partners touched them in a way they liked, they reinforced that specific behavior. Judy continues to talk about how she has fostered sexual communication between herself and her husband in such a way that he felt reinforced and she got her needs met:

I was shy and didn't want to be overly pushy about my needs in the beginning of our relationship. Over time, he learned what I liked. I would move his hand or I would let him know that I was satisfied after the fact so he would do it again. If something produced an orgasm, or if it was good, I would respond in a positive way with either "Gee, that's fantastic" or twists or movements or moans or whatever was called for. There were times when it was not good, and I nonverbally moved his hands or sometimes said that I was uncomfortable. At this point in our relationship, there is less of that because now I can say "Don't do that," or "That's too sensitive right now" or whatever. Now we both can do that, but at least in the first year I treaded very lightly with him. I felt it was important for me not to shake the really good image he had about himself sexually. The result is that I now have a husband who is very adept sexually and very secure in his sexuality. Now I tell him how good he is and that I'm never going to tell anyone else because all the women will be after him. He runs around with his feathers up and thinks he's the greatest thing in the whole world. But that is important in relationships. For so many years, I didn't know how to say, "Hey, you're great;" not just sexually, but in many different ways. If you let them know that you think they're great, they let you know that they think you're great, too. My feedback was always positive, never negative. I stay away from the negative feedback unless something is really bad for me. If I had been negative, the marriage never would have lasted.

After initial difficulties, Harriet (thirty-four, married ten years) learned a better way to tell her husband what she wanted and he, in turn, was more able to listen to her wishes and be more responsive:

Now I tell him very specifically. I say, "I'd like you to do such-and-such instead of what you're doing." "I'd like you to do it softer, even softer, pretend you're a feather," or "Move over to your right just the tiniest bit." When he finds the spot that I'm into at that particular moment, I say, "That's it," or "That's terrific" or whatever. I give him a lot of feedback. It's something we've talked about because early in our relationship telling him so directly and specifically bothered him. He would rather I'd do it some other way, or not do it at all. What he really would like is that whatever he did would be perfect for me, but that isn't how it is or was. My being direct hasn't bothered him for years and my sense is that's because I've tried to be responsive to what he's told me he likes or doesn't like about my feedback. He told me that sometimes when I gave him instructions about what I liked and what I wanted him to do, he felt like he was working on me and so he wasn't turned on by the process. Also, I used to say things about what I didn't like, rather than what I did like. I would say, "That's too hard" rather than "Could you do that softer?" Now, instead of saying, "That's not fast enough," I say, "I'd like it faster." I've paid more attention to saying things positively and in the affirmative. My basic style, which is to be real explicit, hasn't changed, but the way I do it has.

For many women, talking about sex for the first time can be uncomfortable. Frequently, women are afraid and concerned about their male partner's reaction. Our role-scripting as women programs us to take care of our partner's needs. It is our responsibility to make life comfortable for him. We should make certain he is fed well and clothed appropriately, and that his home is pleasant and comfortable. It is amazing how we are more willing to be uncomfortable ourselves rather than make our partners uncomfortable. We are often willing to live with the constant discomfort of an unsatisfactory sex life rather than risk making our partners uncomfortable for the first ten or fifteen minutes that it would take to begin talking about sexual difficulties.

Asking for what we want is an essential aspect of sexual communication, but conflicts with our role scripting. Again, women are supposed to be good, chaste, pure; in short, asexual and passive. Sometimes it takes years to develop the self-confidence to break free of that rigid role scripting. It also often requires a fair amount of trust between a woman and her partner—trust that he will be supportive, open, nondefensive. Some women mentioned that it took a substantial amount of time for the necessary self-confidence and trust to develop before they could begin to communicate their sexual desires to their partners.

Mary (forty-eight, recently divorced):

At nineteen, I was totally unable to say what I liked or wanted sexually. Then when I was twenty-five it was still very difficult. It wasn't until after fifteen or sixteen years into the marriage that I could actually say what I liked or wanted or appreciated. Before that I was afraid to risk saying I wasn't really satisfied.

Darielle (twenty-seven, married three years):

When we first knew each other, I was a little bit apprehensive about telling him things I did or didn't like. Now that we're married and the relationship feels more stable, I'll go ahead and tell him if I don't like something he's doing. Now I realize it's stupid not to say something. I mean, what good does it do if you don't like something but you never say anything, so of course, it just keeps going on. It's only going to get worse.

An interesting fact emerged from our interviews. None of the women received a negative response from their partners once they were able to open conversations and start communicating about sex. Louise, a thirty-six-year-old widow, found that some men even appreciate a little information:

Several men have said that they really wish women would tell them what they like sexually. One man said, "Women should come with their own individual guidebooks. Different women like different things, yet somehow the guy is expected to just guess it right off and they rarely give you any hints." In my experience, men whom I have met say they like to be told and appreciate the help. I had always thought that men's egos were kind of fragile, that maybe you shouldn't tell them what you want. It's like saying what you're doing isn't okay or something. I used to believe I had to be careful not to say anything that might be critical because it might turn them off. But apparently that's not true.

It appears that the main obstacle to sexual communication is within the women themselves and not in any actual negative response from their partners. Still, confronting these internal feelings remains, for some women, an ongoing battle.

Billy (forty-three, married twenty-six years) says:

I believe the ability to communicate should extend into sexuality and that I should be able to say things like, "Hey, I didn't like the way that was." If I can say that I don't like the way a certain conversation is going, I should be able to say I didn't like something we did sexually. I know if I can talk about it, I can get further with solving the problem because maybe he's not even aware of my feelings. When I'm willing to open myself up and risk communicating, sex is better, but I have to start the process. He can't do it because he may not know anything is wrong. But if I do it, then he can respond. Sometimes it takes me a while to do it. I can't always do it right away. Sometimes I can be super open and everything flows, and other times I'm really uptight.

Women worry about the best time to talk about sex and how to bring the subject up in a delicate way. However, waiting for the perfect opportunity could mean waiting around forever, because the perfect opportunity often never arrives. It's difficult to start this kind of conversation in the best of circumstances, particularly if you haven't had any practice at it, so the first few minutes are likely to be uncomfortable for both of you. You might bring it up in reference to a recent conversation with a friend or at a time when you are both sharing past sexual events. You might talk about it after seeing a movie which is somewhat related, or you might even open the conversation as a result of reading this book. You might say something like, "I want to talk to you about some things I've been thinking about, and they have to do with sex. Would you like to do that? When would be the best time to do that for you?" You don't have to decide everything yourself. You don't have to decide where, when, and how this conversation is to take place. After all, it is a relationship problem the *two* of you have to come to terms with.

A technique which helped one woman to begin a conversation about sex was to talk with her partner about her fear or embarrassment before she actually got into the content. We suggest this frequently to clients so that their anxiety is not misinterpreted by their partner as anger or disapproval.

Theresa (thirty, therapist, lesbian):

If I'm afraid, that's what I'll say. I might say, "I'm scared to ask you this," or "I'm embarrassed," or "I'm afraid you won't want to do it," or "I'm afraid you'll think I'm awful, but I'm still going to ask you."

For example, I've suggested masturbating together to many of my clients and friends. They say it sounds great, but when it came down to doing it myself, it was another story. I was embarrassed the first time I asked my lover. I think I said, "I'm so embarrassed to ask you this, but. . . ." And she said, "Ask me what?" And even though I was nervous, I said, "I want to use my vibrator and masturbate." She was totally supportive and said, "Great, that sounds neat. I wish I had enough energy to get into it, too, but I don't." It's been interesting to see all these issues of guilt and embarrassment come up for me and to take a chance and ask anyway.

Cleo, a thirty-two-year-old newspaper editor, who lives with her boy friend, Peter, and seven-year-old daughter, used the following method to begin talking about sexual preferences:

Peter didn't like to talk about sex. He believed it took all the mystery out of it. The problem was, I never felt like I turned him on. If I even touched him, I felt like I was intruding on his space. So I finally started to ask him what he liked; how he liked me to touch his penis, what he liked and what he didn't like. Even when he balked, I just kidded him into talking. I also told him how I felt, that I was afraid to touch him, so he started to tell me more about what he liked. He started to actually show me how to touch him. I'm sure it was the first time in his life he ever did that. It all came from me sticking up for my own sexual feelings and feeling all right about it. Then he really started to enjoy making love with me and I enjoy making love with him now. It's like we're relaxed with each other now.

The women we interviewed had different ideas concerning the most auspicious time for talking about sex. In general, the consensus was to bring the subject up as soon as possible. Many felt it was easier to start talking about sex at the beginning of a new relationship because of the initial excitement and good feelings each has toward the other. They also saw such a discussion as a way of establishing a positive communication system that would strengthen the foundation of a budding relationship. In regard to an ongoing relationship, the women felt it was important to talk about sex as close to the event as possible to avoid the buildup of resentment. Anna (twenty-eight, married):

It's important to communicate when you've got your act together and not wait until it's blown out of proportion or until you're so hurt it almost kills you. I think communication should be more of a positive experience, so I don't wait until the problem makes long-lasting wounds that take a long time to heal.

Some, like Rosemary (thirty-six, divorced) preferred to communicate—or negotiate—before sex had begun:

I've had a relationship with my boy friend for three years now, so I feel more comfortable about saying when I want sex. I may say, "Let's make mad, passionate love tonight," and he's very responsive because he likes that. He encourages me to tell him that I want to have sex and how I want to do it. Sometimes he'll say, "I want to be in the passive role tonight," and maybe I'll say, "Well, I want to be passive, too"; so then we have to negotiate about who's going to be the active or passive person. Sometimes I may want something special sexually and he wants me to let him know.

Others felt strongly that talking about sex during the lovemaking was an essential part of their intimate relationship. Without the talking, the sexual act became too impersonal for them. Gail (thirty-five and living with her female lover) feels that:

Being verbal is something that has become very important to me. It's important to me to communicate about sex with my partner. I tell her what I want done, like "Put your hand there" or "Touch me here." Talking not only gets me the kind of touching I want, but turns me on as well. I find I need to talk while I'm having sex. Sometimes I even need to stop touching in the middle of sex and just talk about something. I think I need to have that kind of human contact to affirm I'm there as a person and not just as a sex object.

Others had the opposite reaction and found it too impersonal to talk during sex. Anna (twenty-eight, married):

I don't necessarily say what I want right in the middle of everything. I usually wait. I find it hard to tell him right when we're having sex because then it is more like "paragraph two, sentence one"—an instruction manual—and then it completely ruins the mood. But I tell him soon afterward.

Choosing to discuss the specifics of lovemaking either during sex or at some later neutral time—for example, over dinner or during a long car drive together—depended upon the specifics of the situation and the anticipated reaction of the partner. Diane (thirty-two, lesbian) explains and gives an example:

Either I tell them right at the time, "I'd like to have you touch me here," or I might say it after we finish making love. For example, if somebody was really getting into making love to me and let's say she had her fingers in my vagina, which she was obviously enjoying, but which I don't like too much, then I might wait till later. Or I might put my hand on top of her hand and move her hand if I really wanted her to stop.

Many women preferred to talk about the positive things during lovemaking while saving the negative things for afterward. Katherine (forty-two, married):

If my partner does something I really enjoy, then I usually tell him immediately. If it's something that I feel is not quite satisfactory, I usually let it wait until the next day, so as not to interrupt the pleasant feelings that are there. If it's displeasing and I say something, it may put a damper on what has been pleasing. Often that creates a defensiveness, whereas if I wait until the next day, it loses that power to take away from the good stuff.

However, even in this area other women felt just the opposite, as exemplified by Christine (forty-one, married), who prefers discussing the negatives at the time they are happening:

Unless I think it will hurt his feelings, I prefer to tell him right away. For example, if he did something that hurt me physically, I would tell him right away. He doesn't get uptight about those things. He's really very loving and sensitive. He doesn't seem to take offense.

Some of the women mentioned in particular that they appreciated their partner's help in teaching them how to communicate. They felt that their partner was very important in allowing them to be more open and helping them to express themselves sexually.

Lorraine (twenty-seven, single):

Doug is the person who taught me to be comfortable saying things like, "How do you feel?" or "How do you like to be touched?" or "What do you want me to do now?" "Is this comfortable for you?" He taught me to be aware of things like that. The first time we made love, he started saying things like, "Would you touch me here?" "Would you touch my balls?" "Would you rub this?" So I gradually started saying the same thing to him and when I found that I could do it too, I felt so good. Now, even if a sexual experience isn't the most fantastic one I've ever had, being able to communicate makes me feel comfortable and close to my partner and I feel good about that.

Heather (thirty-five, married three years to her second husband):

Usually problems arise because I don't like to talk about things that much, so he has gotten to the point where he asks me—very often—"Is there anything wrong, is everything okay?" Sometimes it takes three times for the question to be asked before I actually tell him. In the beginning of the relationship, it was much worse, but now we're more open with each other. We usually end up discussing it, and he tries to see if there's anything he can do or I try to see if there's anything I can do to work the problem out.

NONVERBAL COMMUNICATION

Although we have been largely discussing verbal communication, nonverbal communication can be equally important. People have all sorts of ways of letting their partners know what they want. Sometimes much more can be expressed by a smile, a sound, or a certain body motion than through words. We are continuously communicating through the use of body language. Although some women preferred either verbal or nonverbal communication, most used a combination of both.

Most of the women who relied on body language found it difficult to articulate the specific ways that they communicated their desires to their partners because they had never had occasion to analyze their particular style before. Those who were aware of the process told us how they did so. Tara (sixty-three, married for forty-two years):

I communicate more by expressing delightful sounds or using more body language.

Billy (forty-three, married for twenty-six years):

I let him know if I'm turned off to oral sex by body language. I can't seem to tell him directly, but I communicate it somehow, because he seems to know. I would say that I have a way of holding his head so that he knows. There's also a stiffness in my body when I'm turned off.

Aruna (thirty-three, married):

If he's touching me in the wrong place, I'll just move his hand to the right place or if I want to touch myself, I'll just touch myself. For example, sometimes I'll turn the whole thing around and begin doing an oral thing on him. I'll turn my body around so he can do oral sex on me, too, which I like because it makes our whole lovemaking much longer and slower.

Some of the women who used nonverbal communication did so because of their partners' discomfort with talking about sex.

Brenda (twenty-four, married):

My husband doesn't feel that comfortable talking about sex. I've tried talking to him after we've had sex and it turns him off to talk about it too much. So I pretty much have to use my body to get what I want. I usually wait until we're in the physical act of making love because I find it easier to physically just do what I want to do.

But nonverbal communication, used in isolation, can have its drawbacks. Jesse (sixty, divorced) felt pushed by nonverbal communication, whereas with verbal communication she felt she had a choice:

I prefer to rely on words. Although I rarely need to say "My breasts are very sensitive," on occasion this is ignored, so I pass on this information. I resent being manipulated, as I sometimes feel, if my partner takes my hand and actually places it on his penis. I resent this because it's something I would do eventually, but then I feel pushed into it. So I would prefer words and I ask him to tell me what he wants, too.

One woman liked to have her ears kissed, so she would frequently kiss her partner's ears in hopes that he would reciprocate. However, he never seemed to get the message, or so it appeared, because the more she would kiss his ears, the less he would kiss hers. One day the couple finally talked about it, only to learn that he hated to have his ears kissed—which he was attempting to communicate to her by not kissing her ears. After they talked about it and realized the other's preferences, he started kissing her ears and she stopped kissing his.

In an ongoing relationship, many women observed that, after a period of communicating by either verbal or nonverbal means, both they and their partners began to learn each other's likes and dislikes and less and less communication was required.

Of course, there are many times when sexual desires differ, when one person is generally more interested in sex than the other and no simple solution seems available. In cases where compromise is not easy, it is often easier to blame the other person rather than to look at ourselves. Raisin, a thirty-one-year-old lesbian living alone, has an enlightening perspective that helps keep destructive blaming down to a minimum:

I think it's very easy, in sexuality, as in any other area, to blame, to get into a space where it's the other person's fault. What my lover and I do instead, whenever we have differences, is take some time to figure out and talk about what our *own* part is in the problem. There really isn't any need to comment on anyone else's part. For example, my part in our relationship problem has to do with the fact that I withhold emotionally in certain ways. Whatever else she may do, I know if I would change that, our whole relationship would change. Since I know I have the power to change things, then if Rosie and I have a disagreement, I have to look at why I'm still withholding, and not just say, "It's all your fault because you did . . ." I try to be very aware of what my part is in the difficulty. Things get resolved much sooner when we each take responsibility for what our own part in an argument or difficulty is. We don't spend a lot of time telling one another what it is that the other person is doing wrong because we have respect for the other person's own process. If the other person is only evolving at a certain rate, I can't change that. All I can do is to lay a guilt trip on somebody by blaming them. If they're not ready to hear something they're not going to hear it anyway, and if they are, they'll discover it for themselves.

In the end, however, differences may be too great and it may be impossible to be comfortable with a particular partner. In those cases, some women decided to end the relationship and look elsewhere for a more compatible partner.

Judith (forty, married, bisexual):

I can't function sexually with men who can't handle my assertiveness. And I have had experience with those kinds of men. I had one experience like that when I was at a convention years ago. My warning bells went off about this man, but I ignored them because I was into the excitement of exploring a new relationship. The end result was that I went to bed with him and I don't know what he was doing, but I started using my own hand on my clitoris. He took my hand away and said, "No, we don't do that," and I thought, "Oh!" and decided I didn't want to have sex with him anymore. We ended it pretty fast and I left. He called later and wanted to see me again, but he was so far down the road from any man I wanted to have sex with, if he felt too uptight to let me use my own hand.

In longer-term relationships, however, it might not make much sense to give up so easily. Communication which may require time and willingness on the part of both people is also the hallmark of intimacy. Beverly (thirty-six, married nine years) gives her unique view of a relationship which takes into consideration that there may be times when distance is not only useful but necessary:

The minute I know things are out of kilter, even though I don't know specifically what's wrong, I say what I'm feeling and we talk about it. Maybe in the process of talking about it, I'll identify what it is, but even if I don't have the answer at the end of the conversation, this process always brings me closer to Mark. Afterward I want to share more physically with him and can be more sexual. There are times when I don't feel close to Mark and when I don't want to be close to him, and we talk about that, too. He allows me my space and I allow him his. We don't feel rejected, we just feel apart.

In any long-term relationship, the pattern is moving together and moving away and moving together and moving away and I feel that's a natural pattern. If you're communicating with each other about that, it's not threatening, it's not frightening; in fact, it's healthy. If you're not, then the coming together gets less frequent and the moving away becomes more frequent. When I feel that we're distancing to the point of it being uncomfortable then I really don't feel very sexual toward Mark. If we don't talk about the distance and the separateness, then we'll go without sex. But I can't go for more than a week without sex. I have to talk about it and after we talk about it, even if it's not resolved, I still feel closer to him and I can have sex. Then I can stand the separateness.

CREATIVE COMMUNICATION

A number of people came up with very innovative ways to communicate about sex, ways that enhanced the relationship and were a turn-on sexually. Again, what appeals to some is distasteful to others, so you might find these methods too gamy or too slick or perhaps you just wouldn't feel right using them. While they are not for everyone, they do represent a range of ways people communicate sexually and may spark other ideas or methods that may be more appropriate for you. Penelope (forty-six, married) gives her own version of "instant replays" that have enhanced her communication and sexual relationship with her husband:

Early in our relationship we did something that helped us keep our sex exciting. You know how on TV you see a football play and then you see an instant replay of it? Well, when we fucked, we would spend at least as much time as we had spent fucking, talking about it! "Remember when you were kissing me on the mouth? It felt like my mouth was my cunt. Were you pretending you were kissing my cunt?" "No, but I can see how that might have felt like it."

The whole process was terribly validating for each of our sexualities. We felt like we were getting stroked for our pleasure, saying, "Oh, that was good. You were getting so much pleasure out of that." We were also getting our nonverbal cues clarified as to whether they were accurate. For example, there will be times when I want Harold to come. I'm tired and I'll want the whole lovemaking experience to be as exciting as it's been. I don't want it to continue past my excitement, so I'll want him to come. Then I'll put my hand down and cradle his balls or put my hand on his perineum and stroke it to heighten his excitement. We checked out, on our instant replay, whether or not I did that so he would come, because that's what he picked up on, or whether it was just my trip and what turned me on. So we've gotten to the point where we can pretty much clear things like that up. Sometimes I will touch him in places where I would like to have him touch me, but other times I'm touching him just to express my level of arousal. We have to clear up whether or not I'm giving him the message of "Touch me here, too" or whether I'm touching him as part of the expression of where I'm at.

Sometimes I have to tell him. If I find myself wondering, "Is he going to be confused by this?" I avoid that wondering by saying, "Just keep touching me the way you are right now, regardless of what I'm doing." Because from our instant replays, he expects that I will touch him the way I want to be touched unless I say something different.

Allison (thirty-five, divorced) finds that directing the scene with her lover not only allows her to communicate her preferences, but also adds variety to the usual sexual encounter:

The way it started was that one night Greg said he would do whatever I wanted him to do sexually. So I told him what to do to me every step of the way, from kissing to squeezing to fucking to eating—anything. It was like at the moment I wanted something, I told him and got it immediately. It was incredibly exciting, giving directions and getting exactly what I wanted. Best of all, it was immediate gratification. It was really like being a child again and getting all your needs met immediately. And it wasn't controlling. It didn't make him feel like he didn't know what I want. It was almost like getting into a slave thing —a playful slave fantasy. It was also fun and at the same time a way to let him know even more about who I was sexually.

The following two women found creative ways to teach their partners about their bodies and to improve communication, which in turn enriched their lovemaking with their partners.

Rose (thirty-six, single):

One night my lover and I were lying in bed naked, fondling each other, and he began to ask me about my experiences with other lovers. At first, I wasn't really sure what he was asking, then I began to realize that he was curious about other men, what they were like as lovers, but more specifically, how large their penises were. I realized that part of his insecurity was based on the fact that he rarely ever saw his whole penis erect because he was always looking down on it, so I reached over and grabbed a mirror that I had on the bureau and by holding the mirror down at the base of his penis, showed him his whole erect penis and balls. It was a good experience for him to see how large his engorged penis looked from that angle. Then I used the mirror to show him exactly where my clitoris was. I was certain that he knew generally where it was, because he's a very effective lover with his hands and his mouth, but by being able to pull back the hood and stretch the two inner lips, he was able to see exactly where it was and what it looked like. We went on to make love and at one point he stimulated my clitoris. Although our sex had always been good, this time his technique was particularly exquisite and our lovemaking seemed to get even better after that. I can't help but think that was because of the good feelings we both had about the sharing we had done. And also because he now had much more detailed information.

Renée (thirty-two, divorced seven years, educational consultant):

The intensity of my orgasms tend to be much stronger when I masturbate than when I have sexual intercourse. That's because I know my body and my sexual pattern of arousal so well. As a result of that, I now institute "anatomy classes" with any lover whom I'm "serious" about. What I say is, "Let's do a basic anatomy class and take our clothes off and do some touching first and just figure out what areas of our bodies are the most sensitive." After we get through the touching and stroking, we get to the primary erogenous zones, the genitalia, and figure out whether each of us likes a lot of pressure or just very light touches; whether we like nails or we don't like nails, that kind of thing —mouth, tongue, that whole trip. As a result I think my sexual experiences with men have been really together!

The way I introduce the anatomy lesson into the relationship is to wait until we've had a series of very positive sexual encounters so that it's presented as an enhancement as opposed to "Let me show you what I want you to do because you weren't turning me on." For example, at the end of a really great lovemaking session, after I told him he was a great fuck, I'd probably say, "Next time why don't we do a basic anatomy class? You know, if it's this good now and I don't know you very well, we could probably be fantastic with a little bit of work." Generally they say, "Cool!" Then the next time you've already laid the groundwork so that it doesn't come as a shock. Sharing that detailed information gives me a better chance of having those same intense orgasms with him as I have in masturbation.

INITIATING SEX

When we asked women how they initiated sex, most of them had to think about it before answering. Some, like Marie (age thirty-three, married ten years), felt that they never initiated sex:

I have a problem with that. This may sound strange, but I don't think I have ever initiated sex. Usually my partner does. My husband says that I never initiate sex, so I don't think I do so consciously. If I do, it's subconscious. If I indicate any desire, it's through body language. It certainly would not be verbal.

Others, at first, felt that sex just occurred spontaneously, that they didn't do or say anything specific, but upon closer examination they realized that they had developed specific patterns of communicating their desire for sex to their partners.

Many women had a great deal of difficulty overtly initiating sex, again because our culture teaches that women are not really supposed to be sexual beings. According to this role scripting, women should only be responsive to the male sexual drive, and should have no sexual drive of their own. Women who are active sexually have been labeled promiscuous, sluts, oversexed nymphomaniacs. All sorts of negative labels have been used for women who are "too" interested in sex.

Women are also concerned about appearing too aggressive, and hence unfeminine. Consequently, many women who did initiate sex often did so in a disguised manner. They might just get into bed nude and be covertly seductive—or, like Connie (twenty-six, widow), use a more subtle approach which was sometimes understood and acknowledged and sometimes not:

I'm trying to remember situations where I initiated sex . . . and probably the only way I've done it—and it's a subtle approach—was to allow or encourage the discussion to take a more personal and intimate note. Otherwise, I guess I more or less waited for my husband to make the first move.

A large majority of the women in our sample did initiate sex and many were very proud of that fact. They felt that it had taken them a long time to finally get to the place where they felt okay about initiating sex. For many of these women, this process took years or several marriages and was based on finally feeling good about their own sexuality. Being able to initiate sex also made them feel more equal with their partners, more powerful as sexual beings.

Women seemed to have two major ways of initiating sex: either talking about it or doing something physically that would communicate their interest to their partner. As with the general issue of sexual communication, some women preferred to tell their partner verbally what their desires were and others preferred to let them know through body language. Sometimes a combination of the two was used.

The women who had difficulty talking about sex used nonverbal cues. They found that it was often easier to let their partner know that they were interested in sex by the way they touched or looked at them. Some were direct and others more indirect in their sexual overtures. Many women mentioned that this form of sexual initiation evolved naturally. Mary (forty-eight, divorced):

It always just seemed to happen, but of course that's probably not true. It seemed to me as if the conversation would turn to more feeling, intimate things. Then there might be hand-holding or other physical touching, and then kissing, and it would go from there.

Of course, since we often touch our lovers at times when we are not primarily interested in sex, it is important to be able to distinguish between an affectionate squeeze and one that means "Let's go to bed." Most of the women we talked with didn't know, upon reflection, how their partner could distinguish between a hug, kiss, or squeeze for affection without sexual intentions, and a sexual overture. Those who could distinguish between the two talked about subtle nuances. When they were interested in sex, their kisses would be longer, or in the ear rather than on the cheek, or the eye contact would be more intense. Sometimes couples developed special signals after being together for a period of time. Tara (sixty-three, married):

I guess I let him know mostly just by a touch. In bed, it's just a touching and reaching for him. When I'm interested in sex, I guess I touch him differently, I stroke him in a more sexual way.

Beverly (thirty-six, married nine years):

Sometimes at home, if my husband is reading the paper or something, I'll put the music on and start dancing in a suggestive way. This way I get his attention. Sometimes I like to go up and just hug and kiss him when I don't have underwear on. Usually I wear a bra and panties, so when I don't, he gets really surprised and excited and it's a neat lead-in to sex. I don't like to stick with one way of initiating sex; it's so boring, it just becomes habit. It loses the excitement for me.

Allison (thirty-five, divorced and living with her boy friend) has a unique way of initiating sex:

We sometimes go through periods of not having as much sex, particularly in the winter. That's because we keep our house very cold and we're usually bundled up with blankets and in pajamas. He may also go through a period of being preoccupied and tired and won't want sex for a few days. Then I might display parts of my body just to sort of remind him that it's still there. If all of a sudden, he sees my bare rear end or my cunt, it reminds him and he thinks, "Hmm, maybe that's not such a bad idea after all." He starts to remember how nice our lovemaking was. So I'm just conscious of occasionally displaying various parts of my body to him so that he remembers that sex was something very nice and that he'd like to do it again.

Susan (thirty-six, married):

I make sure I go to bed at the same time he does. Both of us are usually so tired at night that we wind up going to sleep as soon as we hit the pillow, but if I'm interested in sex, I won't let him go to sleep. I'm not very subtle either. I'll talk to him and make sure he stays awake long enough to know that I'm interested. And I touch him and caress him. It's not very difficult to do now, but I know there are a lot of women who cannot reach out like that. It took a while for me to be able to do that too. It took me a while to feel that kind of trust, that I wouldn't be rejected.

Fear of rejection seemed to be a common reason why women only tentatively initiated sex. As with communication of sexual preferences, women sometimes assumed that if their partner was not in the mood for sex, it was a personal rejection.

The truth is that it can be liberating to have a partner say no to a sexual invitation. This could give the woman the permission she needs to not always have to accept his overtures. Many women we interviewed went through their whole married life never being able to say no to sex directly. They could say no if they had a headache or maybe if they had their period or if their child kept them up the whole night before, but they could not say no simply because they didn't feel like it. They didn't feel that they had that right. They felt sex was their husband's privilege. Consequently, they reluctantly acquiesced and frequently felt resentful.

Louise, age thirty-nine, married for two years to her second husband:

In my first marriage one of my most damaging beliefs was that women did not say no. That if you were a good wife you consented to having sex at the demand of your husband. Therefore I did not initiate a lot. My husband was the initiator and the teacher. I got the message from my family that I was fortunate to have married a man of means, and that I needed to take care of him. I got messages from other friends who said you don't want your husband to wander and look for something he's not getting at home, so I did a lot of agreeing and submitting to sex even when I did not want it, hoping it wouldn't last long.

So over the years I became a passive recipient during sex. I still carry a lot of resentment at not saying no. So in my present relationship, saying no is very important. It is very important to stay with what I feel, either yes I want to or no I don't. I have never said yes when I didn't want to, so I am very proud of that record.

When someone never says no, resentment can build up which overflows and contaminates what would otherwise be a positive experience. Consequently, many women who never said no to sex found that they would withhold in other areas. It turns out that when both people can say no to the other's overtures their sexual relationship can actually be enhanced. Then they are free to have sex when they really feel like it, thereby ensuring a good experience.

Also, saying no to sex is not necessarily a rejection: there are many reasons why a person might not be interested in sex. And there are many ways to say no that reaffirm your positive feelings for your partner. It's possible to say, "No, I'm not interested in sex right now because I'm too tired, or because I've worked too hard today, but I'd like to cuddle a little or just to sit and hold you and maybe tomorrow I'll feel more like it." It is also possible, if your partner says he is not in the mood right now, to let him know that you would still like some physical contact if that happens to be true. For example, you might say, "I understand that you're not in the mood for sex now, and that's fine, but I would like a hug. I'd like you to hold me for a while. I need that kind of touching now."

Nell (thirty-six, married eight months) describes how she adjusts the way she initiates sex to her assessment of her partner's likely reaction:

I ask him straight out if he wants to make love and let him know that I want to. I have finally learned to take his responses to my initiatives at face value. It used to be that if I was in a terrible, terrible mood and he said no, I would conclude that I was so ugly that he'd lost interest in sex with me altogether. Now I realize that 99 per cent of the time he refuses, it's a very simple kind of thing. If he says he's tired or preoccupied, then he really is tired or preoccupied.

If we're in a situation where it's possible to have sex, I might just come over and massage his neck or start taking off his clothes or taking off my clothes. I don't do those kinds of things unless I'm pretty sure he's feeling positive, because those actions sort of commit him to saying yes rather than asking, which leaves him open to saying no. I feel like I know which approach to use when.

Other women were quite bold in their initiation of sex, particularly if they were feeling secure in the relationship.

Darielle (twenty-seven, married) says:

When the relationship is going fairly well, there are a number of things I do when I want to have sex. I'll go up to him and sort of tease him or kiss him in a playful or seductive way. I'll say things like "I have a surprise for you" or I might say, "Come in here, I want to talk with you" in a sort of ominous way, but he knows what I mean. I might start undressing him. I might start playing with his penis. I might go up and hug him and really press my pelvis against him, or if we're in bed in the evening, I might just get on top of him and begin stimulating him and playing with his body. Sometimes if we're in the car, I might put my hand on his penis and rub him a little bit so he'll know that when we get home I'd like to go to bed.

Couples need a certain amount of time to develop the necessary level of intimacy required to understand their partners' subtle nonverbal signals. Even then, some signals are missed. Therefore, some women prefer to communicate with verbal language instead of body language. A number of phrases used by women have already been mentioned. Here are some others: "Feel like making love?" "Do you want to fool around?" "Let's go to bed early tonight." "Want some nooky?" "Do you want to fuck?" or "I want to make love. Do you?"

Initiating sex with a new partner has its own special pitfalls. Most women we interviewed had no difficulty being warm and available if they were sexually interested in a new date, but few in our sample overtly initiated the first sexual experience.

Jane (forty-two, teacher, divorced) says:

I rarely initiate sex at the beginning of a new relationship. It just happens. I guess a typical scenario would go like this: We're laughing, talking, having a good time, and very often the gentleman asks me to go to his apartment with him or go home with him for a drink or whatever and I do, and we end up in bed. I think probably, when I'm having a good time and I'm interested in someone, I come across as being very affectionate, very warm, very sensuous, and I'm sending a message that I'm willing.

Alexandra (thirty-two, divorced) explains how she indirectly lets her date know she's interested:

When I'm with someone I don't know well and I want him to know I'm sexually interested, I convey that message by using a subtle kind of flirtation: things like brushing by someone's body, looking at them a glance longer than necessary, a handshake that holds on a little longer than would be expected, a tone of voice, or maybe saying something provocative that can be taken a couple of ways.

Because of the reverse role scripting, many lesbians are more practiced at initiating sex with a new partner than are most heterosexual women. Theresa (thirty, lesbian, living alone) described a recent experience:

I sat very close to this woman I was real attracted to. I had set up this thing where we would all go out to dinner, about six of us, and I made sure I sat beside her and kind of played footsies every once in a while under the table. I talked to her very intently and made sure that she knew that I was interested in her. Then I put my arm around her and asked where she lived and if she might like to come over to my house and have some tea. She grabbed me and kissed me and we were off and running! That's how it happened.

I think that when you are first coming out as a lesbian, it's really hard to initiate sex because you've never been overtly sexual with a woman. So it takes some practice.

Again, fears of rejection limit women's sexual assertiveness with a new or potential partner. Suzanne (thirty-seven, bisexual, divorced) has an unusual way of looking at assertiveness in initiating new relationships, an outlook which enables her to maximize the possibility of developing a good relationship:

I'm generally rather assertive in my life. If there's something I want to do or somebody I want to spend time with, it's fairly easy for me to be open and tell that person how I'm feeling. If there's a man I'm attracted to, I don't hesitate to call him up or tell him I'd like to spend time with him. If there is somebody I'm attracted to as a friend or lover, then I'll just put it out there and say that and then they can respond in a positive or a negative way. What I've learned is if somebody isn't interested, I don't have to feel bad personally and feel something's wrong with me. There are a lot of people in the world and some are going to reciprocate my feelings and others are not. If I didn't show some assertiveness there might be a lot of relationships and wonderful experiences lost.

Ariel, who was recently separated, has been practicing being straightforward with some new acquaintances. However, she finds it safer to practice this new skill with men who are not really possible future partners, as a way to buffer the pain of a negative response:

I've been working on being more willing to take risks to meet men. I'm still not the most terrific risk taker, although I will go out for something I want now. In most cases, my approach hasn't been very romantic. It's been much more straightforward. I did tell one friend last summer that I felt like a fifteen-year-old boy who had just scored. That was because I had learned how to ask somebody out, how to make it clear that I wanted to go to bed with them, and how to be prepared that they might say no, which is really, really hard. I did this successfully with a guy I met at work this summer. It was wonderful. I planned the whole thing! I took him on a picnic. He was from Africa and just visiting, so he didn't have a car or anything. I took him on a picnic to the park with all this glorious food and everything. It worked out beautifully, so then about three weeks after he left, I met another guy and I did the exact same thing, I mean the whole same scenario. Then I said to myself, "I really am like a fifteen-year-old American boy who finds one way that works and scores and then uses that way again and again."

In neither case did I really care about the people, so it was safer than some other situations. That way, if I had been rejected, it wouldn't have been too much of a thing. They were both leaving town. You know, if I'm going to take a chance, it has to have a couple of safety valves built into it.

As difficult as it is for women to initiate sexual contact, it is equally difficult for them to be assertive enough to say no to someone who takes the initiative sexually when they are uninterested. Many unattached women find themselves in bed with a partner that they don't really want to be having sex with, but it is easier to go along with his wishes than to assert themselves and possibly hurt his feelings or have to deal with his anger.

Connie, a twenty-six-year-old widow and businesswoman who lives with roommates, gave an example of how she cleared up a potentially uncomfortable situation by dealing with it early and directly:

Let me explain how I have said no. Actually, this is an example that just happened the other night and I know this guy didn't believe what he was hearing. He is an older man and we've been friends and business acquaintances for a long time, so when he called up and said, "Let's go out for dinner, but I want to make it perfectly clear this isn't business." I said, "Okay, this is for fun." I realized after the champagne cocktails and the escargot that this guy pretty much had in mind coming back to my house, sitting in front of the fireplace and . . . So by the time dessert rolled around, I said, "You know, I've got to tell you this because pretty soon the waiter is going to bring our coffee, we're going to walk outside, and you're going to say, "Where are we going to go?" and I'll say, "Not to my house" and you'll be offended. So before we get to that point, let me say that for these reasons I really don't choose to have a sexual relationship with you."

I explained that I felt the differences between us that were attractive in a business and friendship relationship probably wouldn't be attractive in a sexual, intimate relationship, and he understood.

Saying no is also difficult for married women or women in long-term relationships. Fear of hurting their partners' feelings causes many women to participate in sex at times when they really don't want to in the name of being sensitive to their partners. The following women, however, had, over time, worked this often sticky issue out. Billy (forty-three, married):

With Fred, it's not hard to communicate that I want sex. All I have to do is snuggle up. I think I also have a right to say that I don't want to have sex and that this is nothing personal. He understands that now, where before it used to really hurt his feelings. It's so much better to be able to say it outright and still be able to cuddle.

Sarah (twenty-nine, married):

I tend to be very direct with him and ask him if he's interested in having sex with me. I've found that being indirect has not worked very well because often one of us has one thing in mind and the other has something else in mind. If I'm clear about what I want, then I can make it clear to him right from the beginning. It took me a while to find a way to let him know when I didn't want to have sex with him. I've found telling him that I don't want to have sex, but I do want to be physically close to him, by holding him or massaging his head or his back or his whole body in a nonsexual way, prevents him from feeling rejected and yet lets him know where I'm at. That works much better than both of us feeling close and affectionate and finding out that he's really interested in having intercourse and I'm not. It's been much more useful for us to be very direct about it right from the onset. If, in the process of being close to him, I decide I want to have sex, we can go ahead and have it. Frequently when I do get close to him, I get interested in having sex, and he's always very willing to continue.

CREATIVE INITIATION

If you are in a long-term relationship and you get stuck in predictable sexual patterns, it might be interesting and exciting to find new ways of initiating sex—something that adds variety and helps to keep the relationship vital and alive.

A few of the women described particularly unique methods of initiating sex. They had devised agreed-upon signals with their partners and made initiating sex into a game. Iris (thirty-two, living with boy friend):

One day while I was antiquing, I came across a basket of brass reproductions of "screw checks" used in saloons and whorehouses in San Francisco during the gold-rush days. On one side they read "All Nite Love Check," and on the other side "Red Door Saloon, $3 a Nite." So I bought one and, on days when I find myself in a romantic mood, I just slip my boy friend this token so he can be prepared to make love later that night or, sometimes, when I give him the token we make love right then. He liked the idea so much that he wanted a token of his own so he wouldn't have to wait for me to give him one. With two tokens, we can pass them back and forth all the time. Sometimes, we give the other person two of them for a "special $6 night." And if one of us is tired one night and only half into it, we joke about crediting the other person $1.50 toward the next time.

Morgan (forty-two, married nine years, hospital administrator) and her husband sometimes use an antique Japanese doll to communicate their sexual interest:

We have a little ivory Noh doll whose face reverses from a human smiling one to the face of an angry lion. (Noh is a kind of traditional Japanese theater play where the actors wear masks, changing masks as they change characters.) The lion's face is all screwed up and scowly and the human face is very placid-looking. If we're feeling snarly or not interested, the lion face is up, and if we're interested, then the human face is up.

The game Harriet (thirty-four, married) uses is one we have suggested to our sex therapy clients to help them determine their level of sexual interest and to communicate that information to their partner:

We have this number system that goes from zero to ten. It's something we call our "sexual readiness scale." If I'm interested in making love, I might say to him, "My number is eight" or six or ten, or whatever I happen to be at that time. Zero means I'm not interested at all, with ten being I really, really, really want to make love. Five is, well it would be nice but it doesn't matter. I usually initiate if I'm about a seven or eight. I might say to him, "I'm a seven—what's your number?" Then, if he's a three and I'm a seven, I know I can get him! We have this joke which is, if you can get it up, you can have it. So I'll say to him, "Well, if I can get it up, can I have it?" If he were a one, I'd probably masturbate instead. Generally, we're pretty obliging to one another, so that if I'm a three, for instance, and he's a seven, I would probably be open to going ahead and making love so long as he understands that he shouldn't expect me to get very passionate. I make a distinction between passion and something else—I don't even know what I call it. There are times when I'm quite open to having sex, when I'd like to be close in that way, when I want to pleasure him and have him feel good, but I have no intentions of putting a lot of energy into getting real turned on myself. I just don't feel like it. When I'm real turned on and want to make love, that's passion, and otherwise it isn't. So my preface has been, "Don't expect me to be passionate if I'm a three." That means, go for yourself, have a good time, don't worry about it and don't have any expectations about me. It's important to give myself permission not to get real turned on, to take any pressure off myself. When I do that, I frequently get real turned on. But I have to have that freedom to have sex and not be passionate. We agreed once that whenever we totaled ten or more, we'd have sex. If one was a ten and the other was a one, just on good faith we'd have sex. We use the scale all the time. If I come up and kiss him in a certain way, he may then say, "Hmm, what's your number?" and I'll say, "See you in the bedroom," or I'll say, "No, that was an innocent kiss. That was only a three." The scale can be used in a whole lot of ways, like when we talk about a restaurant. "How strong are you about this restaurant?" "I'm an absolute ten, I must have this restaurant." The scale cuts through a lot, it gets right to the point.

Good communication in a relationship is similar to a solid foundation in a house. If a house is built with a strong foundation, it will be able to withstand the stress caused by such natural disasters as hurricanes or tornadoes. Even if the rest of the house is damaged or destroyed, if the foundation is solid the house can be rebuilt.

Stress can arise from numerous natural situations that impinge upon all relationships, such as deciding to have children, buying a house, changing jobs, or moving to a new city. However, a relationship based on open and positive communication is more likely to survive these outside stresses intact.

Those of you who feel that the foundation of your relationship is shaky at best, or who have existed together for a long period of time without this kind of communication, may find yourselves concerned about the future of your relationship. Although communication is an essential ingredient of a relationship which is flexible enough to adapt to the outside pressures it encounters, many, if not most, relationships initially lack this level of communication. For most, this foundation is really formed and strengthened as the result of the various problems the couple encounters in the early days or years of their relationship. These problems themselves actually catalyze the need for and development of communication skills which will be necessary to carry the two people through their life together. Within a problem often lie the seeds of greater intimacy.

The following chapter is devoted to a wide range of problems which affect sexuality. We have culled from our interviews the ways in which the women successfully coped with their particular problem, so that they were still able to maintain an active and satisfying sexual relationship.

6

What to Do When You Run into Trouble

Although problems are always unwelcome, the process of resolution may help us to develop some very important skills. In this
sense, problems can be seen as challenging our creativity and adapt-
ability. In encountering problems, we are forced to develop the
flexibility, acceptance, and communication skills necessary to overcome the trying situation. Indeed, experiencing and coming to grips
with various dilemmas in our lives give us inner strength, new
levels of understanding, and add to our richness as human beings.
And it is understood that we are not expected to solve each and
every one of these problems by ourselves. If necessary, we can turn
to our spouse, lover, friend, relative, or a professional for help. The
same, however, is often not true of sexual problems.

Perhaps as the result of cultural myths, we expect ourselves and
our partners to be sexually omniscient. We expect, without any information or experience, to have all the necessary knowledge to
deal with the many facets of sexual functioning. It is similar to expecting to get a college diploma without attending any of the
courses. We might obtain some of the information through the

process of daily living, whereas other information may never present itself. Similarly, experimentation and practice with different sexual partners might provide us with some of the information we need while not providing sufficient tools to cope with more unusual or individual problems that may be encountered.

The existence of a problem that affects your sexuality may not indicate any inadequacy on your part as a healthy and well-functioning male or female. Neither is it necessarily an indication of some deeper, more serious problem in the relationship with your partner. It may mean that, for the moment, you happen to be stuck, in that no solution appears workable.

This chapter, then, is a compilation of the various sexual problems experienced by the women we interviewed and the solutions they arrived at. Interestingly, there was virtually no woman who did not, at some time, experience a problem which affected her sexuality. This is particularly noteworthy in light of the fact that the women we interviewed generally felt very positively about their own sexuality. Yet the material we amassed for this chapter exceeded that for any other.

It is encouraging to realize that it is possible to have a sexual problem and overcome it. Sometimes, when we are in the midst of difficulty, we feel alone, as if we were the only one who had ever had such an experience. We lose sight of the fact that a solution can evolve.

The women we interviewed found a variety of ways to solve their problems. A few sought professional help, but they were by far in the minority. Most who succeeded in overcoming their problems did so on their own or with the aid of their partner. The women who never resolved their sexual difficulties continued to experience the repercussions of their unresolved dilemmas and expressed their pain quite poignantly during the interviews. These interviews were like therapy sessions, and since these women had found no solutions, we chose not to include their transcripts in this chapter.

Some of these solutions may seem superficial to you, or not quite appropriate for your unique situation. It may be that nothing in this chapter will present you with the exact answer you are seeking. Our hope is that reading about the ways other women have solved their sexual problems may generate more ideas of your own or suggest some options you had not considered before. Anything that gives you a slightly different perspective on your situation might enable you to create a solution.

Organizing this chapter was very difficult because of the overwhelming amount of material and the complex etiology of the various problems. Consequently we decided to present the material in the following order: First, we viewed the effect of work and family stress on sexuality. Then we looked at sexual inhibitions (oral sex and nudity) and sexual dysfunctions (lack of orgasm, sexual disinterest, erection problems, and rapid ejaculation). The second half of the chapter addresses various medical problems (ranging from contraception and relatively minor vaginal and bladder infections to more serious medical conditions) and their effect on sexuality.

LACK OF TIME

An overriding concern of almost all of the women we interviewed was that of finding sufficient time from their harried schedules to enjoy sex. To us, lack of time often seems to be more of a cultural problem than a problem in terms of sexual functioning, but without a doubt this situation certainly interferes with achieving a good sexual relationship.

Due to the time constraints on their lives, women unhappily acknowledged that sex had to be planned for. In a marriage or a living-together situation where time is at a premium and each person has multiple roles, women reported that sex often ended up taking the lowest priority—occurring after work, after meals, after taking care of the children, after the household chores were completed—and then only if there was time and energy left over. The result was that sex was often completely omitted, or squeezed in when either or both partners were too tired or preoccupied to really enjoy it. The interference of work and stress on sex came up over and over again in our interviews.

Anna (twenty-eight, married):

We tend to fall into it because there's so little time. We're tired, yet we want the closeness of making love so we'll do it. He'll have an orgasm and then I'll masturbate with him still in me. I'll reach orgasm, too, and that'll be it. There isn't much foreplay or caressing. It feels sandwiched in particularly when our days are really hectic.

Many people have difficulty accepting the fact that they must include time for sex in their planning, because they operate under the myth that sex should be spontaneous. Although other activities are planned, sex should not be. They tend to think that during their dating period, sex always occurred naturally and that only after they started living with someone or got married did finding time for sex become a problem. But the fact is, sex never was truly spontaneous. During dating, specific periods of time were set aside consciously or unconsciously for sex and certain preparations were made so that the time together would be particularly good. Time was set aside to be together without outside distractions, underwear was carefully chosen in case the evening ended in sex, showers were taken, perfume worn, the diaphragm or other contraceptive methods made accessible, and sometimes the house was even cleaned. But once a couple decided to make the relationship more permanent, more intimate, these preparations were often no longer attended to.

However, we found that when women were able to acknowledge the energy they had previously put into preparing and planning for the sexual part of their relationship, they could consciously continue to put this same energy into a living-together or married relationship. This conscious preparation was a way for couples to maintain an exciting and satisfying sexual relationship.

Judy (thirty-one, married):

We make dates with each other. We let each other know in the middle of the afternoon. One of us will say to the other, "Could I have a date with you for tonight?" Then there is that sense of anticipation and we like that. David reads a lot at night and unless we make an absolute plan to get to bed early, sex is much quicker and not as nice as when we really make space and time for each other.

Some people's schedules conflict or their lives are so busy that they would never have time for sex if they did not prearrange it.

Brenda (twenty-four, teacher, married to Dick, a repairman, for three years):

I really have to plan in order to have time to make love. Right now Dick is working day shift and I'm working about three or four nights a week, so it's really hard to find a day when we're both not tired. I usually start about two days before I want to have sex by telling him that I want to see how we can set some time aside. Dick has one day off a week and I request that night off from work so I can go to bed with him. I also have to plan to come home to get eight hours' sleep the night before, so I won't be any more tired than he is. A couple of days ahead of time, I have to approach him and let him know, so he'll be sure not to be too tired either.

Theresa (thirty, psychologist, lesbian, living alone) and her lover, Betty, a carpenter, set up specific times for sex:

I really plan for sex by unplugging the phone, and making sure I don't have too many appointments crowded together. But that's my bias, to make definite plans so sex counts. It's like you make plans to go to the movies, you don't just all of sudden find yourself in a movie theater, and I think that it's the same thing with sex.

Some women feel that planning sex builds in pressure to perform. What happens when you've planned Wednesday night together and Wednesday arrives and you're not feeling turned on? This fear leads some women to avoid planning. Alexandra was concerned about this so she devised the following way of handling it. She and her partner have an understanding that it's okay to say, "I'm really tired tonight. I just don't feel like sex, even though we planned to make love tonight." Knowing this is part of the ground rules frees both of them up to plan for sex without feeling that they have to go through with it no matter what else comes up.

Penelope (forty-six, married) did not exactly plan for sex, but found a way to change her evening routine so that it was easier to have sex if they were so inclined:

When I was working a lot, we had a certain routine. We'd come home from work and before we got into the evening, we'd share what our day had been like. That sometimes took up the whole evening. We'd sit at the table and talk about our day and then we'd be tired and he'd say "Want to play Scrabble?" and I'd say "Yeah." Finally I said, "You know, we're not making love as much as I'd like to, so let's talk and play our game in bed and then if we want to make love, we're right there." Then our frequency went up. When we were through telling each other about our day and deciding what to do with the rest of the evening, we didn't have to go through a transition. This way, we were already in bed and touching each other while we were sharing our day's adventures, so making love was easy and natural.

STRESS

Another culturally induced problem like lack of time is the effect of stress on our sex lives.

Work stress was the problem most often mentioned, since so many of the women we interviewed had careers in their own right. Many of these women found themselves having to juggle their job as well as their family and home responsibilities, and frequently found themselves too drained for sex when the time was available. Men have historically had their sexual energy sapped by pressures at work; now women are facing the same problem. Without the benefit of role models, the women we interviewed were attempting to solve the problem through trial and error. Some had found solutions, while others were in the midst of the struggle.

Gweneth (forty-four, nurse practitioner, married, mother of three teen-agers) asserted herself and got her family to help with the household chores:

I just give everybody certain jobs to do so I'm not overwhelmed on the weekends. If you're working and trying to do all the housework too, it can get to be too much. We can get the whole house cleaned in three hours. Now everybody does their part and we clean the house once a week. That's a big change for us and it's worked out well.

Diane (thirty-two, lesbian, living with foster child) scheduled in a cooling-out period:

When I get too involved in my work, it creates a bad situation. I get so immersed in it that it's really hard for me to forget it when I go to bed. What I've done is to try and end whatever I'm doing earlier, so that I have a period of time to cool out first. I bring a lot of work home since I'm so much more productive at night. Now I try to end work an hour earlier so I can relax before I go to bed. That way I have the energy and peace of mind to be there sexually for my partner.

Marie, a thirty-three-year-old college professor who has been married ten years, says:

The main thing that interferes with sex is something that has nothing to do with sex and that's my being preoccupied with work or personal problems. Sometimes I have a difficult time making the transition between something that has happened during the day and having sex.

If I've been in a meeting or if I've had a rough time in the library, it's hard for me to turn that off in the evening. It takes a very deliberate effort to forget about that for a few hours. It also helps if my husband is sensitive enough to realize that I'm preoccupied and lets me work that out myself at my own pace and doesn't try to rush me. If I don't get my mind off my work, if I go to bed anxious, I won't be in touch with my body, nor with his. I'll be preoccupied, tense, and probably angry because I'll feel I've been taken away from something that I want to do or ought to be doing that would ease my mind. Then I'll feel compelled to be sexual, but I won't really want to, so I won't really be there emotionally and it won't be a very good experience.

Theresa (thirty, lesbian):

My lover is a carpenter, so she's physically tired at the end of the day and it's rare that she has energy for sex during the week. I'm really into sex lately, so I've gotten into masturbating while she's holding me, just before we're going off to sleep. That's great for me.

FEMALE SEXUAL DYSFUNCTIONS

A person with a sexual dysfunction—lack of orgasm, erection difficulties, rapid ejaculation, sexual inhibition, sexual disinterest —often experiences it as a statement about his or her adequacy as a functioning male or female. It seems to imply a basic deficit.

In almost any other area of functioning, we think nothing of reaching out to a friend, family member, or professional for help. However, this is often not true of sex. It is difficult to talk about it to others, relatively few classes and useful books are available, and not many people are well informed on the subject. Besides, it is not quite socially acceptable to discuss your sex life. But, more importantly, one doesn't even want anyone else to know that the problem exists. As a result, all avenues to the usual ways of solving problems are closed, exacerbating the difficulty as it remains clothed in secrecy.

The result for many people is that they are unable to seek help from others. They feel compelled to face the problem alone, to solve it on their own, which would somehow prove that they are not in fact inadequate. Yet, without the necessary information and skills, this task can be overwhelming. And feeling so helpless then only increases the already existing feelings of shame and inadequacy.

Sexual Inhibition

Sexual inhibition is not a sexual dysfunction in the true sense of the word; however, strong inhibitions can have a deleterious effect on a person's sex life. Not only is the partner with the inhibition constantly anxious and uncomfortable during sexual encounters or with certain sexual activities, but the other partner often experiences constant frustration, which can make the inhibited partner feel even worse.

The most common sexual inhibition by far was discomfort with oral sex. Some women were uncomfortable with cunnilingus, especially if they had negative feelings about their genitals. However, of those who disliked oral sex, most disliked fellatio either because it made them choke or because they didn't want their partners to ejaculate in their mouths.

Many of the women wished to overcome their distaste for oral sex, and many had. However, others felt that by adding variety in other ways to their sexual relationship, they replaced the need for oral sex, and that solution was satisfactory to both people.

Christine (forty-one, married nineteen years) said:

One thing I really hate, that turns me off, is when he kisses me down there, yet I know he really likes it. I don't know why I don't like it, maybe I'm just conservative. I guess the cleanliness part bothers me. I think that's what it is. It's just not my bag. So I try to please him by doing different things and by using other positions.

Others, however, did feel that their dislike for oral sex was causing difficulties in their relationships and they were interested in finding ways to enjoy oral sex more fully.

Beverly (thirty-six, married nine years) shared how she overcame her aversion to both cunnilingus and fellatio:

From the very beginning of our relationship, I had a lot of hang-ups about trying new things sexually. My whole background was rather restrictive in regard to sexuality. But I was naturally inquisitive and adventuresome and that got reinforced by my husband. He introduced me to many new things sexually and I was willing to try them. We would talk about my mixed feelings, about the discomfort and the guilt I felt. He constantly supported me and I wanted to learn, so that really helped. One of the big hurdles I've gotten over is my feelings about oral sex, and I did that through a combination of talking about my feelings and doing a lot of reading. My husband had already reinforced the view that oral sex was not perverse, or abnormal. Although I could hear what he said, I couldn't believe it. Finally after doing a lot of reading and a lot of reflecting and talking to him, I got to the point of thinking, "God, how could something so pleasurable be so awful?" And over time, I've become comfortable with it.

Her approach to learning to like fellatio, however, was even more creative:

There are two ways I've overcome my aversion to fellatio. One was to start by kissing, licking or touching his genitals in a way that I felt comfortable doing. I would do that for as long as I felt comfortable, and then when I got uncomfortable, I would stop. Another way was to use whipped cream. I put it on his penis, his balls, and especially the glans of his penis. That's the neatest place to put it on because it's so sensitive and smooth and feels so good. The glans is also small and manageable, so I can handle that. It's nice, really nice. Then I imagine that it's an ice cream cone and I lick it off by swirling my tongue around it, just like it was ice cream. The texture, the taste, and the flavor are really nice. That way, I've been able to suck and lick his penis longer. I can do it even after the whipped cream is gone, because I still have the image of the ice cream in my mind.

Another solution helpful to Rose, a thirty-six-year-old single woman living alone, was:

If I clasp my hand around my partner's penis at the base, I'm less afraid of choking. This way, I know my hand will stop his penis from thrusting too far into my mouth.

A few women talked about how discomfort with nudity or a dislike for their body caused problems sexually. One woman was unable to fully enjoy lovemaking with her partner when he tried to give her pleasure because of her negative body image, nor was she able to feel free about using her body to give him pleasure. Her solution to this problem was to begin looking at her body in a mirror in a new way. Combining the frequent mirror observations with yoga helped her to appreciate her body and to be more comfortable with it.

Some women had grown up in families where bodies were always clothed. They had never seen their father, mother, or siblings undressed and had never been naked in front of another person except their lover or husband. The discomfort they felt with nudity made them less spontaneous in bed. Beverly (thirty-six, married) took the following approach to easing her discomfort:

One thing I've overcome is the discomfort with nudity I felt early in my marriage. When I was first married, I always had clothes or something on. I was twenty-five years old then and I had never worn a bathing suit in public, not even in my own back yard. My body was not something I wanted to show off to anybody. When I got married, I was suddenly supposed to be able to show it off to my husband. Obviously, I didn't feel comfortable doing that and so the nudity would be under the cover with dim lights or no lights. I overcame this by talking about it and gradually disrobing more and more. My husband insisted, I mean he just insisted that we have the lights on, that it was really okay to view my body and for him to view it, and that was nice. Now I just walk around nude when we're alone and I feel comfortable doing it.

Lack of Orgasm

Not being able to experience an orgasm was the major sexual dysfunction encountered by the women we interviewed. Some had never had an orgasm, while others had experienced orgasm during masturbation but never or only rarely with their partner. The women who had very little experience having orgasm generally required more information to make the experience of orgasm available to them. This information was often acquired through various sources, such as reading and educational classes, in conjunction with a loving partner.

Alice (thirty-eight, single):

There was a time when I just hadn't experienced orgasm at all. I didn't understand what my partner was talking about when he said he wanted me to have an orgasm because I didn't know what I was supposed to be experiencing. Then we both decided to read some sex books and we came across the whole idea of women needing clitoral stimulation. First I tried stimulating myself during masturbation and it worked. Then my partner started to do it during intercourse and that helped me to have an orgasm, which definitely improved the quality of our sexual relationship.

Judith (forty, married eight years to her second husband):

With my first husband my orgasm became the goal of our whole sexual experience. That just totally bottomed it out for me. It was almost impossible to come under those circumstances, so I avoided sex a lot, even though technically he was a proficient lover. Nathan was much more physically loving. Every time he touched me it didn't mean he wanted to go have sex which had been my experience before. He was so warm and would hold me or touch me a lot, and it wasn't necessarily sexual, so a lot of my barriers started breaking down.

The other thing that really helped was taking some sex education classes. I don't know if it's true for everybody, but even though I'm intelligent and well educated, I found that I didn't know nearly what I needed to know about sex. Once we completed the university course, we didn't have any sex problem—all we had needed was information that we had not had before, and permission to let whatever we were experiencing be okay. We found out, for example, that a great percentage of women don't come every time. I had thought since I didn't, I was deficient.

Other couples got help by talking to friends or health professionals. Bernice (sixty-seven, married forty-two years):

I had orgasms before we were married when we were just fooling around, but after we got married and started having intercourse, they stopped. My husband and I talked about that and he was frustrated and I was too, but neither of us knew who was failing who. My husband talked to our family physician. I had a whole group of young married women friends, and we'd talk about things like that, like why we weren't having orgasms. We were knowledgeable about sexuality, we knew what we wanted, but it wasn't happening. Our family physician was a German doctor who had come over in 1936 just before the war and he was just great. When Alan talked to him, he gave him information on how to stimulate me clitorally. He did that and I became orgasmic.

In some cases, as with Paula, a partner was sufficiently knowledgeable to teach the woman:

I was twenty-three and had never had an orgasm when I met a guy who was really considerate. It was my first experience with a guy who was interested in my having as good a time as he had. Many of the things I'm comfortable with now I attribute to his being willing to take some time with me and to care about me, although at the time this was really embarrassing. He would talk to me while we were just fooling around, before we had intercourse, and would insist that I tell him whether things felt good. That was uncomfortable and difficult to do because in the past I would usually just clamp my mouth shut and say to myself that I'm supposed to enjoy this. Although it had been enjoyable in the past to some extent, most of the time I didn't always know what felt good because I had never focused on it before. He also told me what felt good to him as it was happening. He was really responsible for my becoming more at ease with my body because he made me feel that my feelings and my satisfaction were important, too.

A partner's acceptance, support, and reassurance can be of paramount importance in enabling a woman to relax and gain sufficient comfort to learn to experience orgasm.

Florence, a thirty-four-year-old businesswoman and lesbian who has lived with her lover Kate for two years, discovered that over time and with the loving support of her partner she was able to become orgasmic:

Prior to the time I was married, I really had very little sexual experience with men. I just simply wasn't turned on by men. I was, however, turned on by women. I had had an experience starting when I was in the seventh grade with a woman that lasted intermittently for thirteen years, but I did not have orgasms with her. When I was finally married, the guy that I married didn't turn me on particularly. Although I had masturbated to orgasm for years and I knew what turned me on, somehow I couldn't make that transfer to having one with him. Then I realized I was really gay, that I was a lesbian. We were divorced and I came out. But even with women, I never had an orgasm. I enjoyed it, but I still faked orgasms. I still didn't know how to make that transfer and I was too embarrassed to say to my women lovers that I didn't have orgasms. I assumed everybody had orgasms with other people except me, and I didn't want to be different, and so therefore I couldn't be honest about it. Then I met Kate, a feminist, who was very aware of female sexuality. Since I cared for her and she cared for me, I knew that I was going to have to come clean. If we were going to continue our relationship, I was going to have to admit where I was, which was preorgasmic.

We talked and I told her my deep, dark secret—that I had never had an orgasm with a woman, with anyone. So we began there. It has been a three-year process of Kate helping me. It's been interesting, it's been fun, but it has also taken a long time to be able to emotionally and physically trust another human being that much. I also needed to learn what to do technically. I had to get down to the real clinical aspects of orgasms. Kate had to teach me some of the basics about sexuality. Kate explained to me that you don't necessarily get turned on every time you're making out. Sometimes you don't get turned on until you actually have oral contact, oral sex.

We had what we called "clinics," lovemaking sessions where there were no expectations since expectations is a big word. We would simply practice. She would kiss me, and make love to me orally, and I would concentrate only on the feelings. One of the fears that came up in our clinics was that I would get turned on and suddenly feel that I had to urinate and so I'd stop. Finally I told Kate that I felt like I was going to urinate. She explained that as I became aroused there was more pressure on my bladder. That took away the anxiety. I was then able to relax and we went on from there. I don't remember when I first had an orgasm, but it was wonderful. We both were elated.

What I learned is that it's important to realize that you're not always going to feel turned on when you start making love. Sometimes you may not be that turned on throughout the sexual act, but your partner might be. So you simply go with whatever is there instead of worrying about what you should be feeling at the time.

Sometimes when it was possible for a woman to have orgasms during masturbation but not with her partner, the problem resided in feeling too much performance pressure; too much focus on the fragile orgasm seemed to frighten it away.

Rosemary (age thirty-six, divorced) explained how she coped with that:

I experienced a problem right after I started having orgasms for the first time. I was having them pretty regularly, although not every time I had intercourse. This was very pleasing to both my boy friend and me, but then for some reason, I stopped having them as frequently. We both made an effort for me to have an orgasm; we would try real hard in intercourse, but I just couldn't seem to make it and I felt angry when I didn't have one. Sometimes I was so angry at Steve because I felt hurt and disappointed. I felt as if it was his fault even though in my head I knew it wasn't. I knew he couldn't make me have an orgasm. Steve also felt guilty because he thought he'd let me down and we talked about that a lot. He said that his self-image, his masculinity, was diminished because he derived a lot of satisfaction out of pleasing me. His identity was linked with pleasing me. We analyzed it over and over again, and then I decided to go back to a way of thinking about sex that I had before I started having orgasms. I decided to simply enjoy sex; the whole process of it. I did not concentrate on having sex or intercourse to reach an orgasm, but instead I concentrated on enjoying how the whole thing felt—the pleasuring, his penis inside me. The fact is, I do enjoy sex. I do enjoy intercourse, even when I don't reach orgasm. I stopped being so preoccupied with having to have an orgasm. I stopped feeling that intercourse wasn't complete or satisfying unless I orgasmed. We also started having other kinds of sex more often. We used different positions and began to have more oral sex. And perhaps, because we were relaxed and our communication was so open, I started having orgasms again. It just sort of happened once I relaxed and wasn't so uptight about sex.

Lack of Interest

The second most pervasive sexual problem expressed by the women was not feeling turned on often enough. Lack of desire for sex can stem from anxiety, outside stress, insecurity about being an adequate lover, or it can be a reflection of other relationship problems. Sometimes it isn't a lack of interest at all, but rather just a difference in the two people's libidinal levels.

Sage (thirty-five, lesbian), dealt with her feelings of anxiety which dampened her sexual interest by adopting a new attitude:

I used to feel terrible performance anxiety because of the sexual image I feel people have of lesbians. It's like if I'm not a good lover, and I'm a lesbian, then, what am I? I used to have terrible self-doubts if I couldn't come fast enough or if I didn't get my lover excited enough. I just really got into negative patterns and then it got worse and worse. I would get into bed and usually I would start to feel anxious and I wouldn't feel turned on. I really worked on that for a long time. It is still hard for me to accept lying in bed with someone and not feeling turned on. I still have that from time to time and I always have to talk to myself to get out of that way of thinking. I have to detach myself and say to myself, "It's really nice being with this person and my presence alone is more than ample. It's okay if I'm not turned on." I keep reminding myself that my whole self-esteem does not hinge on whether I get turned on at this moment.

Often, what women perceive as a lack of interest may not really be that but rather a level of sexual interest which is lower than their partner's. Ruby (thirty-nine, married eighteen years) handled this discrepancy in the following way:

My husband has always felt that his sexual need was greater than mine and my response to that has been "Wait a minute, you're not giving me a chance." So in recent years, when I sense he wants to make love, but he doesn't want to make the request because he's afraid I'll think he's being too demanding, or too masculine, I'll surprise him by taking the initiative. I might come in nude or be physically aggressive in some other way and he responds immediately.

A sexual relationship, obviously, does not exist in a vacuum. Other areas of one's life affect sexual enjoyment, functioning, and interest. In addition to work stress, family problems, chronic financial problems, illness, or emotional problems can create sufficient tension to strain a sexual relationship. It's not uncommon for communication problems with a partner or unresolved issues to result in sexual problems as well. The effect of nonsexual problems on sexual relations is far greater than most people are aware. People very often see the sexual difficulties as The Problem and blame the other person for not being loving or not caring about them when, in fact, the sexual difficulties are merely a sign that something else has gone wrong in the relationship.

Heather shares how she and her husband respond sexually when they're experiencing problems in their relationship:

If we're really upset or dissatisfied with each other, sex is not particularly something either he or I want. We take the tack that we'll work out our problems and then we'll get back to having sex. Obviously, this doesn't go on for a very long period of time. But I don't try very hard to communicate about sex when I feel that there's a lot of tension going on about other things.

Billy (forty-three, married for twenty-six years) found that counseling gave her a perspective on her sexual disinterest which reflected other feelings in her relationship:

I went through a long period of really not wanting sex for a variety of reasons. One was being afraid of getting pregnant. Another one was that Fred always came really fast and that left me feeling really strung out and mad at him. Then I would wonder if there was something wrong with me.

At the time, I was going to this counselor for some other problems. I remember telling him that all Fred wanted was sex and that if I gave it to him every time he wanted it, that's all we would be doing is having sex. The counselor didn't believe that. In talking to him, I realized what was going on for Fred was that my not giving in sexually made it even more desirable. I don't know if I was holding back as a punishment or what. I know I was not overly happy being married at that time. I had a lot of feelings I couldn't deal with and maybe I held back sexually because it was a giving of myself. I wasn't at all sure that I wanted to be so giving. Anyway, going to the counselor helped me work through some of these problems. Then I was more relaxed and I enjoyed having sex more. It also helped me talk to Fred about it more easily.

Sex sometimes acts as a barometer measuring the close or stormy times by the presence or absence of sexual activity. It was not uncommon for women to state that when they were angry with their partner, sexual activity ceased until the nonsexual problems were resolved. The methods used and the ease with which a couple could resolve such problems depended on many other aspects of their relationship. Just talking about the difficulties was sufficient to clear them up for some women, such as Alexandra (thirty-two, divorced):

I am not always aware of when other problems in the relationship are affecting me sexually. I might be upset and angry and not really realize it except that I will not feel turned on in bed. Then Ralph will pick that up and feel hurt. Sometimes I get scared that my sexual feelings will never come back. I worry when I'm not turned on, that it's the end of our relationship, or that there's something wrong with me. But when we're able to talk about what's bothering me, my sexual feelings come back very quickly and it's always a relief.

A few couples have a rule that they never go to bed mad, and in that way resolve their differences on a daily basis.

Judy (thirty-one, married two years):

We have a nightly ritual of cuddling regardless of the outcome. We don't just get into bed and go to sleep. If we are angry with each other, we don't turn off the light until we make up. We could be up until five o'clock in the morning working something out. We have never once turned off the light without working out our anger and then cuddling and kissing before we go to sleep. And it has never been phony.

Some couples were not able to resolve the anger by discussion, but had methods by which they could successfully dissipate the anger through their physical relationship.

Judith (forty, married) found wrestling to be one good way:

We do a lot of wrestling. If we've built up a whole accumulation of minor irritations it frequently evolves into a physical thing like wrestling, and that may evolve into a sexual experience. Not necessarily, though, since sometimes the wrestling dissipates our frustrations and satisfies us. However, other times it's very simple to go ahead and be sexual afterward.

Some express the anger and aggression sexually, like Elaine:

I use sex to get rid of all my anxieties and my anger. I could jump in bed in the middle of being angry toward my husband, although then I might be more mean sexually and take out my aggressions that way. The interaction usually ends up with both of us being delighted by the time we get through. An hour later we're both glad that it came to that because the anger is gone. It's over and done with. As a matter of fact, my orgasms are probably more intense, more sensual and magnificent then—maybe because of the anger.

SEX AFTER DIVORCE

Women who were divorced after a lengthy marriage or women who were widowed often had problems being sexual with new partners. Some felt inexperienced and often undesirable, especially if their sexual activity had diminished toward the end of their relationship due to constant conflict or illness. Suzanne (thirty-seven, bisexual) used affirmations to help her get through this period successfully:

When I split from my husband there was a three-month period where I didn't have sex at all. It's very rare for me to go for a prolonged period without sex, but even though I thought about sex a lot and was very frustrated, I couldn't bring myself to have sex with anybody because my husband was the only person I had ever had sex with. I felt scared and reticent. You see, I was so used to having only one sexual partner that after I separated from my husband, I would be with men and feel turned on, but then I'd close up. It took me three months to finally feel open enough to have sex with someone.

Finally, I met a man that I felt very turned on to and had a wonderful experience with him. We related sexually for a few years, on and off; we never had a really meaningful relationship, but it was a wonderful opening-up experience for me. But the way I got through those three months was by talking to myself. I used affirmations or messages that you tell yourself. I told myself, "You've closed up perhaps because your body needs a rest, and needs time to reevaluate things. You've set up this barrier because you need this period of time to shut down. When you're ready to trust again and to open up again, you'll do that."

People close down because they are afraid they are going to be hurt again or that they can't trust again or that they are not going to enjoy sex. If you really want to open up faster you can give yourself positive internal messages like: I want to open up; I want to experience good sex; I want to be open to people; I'm feeling very horny and I want to have that release, not just in masturbation but with somebody else too. The more I would tell myself that the more I'd be able to open up to it.

Nell (thirty-six, second marriage) describes how she broke the ice and had sex for the first time after her divorce:

We first met when we were doing volunteer work—like stuffing envelopes—for a political group. We had said to each other that we must get together, but it never happened. I was almost writing him off when all of a sudden he suggested spending some time together. And lo and behold, we spent a long, wonderful day together. It was very late when we got back to my house, and I was feeling a growing affection for him and I was really amazed because this was only six months after leaving my husband. Those six months had been dreadful, but there we were in February and everything suddenly seemed to be healing, like Christ doing a laying-on of hands. I was feeling so whole, and he was very funny and I was laughing a lot. Here it was ten years since I had had any interaction with a male as a potential lover other than my husband, so I was really in new, strange waters.

I really wanted him to stay over and yet I was also obviously conflicted about it. So he said, "Don't worry, I see there's only one bed here, so I'll sleep with my underpants on," and I remember thinking to myself, "What good is that going to do? I mean, that's never stopped anybody before." Then I realized I didn't want it to stop but I had been married for so long that I really didn't know what to do, so we got into bed and he fell asleep on the other side of the bed and then I sat up for two or three hours just looking out of the window and thinking what does a girl do in a situation like this? I could just wake him up and say something humorous like, "Are you sure you want to have your pants on?" I finally woke him up at about four in the morning and I said something real corny about thinking it would be okay if we "did it." He understood and the lovemaking turned out to be more natural and easy than I thought. It was also fun in the way that children who really like each other have fun together, which has characterized our relationship ever since.

SEX WITH A NEW PARTNER

Another common problem for single women was finding that when they jumped into bed early in the relationship, they often would feel dissatisfied sexually or not personally respected. As one woman put it: "I don't like hopping into bed with someone the first day. I've done it and I don't like the way I feel afterward, so I'm not going to do it anymore. I don't like it." Some women got out of this by learning to say no to casual sexual encounters until they felt more certain of their feelings about the person.

Some women found that although they cared about their partner, their partner refused to respond in a caring, loving, and receptive manner despite their attempts at communication. Many of these women decided to end the relationship rather than continue to feel unrespected and used. Cortney (thirty-one, divorced):

I went with one guy on and off for three years. It was a real unhealthy relationship, but we had great sex, except that I didn't really get anything out of it. It's hard to explain. I was always really excited by him and I always told myself that he was the greatest lover I'd ever had in my life, but after a long time I realized that I wasn't being honest with myself about the sex. I told myself he was so terrific because he made me feel so feminine. He was real good in bed, but he almost never got me to the point where I could finish and have an orgasm. It wasn't a giving relationship on his part—he was doing the taking and I was doing most of the giving. I loved sleeping with him, but I was very frustrated because after he had come, that would be the end of it. I mean, he was great while he was doing it, but when it was over, he really didn't care whether I had an orgasm or not. I remember I tried to be really honest with him one time and said, "I'm really frustrated and I really want you to finish me. I don't care if you get hard again or not, just use your hand, anything. I just can't stand this. This has been going on for two hours and you're all through and watching a football game and I'm lying here going nuts!" And he just said, "Later." So I started thinking, wait a minute, what's this all about? It had taken me such a long time to get to the point where I could talk to him, and his reaction had been such a letdown. I think that is what finally got me out of the relationship. I just thought, that's not right. I mean I already had a list of other things that were wrong with the relationship, and if the sex wasn't good, what was I doing here? But I was always kind of insecure and afraid I couldn't find anybody else so having him was better than not having anybody.

Ariel (thirty-three, separated one year) found that being alone wasn't as bad as she had thought. She talks about how she chose temporary abstinence as a solution to unsatisfying relationships:

If I wanted to, I could still be doing the quickie scoring number that I was doing this past summer. That was fun, but it paled very quickly. I don't want to do that anymore and yet I have not met somebody I can have a multilevel relationship with. The trick is to choose abstinence instead of cursing each day and saying "Oh, poor me" and feeling sorry for myself. Right now I am abstaining from sex even though there are plenty of folks out there that would fuck me if I chose to deal with it at that level. I've decided I'm not interested in just a sexual, physical release, so I've chosen abstinence. It makes me feel better about myself having made this decision because then I don't feel, "Oh, woe is me, why can't I find somebody?" I am accepting emotionally what I already know intellectually, which is that this is not the way it will always be, that there are people out there that I will like, and that this is just a phase in my life.

MALE SEXUAL DYSFUNCTIONS

A male's sexual problems can also interfere with a woman's enjoyment of sex. The two most common problems men experienced were difficulties with erection and not being able to last as long as they would like before they ejaculated. Some of the women we interviewed found they could be quite helpful to their partner in overcoming his sexual concerns. Allison (thirty-five, divorced) shares an episode in her marriage where she helped her husband with erection problems through an outside affair and new sexual information:

There was an interesting way we got through a sexual problem in my first marriage. My husband Murray started to experience some problems not only with maintaining erections but also with coming very quickly. He'd be in for just a few minutes and would come. Sometimes it wasn't that short, but often it was and therefore the only way I could come was through oral sex and not through intercourse. After years of this going on, I slept with somebody else who was also Jewish and who was able to maintain an erection for at least twenty minutes. My feeling before had been that, like in the movies, James Bond could fuck for hours but Murray couldn't because he was Jewish. But there was this Jewish person who could fuck up a storm, so if he could, Murray could. When I told Murray about sleeping with this guy, my comment was, "If this guy could do it, you can do it, too." And that's what I decided. I decided he should see this as a problem to be worked out rather than just accepting it as the way he was. I remembered reading some articles in magazines about how to help men maintain erections. I got Murray to agree to try some of the exercises. I learned how you hold the penis to squeeze it and in about two or three times, everything was fine. Then he was maintaining an erection for forty minutes or close to an hour.

Rather than trying to change the situation, other women we interviewed were very emphatic and accepting of their partner's difficulties in attaining erection. Many, like Penelope (forty-six), felt that lack of erection was not really a problem for them:

There are times when Harold doesn't get an erection, but it isn't a problem. I don't consider it a problem. It's only a bummer when he tries so hard to get an erection that that's where all his energy is going. Then he's not really there anymore. He's not really able to enjoy it and neither am I. When that happens, he stops trying to get an erection and we just continue holding or cuddling or loving each other in other ways. That feels fine to both of us.

Once the focus on the erection is dropped, it is possible for the couple to have a very satisfying lovemaking experience without including intercourse. Roberta said:

When we had problems sexually, we handled it by talking about it. We would tell each other how we were feeling, whether I wasn't feeling like having sex or if he was feeling like it and I wasn't. Then if I felt like satisfying him I would masturbate him or suck on him. If he couldn't get an erection, we would just talk about it so that it would be out in the open. I would say, "Well, let's be close then," and he would say, "My mind is really into you, but my body isn't right now, for whatever reason." Then we would just hold each other and feel close. If I wanted more sex than he did at that point, I would masturbate and he would touch my breasts or whatever I wanted him to do if he was into that.

Billie, age fifty-four, with one grown child, has been married for five years to her second husband John, age sixty-two and retired:

John has been having more and more difficulty getting erections. When he can't get an erection, he uses manual sex on me, which provides a kind of closeness, because I can have an orgasm this way and he feels very good about that. I enjoy it as much as intercourse. He will usually stimulate me enough so that he can have an orgasm just by trying to penetrate me, so he is satisfied, too.

Sonya helped her partner creatively solve a less common problem, that of being unable to ejaculate inside her:

I had a relationship where my partner was able to maintain an erection for a long time but unable to ejaculate inside me. Once he let me know that he could bring himself to orgasm by masturbation, I encouraged him to do that. I held him while he masturbated and it was really a loving part of the whole experience. I shared what he was doing by watching him, holding him, touching him, and by being with him. It really didn't take away from the intimacy of our experience at all.

HEALTH PROBLEMS

Contraception

Although contraception is not really a health problem, the ramifications of the contraceptive method used often affect the woman's health and her sexuality with her partner. Most of the available contraceptives have their drawbacks. Vasectomies and tubal ligations are viable alternatives only for people who have already had the number of children they want, or for people who have definitely decided against children. As one woman enthusiastically said:

I'm delighted I don't have to mess either with birth control pills or a diaphragm. I didn't like birth control pills and the diaphragm and I were not made for each other. It was just too difficult, too slippery, and took too much time, so my husband had a vasectomy. It makes things a hell of a lot easier.

Those women who had not yet started a family or were not quite sure if they wanted additional children generally used one of three contraceptive methods: birth control pills, an intrauterine device (IUD), or a diaphragm. Contraceptive foams and suppositories as well as condoms were used more on a temporary basis when other methods were unavailable.

Our interviewees were aware of and concerned about the possible negative effects of birth control pills. The IUD often caused midcycle bleeding and increased cramping and bleeding during the menstrual period. In addition, many male partners complained of getting impaled on the IUD string when it had not been cut short enough. As a result, many women preferred the diaphragm, even though they considered it less carefree than the IUD or pill. They felt that the diaphragm cut down on the spontaneity of lovemaking; it was messy; and the cream or jelly had an unpleasant taste and odor that often affected their lovers. In addition, some men reported that the diaphragm cut down on the sensation they experienced.

This latter problem can often be ameliorated by changing diaphragm type. There are three different types of diaphragms: the coil spring, the flat spring, and the arching spring. Different styles work better for different women. In terms of interference during lovemaking, a number of women devised ways of using the diaphragm so that it interfered only minimally. Some of these women suggested using the diaphragm regularly, so as to not break the flow of lovemaking. They would insert it every night before they went to bed, if they had a regular partner or if they thought an evening might end up with sex.

Suzanne (thirty-seven, divorced):

If I'm going out with a man I think I'm going to be sexual with, I put my diaphragm in before the date. That way, when I'm in the middle of some passionate scene, I don't have to run into the bathroom to put it in.

Allison (thirty-five, divorced) had a helpful hint for women who had difficulty putting the diaphragm in:

I always had trouble putting in my diaphragm standing up. I found an easier position to be lying on my back with my knees bent and my feet on the floor or bed slightly spread apart. The diaphragm seems to just slip in place very easily in this position.

One woman mentioned the importance of washing the vulva with a cloth afterward so that the taste and smell of the cream was minimized. Another woman preferred Ortho cream over Ortho jelly because of its more pleasant scent.

A few women suggested not putting the diaphragm in beforehand, but instead integrating it into the lovemaking process. Harriet (thirty-four, married ten years):

Tom almost always puts my diaphragm in as a part of our lovemaking. He doesn't like the taste of diaphragm cream, so putting it in ahead of time isn't too good and it's a drag in the middle of a high-pitched session to say, "Okay, hold everything while I go to the bathroom." So what we do is when we decide to make love, I'll get out the diaphragm and put the cream in. Then while he's kissing me and stroking me, he puts the diaphragm in and usually while he's putting it in, he'll either be stimulating my clitoris at the same time or my breasts or whatever. That way, it's not a break from our lovemaking. Besides, he can get it in quicker and better than I can.

The problem of wanting to make love and not having the diaphragm close at hand was solved by a number of methods. For regular bedroom sex, keeping the diaphragm and cream on the nightstand or in a specially designed pouch which attached to the bed eliminated the need to dash into the bathroom just when sexual passion was at its peak.

Harriet had an ingenious solution which enables her to make love anywhere and at any time:

I have two diaphragms. I keep one by the bed and I keep one with me in my purse. That way I never worry. If we're going off on a trip or if we're off in the woods taking a walk and it seems like a perfect time for making love, I always have my diaphragm.

Alexandra had a great idea for a diaphragm case that enabled her to carry it around in her purse inconspicuously:

I hate that ugly plastic diaphragm case. I'm embarrassed that someone might notice it in my purse, and besides, they always seem to break on me. But I have discovered a wonderful new creation. Those circular flavored candy containers with flowers painted on the top are just the right size for my diaphragm. I just cut out a piece of felt for the bottom to absorb the moisture and no one can tell that my mint candy box contains my diaphragm.

Some women did not like having the contraceptive cream slowly drip out of them over a period of a couple of days. One woman suggested the following way of feeling cleaner.

Marie (thirty-three) says:

I use a Norform, which is a douching solution that's in a suppository form. I just push it up with my finger as far as it can go. Then my body heat melts the suppository and releases the douche, which cleans me out. I carry a Norform in my purse to clean myself out if I use a diaphragm with spermicidal gel or cream. If I have intercourse repeatedly, I find I have an accumulation of cream inside from the spermicide and I start to get infections. So I usually just douche with water to clean myself out. But if I'm traveling, it's bulky to take a whole douching outfit with me, so Norforms are easier to travel with. However, it is always important to wait six to eight hours after intercourse before using a suppository to ensure that the Norforms do not interfere with the effect of the spermicide.

Common health problems are not usually a cause for alarm, but can create physical discomfort in a sexual relationship. Intercourse is no fun in the midst of an irritating or painful vaginal or bladder infection. Water retention prior to menstruation or menstrual cramps can interfere as well. The women we interviewed had developed their own personal solutions to these and other common problems.

Vaginal Infections

The vagina has natural secretions that are perfectly normal and healthy and, unless they are accompanied by itching, odor, or pelvic pain, there is no cause for concern. Consequently, under normal circumstances, douching is not necessary and can actually even cause vaginal infections. Stress and excessive irritation of the vagina can also cause vaginal infections:

I have found that douching has been a real no-no for me, says thirty-five-year-old Roberta. I had an infection once for about two years and I was douching every day with vinegar and water as my doctor had told me to do. I wasn't getting anywhere at all, so I went to another doctor. He told me that I shouldn't douche at all because it washes out all of the flora of the vagina and changes the natural pH of the vagina, that any of the douche products you buy over the counter in the drugstore are no good either, because they alter the natural pH of the vagina, which is specifically designed to prevent overgrowth of bacteria or yeast. This pH can be altered by your period or pregnancy or stress. I realized that during this past two years I was undergoing a great amount of stress and that my pH was constantly altered. I realize now that if I'm under stress the first place it will show up is in my vagina, and I'll come down with another yeast infection. I've also found that if I don't use enough lubrication like saliva or mineral oil on my genitals when I have intercourse, I invariably come down with a vaginal infection. My tissues are very, very sensitive, and I've got to be very careful that I have adequate lubrication.

Vaginal infections can also be caused by constantly keeping a diaphragm (or a tampon) inside, because natural secretions are not allowed to drain, causing the bacteria to become overgrown.

Women who commonly encountered yeast infections recommended eating yogurt daily or occasionally douching with it (the bacteria in the yogurt seem to supply or replenish the growth of bacteria which fight vaginal infections). They also suggested using Albolene cream, K-Y jelly, or baby oil to ensure sufficient lubrication during intercourse or periodic baking soda douches as preventives. As one older woman said:

If I'm not having any problems, I don't need to wash after sex. If I'm on the verge of some kind of vaginal infection, I'll frequently want to wash right after I've had sex. I don't douche ordinarily. I just wash. Every so often, I douche with baking soda. It keeps yeast infections down and helps with odors. I use about ½ teaspoon of baking soda to about a glass of warm water in a little douche bag. Even though I don't have periods anymore, when I did, it was especially nice at the tail end of my period when everything was sort of yucky. It's good for clearing out all the rest of that stuff and it keeps vaginal infections down enormously.

Once a yeast infection was actually contracted, plain yogurt was again suggested. This time, however, douching with yogurt or inserting a tampon in the vagina with its tip drenched in yogurt was recommended, in addition to eating yogurt. Vitamin E oil was recommended to relieve itching and to soothe irritated tissues that are common side effects of vaginitis. Vinegar or boric acid douches are recommended for fighting hemophilis or trichomoniasis, two other very common vaginal infections. It is also not advisable to wear tight pants, nylon pantyhose, or nylon panties when a vaginal infection is present.

Bladder Infections

Intercourse can irritate the bladder and cause bladder infections, or cystitis. One commonly used preventive is urinating immediately before and immediately after intercourse. Elaine, a medical professional, has another suggestion for preventing or alleviating bladder infections:

People who use a diaphragm tend to have more bladder infections because the diaphragm puts pressure on the urethra. So it's important to drink lots of cranberry juice so your bladder has the right kind of pH. Things that aggravate bladder infections are coffee, tea, chocolate, spicy foods, and alcoholic beverages. And any time women are going out drinking, I tell them they should drink cranberry juice and vodka as opposed to a regular drink. Then they're countering one with the other.

Women who are confined to a wheelchair constantly have to deal with bladder infections. Jill, a thirty-four-year-old unmarried teacher who has been confined to a wheelchair for sixteen years, has minimized this problem:

Women who are sitting all the time like someone in a wheelchair or someone who is arthritic often have smaller vaginas and increased infections because they are not getting much circulation of air in the vagina. If you have a sanitary napkin on all the time, you're setting up the same situation. You see I am forced to wear a sanitary napkin for drainage, even though I am not catheterized. So it's important for me to remember to remove it periodically to aerate the vagina. It is very easy for a person in a wheelchair to have urinary tract infections. I've been in a wheelchair now for sixteen years and I've never had a urinary tract infection because, as I've said, I periodically remove the sanitary napkin and I also wash with mild soap and water after I urinate. I also swim a lot, which helps aerate the vagina and keep it clean.

Menstrual Discomfort

Some women retain fluid prior to menstruation and find this very uncomfortable. Reducing salt intake or anything which contains sodium (diet sodas for example) can reduce fluid retention. Alexandra (thirty-five) found a diuretic to be very useful in this situation:

Sometimes around my period, my nipples get really sore and I take diuretics to release the water. That way they don't get so engorged.

A couple of suggestions were made for relieving menstrual cramps. A common one was to have an orgasm:

When I'm first getting my period and feeling bloated and uncomfortable the best thing is to have an orgasm. If my husband wants sex, then we have it. I may not be feeling like it at the moment, but I know that the orgasm is going to alleviate the cramps.

Another suggestion was to take fifty milligrams of Vitamin B₆ per day. Alexandra took vitamin B-complex throughout the month. She felt it helped alleviate her menstrual cramps and depression and curtailed a premenstrual hungering for sweets. She cautioned however that it takes a few months before the effects are noticed.

Venereal Disease

Women who related sexually to more than one partner at a time were understandably concerned about contracting a venereal disease. Syphilis, gonorrhea, and herpes were the infections mentioned most frequently. All three are communicable. Treated effectively, syphilis and gonorrhea can be cured, although some strains of gonorrhea are highly resistant to the antibiotics used to treat them. Herpes, on the other hand, has no known cure. There are two types of herpes: both look like a blister or cold sore and one is found on the mouth and the other forms on the genitals. However, recently, the type of herpes found on the genitals has also been found on the mouth and hence can be transmitted through oral sex. Lesbians, who do not normally have to deal with the usual venereal diseases, are now finding herpes a problem. Once communicated, herpes infection can recur whenever the man or woman is under stress. In general, women suggested abstaining from sex when they felt a herpes blister beginning. Alexandra, had this recurring problem for quite some time and created this inventive solution which worked for her:

We couldn't have sex because the herpes was so painful. We had both been wanting each other so badly and here I had this herpes plus a cold and I felt horrible, embarrassed, and humiliated. Basically my partner was very understanding and warm and affectionate. What ended up happening was that we had anal intercourse. That was the first time that I really enjoyed it, I mean *really* enjoyed it. Not only did we have it that one time, but as soon as we finished, we looked at each other and said, "Well, I guess we're a little perverted," and did it again. We continued to enjoy it until everything went back to normal and I was able to have vaginal intercourse again, but it was like we had this secret. He told me he thought I was extremely lucky because I had two cunts, and he said that's why God made anuses—in case something went wrong with the first one, then you had the second one.

One way to protect yourself against venereal disease is to use condoms. To help make condoms more fun, one woman suggested the following:

Shop around and find rubbers you like. Get lots of different kinds in small amounts, like three or four to a package, which is cheaper Take them out and try them on your finger to see how it feels and how you like it. Try the colored kinds or a French tickler for variety. Your partner will think you're kinky. I test mine by filling them full of water to make sure there are no leaks.

Pain

Health problems that result in pain interfere with sexual enjoyment. Pain experienced in any part of the body can have a detrimental effect on sex.

Pain during intercourse was found to be a fairly common problem for women. It was sometimes experienced during deep thrusting in certain positions and at certain times during the menstrual cycle, particularly during ovulation. Women found that limiting themselves to a few comfortable intercourse positions was a way to solve this difficulty. Allison (thirty-five, divorced):

Sometimes when I'm ovulating, I'll feel a pain during intercourse on one side of my ovaries. I tell my partner that it hurts so he doesn't go in as deep as usual. Then I turn my hips a little bit and he goes in at a different angle, and I don't have any pain.

Having an orgasm was suggested as offering relief from bodily pain as well as for menstrual cramps.

Olive, age thirty-five, a student living with Ben, a salesman, and her two children, explained:

I have degenerative arthritis of the cervical spine. It means I have pretty chronic pain, a lot of muscle spasms, and some limitation in the use of my right arm. I can't lift heavy things like I used to. I can't turn my head in both directions as far. Having orgasms and masturbating really helps me control the pain. I heard something on the radio that said when you're sexually aroused and when you're orgasmic, your body actually secretes a certain substance which is like cortisone and has a direct chemical effect on the pain. I never really conceived of it that way. I think, for one thing, sexual arousal is a distraction. I really get into feeling sexual and I don't concentrate on the pain as much. My right hand is the one that's most affected, and if that really hurts, I might use the vibrator to masturbate. The relaxation and release of orgasm is very helpful for me. It really helps the kind of muscle spasms that I have. And I find it really easy to sleep a lot of times when I might otherwise be very tense and in a lot of pain. It's a nice way to be good to yourself when you hurt.

However, in order to get to the point of orgasm, a blocking out or reduction of pain is required. Katherine suggests self-hypnosis for relief of lower back pain which in turn enabled her to be more sexually available:

I decided to try hypnosis for some relief from the pain, which was very helpful. I worked with a hypnotist for only three sessions. The first time was an interview, the second a demonstration of how to hypnotize myself and the third time was to make sure I got it right.

I used the hypnosis to block pain. I would put myself into a light trance and would picture myself turning off a water tap; turning it all the way off so that there was not even a drop coming out of the faucet. That water represented my pain and when I turned the water tap off, I turned the pain in my back off.

Surgery

Quite a few women we interviewed had had a hysterectomy. Although a hysterectomy does not have to affect a woman's sex life, many women reported positive as well as negative effects of their hysterectomy. Although most of the effects were psychological and emotional, some were physiologically based. The majority of the women reported that the hysterectomy had had a positive effect on their sexuality. As one woman put it:

I knew I couldn't get pregnant, and so in a way I felt freer sexually. I guess I feel I can do what I want anytime and I don't have to worry about it.

Penelope (forty-six):

I had a hysterectomy and that had a tremendous effect on my sexuality. It was similar to women who talk about not feeling good on the pill and not even being aware of it until they go off the pill, and feel so much better. I am so aware now of how much more open I am to sexual feelings than I was with the diaphragm. If I wake up in the middle of the night and I'm feeling sexual, there's no hesitation about having sex. So our frequency has gone way up. It seems to me as though my staying power with pleasure is longer now too. I don't get so concerned about conserving energy for that last orgasm. I always seem to have it. On the other hand, my orgasms are different now than before when I still had my uterus. They're not as good. I liked my uterus. I got a lot of sexual pleasure out of it since I always felt my uterus and my cervix during my orgasms. In fact, my favorite way to orgasm was for Harold to stay still with his penis stationary while I contracted around it. And part of the pleasure was having my cervix come down and ride back and forth over the top of the penis as I contracted around it. Now the orgasms are much freer than before, but that quality is missing with the uterus and cervix gone.

The women who felt that the hysterectomy had had a negative effect on their sexuality responded primarily to their physician's lack of preparation and sensitivity as well as to the trauma of the operation itself. Consequently, a few women strongly recommended that a physician be picked carefully and that several medical opinions be obtained before deciding on surgery. Rosalind (thirty-five):

I think it would be helpful for anyone to have a female gynecologist. That's not to say that there aren't any good male doctors. But I think one has to be able to sit down and figure out what their requirements are for a good doctor. For me, it was easier to relate to women, particularly the female gynecologist I chose, because she was so comfortable with everything, including sexuality. She was very easy to talk to.

Another important thing is to get several opinions before making a major medical decision. When you're faced with traumatic issues, like a hysterectomy, as I was, it's very hard to be that assertive. I felt so vulnerable and devastated at that time. I needed someone to help me. Fortunately, a friend who's a doctor told me to get another consult. He was emphatic and said, "Don't take what one doctor says as the law, not when it affects your body and your life. Get some other consultations." That never crossed my mind. I didn't feel I had the energy or the strength or the right to get another doctor's opinion.

After the surgery, because of the need for sexual contact and the inability to have intercourse, many women's feelings resembled those of women who had just delivered babies. For some, the need for sexual intimacy and contact at that point was great. Judith (forty):

I had a hysterectomy last April and we were told by our doctor not to have sex for a certain period of time. But the experience of being in the hospital for eight days was very isolating and impersonal. Having strangers do very personal things to your body was very alienating, so when I came home I wanted sexual contact with my husband Nathan.

It wasn't so much that I wanted an orgasm, but rather that I wanted the contact, the communication, the feeling of concern from him to sort of rejuvenate myself. So we started to have sex but were very careful not to have any intercourse. It wasn't a nightly thing, but it was enough for me to make the contact, and to be satisfied with the bodily comfort, the touching and sensuality. I either had him hold me while I masturbated or we masturbated together. We found that we can have orgasms together when we're both masturbating. The timing, somehow or another, is synchronized, so it worked out well.

Evidently the uterus has contractions of its own when you have an orgasm and initially my orgasms felt diminished. They weren't gone, but there was less sensation. When you have an incision, the whole area is sensitive and not real amenable to the kind of movement you make when you're approaching an orgasm, but once the healing took place, I didn't notice any difference. Since I was still sore, rear entry with me on my side was the only position that was feasible, as I didn't have to support my weight that way. I also used a vibrator by myself and with Nathan, which made it much easier for me to be aroused. You see, there was a whole dampening of my sexuality as a result of my hysterectomy. I felt that my body had betrayed me in some way. It had tried to kill me by bleeding to death, so I had a lot of anger, resentment, and bad feelings about my body. It was especially hard for me because I had been very healthy before all this started.

Another thing that made having a hysterectomy harder for me was my age. I felt like I was going over the hill at forty anyway, and then to have them cut out all my parts! I felt like I wasn't going to be a woman anymore, at least not a real woman. I had a lot of fears and a tremendous sense of loss.

What really helped was the fact that Nathan never withdrew, never pulled away his emotional support. He didn't act as if he found me any less attractive, and was extremely supportive of everything I was going through. It was reassuring to realize that his caring for me didn't depend on my looking beautiful or attractive all the time and that he was still turned on to me.

The sexual techniques used to resume sex after a hysterectomy resembled those that helped women resume sex after childbirth. Bernice (age sixty-seven):

After the operation, if I couldn't have intercourse I would bring my husband to a climax by masturbating him. I might start orally, and then finish manually. Once after his prostate operation, he got an infection and was ill for months. Then he had trouble having intercourse so he did the same for me, he masturbated me.

Ann (fifty-nine):

My husband felt I was very tight after my hysterectomy and intercourse was painful for me. I remember going to a doctor and having a thorough exam because I was worried. He inserted a number of different-sized speculums, but he told me I was normal, that my vagina was tight and that that was good and that there should be no sense of pain. And that worked for me. I really did have a sense I was injured. What reassured me was to check it out physically and find that my vagina was okay. Because I was so tight, we needed to use new positions for a long time—positions that didn't strain the vagina and make intercourse painful. Being on my side, which was never a good position for me before, was more helpful. Another good position was when we were both on our sides, facing each other. The back position, when I'm lying on my stomach and he enters from the rear, was very painful. We really had to juggle around positions and check them out. I had to be very honest with him, because the difference between pain and pleasure is a fine line. Sometimes if I was really aroused I still wanted to go ahead and have sex even though it was painful. Usually, though, I wanted to enjoy sex without the pain, and my husband was very understanding about that. Of course, we've always been imaginative about other ways of pleasuring each other without having intercourse and we still enjoy that.

In many ways, a mastectomy had a more serious negative effect on a woman's sexual feelings and self-image than a hysterectomy. Women who had had a breast removed tended to feel more obviously disfigured, whereas the hysterectomy was less visible. The change in body image often took a considerable period to overcome. Time and a loving partner were the two most important assets that helped women work through their feelings after the operation. Bernice (sixty-seven, married forty-two years):

I had a mastectomy fifteen years ago. Before that my husband and I were very free with each other sexually. I never, for instance, slept with a nightgown on. But afterward, I felt that my body was no longer attractive. I wanted to hide the fact that I only had one breast. So I started sleeping with a nightgown on and continued that for about two or three years. That felt like a rejection to my husband. He was concerned about me and would ask, "What's the matter?" Actually my husband was marvelous about the whole thing. He never in any way indicated that he thought I was marred. It apparently didn't make any difference to him. I was the one who had those feelings. I was also able to talk to my husband about the mastectomy, about my anger and my fears. You know, things like, "Why did this have to happen to me? Why did I have to get cancer?"

It took me years to get over the horror of having a breast cut off. But over time and with the support of my husband, I just started feeling better. Now I can laugh about it. After all, I'm like a tic, tac, toe board —a Cesarean, a hysterectomy, a mastectomy. It just doesn't bother me anymore.

Seventy-two-year-old Glenn describes how she handled the physically and psychologically scarring effects of her bilateral mastectomy without letting it interfere with her sexual life:

I first developed a breast cancer when I was just under fifty. Five years later I had to have my other breast removed. This had been a difficult thing to accept as far as my own sexuality because at the time, the operation was a very, very deforming sort of thing. I had horrible scars, not only on the front of me, but also holes under my arms, because my muscles and lymph glands were taken out, leaving my upper arms flabby and one arm larger than the other. I had a fairly respectable figure before that so the operations were pretty hard on me. The way I've dealt with that is that I have always explained to a sexual partner that I have had a bilateral mastectomy and that I am sensitive about it. While I didn't object to being in the nude, I did object to exposing battle scars, so to speak, so if he didn't mind too much, I was going to keep my bra on. I've kept my bra on with everybody that I have had sex with since. I always wear a bra, even at night when I'm by myself. I don't like to look at myself without one. I was obviously more comfortable sexually before I lost my breasts, but on the other hand, it has worked out that I don't feel that the mastectomy has interfered tremendously and I don't feel embarrassed about it.

Recently, I was on a cruise and had met an officer on the ship whom I liked. We went out to dinner at port and then went out for a walk along the docks. All of a sudden he just turned around, put his arms around me, and said, "Are we going back to my cabin on the ship or are we going to take a hotel room somewhere?" This was the first time the idea of sex had been mentioned between the two of us. Somehow it seemed like a perfectly natural and normal sort of thing. He and I had been seeing each other for a while and it was just a normal outgrowth of the relationship that had arisen between us. So I said, "Let's go back to the ship."

I ordinarily wear a one-piece foundation, and when I go to bed at night, I have just a bra which I wear, so I stopped by my own room and picked up the bra. Then we went to his room. He was so very, very thoughtful about the fact of my not having breasts. He said, "Would you like me to go out of the room while you undress?" And, of course, this gave me a chance to get my disfigurement covered up so that I was not embarrassed about this. I got out of the one-piece foundation and I got into the bra. He was so exceedingly gentle and thoughtful about seeing that I was comfortable about this.

I enjoyed our lovemaking because he was aggressive sexually without being rough, and while he was being satisfied himself, he was very careful to see that I was going to be satisfied too. It is just one of the experiences I'll never forget.

Since we are trained at such a young age that beauty is of paramount importance for a female, many women undergo traumatic repercussions when they experience any physical disfigurement which includes scars from injuries or operations. Once a woman was able to allow herself to be seen by a sexual partner after such an operation, she was already en route to overcoming her embarrassment.

Sonya (forty) describes how she learned to overcome the negative feelings about her body after a serious heart ailment:

Four years ago I had open-heart surgery. I had led a full, active life up to that time. The operation itself was a very traumatic experience. I very nearly died before the operation, during the operation, and after the experience. Once I knew I was going to survive and was on the road to recovery, I made a conscious decision that I was going to live as full and normal a life as possible. That decision included a full, active sexual life, but there were a couple of things that I had to cope with in that regard. One was my concern about my physical appearance. I have a scar that goes from my neck to my navel and I was worried that every man I met would think of me as a freak of some kind. But I have found that the scar has never made a difference to any man—without exception! Not one man has ever found me unattractive. Secondly my heart beats arrhythmically, so sometimes when I have exerted myself too much, my heart beats very loudly and noticeably. I have learned to relax and cope with that. What I think has really made the difference has been my attitude. I have an attitude of health. I know I have a serious health problem that's an ongoing chronic problem, but I choose consciously to live a healthy, normal life. And it's working. It might be that my attitude is why my scars haven't made a difference to my partners. It might be that because I have a lot of zest and spunk and enjoy life so much, they see me rather than my scar.

Physical Disabilities

Women who are disabled are limited sexually by their physical capabilities as well as by society's view of them as asexual beings. If the disability began at birth or early childhood, a woman often grew up with feelings that although boy friends and romantic crushes might be a viable alternative for other girls her age, she was somehow out of the running. Her treatment by physicians as an object, a clinical case, taught her to view her body as something alien. She was also generally overprotected by her parents. Twenty-seven-year-old Lorraine, who is single and disabled with cerebral palsy, is also a peer counselor for the disabled, and describes some of these feelings, so commonly experienced by the physically handicapped:

I have cerebral palsy, which is due to a birth injury. From age two to seventeen I wore leg braces from the waist down and went to physical therapy. That had a lot of negative effects on my self-esteem, particularly as it related to my body and my sexuality. To this day, touching is an issue with me because in the medical treatment and twenty years of physical therapy, I was often publicly displayed in front of medical people and other hospital personnel. The touching I got from these people was very clinical. When people touched me—physical therapists, doctors, nurses—it was always for diagnosis. For instance, during a neurological exam, they would ask, "Is this sharp or dull? Is this hot or cold?" Not, "How does this feel? How are you feeling?" People took a lot of license with my body in how they treated it and I didn't feel that I had the right somehow to claim my body as part of myself and say, "Wait a minute, you're dealing with me here." I think an adult in that situation might well have been able to say that, but growing up in the situation I felt that that's the way things were. Also I had this notion that it wasn't my place to say anything.

I dealt with my feelings of embarrassment and feelings of being just an object by detaching myself mentally from what was going on. As a teen-ager I became more and more aware of my appearance and felt worse and worse about it. I struggled with learning to walk and dragging my heavy braces around. I tried to ignore whatever bodily impulses I got, particularly sexual ones.

As a young child I remember being aware of genital sensations and not really masturbating because I didn't know what that was. I remember being aware of the muscles inside my vagina and feeling pleasure in squeezing them. I did not know that was a sexual feeling. I did not connect that with sex at all. My parents told me about the biology of sex, and reproduction but I also picked up a subtle message from my family that sex wasn't for me because I was handicapped. That message didn't come just from them; it came from the whole society. I just didn't think that anybody would find me desirable or attractive. When I was in high school and began having crushes, I felt I wasn't supposed to have those feelings. I saw other people my age having them and that was okay, but I wasn't supposed to feel them because I wasn't like other people.

The thing that helped me the most was to get away from home and have some privacy. I didn't really have that much privacy at home even to masturbate. Getting an apartment and coping with being by myself was a big turning point. I also met a woman who became a close friend. Making new friends and living on my own really bolstered my self-esteem and helped me develop more positive social skills. And that gave me the confidence to start dating and exploring sexual relationships.

If a handicapped woman is determined enough to fight society's stereotypes and seek out sexual partners, she finds her field of interested partners rather limited. If she is confined to a wheelchair, mobility is a problem and moving from the wheelchair to a couch or bed can be quite awkward, particularly during the initial experiences with a new partner. When in bed, her mobility might be limited, resulting in difficulty with certain positions or in changing positions. Lorraine shares how she handles this problem:

My hip is very stiff. The joint is getting very worn and that means that certain sexual positions are painful. It's not that I can't move, but rather that movement is painful. My handicap has also limited how wide I can open my legs. It's not only getting into positions but also moving around in a small space which is awkward.

If you're dealing with so many things like trying to move around, trying to have intercourse and at the same time trying to stimulate your partner, the man might lose his erection in the process. Then you both have to work at getting excited again. It's more like you have to make pardons and laugh, and feel okay, and be relaxed about it. Occasionally, in moving around, I have poked somebody in the eye with my elbow, because I have to support myself on my arms when I move around. My legs don't take weight as easily, so my mobility is quite awkward and I feel self-conscious, but not nearly as much as I did. When I'm with people for whom physical appearance is an issue, I can feel self-conscious, but I've gotten to the point where I realize that's their problem. They've got a real narrow definition of what beauty is about and I've learned to go beyond that. I may occasionally feel that "Gee, I wish I looked like so and so," but usually I think I'm a very attractive person. It's only when I'm feeling awkward that I wish I was athletic or beautiful like whomever, but other than feeling like a klutz, I don't beat myself with it anymore.

Lydia, a twenty-one-year-old single student who lives with roommates, explains the factors necessary to make a sexual experience a good one for her:

I'm a spinal-cord-injured quadriplegic as the result of a diving accident when I was fourteen years old. Because of my disability, I can't move around and I have to be very specific about the types of positioning that I need and like. So I have to ask for that. I have to ask my partner to move in certain ways or to put me in certain positions so I can touch him or be able to hold him or just so I'm more comfortable on the bed. I also have to talk about the sensations in the different parts of my body. I have total sensations or partial sensations in certain areas and I have to be very specific about them and explain how my body works—what I feel and what I don't feel and what feels good to me and what type of sensation is likely to cause some kind of complications. Like, I don't like direct clitoral stimulation. What happens is that I get a kind of dysreflexia, where my blood pressure gets really high and I start having severe spasms throughout my abdomen which are really uncomfortable for me. So, with genital stimulation I like less direct stimulation like penetration and having the lips of my vagina rubbed.

I was taught that I was paralyzed and that I didn't have sensations, because when people stuck pins into me, I didn't feel it. I believed that for a while, and then I began thinking that there is a lot more to the body than getting pinched, you know. I became aware of feeling pressure and being aware of feeling hot and cold in my body and just becoming a lot more aware of my body sensations and what my body felt like. I began relearning the old sensations and noticing new sensations that were different from what I had before instead of believing that I didn't have any sensations at all. I have been really surprised by the different things that would turn me on. I had an experience where my inner arms were being stroked and it was really pleasurable! I had never thought about the inside of my arms before and it just really surprised me. It made me think about other parts of my body, too, that I wouldn't necessarily consider as being sexual.

It is common for women with certain disabilities to have inadequate control over urination and defecation. Hence, bladder and bowel control is often of concern. Jill, who is disabled with multiple sclerosis and is in a wheelchair, is not catheterized. She handles bladder and bowel problems mostly through control of her liquid and solid food intake:

The first thing I do is to let my partner know that urinary incontinence might occur and that he should be aware of it. I try to prevent that by not drinking a lot of liquids before having sex. I have to drink liquids fairly constantly; otherwise I'd shrink my bladder and that would create more complications. That's a very easy thing for people in wheelchairs to do. So I just watch how much liquid I drink just before having sex and I also try to urinate immediately before sex. I also suggest that we both take a bath before fooling around. That is fun by itself and then I'm sure there isn't any urine odor.

The whole issue of fecal incontinence during sex is also a problem and I try to control that by watching how much or what foods I eat.

That way I'm able to modify some potential complications. For example, I would not eat a high-roughage diet just before I had intercourse because the roughage would tend to go right through me. Bread, rice, bananas, meat, and chicken, for example, digest more slowly. However, each person needs to figure out what foods digest more slowly than others for them.

Lydia, who is catheterized, finds that the catheter doesn't interfere with sex if she tapes it to her body:

I have a catheter, but it doesn't get in the way of intercourse or masturbation. I tape it to my side so I don't have to worry about it being pulled. Otherwise, I'm afraid it might get pulled out or jerked out, but it hasn't been a problem. Also, that way I don't get irritated from any rubbing on it during intercourse.

I've rarely had any problem with bowels, either. One time I had an accident during sex. But it only happened once and it was with somebody I felt really safe with, really secure, so it was kind of hilarious, actually. I had heard about it happening to other people but I never thought it would happen to me. So, I always like to let people know ahead of time that there is always the potential for the catheter to be pulled out or for me to have some type of bowel accident. So, if it did happen, my partner would be prepared for it.

Some medical problems can result in malfunctioning or removal of the intestine. These women may be required to wear a bag that fills with waste matter. Thirty-five-year-old Maggie, a university faculty member who is single and living with her boy friend, had an ileostomy as a result of ulcerative colitis:

Nine and a half years ago, I had an ileostomy and since that time the focus for me has been dealing with having this bag for the rest of my life. I've struggled with incorporating that into my image of myself in a positive way and not feeling that the ileostomy is all that defines me.

Sexually it has caused several problems. One is an actual logistical problem caused by the fact that I have this bag there. When I am close to somebody, it's between us and it flops around because it's connected in one place but hangs down four inches. I'm always very aware of it and always have to make sure it's in the right position, otherwise it's going to get in the way. There's a clip on the end of it, which is the opening. Every once in a while my pubic hair or the man's gets caught in the clip, although that doesn't happen very often. The other thing logistically is that it is possible for it to come off with vigorous sexual lovemaking. That has happened maybe three or four times, which is not much in ten years, but the possibility of its happening is always there, so I'm very aware of this and frequently check with my hand just to make sure it's not gotten loose and come off. I used to wear a belt to keep it on but the belt would come loose from moving around during sex. Now I have tape around the clip which is better. The tape is called Nu-Hope and is made by Nu-Hope Laboratories in Los Angeles. It's called extra-wide adhering tape strips, and it goes right around where the bag is actually glued to my body. It has helped in the sense that even if the bag loosens a little bit, it will stay on for at least some time before the waste matter starts seeping out around the edges, which is the part that gets really embarrassing and problematic.

The other difficulty sexually is that I don't have any control of when the bag fills up. When the bag is empty it's flat against my body so somebody can lay on top of me and it's not awkward. But it can fill up either with gas or with fluid or waste matter in a very short period of time, and I don't have any control over that. That means I have to get out of bed and go to the bathroom. So before I go to bed with somebody, I go to the bathroom first to empty it. I have learned over the years to anticipate when it is going to fill up; like going to bed with somebody right after I've eaten is not a good idea. The only thing I can really do is just go to the bathroom immediately before I go to bed and if I wake up in the middle of the night, and want to have some kind of sexual contact, I generally have to get up and go to the bathroom first. I can never go for eight—or even six—hours without emptying it.

Another logistical problem is that the ileostomy has definitely changed how I deal with people sexually since I can never go to bed easily with somebody for the first time. I have to first have a serious conversation. There is no way for it to be just a quick fuck or anything like that. Sometime very early on I decided for my own protection that I would never go to bed with somebody if I had just told them I had an ileostomy. I would tell them and then see them again before I would have sex with them. That way, I would be sure they would not be carried away by the passions of the moment, and then be really repulsed by it. I wanted to give them time to think about it and deal with it before I made myself vulnerable. One of the problems with this approach is that many of the people I went out with didn't feel comfortable saying that they were bothered about it. I also got to the point where when I was telling them about it I would show it to them so that they would have seen it before we went to bed. I would tell them some of the problems with it in terms of screwing, that it is possible it will come off. This was during the period when I was really starting to explore my sexuality and needed to feel freer. The ileostomy always made things very serious and so it was difficult.

Some degenerating diseases, such as multiple sclerosis, often result in a lessened ability to experience orgasm. Sometimes a vibrator can assist in this situation, but perhaps even more important is a change in attitude about the objective of sex.

Jill, who has been confined to a wheelchair for sixteen years due to multiple sclerosis, describes the approach that makes sex most meaningful and enjoyable for her:

Sometimes it takes longer to come and I need more stimulation or it might not be possible to orgasm at all. But I love a lot of kissing. I try to remember that the enjoyment of the lovemaking comes from my partner too, not just from me. I try to enjoy what I do have by focusing on areas of my body that are still sensitive. We usually think of the genitals as being erotic, so that's what's usually stimulated. Actually there are many other areas of my body that are sensitive and seem to become more erotic the more attention they receive. The biggest thing, however, is that I don't play an orgasm trip on myself. My partner and I just enjoying loving each other—enjoying the lovemaking is what counts. It doesn't have to be orgasm all the time. Lovemaking is more than just orgasm. It's enjoying the lovemaking; the comforting, nurturing, loving, and stroking. Just the touching and cuddling is magnificent.

It seems fairly clear that women managed to find solutions to problems that infringed on their enjoyment of sex and to make even the most adverse circumstances workable if they were sufficiently motivated. Since our sample of women with serious physical problems is quite limited, we have presented only a fraction of the solutions available. Our hope is that the ones we have chosen will give you some new ideas about ways to approach your particular situation, thereby making you aware of more options than you might have thought possible in the past. But even now, you might feel that your situation is so unique and so unusual that nothing you have read relates to it sufficiently to be of use. This may be true. On the other hand, consider the following two possibilities as well. The first is that you really feel the problem lies within your partner and that it is necessary for your partner to change in order for the problem to be solved. If this is your only solution, we would like you to recognize that your chances for change are slim. It is very difficult to make someone else change. A person changes only because he or she is sufficiently uncomfortable with the status quo that they are willing to go through the discomfort and anxiety of trying something new. Consequently, in this case, you may be putting all of your hopes on your partner's acting or being different. You may not be doing anything sufficiently different yourself to bring about a new outcome, or you might be rejecting those things you could do because of the discomfort they might create for you.

If your partner is not the problem, then we recommend that you look to see if the problem you are experiencing is serving any positive function. This is the second most frequent reason someone is unable to find a solution to a sexual difficulty. In this case, it is easier to live with the problem than it would be to deal with the repercussions of solving it. For example, a woman might not be turned on to sex and no matter how hard she or her partner tries, she still feels asexual. What may actually be operating is that not feeling aroused is a way for her to say no to sex. If she were turned on, her fear might be that her husband would have such a high sex drive she would be having sex all the time. Another woman found that being turned off was a way to maintain some distance between herself and her partner. By being turned off she could control her fear of the kind of intimacy that could result if their sexual relationship were too close. In both of these cases, the fears were unconscious and required some professional help to make the dynamics conscious. Once that happened, the women could explore their fears and decide what changes they wanted to make in their relationships. We recommend first trying to get in touch with the unconscious material yourself by trying to see what negative repercussions might result if your sexual problem were solved, and second discussing these fears with your partner. If you are unable to identify these unconscious fears, and you have been unsuccessful in trying to resolve the problem on your own, outside help in the form of counseling or therapy may prove useful.

7

Being Pregnant and Being Sexual

Although you can't have children without sex,* once the couple
has become pregnant, the issue of sexuality is forced underground,
almost as if the two had no connection. However, pregnancy and
childbirth have a tremendous effect on both the woman's own sexual feelings and her sexual relationship with her partner. Yet very
little information is currently available on how pregnancy affects
sexuality. There are few books to read, fewer movies to see, and
even most doctors are unlikely to have much information on the
subject. Also, like other sexual subjects, it is not one that is
discussed freely.

Almost none of the women we interviewed had ever talked to
anyone about the effects of pregnancy on their sexual feelings and
responses. Although they would often talk with their husbands,
parents, friends, and physicians about the physical changes they
were undergoing—such as morning sickness, stretch marks—and
fears of childbirth, their explicit sexual reactions to their pregnancy
were never discussed. Consequently, most women were delighted

* With the possible exceptions of artificial insemination, the Immaculate
Conception and cloning!

to finally have an opportunity to talk about these matters—and for many, the interview brought back very special memories of that time in their lives.

One reason pregnancy and sexuality is discussed so little is that if women in our society have difficulty talking about sex, pregnant women have even more difficulty. Being pregnant is seen as the antithesis of sexuality. People use phrases such as the "little mother" and "blessed one" when referring to a pregnant woman. Motherhood is viewed as a kind of holy and sanctified, almost virginal state.

The clothing manufacturers certainly don't help. Most maternity clothes are decorated with little pink and blue bows or ducks or birds or something equally asexual. If a pregnant woman walks down the street in tight pants or clothes that show off her body, she is looked at askance.

A pregnant woman is treated differently, as if she had been transformed into the madonna. One woman mentioned that before she got pregnant, she would frequently get together with her coworkers to gossip or tell racy stories. Suddenly, after she was pregnant, her coworkers would start saying things like "We shouldn't be saying this is front of the little mother" or "The baby shouldn't hear such things." What is clear is that somehow her sexuality had vanished.

In addition, very little information on sex and pregnancy has been available through professionals or other resources. Most physicians are not comfortable discussing sexuality, perhaps because most were not trained in this area. Human sexuality courses were not even taught in medical schools until recent years. And many women, like Ruth, feel uncomfortable talking to a physician, particularly a male physician, about something as personal as changes in their sexual interest or their sexual response. Consequently, few women receive any preparation for the possible changes in their sexuality as a result of the pregnancy. For example, one woman told us this story:

I asked the doctor, in a sort of roundabout way because I didn't feel comfortable with him to begin with, "Well, do women report changes sexually during their pregnancy?" I made the question sound as if it had nothing to do with me, and because of his archaic professional jargon and impersonal manner, I didn't even understand his answer.

In her eighth month of pregnancy, Judy said that there had been no mention of sexuality in her Lamaze class until just recently, when one woman asked if intercourse would hurt the baby:

The major concern of my husband (and all the other men in my Lamaze class) was that he would hurt the baby if we had sex. As soon as he was assured that that was not the case, he stopped worrying.

Without good information, myths and superstition abound. One woman was told by her psychiatrist that the sight of a pregnant woman's naked body could turn her husband off sexually and that pregnant women emit an unpleasant odor, so the best thing she could do was to undress in the dark. Consequently, she undressed in the bathroom until her husband noticed it and asked her why. When she told him, he responded by saying that it wasn't true, and although he did not find pregnancy much of a turn-on sexually, he loved looking at the changes taking place in her body. He said he really liked touching her because the baby was just as much his as it was hers, and that way he felt more involved in the pregnancy. Touching her made it feel more real to him.

Other women mentioned that they did not experience the changes they were led to expect would occur when they were pregnant, such as stronger orgasms or multiple orgasms, heightened sexual feelings, or lessened sexual interest. They had received this information through the grapevine, and when their reactions were different, many wondered what was wrong with them.

Consequently, what we have tried to do in this chapter is to pool information from sixty-one women who had been pregnant in the past and eleven other women who were either pregnant at the time of the interview, or who had delivered within the previous year. In addition, we interviewed most of the pregnant women a second time, within six months after their delivery.

GETTING PREGNANT

Getting pregnant is not necessarily the joy that most couples anticipate. After spending years conscientiously using contraception and worrying over false pregnancy scares, some couples found conceiving a very difficult task. When this was a problem, many uncomfortable emotions were stirred up as one woman explained:

> I feel dead inside. I feel like a loser. I think of Henry VIII and how he killed all his women because they didn't bear him children and all those other cultures that would throw infertile women out. And I think, I'm one of those women that would just be discarded. So I feel like a discard. It's almost like I'm breaking a covenant with God and somehow I'm disconnected, out of sync with the universe.

Not only did the women experience fear that they might never become pregnant, but they and their partners were forced to proceed with the dehumanizing process of tests and examinations to determine the source of the difficulty. In these situations, considerable strain and anxiety was often placed on their sexuality with the result of turning a previously joyful and often spontaneous event into a planned and programmed task which ended up stressing the entire sexual interaction.

Eve, a thirty-eight-year-old social worker, married sixteen years and the mother of two sons aged nine and eleven, described what this situation was like for her and how she found some ways to ease the strain:

> Our first pregnancy came after such a long time that I had almost given up and thought I was never going to be able to have a baby. We had been so programmed to time our sexuality with ovulation that intercourse became a demand rather than something we really wanted to do. Once I got pregnant, though, that pressure of "Are we going to be successful this time?" was removed and we were able to make sex a much more normal part of our relationship. That period of trying to conceive put a real strain on us. There was a period of months where we had to do things like rush the sperm to the doctor and have intercourse at planned intervals. Sex was no longer spontaneous, which was

really a problem, but having a child was very important to us; we felt willing to go through it all.

What helped us through that period was to do fun things on the spur of the moment to balance the fact that intercourse had to be so planned. We would do little things like deciding in the middle of the day that instead of going home right away after work, we'd meet and go out to dinner or maybe have a picnic. Just small things usually, but it was a way of putting some spontaneity back in our lives again.

Naomi, a thirty-three-year-old health counselor, who had been trying to get pregnant over a period of ten years, related how attending a Resolve Conference with her rabbi husband, Isaac, seemed to ease the emotional distress somewhat:

One thing that was helpful was attending a Resolve Conference, a conference which is for people who are infertile. This organization puts out information and has support groups and counselors to help you deal with being infertile. I went to their conference and sat in the audience with all these people who had the same problem. It was like coming out of the closet. It was real strange to see all these people who didn't look like lepers. I looked around at the other women and they looked pretty and I thought, "Well, it's not because I'm ugly." Men were sharing too. This one guy expressed exactly the thoughts I had had so many times about seeing rotten people with kids and wanting to snatch their kid. Everybody there at one time or another had one of those negative fantasies like wanting to kick a pregnant woman in the stomach. All of those terrible things. It was real nice to know that others had similar thoughts.

There was a clinical psychologist who was wonderful. I just sat there and cried while he was talking. He helped us understand why we used to fight a lot. Isaac would say, "What do you want from me?" And I would say, "I don't know what I want from you." But I wanted something. And he's the one who suggested just holding; he said just hold your wife. You don't need to say anything; she just needs you there for support. And once we started doing that, Isaac felt the pressure off him to do something about the fact that we couldn't conceive.

Isaac also helps me with sex when I'm trying so hard I can't relax and enjoy what's happening. This happens when I look at a calendar and it doesn't matter how I feel, but I see that today is the day I'm probably ovulating so I think I'd better get into it.

Then he says, "Okay, hey, let's not do it." Or else he's real good at just saying, "Relax, let go. Slow down. Concentrate on your own pleasure. Just take it easy. We have all night." He sort of coaches me to not try so hard and that helps.

From this conference, Naomi also learned that the following commonly believed reasons for infertility were merely myths:

There are a lot of myths around about what it takes to get pregnant and they can really affect you when you're making love. For example, right after the man comes, the semen is in a real liquid form for just a second, and the sperm immediately leave and then the semen turns into a gel. Then within just a matter of minutes it melts down again and you feel it running out. I always thought—and I don't know of anyone who hasn't thought this—that the sperm is coming out too. But the sperm's already had a chance to get on its way so you don't have to sit there and hold it in, even though I'll bet you there's 99 per cent of the medical profession out there saying, "Hold it in, stand on your head, put your legs back, because otherwise it'll all run out." Learning that was a relief. I also had this thing in my head that if I didn't have an orgasm, I wouldn't get pregnant. And so, if ever we made love and I didn't have an orgasm, I'd freak out thinking I had just lost my chance. I'd think I'd better have an orgasm—so, of course, I never had one. Isaac said, "You know, my mother had three boys and she didn't have an orgasm until she was fifty." I'd go, "Oh, yeah, I forgot." And then it was okay.

I also get real tired of people telling me to relax. Also people who say, "Don't think about it. If you want to get pregnant, you will." In one of the books I read, a doctor told this woman she was too neurotic to get pregnant. She said, "If you think I'm neurotic, you should meet my mother. And if you think she's neurotic, you should meet my grandmother!" It's real hard, when you know someone is trying to be sensitive, to say, "You're not being sensitive, in fact you're really being cruel."

EMOTIONAL CHANGES

Once a woman has become pregnant, her body undergoes tremendous physiological changes. These changes affect each woman differently. They affect not only her sexuality but her whole emotional state of being, which in turn also affects her desire for and experience of sex. Some women described a fluctuation in mood which left them feeling ecstatic one minute and depressed the next. Sue, a thirty-four-year-old housewife, married five years and the mother of two young children, said:

I experienced something in my first trimester [first three months of pregnancy] that I call "emotional salad." It felt like I was in an emotional toss-up. Little insignificant things could trigger a whole range of emotions—anger, rage, sadness, and hurt. It seemed to be a whole set of irrational feelings. Whenever that happened, of course, I had no desire for sex and I handled it by withdrawing a bit since I did not want to lay it on my husband. He was great about it because he understood what was happening, and the withdrawal only lasted for about six hours or, at the most, a day. I definitely think it was hormonal. It had the flavor of the premenstrual blues that I used to go through just before my period.

Even though I experienced this emotional salad during the first three months, generally speaking, the whole pregnancy was one big high. I loved the experience of having a baby inside of me. I was always aware of the baby, even in my sleep, because at night the baby would kick. This was an exciting sensation.

Some of the women experienced a conflict within themselves between their roles as a sexy wife and as an expectant mother. This conflict created ambivalent feelings that had to be resolved. Ruth, a thirty-three-year-old housewife, married eight years and the mother of a fourteen-month-old son, said:

Somewhere in my mind it seemed that maybe maternity and sexuality conflicted with each other, or were mutually exclusive, so I had to work that out because I still had to carry on with my sexual life anyway. I thought, how can I carry a baby and keep myself healthy and wholesome, and yet be masturbating and having sex? It seemed like my main function at the time was to be a vessel for nurturing this baby. Yet there were all these personal, sexual feelings inside of me that had nothing to do with the baby, so I knew I wasn't just a maternal being. I had to think that one through because I really wasn't sure about my role.

SEXUAL INTEREST

The scarcity of research on pregnancy and sexuality is truly amazing. However, some research shows that women tend to have less sexual intercourse as the pregnancy progresses, particularly during the last trimester when the women are more apt to be uncomfortable due to their physical size.† However, this was by no means true of every woman we interviewed.

What was most interesting about the group of women we interviewed was the diversity of their reactions to sex over the course of their pregnancies. The more women we interviewed, the greater the variety of patterns of sexual interest and disinterest emerged.

A number of the women we interviewed found sex totally unappealing during the early part of their pregnancies because they were feeling so nauseated much of the time. Rebecca, a thirty-two-year-old nutritionist, married for five years to Richard, a consultant, and eight months into her first pregnancy, said:

For the first three months I was almost always feeling nauseated. I wasn't throwing up, but I just felt like dying, like I was seasick all the time. I'd have my better moments, but most of the time I just felt awful and I think I reflected that in not only the way I was feeling inside, but also in the way I presented myself sexually to my husband. So I became less sexually appealing to Richard. Although that bothered me, I was tired a lot anyway, so when I got in bed, I just wanted to go to sleep to get rid of the nausea. At that point sex was the furthest thing from my mind.

Nell, a thirty-six-year-old teacher, married for the second time and eight months into her pregnancy, said:

Sexuality was a little eclipsed as an issue because I was sick a lot; that is, my sexual activity didn't really change, but my focus did. We're usually very active sexually, so that continued, the way eating and sleeping and walking do; but I was really focused on being sick all the time because I'd never been sick in my life and this was day-in and day-out, of just feeling rotten. It was like a flu that lasted for four months.

Betty went back thirty years and remembered that she switched her usual sexual routine to accommodate the nausea:

† A. Castellano and G. Giraldi, "Sexuality During Pregnancy," paper presented at the Third International Congress of Medical Sexology, Rome, October 25–28, 1978.

During my pregnancy I wasn't the least bit interested in intercourse whenever I had morning sickness. That was a particular problem with my first husband because our pattern was to have sex in the morning, so what we did was to shift to having sex at night.

Many of the women who were not nauseated were aware of feeling sexually turned on, but were frequently too exhausted to have sex, especially if their usual pattern was to have sex in the evening before going to sleep as in Harriet's case:

I was very tired and sleepy the first trimester and so sometimes I'd feel real sexy, but hell, by the time we were ready to make love, it was eight o'clock at night. By then I was ready to go to sleep. Sometimes we'd be just eating dinner and I'd fall asleep! It was better to get me in the morning or on weekends. So during the first trimester I mastur- bated more. Oftentimes it was two o'clock in the afternoon and I was turned on and Tom wasn't available. We were both working and by the time we'd get together, I'd just be too tired. So we didn't make love nearly as much that first trimester, but then I sort of woke up and got my energy back the second trimester and we made love a lot more.

Some of the women who were turned off early during their pregnancy gained sexual interest as the pregnancy progressed.‡ Others who were turned on initially found that their interest decreased, especially during the last weeks as their bodies became larger and less manageable. And the interest of some women, like Aruna (thirty-three-year-old mother of two sons, ages five and four months, living for six years with Philippe, a construction worker), seemed to go up and down.

The second three months I noticed a definite lowering of sexual in- terest. Our normal pattern was to make love twice a week. The second three months we made love maybe once every two weeks and then the last two months I had a heightened sense of sexuality which I thought was really interesting. Somewhere very close to the end of my preg- nancy I felt horny a lot, but I felt frustrated too because I couldn't move around more in the sexual act. I felt like a beached whale, you know?

‡ William Masters and Virginia Johnson, *Human Sexual Response* (Boston: Little, Brown, 1966).

Ruth, thirty-three, mother of a fourteen-month-old son, confided:

After the first three or four months, there was a very demarcated change in me—in fact it seemed like I just woke up one morning and felt much more sensitive and sensual. I knew that there was a definite difference in my body. In fact, I remember that at that time we went away to the Pennsylvania Dutch country for a vacation and I told my husband I was feeling almost ravenously sexual. We stayed in this Mennonite farmhouse and had great sex. The next day we were driving home and suddenly I felt I couldn't just sit there in the car any longer feeling so sexual, so we took a rest stop. We were resting in the grass and honestly, just from lying on the grass face down and pressing against the earth I had an orgasm, that's how sensual I felt!

There were other things going on beginning the fifth month that took my attention away from my sexual sensitivity, or maybe it just wasn't as marked. One thing was that I was getting bigger and sexual positions had to change. Then the feeling of my body being almost like a finely tuned instrument changed and became more, I almost want to say animal-like, but I don't know how to say it. I became very sexual in a different way in the last three months. It was more like a hunger, a bodily hunger that felt sort of ferocious. I remember having this incredible penis envy which is something I've never thought about or been conscious of before, but it was like I wanted a penis and I wanted to have the kind of sexual intensity that only a man can feel with his penis.

Monique, thirty-two, mother of a boy, five, and girl, four months:

I noticed that my sex drive decreased at some points during the three trimesters. I can't really say that about my first pregnancy, but during the second one it did that because the pregnancy itself wasn't that simple. It happened to be August, I was in my third trimester, and it was about 95 degrees. All of this made it very hard to get comfortable. The only way we could have sex was either side by side or when I was on top. The idea of even having him on top, let alone actually experiencing the weight of his body, was enough to turn me off. My sexual drive ebbed and flowed according to several factors, like fatigue and anxiety. I had a five-year-old son, we were in the middle of a major renovation in our house, and I was anxious about having another child. I was also afraid my marriage would fall apart like it did the last time I had a child, so I can't really separate out what changes in my sex drive were physiological and which were psychological because there were so many things going on in my life. I did a lot more masturbating the third trimester because I was more comfortable doing that than having intercourse and we did more mutual masturbation rather than actually having intercourse throughout the pregnancy.

There were some women who said that they were never turned on during the entire course of the pregnancy. Six years after being pregnant, Cortney recalls:

I felt very unsexual during my entire pregnancy and I was very insecure about it. Most of the people I knew and the books I had read said your sexual feelings should be heightened during pregnancy. I knew I was frightened about the pregnancy so I figured that was part of the reason I couldn't have an orgasm, but I was still concerned about what was wrong with my body. From the time I found out I was pregnant, I went for eight months without having an orgasm. My husband found pregnancy very exciting. He was at me all the time—maybe a couple of times a week—and I was so uninterested!

In her eighth month, Rebecca still hopes things will change:

Sex has run totally downhill. Every time I get a little bit aroused, I think, "Ah, it's going to start." But it never has. We really haven't made much of an effort to improve matters. It's not like I've been horny at all except for twice when I've had dreams about sex.

And there were some women like Ruth, who had never felt more turned on in their lives:

It felt like I was under the influence of a strong aphrodisiac. I wanted to know what was causing it and I wanted to know how long it would last because I was really hoping that this was now the true sexual me, that I had come into my own sexually and it was here to stay.

It was not unusual for those women who maintained sexual interest to continue having intercourse until the very last moment, as in the case of Ariel, thirty-three with a five-year-old daughter:

My doctor said we should really cool it by the end of the eighth month, but I was ready to go right on with sex right up to the day I went to the hospital. I was after my husband all the time and I just felt very secure about it. My husband went along with this partly because he was happy to see me being so sexually aggressive and also because we were going to natural childbirth classes together. He didn't get real uptight about my stomach like a lot of people do in the later months. Now by the time we were into the ninth month, he would say, "Are you really sure we should be doing this?" but it didn't bother me at all. I felt very secure and so I would say to him, "Don't worry, it's okay, the baby's really liking this! I'll tell you if it's a little too much," or something like that. I would say we made love until maybe the last two weeks.

Some women continued masturbating in the latter stages of pregnancy if their husbands were fearful of injuring the baby. Ruth, age thirty-three, son fourteen months:

A lot of masturbation went on in the last three months and right up until childbirth actually. I'm sure people picture a nine-months-pregnant woman as sort of asexual, but I wasn't at all except that my husband and I couldn't get together that much. It just didn't seem appropriate to him to have intercourse when I was so pregnant.

Nell (thirty-six, eight months pregnant):

Masturbation wasn't very important before the pregnancy. Sex with my husband usually took care of that rhythmic need for the relaxation of orgasm. Later in the pregnancy, when I started to go out to work less, and did more work at home, I found that sometimes I'd get tense and feel all these little tics, itches, and squirms. I'd be sitting at the typewriter, unable to work, and I'd think, "Gee, I wish Frank were home." I knew I needed to have an orgasm. Then I'd start worrying that maybe if I masturbated I wouldn't be receptive to him when he came home. I'd go through this big questioning process with myself, but finally in the last six weeks I decided to try masturbating. I convinced myself I wasn't going to go off and completely not need other people for sex. That's always the bugaboo that was told to me, that I'd become the equivalent of a solitary drinker. Anyway, masturbation was really helpful physiologically. I mean, of course orgasm was nice, but the best part was afterward, feeling this incredible calm like the ultimate hot bath that took away every little bit of tension.

Women who were more sexually interested attributed their increased interest to changes in their hormonal levels, feelings about not having to worry about getting pregnant—which in turn made sex more spontaneous—or feelings of increased self-confidence. Thirty-three-year-old Ariel, separated and living with her five-year-old daughter, said:

In the whole time we were married, the one period I was turned on sexually was when I was pregnant, and my husband was just thrilled! At first he was surprised and then he relaxed and enjoyed the fact that I would initiate sex with him. Whatever insecurities that make it normally hard for me to initiate sex didn't exist then. I felt terribly confident. I felt who could not want me, and of course when you feel like that, who couldn't want you? So there was a lot more sex. As a matter of fact, I think I got hornier and hornier as time went on. Part of that again had to do with all the hormones and stuff pumping through me and the baby's head pressing down, giving me additional pressure and friction down there. I think I had intensified orgasms because of that.

ORGASM AND PREGNANCY

Changes in intensity of orgasm during their pregnancy was mentioned by other women as well. In her eighth month of pregnancy, Judy said:

The only way my masturbation has changed during the last few months is that I've had more intense orgasms and I think that's physiological. I'm aware that my uterus contracts more and I find I will have to lie and rest for ten or fifteen minutes after intercourse because the contractions exhaust me and it hurts if I get up too soon.

I've been afraid at times. I'm very multiorgasmic and I have been afraid of having too many orgasms because I'm worried that too many contractions of the uterus will cause a premature birth or that too much thrusting will hurt the baby, even though I know intellectually that there is nothing going on that could be harmful. So sometimes I hold back a bit sexually and don't go as far as I would if I were not pregnant.

Some women felt the orgasm was of great importance as a way of releasing tension even though they were not often clear about whether the tension was greater due to the pregnancy or the result of other life circumstances.

Thirty-nine-year-old Ruby, an actress married eighteen years to her artist husband, and the mother of a boy, seven, and a girl, four, recalled:

In the second trimester, I was feeling okay physically, and that was a big change. I don't know whether it was really just that sexuality finally had stopped being eclipsed by feeling physically ill, but with my last pregnancy in particular, sex was very enjoyable and extremely relaxing. One of the things that happened in the last trimester is that I found myself getting tense unless I walked about two or three miles a day. I was tutoring and sometimes I would be sedentary all day and at night I would be full of a thousand little tightnesses and tensions. I did all the standard things you know, like relaxing my toes and feet, but I don't have the kind of mental control to make that work. Besides, orgasm for me is so totally relaxing that it didn't make sense to do anything else. I need that complete, overwhelming experience that leaves me in a beautifully tired, mellow, ready-to-sleep state. I don't mean to make sex wholly utilitarian, but it's absolutely true: that there's no comparison between a night of trying to sleep without having an orgasm versus having had one.

BODY IMAGE

The sexual self-image of many women was affected by the changes their bodies were undergoing during pregnancy. For some women these changes were positive, for others they were negative. Some women, like Rebecca, began to feel less and less sexual as they experienced their bodies getting larger and "fatter":

My body was changing and I saw myself getting fat—I wasn't getting fat, I was getting big, but it looked fat to me. I feel fatter than I've been in a very long time. Instead of feeling like I have this cute little stomach, I say, "Look how fat I am." And I feel very unattractive.

Rebecca helped herself somewhat to overcome these feelings by looking at nude photographs of women:

My gynecologist has several pictures of pregnant women in his office and they are really beautiful. I thought, "Well, if those pregnant bodies look really pretty, then maybe I'm not looking at my body in the same way," so then when I looked at my own body differently, it looked better to me. It was hard to accept that feeling because in books on pregnancy, you see pictures of pregnant women who aren't attractive at all because they're fat. I think they just let themselves go. There's only about twelve women in this exercise class for pregnant women that I go to that I think look okay. My stomach is nice and round and hard, so I should think mine looks better. I like it more now than I did. I feel more adjusted to it.

I think I've almost had a preoccupation with what my body will look like after I deliver. I want it to look like it did before I got pregnant and I'm not sure it ever will, and that bothers me. My stomach has always been flat and hard and I don't know what you do with all that extra skin. I'm doing a lot of abdominal exercises, which is all I can think of to do.

Joan, a thirty-one-year-old dance therapist, married nine years, was seven months pregnant at the time of the interview. She had had her husband take photographs of her in the nude to record her body's changes which also enabled her to feel better about them:

Throughout my pregnancy, my husband has been taking pictures of me in the nude. That has made us feel closer, more intimate, and has also helped me to feel good about the physical changes in my body. It's great to see the pictures and then to lay all of them down side by side and really see the changes my body has gone through. And I think being in the nude is nice too. Just walking around nude looking in the mirror at myself is fun. I think I look so much better nude than I do in clothes. The clothes cover me up and when I'm nude I can see everything bulging out. And taking the pictures makes me feel closer to my husband because we're doing it together. The whole process feels kind of erotic and helps me feel good about my body.

The majority of the women we interviewed felt good about their bodies' changes during pregnancy. Many women had sizable breasts for the first time in their lives, and, particularly in the early part of their pregnancy, before they started to "show," had a chance to experience a different and—for some—a more sexual self-image.

Jane (forty-five, two teen-age sons):

I felt very good when I got pregnant. I had a feeling of being "whole." I felt more voluptuous, more feminine, more womanly, as my breasts and my body got bigger. I felt more like Venus de Milo, like one of the Roman or Greek goddesses. Since I had been so very spare before, I was proud of how my body was blossoming. I was also really looking forward to having children.

Some women didn't really feel any sexier, but treated the changes with affection and even humor, which seemed important, particularly during the final months.

Judy, a thirty-one-year-old teacher, eight months pregnant, married two years, tells how her husband David, a rabbi, affectionately treats her pregnant belly:

It's like my tummy is another part of our sexuality. My husband makes it part of his loving me. He loves to touch it. There's also a lot of joyous teasing that goes on about it. David will come in and give me a hug as he turns sideways, like a pregnant woman does. Sometimes he'll come in the kitchen and grab me from behind deliberately around the tummy. Or he'll look at me a lot and I'll say, "What are you looking at?" He'll say, "You've got a *big tummy*."

THE PARTNER'S REACTIONS TO PREGNANCY

Not only did the women's internal feelings about the physical changes they were undergoing affect their own sense of their sexuality, but their partner's reactions affected them as well. A couple of the women discussed their husbands' negative reaction to pregnancy and their responses to that reaction.

Elaine didn't let her husband's distaste for pregnancy get in her way. She had three children and didn't seem to feel it affected their sexual activity much:

I was pregnant with my first husband, and he hated pregnant women. I was more sensual then and enjoyed being pregnant, but he made me feel very unglamorous because I was big and fat—I couldn't even tie my own shoelaces. He made little derogatory comments, but it never really bothered me that much because I just said to myself, "Look, you married me, I'm pregnant, it's your child, so now live with it." Sexwise, we had intercourse right up to the night before every one of the children was born. So I never deprived him at all, except for a couple of weeks after the first two children, when I was too sore.

For Monique, mother of a son, five, and daughter, four months, the sexual disinterest mirrored other problems:

It's very hard for me to talk about the changes in my sexual drive during my pregnancy without talking about what was going on between my husband and me, because they were integrally connected. In my first pregnancy, my marriage was shaky and, not coincidentally, my husband left after the baby was born. It was quite apparent to me during the pregnancy that he was becoming less interested in me, that he seemed more ambivalent about being married and the oncoming responsibilities of parenthood, so naturally our sex life degenerated. I noticed his withdrawal and asked him about it, but I think he felt so guilty that he couldn't really express his negative feelings about the changes in my body and the idea that he was about to become a father. The second pregnancy was very different. Our marriage was much stronger at that point and he was the one that took the initiative in wanting to have a second child. We talked much more about the physical changes in my body and his feelings about becoming a father.

On the whole, however, the large majority of the partners were not only supportive of the women during this time, but many were sexually turned on by their wife's pregnancy.

Barbara (twenty-nine, married eight years, eight months pregnant, and the mother of a girl, six, and a boy, four):

My husband likes my bigger breasts. He always says that's the gift of pregnancy, and then as my stomach has gotten bigger and bigger, he has tried to make me feel better about it.

Nell (thirty-six, eight months pregnant):

Frank was as excited about the pregnancy as I was. He really was delighted in the physical changes, which helped me delight in them too.

Thirty-eight-year-old Elaine recalled:

My second husband used more imagination sexually because my pregnancy excited him. He used more oral sex and he liked to look at my body, to just touch me. He liked me to walk around without any clothes so he could look at my stomach.

MAINTAINING INTIMACY

Given the changes which take place over this nine-month period, couples must readjust many aspects of their lives. Some of the women we interviewed had devised their own ways of creatively handling the impact of pregnancy on their sexuality.

Judy made an effort to maintain "business as usual" so as to keep the pregnancy from too greatly disrupting their life together:

If I had made more of a thing out of being pregnant, it would have rubbed off on my husband. So I made an effort not to do things any differently, not to treat him or my body differently. We just incorporated this pregnancy into our sex life. Had I gotten in bed, as lousy as I felt at times, and complained about it, we wouldn't have had any sex life. If you plant a seed that there are a lot of changes going on here and you feel different sexually, you will in fact feel different and so will he. I tried to keep things as normal as possible and although sometimes it just wasn't possible, I always made an effort. If I allowed myself to feel all my fears, they would have overpowered me. The thought of all the changes that were going on in my body and of childbirth itself was absolutely terrifying. It terrifies the "little girl" in me. It is a big undertaking and a big responsibility. If I want to make the stretch marks on my tummy ugly in my mind, they will be. My breasts changed and instead of saying, "Oh, God, they've changed," I could say, "Look how they are changing." I could do it both ways. I think that one has to keep an element of positive thinking rather than an element of negative thinking or fear. Otherwise, I'll project that negativity to my partner and destroy myself as well.

She even maintained her usual ways of turning him on—despite her changed figure:

I wear flannel nightgowns almost all the time because I'm always freezing at night. We laugh about it. He thinks it's cute. But every once in a while I'll put on something very, very sexy and he loves that. That's an instant turn-on for him. Much more so than even if I come to bed nude. I only have one now that I can still wear being so pregnant, but sometimes I'll surprise him by wearing it. It's particularly good if he has been out in the evening and he comes home and finds me like that. He really loves that.

For couples who are having very little sex due to many of the problems addressed earlier, it seems important to continue some form of intimacy through touching. Rebecca, who had not felt sexual for the entire previous eight months of her pregnancy, did the following:

We get sexual fulfillment in nonsexual ways, like sitting on the couch watching TV and just hugging and snuggling. I get fulfillment out of hugging my husband and stroking his hair in a very nonsexual way, just like you would a baby. We often hug for about five or ten minutes in the morning when we wake up. Lately, we've had more contact during the day by talking more on the phone. Taking a bath together has been something else that we've done. During my most stressful period, taking baths together helped me relax and also be with him. I would run a bath when I got home, and by the time he got home it would be ready. We would talk. Sometimes I asked him to put the oil on my stomach. That's nice because it makes me feel he's touching the baby and it's also nice to be touched and have someone massage you. It also gives us both more contact.

Harriet had a very traumatic pregnancy and, although she eventually lost the baby, continued to be intimate with her husband by doing the following:

I had to spend two months in bed lying on my left side for sixteen to eighteen hours a day to try to save this baby! That's how I got so debilitated. I had back trouble for God only knows how long after that. So we had sex mostly in bed because I was so weak and that's where I was most of the time. Sometimes I'd get up and lie on the couch or we'd lie in front of the fire, on my left side, but it usually happened in bed. Afterward, when I wasn't pregnant anymore, but wasn't ready to have intercourse because I was grieving over the loss of the baby, I masturbated him a lot. I didn't feel sexual at all, but I still felt really close to my husband so I stroked him a lot and honed my fellatio techniques to a fine edge. That was fine. I really enjoyed pleasuring him, but I wasn't into it for myself. That bothered him a little bit, but basically because we had those real close times—even though we weren't fucking, it was okay. I felt turned on in a full way, just taking care of him.

In terms of pragmatics, a number of difficulties arose during the final month because the woman's large stomach interfered with the usual ways of making love. During this part of the pregnancy, many of the couples engaged in oral and manual sex. Those who engaged in oral sex were careful not to have their partners blow air into their vagina which can cause an embolism and possibly prove fatal.

Twenty-nine-year-old Barbara (a clinical social worker, married to Steve, a physician, has a daughter, six, and son, four, and is currently eight months pregnant) said:

In the middle of my last pregnancy, I was not that big, so I could still get into many positions during sex. Sometimes I liked to have sex on top because I reach orgasm better that way, but when I reached my third trimester, I was too big and awkward to use that position. In the last month or so, it was especially difficult and also uncomfortable to have intercourse. What happened was that as I got closer to the end of my pregnancy I had more contractions, which were not comfortable. Oral sex did not seem to contract the uterus as much as intercourse did. Maybe because the weight of my partner was not pressing down on me. So we had oral sex more and masturbated more at the end.

Gweneth recalled:

We would have oral sex and lots of manual stimulation. We called it "outer sex" rather than "inner sex" and that's a good term for it. We used to call it "outercourse."

INTERCOURSE POSITIONS

Intercourse is generally considered safe up until the cervix has dilated two to three centimeters.* Women's responses about comfortable intercourse positions toward the end of their pregnancy were interesting. Almost all of the women felt that it was difficult to find comfortable positions, yet the ones they ended up using covered the whole spectrum. From the following excerpts, it seems obvious that the choice of intercourse position depended upon the

---

* However, there is ongoing debate about the safety of intercourse during the last month of pregnancy due to recent research by Richard L. Noeye ("Coitus and Associated Amniotic-Fluid Infections," *The New England Journal of Medicine,* November 29, 1979, pp. 1198–1200) which indicates increased frequency of infection in women who reported having coitus once or more weekly during the final month of pregnancy.

anatomy of the two people and the size of the pregnant stomach. In all cases, both the mother- and father-to-be were aware of choosing positions that would put the minimum of pressure on the unborn child. The most preferred positions entailed rear entry:

One position we have really used is rear entry, but with me lying on top of him on my back. That way my head is resting on his chest and I'm looking up at the ceiling.

Sue (thirty-four, mother of a boy, three, and a girl, one):

Except for the first three months, the whole pregnancy was really a sexual high. We had sex throughout the pregnancy even up to the last few weeks. Even though I got pretty big, there wasn't any problem. It was just a matter of positions. The way that worked best for us was having both of us on our sides with my husband behind me facing my back, like spoons. I had a pillow between my legs and one under my abdomen. Then when he entered me, my abdomen was supported by a pillow.

Another position that we still use is where I'm on my knees and bent over with two or three pillows under my head and my husband enters me from the rear. There's much more sensation that way for me. I almost always had an orgasm and there was no pressure on the baby at all.

Judith advocated sitting on a chair:

It's also easy sitting up on a chair. He would sit on the chair first and then I would sit on top of him facing him. My stomach didn't get in the way, either.

Other women used variations of the side-to-side position, but while facing one another.

Eve, thirty-eight, mother of two boys, nine and eleven, recalled:

We liked to be on our side facing each other, but with my husband lower on the bed so his head was level with my chest. He was kind of cupped around my belly. That way there wouldn't be much pressure on my belly, which was the main thing I was worried about. Sometimes I would be on top of him so that there wouldn't be any pressure, but I didn't find that as satisfying.

Ruby (thirty-nine, mother of a boy, seven, and a girl, four) said:

The position we used most was side by side, although as you can imagine there was a great gap between our bellies, so it was more like a "V" on our sides.

One of my legs would be under one of his legs and on top of his other one so he would be in between. Sometimes his leg would be on the bottom, then mine, then his, then mine. It was not comfortable to have both of mine in the middle. I had to have my legs separated since I couldn't get them together to begin with because of my stomach. The other position that was not quite as comfortable for me, but that we did use, was rear entry. The missionary position was not comfortable at all and my being on top didn't work either because I couldn't keep my balance.

Yet other women managed to use the missionary position and/or the woman-on-top position. To maintain the missionary position Judy's husband went to the lengths of working out at the gym to build his arms up. Elaine continued to use the female-superior position up until the end:

I didn't do much in the way of changing positions during my pregnancy. It was pretty much me on top most of the time or sideways.

When positions changed during intercourse, the man had to do most of the moving around. The women, due to their size and consequent lack of mobility, often found changing positions clumsy and awkward. But for thirty-six-year-old Nell in her last month of pregnancy, being awkward and clumsy freed her up to be more emboldened sexually:

There can't be any illusion about being a femme fatale, being so pregnant. I mean I think I look kind of funny. I'm fairly clumsy right now. Actually this has freed me up and allowed me to be more playful. It's made me realize that it's possible to look silly without it being a really scary thing, because I can laugh at myself for being so clumsy. For example, if I'm on top during sex and I fall over on the bed or fall out of position, I just think it's funny and we both laugh. I don't think I'll go back to feeling that there's a set way of being seductive. I hope I remember this emboldened behavior and if something goes awry later on, if I tumble over and fall or do the wrong thing, I can just see it as part of the humor of it. I mean, being so pregnant has been a bonus because I think it's much nicer to have a variety of ways you can feel sexually. Sometime in the future I will probably feel seductive, I guess when I'm lithe and thin again, but I'll never forget this period of being kind of klutzy.

DELIVERY

All of the women we interviewed were interested in talking about their deliveries. They had spent nine months preparing physically, mentally, emotionally, and spiritually, so each woman highlighted the event, whether it was a positive one or a negative one. For some it was wonderful, for others it was very difficult and traumatic. The negative experiences seemed to reflect either unforeseen physical complications or problems in the relationship that were not effectively dealt with.

For women in satisfying relationships, the delivery was a very intimate experience. In fact, some of the women reported that although the experience of delivery was not sexual, the intimacy of the experience was reminiscent of sexual intimacy. This was because of the depth of this shared experience. A number of women, however, experienced the delivery as a specifically sexual event.

Roberta (thirty-five, daughter ten years old):

During the whole birth process I was awake and aware of everything that was going on. It was a very exciting moment and just pushing her out was in itself very, very sensual for me. It felt like an orgasm, it really did! The pressure was what was doing it. It felt like a real sexual release, not exactly like an orgasm, but a definite release when her head came out.

Ruby (thirty-nine, boy, seven, girl, four):

It's hard for me to say that my deliveries were sexual because they were so far above and beyond any sexual experience I've ever had and I've had some good ones. I was totally transported—it was ecstasy when I delivered both times, in spite of the fact that the first time I had some difficulties. I had natural childbirth both times, too.

A piece of interesting information we found out was that women we interviewed who were in good physical condition and who had regularly practiced prenatal yoga had easy deliveries. Although this was not always the case, these particular women had short labors and felt that their bodies returned to normal unusually quickly.

Ruth, mother of a son fourteen months, recalled:

I had a very fast delivery—in fact I was lucky to get to the hospital on time. I feel it was because of the yoga I was doing. Some of the postures seemed to increase the dilation. For example, there is a kind of squatting you do in yoga where you actually work on opening up your joints and muscles, and I just felt very open. I've heard that it can lead to an easy delivery, which I certainly had. Also, my body literally sprung back into shape. I mean, one week later, I was back in my jeans that I wore during my third month of pregnancy before my body had changed at all. I know any woman who had not had this experience would resent hearing this, and I don't exactly know how it happened except that it must have been the yoga.

We had always thought that an episiotomy was a standard procedure during delivery. The medical definition of an episiotomy is "an incision of the perineum at the end of the second stage of labor to avoid laceration of the perineum."† This is done to prevent tearing of the vaginal wall as the baby's head, in particular, emerges. Apparently, a tear heals more slowly than a cut. Consequently, we were surprised when a nurse informed us that it was possible, under certain conditions, to give birth without an episiotomy and without tearing. To avoid an episiotomy, the woman and the doctor have to work very closely together. The breathing used is different from Lamaze and allows for the attending physician to massage and stretch the vaginal opening at the appropriate time. Although this is not an alternative for every woman or with every pregnancy, it is an option available to some. Giving birth without an episiotomy facilitated the process of resuming intercourse after the birth because there were no stitches which needed to heal.

Sue, thirty-four, had an episiotomy with her first child, but not her second:

† Clarence Wilbur Taber, *Taber's Cyclopedic Medical Dictionary* (Philadelphia: F. A. Davis Company, 1965).

With my second child I was very careful to pick a doctor who was open to the idea of not having an episiotomy unless it was absolutely necessary. Having one birth with and one without, I absolutely recommend not having an episiotomy, if at all possible. Without having one, I was able to get up the very same day that I gave birth and I felt fantastic. My bottom was never sore and I never had to deal with healing. Other women in the hospital who had just delivered were in incredible pain and could hardly walk. I also resumed sex in less than a month.

Delivery without an episiotomy is very different from the other way. In natural childbirth you bear down with each contraction. It's like trying to defecate a mass, like passing a watermelon. You are bearing down and pushing. When you are delivering without an episiotomy, you have to bear down and then stop in the middle of each contraction and start panting. It's like trying to stop in the middle of massive diarrhea. But if the baby's head comes out too fast, it might tear your innards. The doctor is like the director—he orchestrates when you have to stop pushing down and start panting. It's difficult to do, but it's possible.

RESUMING SEX

Resuming sex after childbirth was a traumatic experience for many couples. Very few were given any information about the healing process, but were generally just told to wait six weeks, although intercourse is generally considered safe once the bleeding has ceased, which is in approximately three weeks. They were not told that the initial intercourse experience after delivery might be painful and difficult, nor were they prepared with techniques they could use during the first few experiences to make penetration easier. Few realized that their vagina might be tighter than usual because of the episiotomy and that penetration might be painful either because of the tightness or because the stitches hadn't completely healed. The amount of time required for the healing process to be completed varied from woman to woman. Many of the women we talked with were surprised at how long it took before they were free of pain.

Eve (thirty-eight, mother of boys, nine and eleven):

I can remember a couple of times when my husband would get almost to the point of being ready for penetration and then he would go soft. I think it was because in his head he was afraid he was going to hurt me. It took some time till I fully healed and got back to normal. It really takes a lot more than six weeks till the vagina heals, even though the stitches have all been taken out. It was another two months before I felt whole and could enjoy intercourse.

Many women expected, because the man in our culture is supposed to be the expert on sex, that he would automatically know how to resume intercourse after the delivery. If he didn't do it right, he was often blamed for being inconsiderate or unloving.

Couples are frequently told to abstain from sex for six weeks prior to delivery and then six weeks after, and this means that some couples have not had intercourse for three months. If, during the pregnancy, sex has been infrequent or strained, and if there has not been good communication about these difficulties, resuming sex can be disastrous. The delayed healing, coupled with difficulties and embarrassment in communicating about sex, created a very painful experience for Susan after her first pregnancy eleven years ago:

When I went back to the doctor for my six-week checkup, he said I was not completely healed. I had been waiting that six weeks out like anything. So when I came home I told Paul and he said okay. Then we didn't make love and we didn't make love and it went on and on until I finally said, "It's been three months and we haven't made love." And he said, "I've been trying to be nice about the whole thing." And I responded, "You're breaking my heart." I could not reach out at that point and say, "I really need you." I just couldn't do it. I felt like he didn't want me. It really did bother me because the pain of the memory is still there. I'm sure he doesn't even remember that, but it was so terribly important to me. I guess all my feelings about having the new baby and being afraid that I'd feel I was only a mother and no longer a wife and lover got magnified by not making love. If I had been smart, I would have come home after the doctor finally said I was healed and made a big announcement about it, but I couldn't do that. I just wasn't feeling secure enough. Now I could do it. Now I realize he was waiting for me to say something to make sure I was okay before he would try to make love.

It is often true that the man is more interested in resuming sex than the woman. The woman may feel consumed by the "mothering" experience, particularly with the first child. She is often exhausted from the newness of her role and the concomitant insecurities. Frequently, women also experience postpartum blues because of a drop in the estrogen level following delivery. Meanwhile, the new father is feeling left out of the mothering experience and may feel neglected by his wife as well. Sometimes he interprets her lack of sexual interest or her admonitions of pain as indications that she no longer finds him desirable. As sex therapists, we find that some couples with sexual and communication problems can often trace the origins of their difficulty to resuming sex after pregnancy.

Ruby, mother of a boy, seven, and a girl, four, believes:

I think one of the reasons many women don't get back in shape sooner and don't want to make love sooner is because they are so enamored of their babies. If you wanted the baby, had a good delivery experience, and are nursing, which really bonds you with the child, you're satisfied with just your baby. I had to remember that it was my husband's baby too and he couldn't have that kind of physical experience with it. I think he needed closeness with a body that he loved and that was me. So I was glad to be able to get back into our sex life as soon as possible.

Elaine advocated oral sex during this period to satisfy her husband without putting a burden on herself:

We had never had oral sex even at that point in our relationship and I don't know if I even knew about it before then. That was back in '61, after our first child was born. I was twenty-one and very uneducated about sex. I can remember the night I first did it, the night I got home from the hospital. I gave him oral sex because I felt he was being neglected and I thought I should take care of him because we had always had lots of sex. So then when intercourse was still painful, I just did oral sex on him. He also manually massaged my clitoris, until we could begin having regular intercourse.

Women had numerous suggestions of ways to help relieve the stress and fatigue involved during the initial weeks after a baby's birth. Some women recommended that their husbands be more involved. One woman shared the following, "My husband helped more with the baby and with the house so that I could get some relief from feeling so overwhelmed by the baby."

Ruby, mother of two children at age thirty-nine, had a number of simple but excellent suggestions that seemed to ease the situation for her:

One of the most dangerous things for a mother during the postpartum period is fatigue. It hits her pretty hard, so I think it's important for her to rest or else she's not going to be worth anything to anybody, especially her husband. If she's tired and especially if, as in our situation, their lovemaking takes place at night, she needs her rest. That's the end of a long day after a longer night of getting up every couple of hours, so what I did after both pregnancies was to rest several times a day. I would lie down and nap in the afternoon when the kids napped. A lot of things in the house went by the wayside, and I wasn't able to rest as long as I would have liked, but it really helped.

Another thing I would advise is to get out with your husband once a week, come hell or high water, beg, borrow or steal, even if you have to trade your children off! It might even be something simple like taking a walk, but it should be something between the two of you that is just for both of you. Try to talk about something besides the kids then. It's very, very difficult, especially when you've got a new baby, and there's so much to say about him, but spending time alone and talking about other things helps you both to stay alive toward one another. I know I didn't do enough of that so I would certainly pass that kind of advice along.

We were financially strapped after the birth of both of our babies, so I wasn't able to have someone come in and help. My mother came over after both deliveries, but that wasn't until three or four weeks after the birth of each baby, so those first two weeks were pretty tough. However, I had a number of friends who were very helpful and would try to bring food. I had one couple who came over and cooked a great huge dinner in our kitchen, did the dishes, cleaned up, and even left the leftovers in the refrigerator. Another friend gave me a gift of two months' diaper service, which was heavenly! I would recommend that, because it's such a time-consuming, fatigue-producing operation to do all those diapers. If you can't afford it and your mother-in-law wants to know what you want as a gift, tell her two months of diaper service or Pampers and you'll feel a lot better.

Those women who were not overwhelmed with fatigue and the adjustment to being a mother reported feeling their own libido surface again soon after the delivery. In those cases, they were anxious to begin sex sooner. Ruth, thirty-three, mother of a son, fourteen months, reported:

After the baby was born we were told to wait six weeks to resume sex, but I felt that I could have started after three weeks. In a way I enjoyed putting it off because of the anticipation. That was a very sensuous time. Being prohibited from having sex made it almost salacious. It was like being married and having some stipulation that for a week you can't cross over to the other side of the bed. It creates such a buildup to having sex again because you know it's just around the corner and you're getting so close to it and I really did build it up in my mind. I felt very attracted to my husband and I felt attractive again myself for the first time in a long time. I was really looking forward to making love face to face. My dream was of pulling my husband down to me, having him close to me, lying on top of me, things we hadn't been able to do since I was five months pregnant. He was excited about just being able to hug me close and press himself to me. As for actually making love for the first time after the birth, there was no problem.

Ease in resuming sex was frequently greater after the second or third child as evidenced by Monique, thirty-two, mother of two children, ages five years and four months:

I remember the second time around feeling ready to resume sex much more quickly than after the first pregnancy. I was much less fearful of the possible physical pain due to the unhealed episiotomy and I remember at about four weeks Brent was chomping at the bit ready to resume sex. I was also much less tired the second time around and felt much more comfortable about the baby, my mothering ability, and our relationship. We did a lot more talking and kidding about it, with more ease on both of our parts about what might happen or what it might feel like. He wore a condom mainly for birth control, but also because I was afraid I would be nervous and wouldn't lubricate enough. The condom just took care of that because it was prelubricated.

The first experience was one of the most passionate sexual experiences I have ever had with Brent. It didn't hurt at all, maybe because I was much more relaxed. We hadn't done it in maybe six weeks so the pause in time made it even more of an exquisite experience. I remember we made love for what seemed like hours, although it was probably just half an hour. The times right after that were also sensational.

A number of things can be done to facilitate the first experiences of intercourse after childbirth.

Nell used a dildo to stretch her vaginal opening:

We used a dildo for two and a half months to stretch me before "the real thing." It worked wonders and had the positive effect of making sex enjoyable again after ten very sore weeks.

Ruth discovered a novel technique for soothing her tender vagina after an episiotomy:

I was in the hospital for only two nights and came home on the third day. The first week home I felt really sore from the episiotomy. I had to use little steps and then after walking around a while, I felt really, really sore. I couldn't take a bath because I was still bleeding and couldn't use the heating pad because I couldn't put it right next to myself. Then I got this stroke of genius, which was to use my hair dryer with the diffuser attachment on a medium heat setting. I just aimed it at my stitches and turned it on. It was extremely soothing. The heat made my skin feel like it was melting into soft pliable skin instead of being tight and taut. I used it several times a day and really felt that it also helped me to heal faster.

Other women recommended sitz baths with warm milk and 50 to 100 milligrams of powdered magnesium.

Some women used other forms of self-healing. Research by the Simontons in Texas shows that it is possible through various visualization and meditation techniques to reduce the size of a tumor and reverse the cancer process.‡ Self-healing works basically by attaining a meditative or trance state in which you imagine or see yourself completely healed. In situations where there has been an episiotomy, this can be done by imagining the cut in the vagina healing and the tissue becoming pink and healthy, as well as by

‡ Simonton, Carl, et. al. *Getting Well Again: A step-by-step self-help guide for cancer patients and their families.* J. P. Tarcher, 1978.

imagining yourself sitting and walking naturally without pain. If this process is engaged in for a few minutes twice a day, it appears to accelerate the body's own natural healing process. No one yet knows exactly how or why this process of self-healing works; we only know that it does work for some people.*

The Kegel exercises were also recommended to tone the vaginal muscles and get them back into shape after childbirth.† The women we interviewed almost unanimously recommended doing their "Kegels" to get their vaginas back in shape after delivery. As one woman said:

I think it's like any sprain you get, the sooner you can begin to gradually exercise it, the sooner the muscle regains its flexibility and strength.

Others felt that doing their Kegels also increased their sexual desire and made them interested in resuming sex sooner. This would make sense since exercising this muscle often intensifies the sensitivity in the vaginal area and also focuses a woman's awareness on her genitals and on sexual pleasure. Kegels are actually important for all women regardless of pregnancy since, by strengthening the pubococcygeal muscle, they give a woman more control over her body. Many women will contract this muscle consciously during intercourse to increase their partners' stimulation and their own. This technique is sometimes referred to as the "inner kiss."

One woman who had delivered over thirty years ago, before Kegels were developed, advocated intercourse with the woman's legs together to compensate for her stretched muscles after delivery.

I used to worry that there wasn't enough friction to satisfy my husband because of the vaginal stretching during my deliveries. My approach to sex may be an old-fashioned one, but I'm concerned with my partner's satisfaction because knowing he's satisfied gives me

* Further information on this visualization process can be obtained by reading *The Mind's Eye* by Mike Samuels, M.D., and Nancy Samuels. New York: Random House, 1975.

† See pp. 110–11.

pleasure. What I did was to keep my legs together instead of apart during intercourse. I was always on the bottom and when he used a condom it helped to take up some of the slack, too. I used to enjoy intercourse more with a condom than without, because there was more friction. It may be that in those days the rubber was thicker.

In addition to stretching the vaginal opening and practicing the Kegel exercises, women talked about the importance of prolonged foreplay, extreme gentleness, and sufficient lubrication as ways to make their initial sexual encounters more enjoyable.

Sue's experience with resuming sex after the birth of their second child was much improved because of what she and her husband learned from the first experience:

My experience with resuming sex after my first child was incredibly painful. In fact, my husband could not even get in. My vaginal opening went into spasms and the experience was disastrous. If I had been more prepared for the possibility of pain, we would have had more foreplay and gradually eased into intercourse. After that, my husband was great about it. What he did was gradually stretch my vaginal opening by massaging it with his fingers. He spent a great deal of time relaxing me and stimulating me. For the first couple of times, he just concentrated on stretching the vaginal opening, using one, then two, and eventually three fingers. The first time we had intercourse, he only entered partially. It was like being a virgin all over again. I also had less secretion after delivery, so we used a lot of K-Y jelly.

Barbara, pregnant with her third child, cautioned:

The vagina and the area around the entrance of the vagina hurt after childbirth, so sex during that time really needs to be gentle. However, the clitoris doesn't hurt, so you can still have sexual feelings and enjoy being stimulated.

Some positions for intercourse were recommended for easing the pain. The next two women both had delivered within the past year and had the following suggestions to make.

Harriet:

Some positions were more comfortable—like me on top or the missionary position with my legs down—so that he didn't go in so deeply.

Deep penetration was very uncomfortable so we didn't use any positions where the penetration would be that deep. We didn't use the position where I kneel and he comes in from the back because that was too much; but with me on top, I had more control of how deep the penetration was and that helped. We had a much more sedate kind of lovemaking for a while.

Gabrielle:

I tried to elevate myself so my vagina would be on a plane level with him. If I was tilted at all, then he would thrust on the side, which was really painful. We tried to keep penetration in the middle of the vagina so the penis wouldn't press on the opening or on the side.

Although having a Cesarean rules out the need for an episiotomy, a Cesarean delivery has its own particular difficulties in terms of resuming sex. Due to the incision, positions that don't involve pressure on the stomach were, in general, preferable. Cortney, thirty-one, mother of a six-year-old son, said:

I would lie on my stomach rather than having him on top of my incision, which was real sore for a long time. I would be on my stomach with my legs out and he'd come in from behind.

CONTRACEPTION
AFTER CHILDBIRTH

Once women can resume intercourse after delivery, they are faced with the problem of contraception. Contrary to common belief, it *is* possible for a woman to become pregnant soon after delivery even if she is breast-feeding. Consequently, some women decide to be fitted with an intrauterine device (IUD) as part of the delivery procedure. Due to problems with the IUD,‡ however, many women are now searching for other methods. Getting a tubal ligation before leaving the delivery room is also an option, but it is only available to women who are certain that they do not ever want to become pregnant again.

Since the uterus has changed size as a result of the pregnancy, it is generally not possible to use the old diaphragm with security, be-

‡See pp. 195–97.

cause it may no longer fit properly. And since the internal organs continue to slowly shift, it is often a considerable period of time before the changes have stabilized sufficiently for the woman to be fitted for a new diaphragm. With the exception of the minipill, which contains only progesterone, birth control pills are not a viable alternative for women who are breast-feeding since estrogen can reduce the production of milk. Consequently, contraceptive foams, contraceptive suppositories, and condoms appear to be the best options for nursing mothers who don't want tubal ligations or IUDs. Although these methods have their drawbacks in terms of messiness or decreased sensitivity for both the male and the female, they are safe and effective methods of contraception following childbirth.

ORGASM AFTER DELIVERY

After the initial difficulties were overcome, some of the women reported that pregnancy had changed their experience of sex and particularly of orgasm. Heather, the mother of a two-year-old daughter, said:

After having my baby and resuming sex, I experienced much more sensation throughout my pelvic area, particularly the back of my vagina and my vulva.

Secondly, I felt my orgasms were deeper, that my physical sensations were stronger and more powerful. It seemed that having gone through the experience of having a baby and using my system in such a total way, enhanced and enriched the sexual experience at a whole other physiological level. Whereas before I was using maybe 75 per cent of my sexual awareness or my bodily awareness, now it was closer to 100 per cent.

Ruth, mother of a fourteen-month-old son, stated:

I found that for the first time in my life I was multiorgasmic. That was something I had dreamed about, but thought could never happen to me. I felt like all this backed-up sexuality that was in me during the pregnancy was coming into play, coming into full force. It was really wonderful and I thought that maybe it was because I felt more womanly having had a child.

Now the baby has arrived and sex between its parents has been resumed. But with the advent of a new family member, particularly one so helpless and dependent, new strains often develop in the couple's sexual life as they try to juggle the demands of their various roles as husband, wife, provider, lover, and parent. In addition, parents are being asked not only to adapt to the physical changes caused by the presence of children, in terms of making the time for sex, but are also required to be role models and teachers in the sexual area—a task for which they have had little preparation themselves. The next chapter deals with the ways the women we interviewed met this challenge.

8

Parents Are Sexual, Too

When asked about their perceptions of their parents' sex life, most of the women we interviewed felt it was nonexistent, with the possible exception of when they and their siblings were conceived. Although rationally they realized this was not the case, they had this impression because they never received any indication while growing up that their parents made love. These women's parents never announced mysteriously that they were unavailable, their bedroom door was never locked, and the women we talked with never saw their parents touch each other in a sensual or sexual way. They equated this absence of overt behavior with the absence of sex. This, however, was not necessarily the case. While it is possible that sex did not play an important part in their parents' marital relationship, it is equally possible these women's parents had satisfying sex lives, but relegated it to times when the children were asleep or not at home.

Most women regretted that their parents hadn't presented themselves as sexual people, feeling that this would have helped them develop healthier attitudes about sex. It also would have given them some positive role models for being a lover as well as a wife.

Yet these same women, now mothers themselves, are also sympathetic with their parents' dilemma of finding enough time and energy to maintain an active sex life once their children were born.

Without question, children do put a strain on a couple's sexual activity. The prechild spontaneity is often lost as children's needs, activities, and demands lessen privacy and eat into what was once an option of making love whenever it was convenient.

Many women lamented the loss of freedom to have spontaneous sex with their partner after the birth of their own children.

Monique, following nine years of marriage and two children, ages five years and four months, expresses this situation well:

The whole issue of being able to still have spontaneity in your sex life is a troubling one when you have children. The times you can have sex become much more regimented and regularized, either in the morning or at night. It's very hard in the middle of the day unless both children are occupied, to say "Hey, I want you," or "Let's screw!" It means that I have to be much more aware and have to pick an available moment and not let it pass by. I have to grab that moment, because there's less free time to myself. It's so easy to let an opportunity during the day pass and then think to myself, "I'll wait until tonight, until eleven o'clock." Well, often at eleven o'clock I'm tired, I'm worn out, I'm frustrated. I find late at night I'm much more passive, I just want to get it over with because I want to get to sleep or I'm worried about getting up the next morning, or preoccupied with all kinds of things, so I'm not as assertive and integrally involved in the experience. Therefore, it's crucial that I take responsibility for my own sexual needs during the day when I'm more aware and more energetic.

Most of the women developed ways of keeping their sexual relationship active despite having one or more children, but none were completely satisfactory. They couldn't always afford to go away on weekends or pay for babysitters or find couples to exchange babysitting, or didn't have available—or willing—extended family members nearby to help out. Nearly every woman we interviewed who had children was very interested in learning how other parents dealt with this problem. The most frequent response after this part of the interview was, "How do other women cope? Can you give me some ideas before your book comes out?" Consequently, this chapter deals with that need, by providing a compilation of all the different solutions women mentioned.

MOTHERHOOD VERSUS SEXUALITY

Finding ways to keep your sexual life vital in a family situation takes creativity, energy, cooperation from your partner, and, above all, an interest in maintaining an active sexual relationship. We noticed that not all the women we talked with had this motivation. Some were in conflict about combining their maternal and sexual roles, which tended to complicate an already difficult situation:

My feeling about the relationship between sexuality and motherhood is that it's very difficult for me to feel like a sexual being when my identity is tied up exclusively with mothering. I find when I identify myself solely as a mother, I often feel resentful, unfulfilled, and it's hard for me to turn on to my husband sexually. I usually feel more dependent, more needy, so I can't feel as assertive, as feline, as coquettish. Therefore, I'm a big believer in getting as much help as I can rearing the children. Then I can feel more freedom to see myself in a variety of roles. Since both my husband and I have full-time careers, we have chosen to have a housekeeper come in during the week. I have a lovely woman full time, who's very warm and maternal, and we also have an art student living with us. She takes care of the baby from five o'clock to eight o'clock in exchange for room and board, so when I get home from work I can be with my five-year-old, who really needs my attention at this point.

Some women felt that their role as mother was primary in their lives and deliberately put all other interests and duties second. Tricia, however, managed throughout the thirty-nine years of her first marriage to always put her husband first despite having two children, and this, she felt, was one of the reasons they had such a good marriage:

When I had my first child I remember thinking that the child is supposed to come first, but I didn't believe that. The child came first with my husband and me only until it was able to be on its feet. After that, we never let anything interfere with us, never, because somehow or other we knew that that was important for our relationship. Maybe it was easier to follow that philosophy because there were nine years between our two children and that makes a big difference. Each child always had his own room and we always had enough space. Also, my husband was very child-oriented, so he always helped out with the kids.

BREAST FEEDING

Having a baby, particularly if it is the first child, is often physically exhausting. It necessitates a change in lifestyle and adjustment to the new mothering role, in addition to the physical stress of recovering from the delivery. Another issue that added stress for many women, because of the ambivalent feelings it brought up, was breast feeding. Some women who were breast feeding had trouble viewing their breasts as nurturing objects as well as sexual objects. Some women found that the breast-feeding experience led them to consider their breasts more as functional than sexual objects. Barbara, (twenty-nine, mother of two children, six and four:

Breast feeding for me is a very sexual experience. When the baby is nibbling on my breast, it actually feels the same as when my husband does. My husband always makes the joke that it's either the baby or him. It's hard when you're breast feeding to have someone nibble on your breasts sexually because the milk comes out, and you need that for the baby. Other women I've talked to agree that when you're breast feeding, your husband is kind of cut off from your breasts.

Beverly (thirty-six, married nine years to her attorney husband Mark and the mother of a five-year-old son) had some similar feelings but found a solution that met everyone's needs:

I breast-fed for ten months and had real difficulty allowing my husband to suck on my breasts. I was afraid I was going to give all my milk to my husband and not have enough for the baby. The way I solved that was to make sure the baby got fed first. I was still a little squeamish about it, but my husband helped me with that by saying the more your breasts are suckled, the more you will produce, and I always had enough milk for the baby so I assumed that was right.

Other women also found breast feeding to be highly erotic, and seemed to have no conflict about experiencing sensual or sexual

pleasure from nurturing their child. Roberta, physical therapist, recalled her experience ten years ago when her daughter was born:

I really loved breast-feeding my baby. It was very erotic. My uterus
would contract and I would be in an orgasmic-type state when the
baby suckled my breasts. It was very gratifying. I felt kind of funny
having erotic feelings with my baby though. At first, the feeling was
somewhat uncomfortable physically, because of the intense contractions
of the uterus. The uterus would clamp right down and it would feel
like an extra cramp, but after the first few days, it was a much more
pleasurable feeling—the contractions were like what you get when you
have intercourse.

What happens is that a hormone is released when the baby suckles,
which contracts the uterus. The contraction is a very natural process of
getting the uterus back to normal condition, and breast feeding really
aids the woman in getting her body back into prepregnancy shape, by
producing those contractions. I can't imagine any woman not breast
feeding because it's good for you physically and it's such a warm close
feeling.

One woman didn't experience sexual pleasure from breast feeding, but interestingly, she learned a new respect for her breasts,
and as a result enjoyed more breast stimulation during lovemaking.
Ariel:

I never disliked my breasts, I just discounted them. I'm fairly flat-
chested and I grew up with a hang-up about my breasts, so I have
never felt very much sexual sensation in them. I have really wondered
why men wanted to touch them or suck them because it certainly did
nothing for me. I always just ignored that part of my body. I breast-fed
my baby for a year and never had sexual feelings from the feeding, so I
didn't want to hear about people who had orgasms while they were sitting there breast feeding.

I never had anything like that, but I did develop this real fondness
and respect for the way my breasts functioned, in the way they provided milk. My child had nothing but breast milk for the first six
months of her life and she tripled her weight in two and a half months
or something absurd like that, and that was just on breast milk. Since
that time, I have used my breasts more sexually. I still don't have a tremendous amount of feeling in my breasts. I don't think I will ever be
the kind of person who could have an orgasm just from stimulating my

breasts, but I like them and respect them and feel some warmth when they're touched or fondled. I used to pull them in when someone touched them, now I push them out. Now I use them when I'm making love with somebody, so that's a whole other thing. And now I know there are plenty of men who adore my breasts just the way they are.

A physiological change which might be considered when deciding when to terminate breast feeding is the fact that prolonged breast feeding (generally five months or longer) can sometimes result in temporary atrophying of the vagina, similar to the process that occurs after menopause.* This is because breast feeding creates increased levels of prolactin, an antiestrogenic hormone. Because of this, some breast-feeding mothers experience discomfort with intercourse. The use of local estrogens, which can reduce the flow of milk, or lubricants, such as K-Y jelly, which do not affect nursing, can help to alleviate any discomfort.

FINDING TIME FOR SEX

For a number of months after the baby's birth, the household goes through some degree of chaos as the family adjusts to the addition of another member. When the initial shock has subsided, the difficulty of finding time for uninterrupted sex becomes a major problem. This problem seemed to concern all of the women we interviewed, and although many had some solutions, they were constantly looking for newer or better ones.

One solution was to find ways to occupy the children in order to free up time for uninterrupted sex. The method used, however, depended on the age of the child. Finding ways to occupy an infant or preschool-age child was considerably different from methods used for a school-age child or teen-ager.

Women did not seem to have many unusual solutions for dealing with infants. For the most part, they worked around the child's sleeping patterns when that was possible. Heather, a thirty-five-year-old part-time therapist, recalled:

* See p. 309

I have a two-year-old daughter and it was difficult, especially while she was younger, to find time for sex. For the most part, our sex life pretty much revolved around her nap time. She took a nap very predictably in the early afternoon, so my husband was able to come home from work for lunch, and we would have sex. We could also have sex on the weekend. We used to really enjoy having sex in the morning when we first woke up, but that's just not possible with a tiny baby who wakes up at the crack of dawn. Now that I'm more accustomed to taking care of a baby, I feel more comfortable arranging days and weekends away so we can be together and have some extra time for sex.

Some women recommended waking the baby up to feed it and change its diapers to ensure a few hours peace and quiet. However, even with the best of preparation, some babies seemed to have an uncanny knack for waking up just when lovemaking was in process. Harriet, who took a leave of absence from work for the first few months had the following experience with her now six-month-old adopted son:

Peter was amazing in his ability to wake up and start screaming just when we were about to have intercourse. For a period of about eight weeks, almost every time we started to fuck, Peter woke up! He would be fine through all the love play and all the foreplay, and then just as soon as we got to actually fucking, he would wake up and scream and scream and scream! We would try to ignore it, but it just ruined the whole thing.

He would be sleeping in his room. Music would be on in our bedroom. We'd say, "Okay, Peter wakes up at eleven, so at nine-thirty we're going to start making love; we'll be done by the time he wakes up." Then he wakes up at ten! We couldn't stand it! What we've tried to do is just pay more attention to what time it is, pay more attention to his schedule, and plan to get involved when he's settled. I mean, it really cut down on our sex life, because we'd never done that kind of planning before.

Some women found that consciously manipulating the baby's schedule early on would assist the baby in sleeping through the night and give them and their partner some uninterrupted time for making love. Gweneth remembered:

When my kids were babies, I really missed things like going out to dinner and having a good time with my husband. We like to go for dinner and talk—we like long conversations over dinner—so I started manipulating their schedules so they would sleep through the night and we could be together. I would keep them up after a short morning nap, then put them down for an afternoon nap, and pick them up early. As soon as they could do it, I would eliminate the afternoon nap and put them to bed by six-thirty or seven, and they'd sleep until seven or eight the next morning. That way, we could have a beautiful evening together.

Many of the women we interviewed initially slept in the same room with their newborn and felt perfectly comfortable making love with the baby in the same room.

Gaye, a thirty-three-year-old college instructor, married eleven years:

My children are now eight and two. When they were first born, they slept in our bedroom in a small crib. Although we may occasionally have had sex out of the bedroom during the day or at night, our usual pattern would be to have sex late at night in the bedroom when the baby was asleep. Of course, once the baby got old enough, we stopped doing that.

However, many of the women became less comfortable with this practice as the baby grew older and eventually sought greater privacy from the child. Gabrielle, who at twenty-seven has been living with Robert, an artist, for five years, had the following somewhat humorous experience while making love in the same room with their ten-month-old son:

Children obviously understand more as they get older. My son's at an age where I don't think he understands the moaning or the groaning you go through during sex, but he instinctively thinks something is the matter and I feel uncomfortable with that. Every once in a while, when we're in the midst of making love, I have to look over and say, "Are you all right, Alex (pant, pant, pant)?" and so it just doesn't work out. It puts a damper on our sex life because he's around most of the day. If he is in another room playing or involved in something, he'll crawl over to us. If Mom and Dad are together, that's where he wants to be. There was one time I was going down on Robert. Our bed is on the floor. I was on my knees close to the edge of the bed and Alex was on the floor. He came over and pulled down my underpants and bit me. That was the last time we made love with him in the room. However, I've kidded with Robert that now I can tell my friends I've been to bed with two men at the same time.

As the baby grew older, solutions became more creative. Sally came up with a great idea which, although it only lasted for about the first seven months of the baby's development, was effective while it lasted:

It was difficult to get together in the beginning, especially when we were so tired and were constantly changing shifts. One of us would be on duty watching the baby and the other would be off duty having some free time. Lots of times we would try to make love while the baby was lying right there in the bed with us, although it made me a little self-conscious. But the main thing was that he would interrupt by crying or he would need something, so it was hard. Basically what we relied on was the Wind-Up Swing. We would put the baby in the swing for twenty minutes and be guaranteed twenty minutes of swinging time for ourselves. By swinging time, I meant that we had sex during that time, so we had a twenty-minute sexual rendezvous. Eventually the baby was too big for the swing or not interested in swinging anymore because he was too active. Once I remember being so hard up we put him in the high chair with about a million Cheerios and used that time, but that was an exception. Usually we just waited until bedtime and made love at night when he was in bed.

As the children reached preschool and school age, options increased. Still, mothers preferred to put children to bed early or make love late at night when they were sure the children were asleep. But at least there was time available during the day for people who had the flexibility in their jobs to take advantage of it, as evidenced by the following story told to us by a woman in one of our workshops:

We have two children whose ages are seven and nine. It's difficult to find time to make love other than late at night, after they've gone to bed and we're both too tired to put much energy into sex, or in the early morning. The problem with that is we never know if one of the children will wake up early and wander into our bedroom, so I'm not very relaxed about having sex in the mornings. What my husband did one day was to call me up at home and ask me if I wanted to go to a matinee with him. I thought he meant a movie and I said sure. But later I found out that he meant a sexual matinee. We took two hours for lunch and had a great time, with no one else around. We do this fairly regularly now. He'll call me and invite me to a matinee or I'll invite him, and then we just take the phone off the hook and have fun.

Finding time during weekdays, however, was not an option for most of the working women we interviewed. Sunday school, however, was one way of getting time on weekend mornings. (We always knew there was a good reason for Sunday school, but as kids, we could never figure out what it was. Maybe this was it.)

I know what my parents did, and I don't know why I remember this, except that my mother made such a big thing about our going to Sunday school on Sunday morning. She would get up bleary-eyed and take us to Sunday school and I think that was their time to fuck. I couldn't figure out when they ever did it when I was a kid, other than at night. I know they did it at night because one time I walked in on them by accident. They were both very embarrassed, but I still think they also did it Sunday mornings while we were at Sunday school.

A popular after-school or weekend morning technique for keeping the children occupied involved the use of television. Many people complain about the effects of television on our youngsters, but Karen found a way to use it creatively and in moderation with her three- and five-year-old daughters:

Since we both work, having sex is usually an evening-time thing. I usually put the kids together, either in their room or in the family room, and give them a project to do or let them watch a television program I know they're interested in. Sometimes I also give them a treat, like a Popsicle, carrot sticks, cookies, something I know they want or they've asked for earlier. I usually tell them that if there are any problems they can knock on the door. I just explain to them that Daddy and Mommy have worked all day and we haven't been able to spend any time with each other, so we want to be alone for a little while. They don't really question it.

Another woman knew of a family who had come up with an ingenious solution:

Some people I know have two little girls and they had a clever way of keeping their kids occupied while they made love. They had a switch in their bedroom so they could turn the television on downstairs and in the morning the little girls would go downstairs to the recreation room and get their bananas, juice, and milk, and have their breakfast and watch the cartoons on television while their parents would make love.

Although the children might seem well occupied by TV, some project, or a neighborhood friend, this did not ensure that they might not barge in unexpectedly while their parents were in the middle of making love. Louise, a thirty-six-year-old clergywoman who is widowed, with a son age six and a daughter age three, had a creative solution for this:

I have an intercom that connects the upstairs with the den, which is downstairs at the opposite end of the house from where the children are sleeping. So if I'm with my boy friend in the den and my children are asleep upstairs, I can hear them. If they get out of bed or need me, I can go up to them instead of having them come down and walk in on us.

A more common solution proposed by many of the women we interviewed was locking their bedroom door:

We have a lock on our bedroom door so we feel somewhat relaxed knowing the kids are just not going to walk in, since I don't think that is fair to them either.

Although Elaine keeps her bedroom door closed while making love, she is not upset when a child walks in unannounced:

We are a very close, lovey, and kissy family with lots of cuddling and hugging and touching. If the kids are still watching TV and we want to go to bed, we just go and close the door. Our bedroom door is always open, even at night, but once our door is closed tight, nobody hardly ever enters. I've never made it explicitly clear to them, and, I guess it's not totally understood, because every once in a while one of them will have something important to say and come in when we're right in the middle of things. We just continue lying together cuddling each other. For example, we might turn on our side, stay embraced, and deal with whatever they need. We don't make any big deal out of their seeing us like that and we certainly don't scream at them to get out of the room.

Some women had the luxury of an extra room or two in a separate part of the house that they would use for daytime sex. Sixty-year-old Jesse recalled:

When my children were quite young, it was no problem because once they were in bed they would be settled for the night. I never had the problem of waking children and they really didn't interfere with our sex life at all. Later, when they were older, we had a problem. My husband sometimes spontaneously gasped during orgasm. Sometimes he was quite loud and it sounded like a cry. At one point I was aware that my oldest daughter, who was eleven, had heard this and misinterpreted it in some way as Mamma punishing Daddy. So it was fortunate that my art studio was set up as a combination studio and guest room and we used that room after that. It was very convenient. I think it would be wise if most parents did have a room that was separated from the children's bedrooms so you can have a bit of warning before they come in, as well as more privacy.

One of our clients had an ingenious plan for having some intimate time alone with her husband after he returned from a business trip:

When my husband used to go away on a business trip, I would tell my daughters that he wouldn't be home until four or five o'clock and I would have them stay out and play until then. Well, he actually always got home around noon, but we wanted to have some time alone before the girls came home.

A more common solution was to leave children with someone else, either for the evening, overnight, or weekends. Many women felt guilty about that because they worried not only about their children's safety but about whether they would be emotionally damaged as well. However, getting away from home was the most popular solution suggested by the women we interviewed, both for finding time alone, and for revitalizing their relationship. Ann, a fifty-nine-year-old educator married thirty-six years to Steve, a consultant, recalls:

When the kids were small, and for years later, we would take what we called "orgy weekends" or "orgy holidays." We would take off, leaving the kids in good hands. I know they can hear everything that goes on in the house and I get uptight about that. So we used to go off to a motel in the city for two days, and have all the trappings of a sexy weekend—the king-sized bed and breakfast in bed. We would make love all Friday night and all day Saturday and would come out absolutely soft on Sunday!

Women had various ways of taking care of their children during these sexy weekends away from home. Most women did not feel comfortable leaving their children with strangers for any lengthy period of time. Relatives were favorite choices. Those with the financial resources would hire a babysitter or a live-in housekeeper for assistance. Ann had that luxury:

I was fortunate. I had live-in help from the time Peggy was born. That's what I loved about this house. We had a third floor with plenty of space for private living quarters. Having live-in help made it possible for me to have a career and to pursue other interests as well.

Monique found an inexpensive way to obtain household help:

One thing you can do if you have an extra room in your house or apartment is to contact organizations like the National Student Housing Council and by simply giving room and board you get up to twenty hours of free labor per week. The students are most often from foreign countries but obviously they speak English because they're studying here in universities. The Student Housing Council does some screening, but you could also check their references through the university. In each city you'll find places such as church or religious centers that deal with people who come in mainly from Central and South America. Frequently they don't speak any or much English—you'd have to know some Spanish—but that's another possibility for relatively inexpensive household help.

Other creative and inexpensive solutions concerned trading services with other couples. Child-care switchboards available in certain areas were preferred by some. Diane, a foster mother, sometimes relies on this method:

Occasionally if there is some real special time that I want to spend with somebody, I find other parents through the switchboard who want to exchange children for different evenings or weekends. The way it works is that families with children register with the child-care switchboard. Whenever you take care of another family's child, you get a credit for that many hours. Then when somebody takes care of my children, I get a debit for that many hours. It's like bartering time.

Most, however, preferred to exchange weekends with friends who also had children:

Neither my husband nor I have any family in the immediate area, so we have to rely on friends for some relief from the children and some time to ourselves. When the children were a little bit younger, we would make arrangements to trade children with other couples. They would take the kids for the night. That way we would have a whole evening to ourselves, which sometimes left us feeling awkward with one another. It was almost like we were dating again, getting to know one another, but it was very useful for us. If you're going to have a sexual evening together that doesn't necessarily mean making love all evening, so you need a span of time, like several hours, to let the feelings build up so you can reach a level of spontaneity. You need time to enjoy music or candlelight or dinner or some wine and just grow closer together. When we just rely on making love late at night, it frequently doesn't work out because the spontaneity and the time you need to develop that spontaneity is not there.

Once the children reached teen years, difficulties ceased a bit for most parents. They didn't have to worry about keeping the children occupied or finding someone to stay home and take care of them. In addition, by the time they reached that age, they had become aware that their mother and father needed to have some time alone and did not find this situation a problem. It is important during their preteen years, however, to explain the importance of parents' having time together, especially if sex is not talked about in the household. Louise, a thirty-nine-year-old nurse-therapist, married to Dick, who is a priest-consultant, describes how she first let her daughter know that she and her husband required time alone to love one another:

Janet is now fourteen and when I entered into my second marriage, she was just eleven. That's when I really began to feel good about myself as a sexual person, and to feel I had a right to make time for my sexual life with Dick. He felt very comfortable letting his kids know he was a sexual person. In his first marriage, he would say, "Your mother and I are going to go upstairs. We're going to take some time for ourselves." Dick and I talked about it and I agreed to try it too. So, I took a deep breath and one afternoon said to Janet, "Dick and I are going to go upstairs for a while." Immediately she said, "Well, I'll come, too and I'll watch television up there." I said, "No, we're not going to watch television. We're just going to spend some time talking with one another and loving one another. We'll come down in a little while." I felt if she knew when we would come down, that we wouldn't be spending the whole evening up there, she would feel more comfortable about giving up some time with us. She's an only child and so she expects a lot of attention and likes to have people around her. I'm an only child so I know what that feels like when everybody deserts you and you're there by yourself. The first time that worked well. She left us alone and we spent about three hours upstairs taking a bath, talking with one another, lighting candles and making love. We came down later, fixed dinner, and were eating dinner when Janet wanted to know what loving was. So we had fun talking about that, explaining that it was talking and holding one another. Then she said, "Doing all that stuff?" and we said, "Yeah!"

Another woman obtained privacy by sectioning off an apartment within the house:

One of my daughters was with me for a year or two after my divorce. I set up an apartment for her on the lower floor of our house so she had privacy and separate living quarters. It was like she was under my wing, yet she wasn't; she was only seventeen, and by the time she was nineteen she was on her own.

The women we interviewed varied considerably in their comfort with letting their children know they needed time to be sexual. Some never mentioned the topic with their children and admitted that although they knew it was important, they had not yet been able to discuss it.

Others felt comfortable telling their children that they did not want to be disturbed during a certain period of time. Since they were not as comfortable telling their child they were going to make love and having to explain the process, they used other, less sexual terms such as taking a nap, needing private time, cuddling, or loving each other. Monique said:

Obviously, the answer depends on the age of the children and what they can understand. We've just put a lock on our door. We told our five-year-old, "Mommy and Daddy need some private time. It doesn't mean we don't love you, but we want to be alone right now, and we want you to knock on the door."

Eve (the mother of nine- and eleven-year-old sons) shared the following:

When the kids were younger, we would try to take advantage of nap times, especially on the weekends. We would use this time to have sex even if I was tired and not particularly feeling up to it. Since our children are just two years apart, the older one was still taking some naps at the same time the younger one was, so we were sometimes able to have some time in the afternoon. We still take "naps" on weekends now even though our kids aren't napping anymore. We retire to the bedroom and I don't know whether the kids have caught on that when Mommy and Daddy disappear for an hour or two and take a nap, they're not really taking a nap. If so, I don't know if they have any idea of what we're really doing. I think they're getting to the age where they probably should have some clues that there's more going on in the room than just sleeping. We haven't had direct questions about our sexual activities as such, but I think the older boy is starting to understand that people do have sex for more reasons than just to have babies. In fact, just the other day, he was asking how often people actually have intercourse because he had heard somewhere that it could be more often than just to produce babies.

Christine, at age forty-one and after fifteen years of marriage, simply says the following to her three teen-age children:

"We need to go to bed early tonight." My kids are teen-agers, and I'm sure they know what I mean and that's okay. I mean, for heaven's sake!

However, Cortney has her own rationale for being straightforward with her six-year-old son and seems to be quite pleased with the results:

I've always tried to be real open with my son Benjamin about sexual issues, especially since my mom wasn't like that. She used to get dressed in the closet and here I was trying to raise Benjamin by myself and trying to hide from him. I thought, this is ridiculous, what am I doing? I was doing it because that's how my mother was. After I was in therapy I began realizing how many things I was doing that my mother did without ever questioning them. That's just the way it was. And Chuck, my boy friend, was real comfortable walking around naked. Benjamin asks a lot of questions, like the other morning he came in and we didn't have any clothes on, but we were under the covers. He jumped onto the bed, ripped the covers back and said, "You guys are naked!" I said, "Yeah, we are," and he said, "I think it's really neat that you're lovers," and I said, "We think so too." He is really an open child. He'd have to be, hanging around me, and I decided it's better not protecting him. It's better to expose him to as many healthy things as I can and then he can form his own opinions rather than being sheltered from anything I think he's too young for.

SINGLE MOTHERS

Being a single mother seemed to complicate the already difficult task of finding time to be sexual with a partner. Most single mothers had a tremendous number of responsibilities, since they were the major financial and emotional support for their children. Polly, forty-four, a professional typist, and the divorced mother of a seven-year-old son, says:

The basic everyday problems of being a single parent are maintaining the household financially and otherwise, maintaining the child's physical well-being and then maintaining your own emotional well-being plus that of your child. In other words, you're doing it all. You're doing all the driving, all the shopping, and all the grocery carrying. Those are physical things you can get used to coping with in a fairly short period of time. But on top of that, you have the problems of keeping up with your child's development, realizing at what point he is in life and what kind of problems he is having so you can be receptive, then finding time to be receptive, and then getting yourself into a position emotionally where you *can* be receptive. That's important, because if he thinks that you're busy and under pressure, he'll go watch television rather than come to you with his problems.

Consequently, much of their time as single parents was taken up with running errands, working, and carrying out household chores.

Many of these women already felt guilty enough about not spending sufficient time with their children. This guilt was often compounded when they considered taking a weekend off with a lover and leaving their children with someone else. This was not so much the case if the father was nearby and the children could go stay with him, but since so many divorced women moved to another city when they separated, this meant that the children would have to stay with someone other than a parent. As a result, the single mothers we interviewed were very conscious of setting up support systems in lieu of extended families that were not readily available. Frequently, single mothers like Samantha, the working mother of an eight-year-old son, would band together to take care of children after school or to share housekeepers:

I have a few friends who are single parents and if we want to go out for the evening, if we want to have someone over, or if we want to spend the night out, we call each other and see if one of us can keep our kids. We also do that when cars break down or when someone's got to be picked up at dancing class or at school.

It's really a cooperative idea. For example, one of the ideas I had when my marriage broke up was to buy a big house and fix it up so it would be a two-family duplex with two single women with children sharing the house. That way, the kids would never have to be taken out of their house for us to have a social life. Another idea I had was to cooperatively buy a housekeeper's time. I have a friend who is divorced and has a little girl. She lives about four doors from where I'm going to be moving. Right now, I have someone part time who takes care of light housekeeping and takes care of my son right after school some. My friend and I decided we would each pay for a half week of her time and make her full-time, which means she would take care of both our children after school every day. That way I would not have to worry about rushing home or finding special things for my son to do after school. Single women with children just have to band together and be families for themselves.

Consequently, single mothers were appreciative of a lover's willingness to help take care of babysitting responsibilities whenever possible:

It's important for me to be in a relationship with someone who will share responsibility for my child, even though it's not their child. It's important to find someone who is supportive of the fact that I have a kid. I prefer to find someone as a lover who's willing to either help pay for a sitter or find a sitter or at least recognize that anytime we make plans, deciding what we're going to do with my child is part of making plans. If I'm always the one who has to find child care, it really creates resentment which affects the relationship.

Many women felt it was important to be sensitive about how they presented their child with the idea of a sitter coming in or of going out to someone else's house for the night or weekend. These women were concerned that the child be comfortable with the idea and enjoy the time away from them. Thirty-four-year-old Ariel handles it this way with her five-year-old daughter:

I think it's important not to chuck my daughter out into a foreign land—I started to say "just so I could fuck," but that sounds awful. However, it seems that way when I'm hassling, trying to find a way to spend a night with somebody and of course my child doesn't have a clue as to the full meaning of this. Even though she may know I have invited somebody to spend the night, she doesn't know exactly what that means and I certainly don't want her to feel she's going away from something but rather *to* something. I feel that way about babysitting in general, not that she should be going off to a party, but that she should be going off to be with somebody she enjoys or having somebody coming in that she likes.

Another major problem concerned the women's feelings about having men spend the night in the house. This was a very complex issue which was of concern to almost all of the single mothers we talked with, although women chose to handle it in different ways. A few women, especially those from small towns, did not even date for a long period after their separation from their husbands.

Billie, age fifty-four, with a grown daughter, said:

We were living in Iowa when my husband died. The way I looked at his death was that I had enjoyed my sexual life with him, but since the Lord saw fit to take my husband, it meant I was to do without a sexual life. So I went through this period of not having sex. There were so many survival issues pending that I thought I would have to take care of sex "tomorrow." We were poor and I had to work and raise my daughter. I didn't masturbate during that time because I really didn't know about it. I had no sexual partners then so I didn't have to deal with being a single mother and having boy friends. You see, I lived in this tiny town on a highway and if anyone stopped by, everyone knew about it. I was widowed for thirteen years before I dated, but I didn't think I was missing anything because I was too busy working and raising my daughter. When I think back now, I can't imagine how I could live that kind of a life, going from a happy sexual relationship to nothing. My mind must have been very strong or else I had a very close contact with God; and I felt that if the Lord took him away, there must have been a reason. Anyway, I just accepted it and didn't go looking. Looking back, I don't know if I was happy or content because at the time I didn't know enough to be able to look and evaluate my life.

Anna, age twenty-eight, divorced, with a six-year-old daughter, had had a similar experience before she married her second husband Tyler, an educator, five years ago:

I had a hard time being a single mother and having a sex life because doing that felt promiscuous. I felt I needed to uphold a certain image as a single mother. That was really a big thing to me. After all, mothers don't go out and screw men. At the time I was living home with my parents, which was a heavy-duty thing to go through, but I was putting my daughter Elaine's needs over mine. I thought it was important for her to be involved with family, even though my parents' influence on her was horrible. It was also very hard to have any sort of sex life, living at my parents' home. My parents couldn't accept that. Relationships had to look like they would be lasting; otherwise I couldn't go out. There was no such thing as a one-night stand. And I was beyond the teen-age tactics where you'd say you were going here, but actually would be going somewhere else. I wasn't able to do that— it probably would have been healthier for me to have just been by myself. Finally I realized that if I was going to be myself, I couldn't continue living there. So I moved out when Elaine was four.

Some of the women had sexual relationships, but chose never to have a lover spend the night:

I never had to explain anything to my children because I never had sex in the house. I just would not do it in my house, basically because my kids were like my chaperones from the first weeks my husband left. My oldest son was twelve, and when I came home from a date, whether it was at midnight, nine o'clock, one in the morning, or four in the morning, my son would be sitting in a chair waiting for me. He would immediately get up and shake the guy's hand. If it wasn't him, then my parents would come and stay for four weeks and then go home for two and then stay again for four weeks and go home for two. So I had situations where there was no way I could prevent feeling restricted. Secondly, I did not believe in flaunting new relationships. I did not want to pressure the kids with a new man in the house, be it for sex or any reason.

The major reasons single mothers were uncomfortable having men spend the night revolved around their child's vulnerability. Most felt that their child had already suffered the loss of one man in their life, their father, which left the child hungry for this type of companionship. Louise, a clergywoman, widowed with a three-year-old and six-year-old, explains:

I haven't let Robert stay overnight here, not so much because I want to hide the fact that we're involved sexually from the children, but I feel if he stays all night and he's there at the breakfast table, it seems like he's part of the family, and I'm pretty sure he's not going to become part of our family. I think that's really taking a risk with my children's emotional involvement if they begin to feel that way about him. If he sleeps at our house, and he eats with us and everything, and then I stop seeing him, I think it would be a loss for the children.

They've already been through a real painful thing when their father died and I'm still trying to help them believe that you can love people and it doesn't necessarily mean they'll go away all the time. I don't want to reinforce the suspicion they've already got that somehow when you love people they disappear.

Some women were not so concerned about the child's sense of loss. They would have a lover spend the night, if they felt it was a special relationship that included the child, even if it wasn't going to be permanent. Thirty-one-year-old Cortney, divorced and the mother of a six-year-old son, felt this way before she moved in with her boy friend:

After I got divorced I decided I wasn't going to expose my child to waking up with different people in my bed all the time—not that I was really doing that, but I had never been single in my life and was

excited about all this new sex stuff that was going on, so I avoided exposing my child to the different people in my life. If I was going to
sleep with somebody that night, I would just arrange to do it
someplace else. During the last four years, I've only exposed him to
three people and as far as him walking in and finding someone in my
bed in the morning, they were people I was involved in a relationship
with. I felt that was okay because those men were close to my son and
he felt comfortable with them being there. Benjamin goes to bed at
eight o'clock at night and we wouldn't go to bed until later when I was
sure he was asleep, so we would have sex then. In the morning he
would get up and come in and we'd get up and fix breakfast and go on
with the day. I never felt my personal sexual life was exposed, except
that someone was sleeping in my bed, but it was always somebody he
was close to.

Other women felt that the early morning hours were an important part of their intimate sharing with their child and did not
want to be divided by the presence of a lover, who would also be
seeking their attention at that time. Dora, a thirty-two-year-old psychologist who is divorced and living with her seven-year-old daughter, said:

I never had people stay over because it felt messy and confusing. My
daughter had a lot to work through just with the divorce, and it just
felt like something that would add to her stress and confusion if she
were accustomed to having Dad and Mom always sleeping together
and then suddenly Mom is waking up with different men. In the
morning when I'm with Linda, we spend thirty minutes cuddling.
Well, if I have a man over, does she come join us in bed? And if she
does, who do I focus my attention on? I don't want to get into that
awful place of being divided.

Others, like Sonya, who at forty has four children and is
separated after a seventeen-year marriage, allow a man to spend the
night only if they feel the relationship is going to grow into a
permanent one:

My eighteen-year-old daughter obviously knows about my sexual relations because we're pretty open with each other. We talk very frankly,
but it's my own messages about being promiscuous that get in the way.
I didn't want my children to think I was having sex with one person

after another, and in fact I wasn't. As I recall, there was a period of about six months after my husband and I separated that I didn't have sex at home at all. I took care of my sexual needs away from the house. I dated people who had an apartment or a place where we could have sex. But when I started dating somebody fairly regularly, it became okay with me to have sex at home. I thought that then they weren't going to see me switching men friends all the time. Somehow, in my head, affection and caring are linked and that makes having sex okay. So I introduced them to having one man friend stay over periodically and that relationship lasted for about six months and then another one lasted for about a year, so it was one man at a time and it's still that way. I have changed boy friends several times, but I usually have only one man sleep over at a time.

Others, like Kelly, struggled with the issue and ended up feeling fine about having different men sleep over:

Before I got a divorce I realized it was time to make some big decisions for me alone, and that the children's needs, in a sense, were going to have to take a back seat for the time being. I had hit a really critical point in my life because I realized that I had been denying who and what I was. So I made some major decisions including divorce and sterilization and got a job for the first time in ten years. My considerations about my children really did take a back seat. I knew I loved them and wanted them to stay with me, but I was more sensitive to what I needed to take care of for *me*. So initially, after my husband and I separated, there was someone that stayed with me off and on. He never moved in, but he spent a great deal of time there, including overnight. That memory's pretty vague now. At that time, I needed someone and I felt close to him and comforted by him, but I knew it definitely was not going to be a long-term relationship. The children were four, five, and nine, so they were really tuned in to that. After the first few months of almost being overwhelmed by all the adjustments and turmoil of the separation, I began to really stop and think long-term about how do I approach this, how do I take my children and their needs into consideration and provide good modeling for them? How do we make it go as a family with one adult and how do I continue to meet my needs as an individual? I began to realize that I would feel guilty with different men coming and going, sleeping with me and having sex with me on a very casual basis. Although that might meet some needs of mine, it was presenting a very shallow picture to my children about relationships and about sexuality. On the other hand, I was blossoming sexually and it was important for me at that time to try all sorts of different things. I'd come out of a marriage thinking I was frigid. I was very much a product of middle-class mores about what women do and don't do sexually from a Catholic Church upbringing, and had a lot of negative feelings about my sexuality that had just gotten worse during my marriage. It was difficult to balance both my needs and my children's needs.

It's hard to say concisely what I did about this dilemma. I tried to be sensitive to the picture my children were getting. If someone came over who might potentially become a sexual partner, I didn't necessarily try to make them a part of the family, but at least they knew my children. There was some exposure, and they knew each other as people. Oh, we had some really interesting and funny scenes through the years. Someone would be in my home for the very first time, perhaps somebody I hardly knew at all, and my youngest child would ask him if he was spending the night and should she get out the extra pillow! They ended up becoming very comfortable about it. I can say that over the past five years I've had a number of different sexual partners, but nobody has lived with us. I tried to take it as lightly and as naturally as I could and with as much respect for my children's feelings. I realize that they won't pick up any negative attitudes about it unless I am feeling guilty or upset or unnatural about what I'm doing, so I checked that out with myself and it felt okay. I decided then they just need to accept my life-style and it seems that that has really worked out for us.

The issue of communicating the appropriate values to their children, yet not trying to hide the fact that they were sexual beings, was a dilemma for many women. They did not want to give their children the impression that it was okay to sleep with every Tom, Dick, and Harry because the women would not feel comfortable with their children (particularly daughters) sleeping with multiple partners. They feared giving them excessive permission to experiment sexually themselves, yet they wanted to instill a healthy attitude about sex. Dora talks about her concerns for her seven-year-old daughter in this area:

The other part of being a single parent is that it always meant leaving my daughter overnight with someone so I could go out and have a long night and leisurely morning with someone and that's pretty icky.

I've never yet found a babysitter that Elaine really loved being with. So what I did was allow myself a night like that once a week or three or so of those a month. Otherwise, my boy friend and I would have sex at home after her bedtime and he would leave afterward. I remember one night a man I had been seeing for about six months and I accidentally fell asleep, and about 6 A.M. I suddenly woke up, really worried. He had just shut the front door when Elaine came pattering in awake. It was just cutting it too close for me to feel comfortable.

Part of me feels insecure and ambivalent about my sexual freedom. I really love sex and principally it works for me when I'm in a relationship where there's a lot of loving. It's very hard for me to have good sex with someone I don't know pretty well, so I haven't done very much of that. And I also come from a different era. I never made love until I was twenty-one. Anyway, here's this sweet seven-year-old child of mine and I worry about imparting the right values.

Some women preferred a direct approach, especially with teenagers. This, however, was not always easy for the teen-ager. Even though teen-agers are very aware of sexuality, they are often in the throes of deciding difficult issues for themselves, and the subject is often highly volatile.

Penelope received this response when her twelve-year-old son discovered her birth control pills soon after her divorce:

I don't remember how long I was single before my son, who was twelve at the time, found my birth control pills. He came out and said, "You're still taking birth control pills?" I said, "Yes," and he said, "How come? You're not married." I said, "Not being married doesn't mean that my sex desire changes." He asked, "Well, are you sleeping with somebody?" and I said, "Yeah." Then he asked who and I said, "That's my business and his." To which he replied, "You mean you're not going to tell me?" I replied, "Yeah. I really don't think that's any business of yours," and he answered, "Well, that means that when any guy walks through the front door, I'm going to wonder if he's screwing my mother." I said, "You know, you might be right every time," and he said, "Really? More than one?" I answered, "Well, yeah. I can have sexual relations with somebody and not necessarily have to have a long-term relationship with him. We have fun sexually. We enjoy each other's company, but I'm not monogamous with anyone I'm dating." I knew it would be hard for him to deal with that. He's a very straight kid.

On camping trips, Ray and I would sleep together in the camper and my son would sleep in the camp or someplace separate from us and that was okay, but I never let Ray stay over at the house. I don't know if I would do that today, but that was where I was then. I would probably do it again if my son was at that age and having such difficulty in losing another stepfather, and not being sure what his role was supposed to be around the house. He was confused about whether he was supposed to take over now because my husband was gone. And the confusion of a guy getting up and having breakfast with him would have been too much.

Forty-five-year-old Jane shares some of the problems she encountered because of the way she initially handled her sexuality with her thirteen- and nineteen-year-old sons after her divorce:

When I was first divorced, what I wanted more than anything else was for my two teen-age sons to know that sex wasn't dirty and that it was nothing to be furtive about. So originally, I did have some men stay overnight once or twice when the boys were in their bedroom. Shortly after that happened, the younger boy and I started having fierce battles. At one point he called me a whore during a fight about something else and I put two and two together. I realized that my behavior didn't match what I had taught him, which was that sex was an expression of love between two people. What I've learned from this is that unless you have an ongoing relationship with a person, a committed relationship, you should have sex someplace other than in your apartment where you all live; otherwise you're demanding too much of them.

LESBIAN SINGLE MOTHERS

Women who were sexually relating to women felt the additional burden of not only letting their children know they were sexual, but that they had other women for lovers. When and how to tell the child depended a lot upon the woman's comfort with being lesbian or bisexual. Once the woman came to terms with her own sexuality and had overcome some of her culturally induced feelings of shame and abnormality about preferring female lovers, the children were apt to be more accepting of her sexual orientation as well.

It was also important for the children to be ready to handle the information, although, judging from the feedback we got from the mothers, the children were better prepared for hearing the truth than they were for telling it. Still, not only did the children have to acknowledge that their mothers were different from the norm, but that the situation could affect their relationships with friends in the neighborhood and at school.

Justine, a thirty-one-year-old lesbian who lives with her lover and her two children, ages ten and twelve, had this experience:

I got involved with women and kept that a secret because I didn't know how my children would deal with it. Also, at the time, I was involved with women who were teaching at their school, people they dealt with every day, so it was easier, and I thought better, not to tell them. I also reasoned that when you're a kid and your mom has lots of friends and they're all women, how would you suspect anything? They don't know who Mommy goes to bed with at night. But my rationale was wrong. After I moved in with Ellen, we started having a terrible time with the kids. They were always fighting and sometimes they were hysterical. Then we found notes. I found a note about families—"Families have mommies and daddies and children." So we got some family therapy. That helped, but it was only in the last year that I finally said it out loud that I was a lesbian and Ellen and I were lovers. I thought they knew and I still think they did. But I'd never spoken with them about it directly. Tiffany was nine and Polly was eleven. I said, "We need privacy. We want to be sexual together. Do you know that? Do you know that's what's happening?" And they said yes, and it felt like the tension had broken because something heavy had been acknowledged. They said, "Okay, you can do that." It was a big step! It was like they were finally ready to deal with it even though both of them were and are still angry. Polly, the oldest one, is very conscious of how angry she is that I'm a lesbian. It's a hassle for her. She will get hassled at school if it becomes known. She sees it happening to other kids, but as she reveals this secret to her friends, one at a time, and when nothing bad happens and her friends still like to come here to play, she's not so fearful and not so angry. Her fears were cultural and realistic, so it was hard to argue with them. She said, why didn't we wait ten years, until they had grown up. I said, "I've been waiting a long time and there are things I have to do." I know that anger will be there for a while, but I also know she loves me a lot.

Diane, a thirty-two-year-old lesbian foster mother, gives a good description of how she prepared her eight-year-old foster daughter, Sara, for the possible reaction of others:

There was a lesbian club that had opened up, but it had gotten a poor reception from the neighborhood. I said something to Sara about it—I told her there was this club across the street that people didn't like and had tried to burn down. She asked, "Why didn't they like it?" I said, "The people who went there were mainly lesbians. Do you know what lesbians are?" She said no. I said, "Well, it's two women who like to be with each other." Then I added, "Like I do." I told her some people didn't like lesbians because they thought it wasn't okay for two women to be together. I don't remember if I told her the women are sexual with each other. I explained that she had to make a decision about who she was going to tell and what effect it would have if she told the wrong person.

For about six months she did not say anything about me being a lesbian, and then all of a sudden there was a big to-do in the newspapers about gay teachers in the schools. So I told the woman down the street who had a daughter Sara's age that I was a lesbian and we talked about all the stuff that was happening. I told Sara that I had told this woman I was a lesbian and if she wanted to tell this woman's daughter, who was also her friend, that was okay. She apparently did because the woman told me later that Sara had said I was a lesbian and that a lesbian was when two women kiss each other all the time.

IMPARTING HEALTHY SEXUAL ATTITUDES TO YOUR CHILDREN

An important issue for almost all of the mothers we interviewed was their desire to supply their children with healthier attitudes than they had received from their mothers. They felt they had received the detrimental message that sex was secret and illicit because it had not been discussed in any open and explicit way in their own families. These women felt strongly that they wanted to give their children the exact opposite message, that sex was a normal and healthy process and something that could be talked about openly and honestly. Since they had no good models themselves, most of them were not quite sure how to go about explaining sexual subjects to their children. They were determined, however, to give them a different message. They wanted their children to be able to talk about sex more easily and to treat sex as a more natural part of life than they had been able to do. They wanted them to be comfortable with their bodies, to have accurate sexual information, and to understand that sex is a positive and enjoyable experience that is to be respected and not degraded. They wanted their daughters to be prepared for menstruation and they wanted to acknowledge masturbation as a natural and pleasurable activity. Obviously a tall order, but as difficult as many women found this task, they still attempted to do things differently from their parents.

Many women we talked with were concerned about when and how to best explain sexuality to their children. Most realized that waiting until adolescence was too late, but were confused as to when to begin discussions and how explicitly to present the information.

Basically, it is important to recognize that children are sexual from the day they are born. By that we mean that their bodies contain all the receptors necessary for receiving sexual pleasure even though they may not label those feelings as such. Also, at a very early age, children receive messages from older siblings or peers that something illicit or naughty is somehow connected to something called sex, even though they often do not understand what it means exactly or how sex takes place. Consequently, waiting until adolescence to impart information often means that the child has already received explicit or insinuated input. To ensure that the child's picture of sexuality is accurate requires that parents provide appropriate information.

Information can be presented to children whenever the opportunity arises. Stories in the newspaper or on television about rape, contraception, or unwed mothers, or a pregnancy in the family or neighborhood all present the opportunity to have a discussion about sexuality. Since a child's cognitive development determines the constructs or concepts he or she can comprehend at a given age, it is generally best to determine as clearly as possible the exact nature of the information sought before answering. This can most effectively be accomplished not only by listening carefully to the question, but by asking the child to tell you what he or she thinks the answer is. In this way, you can correct any misunderstanding or any misinformation. It is also helpful to question the child after supplying the information to ascertain whether what you have explained has been correctly understood and if there are any further questions. In general, a sympathetic and straightforward presentation of the information is the approach most likely to bring the best results.

It is also important to realize that children, like adults, receive messages concerning the feelings and attitudes underlying the actual information conveyed. In other words, they may pick up that the conversation about sex is making you tense, although they may not quite understand why. In this case, they may conclude that there is something negative or bad about sex and that is why you are anxious. If, like most parents, you have had little practice with discussions of this type, it is often better to explain your feelings to your child. For example, you might say, "Talking about sex is hard for me because my parents never talked about it with me. But sex is important to me. It's something I really enjoy. So I'm glad to have the chance to become more comfortable talking about it."

This way the child will not be confused by the discrepancy between the words (sex is positive) and the feelings (I am anxious) conveyed.

Finally, the most important information about sex is contained within the attitudes you impart. These attitudes are constantly being conveyed to your children by the way you interact both physically and emotionally with your partner. You give your child a far more powerful message about your positive feelings about sex when the child sees you being physically affectionate with your partner. This does not mean having intercourse in front of the child, but that the child has the opportunity to see the physical affection being expressed in other ways, like the way you hug or cuddle or kiss each other.

A major block to implementing frank, open conversations about sexuality with children or being more affectionate physically with spouses is the woman's own negative attitude about her body. Many of these negative feelings come from the fact that most of us grew up in households where naked bodies were never seen. Many of us felt it took years to gain comfort with our own nudity, especially with having our sexual parts visible. Gabrielle came from such a background:

When I was young, my introduction to sex was not through any formal education by my parents. I don't blame them because it's a cultural neurosis that's kind of passed down from generation to generation. I wouldn't expect my mother to be able to do it if her mother didn't do it; in their generation, sex was simply something you didn't talk about.

My mother's modesty in part came from the fact that she had had a mastectomy. When I gave her her robe, I would have to pass it around through a crack in the door. She would always wear a slip, underwear, and a bra. I never saw her genitals. The closest I got to seeing my father nude was seeing him in boxer shorts, and he would always hold the fly closed. Even in his pajamas he would hold the draw string because there wasn't any zipper. When I was necking in the car as a teen-ager, he would come out in his pajamas, holding his fly closed—as if anyone would be interested in that. The first time I saw a naked man was in some nudist colony magazine that we found on a camping trip. So I have very strong feelings that that is not the way I want my son to be brought up. I think a lot of my feelings of inhibition are due to my upbringing. I'm still uptight when I'm naked. I just want my son to grow up feeling good about his body and know that it's not an unnatural thing to see someone naked.

Anatomy

From the stories told by the women, it appeared that they experienced far greater discomfort than their children when they began talking about sex. When they taught their children to label the sexual parts of their bodies, most children just accepted the information naturally. Some women were even comfortable allowing their young children to examine their genitals as a way to learn about these usually hidden parts and to better explain the process of childbirth. Karen shared this experience:

My husband and I have always been pretty open to walking around in the nude. We don't try to hide our bodies. We take showers together, all four of us, and sometimes if I'm in a rush and he's going in the shower, I'll tell him to take the girls with him. At this age—they are three and five—it's not a problem, but it does bring up issues. My three-year-old asked me a couple of weeks ago where my coochie (their word for genitals) was because all she saw was hair. So I told her it was there and she said she wanted to see it, so I let her look. She examined it and said, "Yeah, that looks like mine," and that satisfied her curiosity.

Louise used a visit to the doctor's office as an opportunity to teach her son about female anatomy:

When I was going to the obstetrician before my daughter was born, I took my three-year-old son with me, mainly because I didn't have a babysitter. I let him come in and he saw the obstetrician examining me. I felt comfortable about his seeing me like that. I wouldn't have felt comfortable at home getting undressed and showing him my body, but at the doctor's office it felt okay to me. I wasn't embarrassed and he actually saw where the baby comes out and got an idea of what anatomy is involved. He said, "Mom, I hate to tell you this, but when the baby comes out, it's really going to hurt!"

I realize that he really did understand some of that because later he asked me, "Wasn't that uncomfortable? Wasn't Daddy very heavy lying on top of you?" I told him no, that it was comfortable and felt good to be close like that.

Ruby recalled an experience that occurred three years previously:

When my daughter was one year old and my son just four, he was still experiencing occasional attacks of "babyitis"—wanting to nurse, to talk baby talk, to be the littlest one. My daughter had gone down for her nap and I was resting on the sofa, leaning way back with my legs crossed yoga fashion. My son curled up in my lap wanting to nurse, which I allowed and which quickly bored him. Next he began chattering about my vagina and uterus and started to lift my skirt. My response was to stop him and get a bit tense, but I sensed a sincerity and something more—a need, perhaps—from him which allowed me to relax and support his exploration. He lifted my skirt and crawled under while talking about being a tiny, tiny speck of a baby inside my uterus. I confirmed his information whenever he asked for it, but didn't need to add much. He asked what my body position had been when he was born, so I put my feet flat on the sofa edge, well apart; my whole body position was then quite similar to what it had actually been in childbirth. All this happened while he was careful to keep himself covered by the skirt. Then he tapped me on the stomach and asked if I was ready; I said "Yes"; and he said, "Me, too. It's time to get born. Do whatever it is you do, Mommy, and I'll come out." Well, I grabbed my knees, raising my back slightly from the pillows, made a few grunting sounds as he raised my skirt and stepped onto the floor. He turned to me with a beatific smile, threw his arms wide, and in a shout of sudden recognition yelled, "Mom, it's me!" We hugged for a long time and then read some books. The entire experience was warm and loving and very satisfactory for both of us.

Some women were able to integrate sex education into their family naturally and preferred to use technical terminology when discussing anatomy:

Well, initially, we started talking about sex when they were very small children. I used to shower with the boys as a matter of expediency. When they were about one and three, as soon as they could stand up in the tub, if I were in a rush, we'd all get in and shower together. I'll never forget when my oldest son—he could not have been more than three years old—stood in front of me about knee level, and he turned me around and looked at my back and then turned me around again and looked at my front. He said, "Mommy, you don't have a penis." I said, "No, girls don't have penises, they have vaginas." Later in the day, we went down to the lake and his little three-year-old playmate next door was swimming in the lake maybe fifty yards out. He ran all the way down the hill screaming, "Cindy, Cindy, Cindy, I have a penis, you don't!"

I can remember, too, when the boys were very little, and I went walking into the bathroom and they were both holding their penises and urinating at one another. They said something about having a swordfight and we laughed and made fun about that. This was when they were preschoolers.

They both went to something called a farm school, which was a nursery school where there were cats, dogs, pigs, and ducks. They watched many an animal being born there. They also discussed at the farm school how plants and trees germinated, so when they asked me how babies were born, I would explain what they could understand at the time. So from the time they learned to talk, they knew they had penises. They weren't called "hickeys" or "ding-dongs." Initially, they "pooped" and "peed," but as soon as they were old enough to learn the word urinate, they urinated. I couldn't stand all those cute little words.

The fact that a little girl's clitoris and not her vagina is the most important part of her sexual equipment is a new idea. Consequently, some mothers have begun equating the penis with the clitoris rather than with the vagina. Ariel, mother of a five-year-old:

Shelly, my daughter, has seen her father's penis and she's seen little boys' penises. Once we were looking at her birth pictures taken the day she was born. There's a picture of her upside down with the cord still attached, and she said, "How did you know I was a girl?" I answered, "Because you don't have a penis, you have a nice clitoris." I try not to talk about the absence of penis, but to talk positively about what she has.

Menstruation

Preparing daughters for menstruation was a common concern. Many women had been totally unprepared by their own mothers and this resulted in their experiencing their first period as a frightening event. Therefore, again these women were particularly sensitive about not wanting to make the same mistake with their own daughters.

Thirty-year-old Karen remembered:

When I was a child, sex wasn't discussed at all. It was something shrouded in mystery, something negative. I can remember in the sixth or seventh grade when they showed us a sex education movie I really didn't understand it. The first time I got my period I used an old rag or something, because I was really frightened. I thought I was bleeding to death. I was really scared! I can remember a girl friend of mine started on her period before I did and I thought once you had a period you were always on it, every day of your life, that you wore Kotex for the rest of your life. One day, I was on the playground with her and she did a flip-flop on the jungle gym. I looked up to see if I could see any Kotex in her underpants, but it was obvious there was nothing there. I asked her where it was and she said, "Well, you don't wear it all the time." My mother had never talked to me about menstruation at all. The only thing she said about it was that when I was having my period, I couldn't wash my hair, take baths, or spend the night away from home. I didn't understand the reasoning behind it, but I never did question it. I more or less accepted it.

Sixty-six-year-old Edith recalled:

It was difficult for me to talk to my children about sex because my mother had never talked to me. In fact, nobody, literally nobody, had ever talked to me about sex in my whole life. I didn't even know when my menstruation started, what it was. I thought I was mortally wounded and that it was all my fault. So I did talk to my daughter about her period. She knew about that. Whenever I would come across an article or got a book or two, I gave them to her and told her to ask me anything about them when she got through with them, but even saying that didn't come out in a natural free-flowing way.

Like Edith, some women relied heavily on written material for their children to digest. Others felt it was important to discuss the information completely in their own words. Louise describes the words she used to talk about menstruation with her daughter:

I don't remember definite talks with my daughter, Janet, about sex. Things seemed to happen more naturally. One day she saw me taking out a tampon and she asked me what I was doing. I said I was pulling a plug. "What's a plug, Mommy?" she asked. "Well, it's a piece of cotton you put inside of you because once a month in the place where babies grow, blood and water come out if you're not growing a baby. Kotex is what you wear if you're afraid your plug is leaking," I answered.

That was just a part of her growing up. And I don't remember sitting down and talking to her when her time came. I was at work when she started to menstruate and she called me. It was four o'clock—I'll never forget it. She said to me on the phone, "Guess what?" I'm saying, "Guess what, what, Janet?" "Well, guess what!" she said it about three times and finally I said, "You didn't!" and she said, "I did!" I said, "Well, what did you use?" and she said, "I went in your bathroom and got a pad out and stuck it to my pants." I asked her how she was feeling about all that and she said, "You know, it's a pain in the neck because I got gym tomorrow and I wonder what I'm going to do." I said, "We can talk about that tonight." "Well," she said, "by tonight I'll have it figured out. I'll probably just take another pair of pants if I leak," and that was it. I've never had cramps so I've never said anything to her about cramps and she's now been menstruating two years and she's never had cramps, which I think is interesting. I'm a nurse, so I have some theories about how we can set up some reactions in our kids that aren't necessary.

Masturbation

Masturbation was often a very highly charged subject, frequently even more difficult for the women to talk to their children about than sexual intercourse. The discomfort not only went back to any negative reactions the women might have received from their own parents, but also had to do with the extent to which they had come to terms with their feelings of acceptance of masturbation in their own life.

Karen, thirty, a saleswoman, married nine years to Gary, a company manager, with daughters, five and three:

A couple of days ago, my three-year-old was rubbing herself between her legs and I said, "What are you doing?" and she said, "I'm just rubbing my coochie." I said, "Well, does it feel good?" and she said, "Yes." My five-year-old says, "It feels good when I do it, it feels like I'm peeing!" It kind of startled me, and I didn't know whether to encourage it or discourage it, so I just said, "Oh, really?" and kind of let it go.

Many women we talked with were well educated and realized not only that masturbation was a healthy and normal activity, but also that it provided the child with sexual learning about his or her own body in a less complicated way than if they initially experimented with another youngster. Roberta approached masturbation in the following manner:

My initial reaction to my daughter's masturbation when she was just a baby was to say, "Don't do that," because that's what my mother told me, but then I started investigating. I read books and talked to my pediatrician, my gynecologist, and even to a psychologist. I finally decided the best way to handle it would be to allow her to masturbate, that it was a natural part of growing up, of learning about one's sexuality, so I didn't tell her not to do it. I simply stated that she needed to do it privately.

Louise found a book that clarified her own feelings about masturbation and shared it with her daughter:

I read a book called *Sex With Love* by Dr. Edith Hamilton that said it is better to wait until you're seventeen years old to become sexually active because a girl needs to learn about her own body, a girl needs to learn how to masturbate and find out what excites her, what feels good, so that she can teach a young boy. That way, she won't get cheated by giving her body away and not getting good feelings and sensations back in return. A lot of girls are nonorgasmic clear through their adolescence even though they've been sexually active, and I've rarely heard anyone say they enjoyed their orgasms when they were adolescents. They were usually too afraid. This book says if you know your own body, your fear dissipates about a lot of things and you really then can teach a young man how to love you. I think this book gave a rationale for feeling equal when you enter into a sexual relationship so you can offer information about how you work to the other person. I really agreed with that value system, so I bought the book and my daughter Janet has read it. Since talking about sex sometimes is embarrassing to adolescents, I advise giving them some reading material and using that as a basis for talking together later on as we did.

However, even with this arsenal of intellectual acceptance, many mothers were personally quite uncomfortable with the whole topic of masturbation, even when they were aware that their child had masturbated at some point. The major concern of the women who were fairly comfortable with masturbation was the issue of privacy. They wanted to convey to their children the message that there was nothing wrong with masturbation, but that it was something done in the privacy of their own room.

Barbara handled the situation this way:

Masturbation was a very big issue in our house. Our daughter started masturbating at about three years old. At first, when she started, it shook us up a little bit because of where she did it, which was everywhere! We couldn't figure out what to do because it felt very inappropriate and so we took out our books on child development and how to raise children, because we didn't want to traumatize her either. We finally decided that, for us, masturbating all over the house just didn't feel right. We told our daughter that if she wanted to touch herself that she could go in her room and do it there, where it's private. Now if we see her touching herself, we'll ask her to go to her room and do it.

If masturbation has not been discussed very early on, sometimes bringing the subject up in later years can be uncomfortable. Jane had a helpful hint about how she initiated the conversation with her adolescent sons under circumstances which she felt would be the least awkward:

The most wonderful time to talk to your children is when you're on a long trip in a car, especially when it involves highway driving and night driving. There's a softness, a quietness, and a sense of privacy about the dark that relaxes everyone. The hum of the engine and the darkness of the night makes the whole atmosphere relaxed, free, and warm. Also, there's not much space in a car, which makes everyone feel kind of cozy. I remember the first time I discussed masturbation with the boys was in the car on a trip at night. They were about eleven and thirteen and I was concerned that they not feel guilty about the things they were experiencing. My thirteen-year-old was reaching puberty. I saw signs of it. So anyway, as part of a conversation, I asked the boys if they ever masturbated, and I think at the time the younger one said, "Yes" and the older one said, "Oh, Mother, for heaven's sakes!" I remember saying, "Your body has nice feelings when you do that," and letting it drop. But nevertheless, in that brief space and without pushing I had let them know it was okay.

Louise remembers that she used a book with pictures as a way of opening up the conversation when her daughter was ten years old. However, she made the subject of the book more real by talking about herself:

I started out the conversation by saying, "Janet, there's something I've been wondering about, and that's if you know about masturbation?" There's a book out called *What's Happening to Me?* that has really funny pictures in it. There's a picture of a little boy on a diving board and he has an erection and the caption says, "It always happens at the most inopportune times." We read that book together and she kind of giggled when we came to that page. Then I told her that girls have the same kind of equipment only they're built a little bit differently, but you can have the same kinds of feelings if you rub yourself and I pointed to where I rub myself. I said that it feels good and you get some nice tingly feelings. I asked her if she'd ever done that, but she said no.

Sexual Intercourse

When it came time to talk about sexual intercourse, most of the women provided information when their children asked questions.

Most were not comfortable bringing the subject up first, particularly with young children. In these cases, they were careful to answer the questions as precisely as possible and in a straightforward manner and hoped their children understood the answers. Since most of them had been raised in a very restrictive environment and had no role models, talking about sex was not easy. Therefore, this difficulty was often compounded with a precocious child, as was the case with Ruby's seven-year-old son:

There was only one time I was taken aback by something my son said and felt I didn't handle it very well. My four-year-old daughter was naked and leaning over the bed and he was checking her out as I was making his bed. It was very casual, he was just looking at her, he wasn't touching her, and he said, "Mama, can boys put their penis in the asshole, too?" For a long enough moment I couldn't find an answer and then I said, "Well, I think you should ask Daddy about that," instead of simply answering yes and letting it go at that. His interest was piqued and I knew it was because he sensed my awkward feelings. If I had simply said "Yes, you can if you want to," and let it go, it would have been fine. All he wanted was an answer. He didn't want to do it or watch anyone do it, he just wanted a simple answer. Every time the kids ask me a sexual question, I try to understand what I'm being asked. Once I understand that, I give the simplest, briefest answer possible. I try to communicate an attitude of openness, warmth, and friendliness because I think the feelings you communicate about sex are the most important thing. They are going to get a lot of misinformation along the way, but as long as they have a basic understanding of the goodness and warmth about sexuality, they'll get it all sorted out.

Again, as with discussing masturbation, the choice of words used is important when trying to communicate a specific feeling or understanding about sexual intercourse. The following two excerpts indicate the difference in parental feelings about the meaning of sexual intercourse and their appropriate choice of words in describing the act to their children. Eve prefers to use the term "making love" when talking to her nine- and eleven-year-old sons:

We started off using anatomical terms with our kids when they were very young, so they knew what a penis and a vagina were, and they knew all the parts of the body by their correct names. When they have asked us questions about sex, we've again used the correct terms. They have asked us about words they've heard at school, like "fuck"—we told them that was not a very polite way of talking about the act of making love. We've called it "making love" as well as "sexual intercourse," although "making love" seems to be the more comfortable for my husband and me. Part of it is that we have tried to convey to the boys a sense that the sexual act is not only a physical act, but also has elements of intimacy and caring. To me, that's the exact connotation of the phrase "making love," so that's what we've used.

Louise, on the other hand, distinguishes between having sex and making love to her fourteen-year-old daughter:

We do a lot of talking about what it means to be sexually active, what it means to have sex. We try not to use the words "make love" because I have a problem with that, I think "having sex" and "making love" can be two different things. I like to draw a distinction there. I think you can have sex and make love at the same time, but I don't think it's always that way.

Most children learn about sex as the result of pregnancy. Mother is having a second or third child, a neighbor or teacher or friend's mother is pregnant—circumstances which pique the child's curiosity. After all, the woman was not pregnant before; how did it come about that she is going to have a baby now? When confronted by this question, a parent is given the opportunity to explain sexual intercourse to the child. Some parents assume that the child could not understand the concept of intercourse so they fabricate an answer—"You go to the doctor's office and the doctor puts the baby inside, and then later, when it is ready, the doctor takes it out"; "When you love someone very much, then you have a baby"; or other explanations that avoid the mention of sex. Unfortunately, although these answers may suffice for the moment, they may have negative repercussions later on as the child becomes confused when friends report different versions. The woman who was told as a child that you have a baby when you really love someone recalls concentrating for days on how much she loved her father so she could have a baby. The result can be frustration, disappointment, and distrust of parental information when the truth becomes known, whereas, straightforward information seems to be well received by young children as indicated by Karen's interaction with her daughter:

About a year ago my five-year-old started asking questions about how babies were made and how she had gotten into my stomach. I explained to her that Daddy's penis goes into my vagina and a baby is made. Then a few minutes later she asked me how Daddy's penis makes a baby and I told her that I'd have to think about it for a couple of days. I needed to think of a way I could explain it to her so that she would understand. I ended up telling her that there is juice in Daddy's penis and when he puts it in my vagina, the juice goes inside and mixes with the juice in my vagina and that makes a baby. Then the baby just grows inside the stomach. It was simple enough for her to understand, and it made sense to her, so she accepted it.

When a description is insufficient, diagrams or pictures can be helpful. Oftentimes in the early stages of cognitive development, words and concepts are more difficult to comprehend than a visual diagram or photograph:

When I got pregnant this time, my daughter, who is seven, wanted to understand how. We had always told her Mommy had an egg and Daddy had a seed and that Daddy's seed made the baby. This time she wanted to know exactly how Daddy's seed got into the mother. We said that Daddy gave the seed to Mommy. "Well, how did you give the seed to Mommy?" Then we told her the penis gave Mommy the seed. "Well, how did the penis give Mommy the seed, through what, how?" We explained it to her verbally, but it really wasn't enough. She didn't understand, so we went to the library and got her some very good books with pictures. The pictures showed the daddy's penis going into the mommy through the vagina. After she saw those pictures, she said to me, "Now I understand." Then she didn't ask any more questions.

Animals also provide an excellent introduction to understanding sex. After all, before people moved to cities, the natural sexual cycles could be readily observed by watching animals, and children raised on farms often learn about sex this way. Pets can serve the same purpose, as Eve discovered:

Another thing that has been very educational sexually for our boys has been just having a pet. We have a dog and we wanted her to produce a litter. So we went through this process of getting her homones. All of this meant a lot of discussion with the kids, who were six and four at the time, about what was going on because we had to take her to be mated a couple of times. There was a lot of joking about how she was going to her boy friend and they were going to try to produce some puppies. It was really an excellent opportunity to sit down with them and use some books to describe what happens.

However, even when the child can understand the mechanics of the process, they are often unable to understand why anyone would want to do such a thing. The response of Samantha's child is not at all unusual:

When my eight-year-old son's teacher was pregnant, it was a class event. The whole class went through the process with her and even made baby announcements for the teacher to send out after the baby was born in the summer. There were nineteen of them and they were very much involved in this whole process. The teacher handled it beautifully, but a lot of questions came home around that time that weren't appropriate for her to answer because parents like to have that responsibility or it should be their responsibility. I guess that's how my son and I got into it. He was reading books so he knew about conception and intercourse, but he wanted to know why on earth anybody would want to do that. I said, "What do you mean, why would anybody want to do it?" "Well, why would a man want to stick his penis in a woman's vagina and pee in it?" he asked. I explained the physiological process and we had some books he could read. Then he said, "I still don't understand why anybody would want to do that." I said, "When people care a lot about each other, they make love and it feels good to adults to do that. It may not be anything of great interest to you right now, but it's something that feels very good. It's something that means two people want to do things that make each other feel good. Part of what happens in that process is that the sperm and the egg unite and the woman can become pregnant and they can have a baby, but there's a whole other process." This conversation continued over about a three-to-four-month period. Sometime later I came home to find my son arguing with an eighteen-year-old babysitter about whether or not people could have sex if they weren't married, which I think is a legitimate thing. I settled the discussion by saying, "Of course they can." I told him marriage is something people do when they want to make a commitment to each other and having babies is part of that, but you can do all of that without being married. He took that in and is in a dormant stage of digesting it.

Most parents find that restricting discussions of sex to describing the mechanics of intercourse is insufficient, especially as their children begin to grow older. During their teen years, especially with the changing attitudes about sex in this culture, many parents wanted to make sure that they instilled healthy sexual values in their child. For some, this meant that sex should be saved only for marriage. In all cases, however, the mothers were concerned that their children treat sexuality in a responsible manner. They wanted them to have sex for the right reasons, as indicated by Sonya, a forty-year-old microbiologist, separated two years and the mother of four children, daughters, eighteen and fourteen, sons, sixteen and nine:

I've also made it clear to my three teen-agers that I don't have a different set of values for my sons and my daughters. I expect all of them to be responsible for their sexual behavior and to be aware of what they're doing. They can have sex if they want to, but I want them to be prepared and take whatever precautions they need. I want them to be responsible for themselves, but also to choose responsible partners. After all, it takes two responsible people to have sex.

They wanted to provide information which would help ensure that their child would be knowledgeable and responsible sexually. Louise had this talk with her fourteen-year-old daughter:

I do talk about sexually transmitted diseases. I say, "Okay, this is the grim side!" I always say, "I really want you to have all the information you need about sexually transmitted diseases and how to avoid getting pregnant, when you make the decision to have sex. When you decide to become sexually active, I hope you plan it by going down to Planned Parenthood. I'll take you or you can go by yourself, but I want you to know those resources are available." I've come a long way to be able to say that. What helped me to be able to say this was giving up feeling that I have ownership of my child's body and to realize that my responsibility is to allow my daughter to own her own body and take responsibility for it.

They wanted to protect the child from having the sexual experience result in pregnancy. Gweneth, a forty-four-year-old nurse, married twenty-one years and the mother of three teen-age children, said:

My sixteen-year-old daughter was going with this darling guy. I just hadn't gotten enough courage to ask if she was sexually active, because you don't want your little girl to grow up, but on the other hand, you do. So I said, "I've never really asked you, if there's a time when you need birth control, please feel free to go to a private doctor of your choice. You don't need permission from me, but please be responsible." I work in a birth control clinic and I didn't want her to feel she had to go there. She said, "Oh, as a matter of fact, I do have strong feelings about Paul and maybe I should get birth control as a preventive, but I want to go to the clinic." She said, "I might as well, all my friends go" —and it just blew all the staff's minds. They were so used to seeing Lilly come in as my daughter and all of a sudden here she is going to see the doctor. Then I thought I'll have to talk to my son Stanley—he was fifteen. And I said, "Stanley, I think we need to talk." And he said, "Mother, if I were sexually active, don't you think I'd use birth control? What do you think I am, an idiot?"

What we realized in doing the interviews was that it was important for the child to have a parent to go to for accurate information about sex. This parent also needed to be open and accepting of the child's attitudes, fears, and concerns. Many of the mothers we interviewed felt that they provided most of the sex education for their children. However, in some cases, the child was more comfortable talking with a man than with a woman. Most mothers were happy to conform to whatever would make the child most comfortable. In general, this meant the mother talking about sex with her daughter and the father talking about sex with his son. Penelope describes the lines of communication between herself, her son, and her third husband:

When my son Joe and I were alone, before I remarried, and before Harold was there, we spent a lot of time walking the dog and talking. That's when we had our best talking. He would talk to me a lot about his feeling ill at ease socially. It was comforting for him to know that females also had a difficult time with dating. He was surprised because he thought it would be so much easier to be asked out than to have to do the asking. Here he was in college going through the same pain

I went through in the fifties. By the time he was sexually active, I remarried and Harold was part of the family. Then he was experiencing ejaculation problems. He would talk to me about problems his girl friends had, but when it came to talking about his own sexual stuff, he was more comfortable talking to Harold about it. He talked to him about his concern that he came so quickly. And Harold gave him some suggestions.

So we see from this chapter that not only is it possible to maintain an active and satisfying sex life despite the presence of children, but it is also possible to grow beyond our parents' limitations in our dealings with our own children. In attempting to be more open with them, we are able to free ourselves sexually from the scripting we acquired from our parents.

Being able to switch roles adds another dimension to child rearing. There is the advantage of having two perspectives on the process: that of the parent and that of the child. Recalling our experiences as a child, and remembering how we wished our parents would have handled the subject of sexuality with us, not only enables us to better understand our own parents' conflicts and difficulties, but challenges us to devise new solutions. It is similar to being an actor on the stage. Playing the role of one leading character allows for insight into that person, but being able to switch roles and play the opposite lead provides us with a whole new level of insight and understanding. With this more complete understanding of the characters, we are given the opportunity to take the risk of improvising our roles. With our greater awareness of both the role of the child and that of the parent, we are uniquely qualified to write a new script and, hopefully, help create more positive and healthy sexual attitudes in future generations.

9

Being Sexual in Your Later Years

It is an indisputable fact that people are now healthier and living longer than at any other time in history. The average life expectancy in the United States is nearly seventy-three years and rising.* As people maintain their health for longer periods of time, they continue to be sexually active for correspondingly longer periods of time. Consequently, there is a growing interest in the part sexuality will play in the later years.

Given the changing societal view toward sex and the fact that women tend to outlive men, many widows, divorcees, and even women who have been married for forty to fifty years are having to face an array of new physical, cultural, and social questions related to sexuality and the maturing process.

Younger women—those in their thirties, forties, and even fifties —were curious about the information we would be receiving from women in their "autumn years." Their questions echoed our own. What do we have to look forward to? Will we still have the same sex drive in our sixties, seventies, and eighties and perhaps even

---

* Diana Woodruff, *Can You Live to Be One Hundred?* (New York: Chatham Square Press, 1977).

our nineties? What will we do for partners? Where will we find them? How will our male partners be affected by the aging process?

It seemed that in this area, as in sexuality and pregnancy, there was relatively little known. There was a dearth of material from older women *themselves* sharing, explaining, or revealing what their lives were like sexually. And, of course, few of the women we interviewed felt that they could personally get this information on a one-to-one basis from women in their own families.

The physical effects of the aging process on sexuality have received scant attention. Few physicians have been trained in geriatric medicine. Lack of medical expertise coupled with the inadequate physiological data available on sexuality leaves information on the sexual effects of the aging process incomplete at best.

Another major issue for older women is the unavailability of men in their age group. Given that the average female's life span is about eight years longer than that of the average male,† and particularly since the custom has been for women to marry men who were three to five years older than themselves, most women can expect to outlive their spouses by about ten to twelve years. Since there are four women for every three men after the age of sixty, the possibility of finding a socially acceptable male partner of the same age or older is considerably reduced once women reach the age of sixty.

Given the general unavailability of older men, other logical options present themselves in terms of sexual expression. However, many of these options were unacceptable to women during their formative years and remained unacceptable in their later lives as well. For example, masturbation, younger male partners, female partners, nonmarital affairs, or sharing their male partners with other women required women to rethink certain moral, religious, and cultural beliefs in regard to their sexual relationships. To further complicate matters, some women had opposed many of these kinds of sexual relationships and activities in their role as parents

† Figures are correct as of July 1979. *Current Population Reports,* Series P25, No. 870 (U. S. Bureau of Census, January 1980).

while guiding their children, which made reversing some of these beliefs even more difficult.

On the other hand, many women found that being in the later years of their lives afforded them a certain perspective, a certain hindsight that placed them in a unique position to reevaluate the importance and meaning of their life, their values, and, in turn, their sexual relationships. Women of this era, with an appreciation of the brevity of life, tended to highlight the qualities of intimacy, companionship, and caring in sexual relationships rather than sexual performance and intensity. It was not that they were uninterested in a satisfying physical sexual relationship but rather that they had put this in a different perspective.

We were surprised, perhaps because interest in this topic was so high, when we encountered such difficulty finding women to interview for this chapter. We had experienced no difficulty locating interviewees for the other sections. We wanted to interview women in their sixties and older who were still sexually active with a partner or by themselves, who felt positive about themselves as sexual women, and who would agree to talk about their sexuality in a taped interview session. Because of our difficulty in finding receptive interviewees, we surmised that most women in this category either aren't having a sex life, don't feel good about themselves sexually, are uncomfortable admitting that they have a sex life, or perhaps—most likely—wouldn't dream of talking about it. Consequently, the women we have included in this chapter may be atypical. There is no way of knowing.

In general, the women we interviewed were unafraid to talk about their sex lives, although some confessed they were nervous, that they had never discussed this with anyone before, or that family or friends would be shocked if they knew what they were doing. Their curiosity, their desire to share their views, and oftentimes their daring at doing something so bold overcame their ambivalence and nervousness.

As a group, the women we interviewed were not afraid to question values, attitudes, and issues and often made decisions that went against popular thought. Some had divorced when there was great social pressure to remain married, some had changed careers late in life or had gone back to school at ages when other women thought themselves to be too old. Many of those we interviewed were highly educated or professional women who were outspoken on many issues, particularly those social issues facing people in their age group today. Their common denominator, regardless of their life-style or educational background, was their interest in continuing to grow and develop. In a sense, they are models for many younger women because they have continued to grow and gain breadth in all areas of life, including their sexuality. For most of them, their sexual life was as important as any other area.

We asked these women why they thought so many of their peers had such difficulty discussing their sexuality. Their answers were interesting.

Janet, age sixty-three, reminded us that women in their sixties and older were imbued with the prevailing Victorian attitudes present at the time of their birth. Sex was not talked about, particularly by women. Sex was sanctioned only in marriage, where its purpose was to produce children:

> Most women in my age group were inhibited primarily because of the fear of pregnancy as much as the stigma of losing your virginity. If you got pregnant out of wedlock you brought shame on the family name. That was a strong attitude, particularly in my family. Nowadays, with the pill, women don't have to worry about that and I'm glad for them. But it was different then, plus the fact that we just didn't talk about those things then. As a matter of fact, I was so naïve when I got married that I didn't think anything was expected of me except to lie there.

Virginia, seventy-five, and a recently widowed drama teacher, feels that her family's religious attitudes and the general attitudes of the times dictated a total avoidance of the subject of sexuality which continues to affect older women today:

> I was raised very strictly as a Methodist. We didn't talk about sex at all. We just were always very proper. I never knew anything about sex. My mother was a wonderful person and taught us almost everything else that we should have known but we didn't learn much about sex and I think that was wrong. No "nice people" at that time taught

their children about sex and about how their bodies worked and I think that was too bad.

Consequently, when I got married I didn't know very much about sex and neither did my husband. Of course, I was a virgin and he was too. I had never read any sexy books, nothing that was "risqué." I had lived a very sheltered life. The result was that we didn't get what we should have out of our sex life. I never enjoyed sex very much because I never had an orgasm for maybe the first twenty years of my marriage.

During sex I would be so frustrated I would cry. It was some relief, but it wasn't the right kind. I think my husband was not a very good lover, and I don't mean any disrespect when I say this. He was just unknowing about how you have a sex life and so was I. My husband didn't do much to help me in terms of foreplay. Later on in our marriage, it was better. We were more relaxed. If he felt like it and I felt like it, we would have sex, but usually at night.

Glenn, a seventy-two-year-old divorced real estate broker, feels attitudes from her generation's era are still strongly entrenched among her peers. For many of them, being open about their sexuality still evokes feelings of shame and ambivalence:

I really don't know any other people my age who will admit to having had another sexual partner other than their own husband. They make the statement that sex is holy and so sex without marriage is something they would not consider. I rather suspect that some of them may have had other sexual experiences in their life that they won't admit to, but they were brought up as I was, to believe that there was simply a "Mr. Right," that sex was a part of marriage and sex without marriage just was not acceptable. And that while they may have had sex outside of marriage, they themselves still didn't accept it and so they weren't willing to admit to having taken part in it.

To complicate matters even further, older men and women also have to contend with the prevalent cultural myth that beyond a certain age people are no longer supposed to be sexual. Older men who are obviously sexual in their dress, life-style, and attitudes, or who make sexual innuendos, are labeled lechers or dirty old men. Women in similar circumstances are considered somewhat ridiculous and are not taken seriously. It is almost as if a sexually active elder citizen were participating in an activity beneath his or her dignity. The following, not atypical, situation took place between Tricia (sixty-seven, divorced) and her daughter-in-law before Tricia remarried:

I met this man in the airport. I was standing in line waiting to check in my bag and he came over to me and said, "If you're going to have a very long wait, I'd like to have dinner with you." I said, "Gee, that sounds nice!" So I checked my bags and he and I had dinner together. I found out a lot of nice things about him and really liked him. Anyway, he said he'd call me in New Jersey where I live and maybe I'd spend a weekend in New York with him. I thought that didn't sound bad. I was on my way to Georgia and he teased me, saying, "Why can't I come to Georgia with you?" I said, "Huh? And meet my son, who'll think I'm nuts?" When I got to Georgia and I described this guy to my son and daughter-in-law, I said, "He was such a nice person. He really turned me on!" At which point my daughter-in-law said, "Mother, not in front of the children!"

There is no question that in the American society sex is reserved for the young. Advertising consistently reinforces this view. Although older women have recently been included in ads for cleaning products and food products and headaches, they are never included in the sexier commercials for perfumes and hair sprays. This notion that older women are not sexual has been internalized by many women. Therefore, the fear that most of us who consider our sexuality to be important is that we will somehow lose this rewarding part of our lives as we grow older.

Apparently this need not be the case; most of the women we interviewed were still very sexual. Some had been married forty years or longer and continued being sexually active. Others were divorced or widowed, and of these latter women, some were still sexually active while a few had not had a partner in quite a while and used masturbation as their main sexual outlet. Of the women who were still active sexually, by themselves and with a partner, the most common response was that sex continued to be enjoyable for them. Jesse, a sixty-year-old artist who is divorced, emphatically told us:

Although my sexual experience now is spasmodic, I find the rare occasions when I have sexual partners very enjoyable because it feels so special and has taken on more of a fun aspect than I ever experienced in my thirty-year marriage. That's interesting when you think about people sixty years old because supposedly their sexual need lessens. Maybe it does, but also there's a greater capacity to enjoy it, at least for me. I think your capacity to enjoy is greater because there aren't the same demands. Hopefully you are in control of situations by this age and you don't need to respond sexually just because someone else is needy. You're reacting to your own sexual needs and desires. There's also no fear of unwanted pregnancies. The result is you can be much freer sexually and much more orgasmic, which is the case for me. Orgasm used to be quite rare in my marriage. Frankly, I didn't know what I was missing, but now, I just expect to have an orgasm whenever I have sex.

THE MEANING OF SEX

The specter of death—their own and their contemporaries'— was much more a part of life for older women and influenced their feelings about sex and relationships. It was not unusual to hear of friends, close or distant, who had recently passed away. Deaths in the family were harder to deal with, but not as unexpected as they would have been when they were younger. For Janet (sixty-three, divorced, retired) death made her more accepting and appreciative of her friends and more conscious of how important a close, loving relationship with a man is for her:

If it does anything, death causes one to accept friends as they are. You're no longer terribly shocked at the death of a friend because so many of your contemporaries are dropping off. Which in turn makes you more aware of your own vulnerability. As the saying goes, you never know for whom the bell tolls. More and more of your friends are dying off, so you treasure those you still have and want to keep them, good or bad; whatever they do, they're your friends. Your older friends who have known you so long are very dear to you. You are more accepting of men in any type of relationship you have. And I'm quite sure that if I didn't have this present relationship, I'd seek another. I don't know how I'd go about it, but I would find somebody. Being close to another person of the opposite sex is very, very comforting at this age.

Self-Acceptance

Living with the daily awareness of death had several profound effects on the women. For many, it caused them to be more analytical about the fabric and meaning of their lives—what they regretted, what they valued. For some it provided the impetus to change certain attitudes or facets of their lives that they were unhappy with while there was still time. As they grew older, the importance of certain activities changed, the meaning of certain relationships changed. One of the most positive aspects that occur as one gets older is greater self-acceptance. People, especially those who have continued to grow, come to grips with who they are or who they aren't. There is an acceptance of their lives with its triumphs, its mistakes, and its limitations. They have made a certain peace with themselves.

Janet, continues, describing how she feels freer and more her own person than ever before:

You can be much more your own person when you're older. The problem of pregnancy is gone. That's no longer a threat. And you're your own woman. You do what you want to. If you want to have many lovers, you can, if you're fortunate enough to find them. In my case, I'm happily situated with this man whom I've been seeing for almost twenty years, so I don't contemplate exploring any further. But of course, I wouldn't throw that out the window if it presented itself. And yes, I feel comfortable with myself. By the time you're sixty-three years old, you know that your career is certainly behind you, and if you haven't saved enough money, invested in something, God help you, so you feel secure financially to a reasonable degree, at least I do. So that's a good thing.

She then goes on to explain how this state of mind affects her sexuality:

I think it helps because you don't have all that on your mind. If you're at ease with yourself and your circumstances, you can relax. For me, good sex has to do with being completely relaxed and at ease with myself. In fact, you almost have to relax to get any enjoyment out of sex, really.

Greater inner peace or inner calm results in greater self-confidence, which has a positive effect on relationships. There is less concern with how others will judge a particular action and less concern that an action will cause a rift in a friendship or relationship. This freedom from harsh self-judgment, this greater sense of self-acceptance can have a liberating effect on sexual relationships. Tara, sixty-three, describes how sex with her husband became better over the years:

We've been married for over forty-two years and our sex continues to get better, mainly because our whole relationship keeps getting better. We're very much in love and we always have been. Over the years we've built up even more love and respect, which increases our enjoyment and ability to experiment and discover new things about each other sexually. When I was very young, and we were first married, we had a lot of sexual inhibitions. There were much stricter sexual codes then, so I think my awareness of the possibilities of joy and experimenting was much more limited, but our relationship helped me to grow beyond those limitations. When I think about the sexual part of my life, I can't separate it completely from my whole life—it's not something separate over here. Our whole life-style, everything about it, has changed quite a lot because we've been open to growing and learning. We've changed our life-style several times and I think that has gone hand in hand with changes in our sex life.

Jesse (sixty, divorced) feels that her years have helped her gain a new perspective of herself and her relationships—a perspective that creates fewer demands and provides her with greater enjoyment:

My emotional maturing has had a tremendous effect on my sexual relationships. I no longer expect the same kind of leadership, I suppose you'd call it, that I expected when I was younger. Then I expected the man to be the aggressive partner, to be the one to initiate any change in the relationship or in the sexual act. This is no longer the case. It becomes more a partnership, almost a working together or playing together, rather than my being the passive one. This has carried over, too, in attitudes that are not directly sexual, but are the result of a sexual relationship, where suddenly you expect much more from someone you have had sex with than you would from a man you have known casually, and I've learned to separate that out. It's sort of complex. Initially, once I had a sexual relationship with a man, I expected him to be much more thoughtful, much more concerned, much more wrapped up in me as a person. I certainly found out that my dependency needs got exaggerated when I had a sexual relationship with a man. I suspect it's a very common thing for women to suddenly become very dependent and put a lot of unrealistic expectations on a man just because he happens to be their sexual partner. Once I was able to spot this, then I could look back over the years when I was much less independent and much less mature where that seemed all right in the framework of the marriage, but now I enjoy sex as a temporary experience and do not let it influence the whole relationship. We remain friends and the relationship is essentially one of friendship without getting caught up in the whole romantic ideal.

Oftentimes, the perspective of the later years helps facilitate a shift in emphasis from sexual performance to the interaction, the intimacy, and the comfort found in a loving relationship. Betty felt this very strongly and shared with us her philosophy and how it reassures her partners:

The whole concept of performance has no place in the bedroom. It's just a hindrance to orgasm. If you start feeling the need to perform in sex, it's going to get in the way. So the first time I have sex with a man, I state that my interest is primarily one of contact, wanting some physical closeness, intimacy, and caring. If I know the man well enough I tell him that it's of very little importance to me, after the many thousands of orgasms I've had in my lifetime, whether or not I have another. That's not my goal. Hopefully, it won't be his either, because in my own experience I have found that when that's the goal, it gets in the way of sensual enjoyment, and relaxation. I must confess that with men sixty and over, this philosophy is an essential part of having a good sexual relationship, because my experience has shown that they often need this kind of help. They are so concerned about performance and orgasm that it gets in the way of having an erection, or sustaining an erection. Any bit of anxiety will just wreck it. I'm especially talking about early encounters, where people don't know each other very well so there's a lot anxiety. It's essential to work to allay that anxiety first, and it has nothing to do with technique. It has to do with caring enough to sense that anxiety and put it to rest.

PHYSIOLOGICAL CHANGES

An important factor determining a woman's enjoyment of sex in her later years is her level of physical health and fitness. After all, sex is a physical activity. The more carefully we maintain our health through proper diet, exercise, and manageable levels of stress, the healthier we will remain. And this health is often reflected in an active sex life.

Menopause

But even given the basic foundation of good health, women experienced some sexual changes as they grew older. However, it was very difficult to tell which sexual changes the women experienced resulted from the psychological changes involved in growing older and which were the result of physiological changes. This interrelationship was even further complicated for women because of the biological process of menopause. In 1900 the average life span of an American woman was forty-eight years,‡ which is usually just at the beginning of menopause. Nowadays, a woman's average life span is seventy-seven.* It's only fairly recently that women have lived considerably past menopause and that there has been a need to attend to the problems of sexuality and the post-menopausal women.

Although menopause is an important part of a woman's maturing process, women have tended to hide its effects and are embarrassed to discuss it. For most women, it is a deeply mysterious topic and, because of its social ramifications, one which they make little attempt to learn about. In actuality, menopause is a natural physical process by which nature prevents conception in women who would be too old to safely bear children.

Menopause is the shutting down of the female reproductive sys-

‡ *Vital Statistics of the United States*, Vol. 2, Sec. 5, Life Tables. (U. S. Department of H.E.W., n.d.).
* *Vital Statistics of the United States*, Vol. 2, Sec. 5, Life Tables. (U. S. Department of H.E.W., 1977).

tem. What happens is that the egg sacs begin to decline in number until they can no longer provide the estrogen and progesterone, the two hormones which cause the menstrual cycle. So the cycle stops. This process is a gradual one and goes on usually over a period of about five to ten years from beginning to end. At the end, there are no longer any functioning egg sacs of any kind. No eggs produced, no periods; the system is completely shut down. The symptoms of menopause are the result of the gradual decline in estrogen production. As the estrogen level declines a woman begins to experience hot flashes, her vaginal discharge diminishes, the vagina itself decreases in thickness due to the loss of its outer cell layers, and the labia lose their fullness. As a result, women sometimes find intercourse painful due to the lack of moisture, the actual shrinking in the size of the vagina, and the vagina's decreased elasticity.

The women we interviewed who had remained sexually active seemed to experience the fewest physiological problems. This appears to confirm Masters and Johnson's findings that a consistent and regular sex life in itself prolongs the ability to maintain sexual activity later in life.† Regular intercourse seems to better maintain the vaginal secretions and retard the shrinking process. Many women don't know that the best thing they can do is to continue having a regular sex life. When they stop, this atrophy accelerates. Women who have continued sexual activity do not exhibit the same dryness, the same painful intercourse, as women who have infrequent sex or no sex life at all. Actually any sexual stimulation —masturbation, oral sex, or intercourse—helps to retard this process because they all stimulate the response cycle and generate increased moisture and increased engorgement. In other words, the longer you continue to use it, the less chance you have of losing it. This makes sense; as with any other part of the body, the more exercise it gets, the healthier it remains.

Edith (sixty-six, married thirty-seven years) tells about beginning to experience a lessening of lubrication which sometimes results in painful intercourse:

During the last year or two, I have had less of a need for a feeling of penetration and more of a need for clitoral stimulation. I guess I

† *Human Sexual Response* (Boston: Little, Brown and Company 1966).

haven't wanted as much vaginal penetration because it was uncomfortable. I've never had any difficulty with lubrication in the past, but lately I've been a little sore. I probably should use a lubricant.

However, it should be noted that there were quite a few older women who said that they had no difficulty with lubrication. For those who did, jellies and creams were recommended, particularly estrogen creams for nurturing the mucous lining of the vagina after menopause, when natural estrogen replenishment had ceased. Another woman who is a nurse practitioner offered older women the following advice:

When women say they're dry all the time, I recommend hormone creams which restore the vitality of the vaginal opening so they can function, and K-Y jelly for penetration. All the women who use the hormone creams call back a month later and say that it works wonderfully and they feel great!

Glenn (seventy-two) has a simple solution for preventing painful intercourse:

Many women I know in my age bracket have vaginitis simply from a dry condition and I've never had that. But I do notice that, if I'm going to have intercourse, it's a good idea for me to find some cream and to use it very discreetly. I put it inside of my vagina, as there is less natural secretion there. It's less embarrassing if I just go ahead and take care of it ahead of time.

The estrogen treatment of hot flashes, which often accompany menopause, and vaginal atrophy is a modern phenomenon. Estrogen is a growth hormone, responsible for all the growth changes in puberty. It causes cells to grow as well as being responsible for the production of cells and tissues in the lining of the uterus, that are then sloughed off at menstruation. Estrogen-replacement therapy will definitely relieve the menopausal symptoms of hot flashes and vaginal atrophy. The secretions will be reestablished, the labia will become fuller and the vagina more elastic.

Unfortunately, estrogen has been demonstrated to cause or accentuate endometrial (uterine) cancer. Research indicates that one to three women in one thousand will contract endometrial cancer per year. After menopause, the risk increases four to ten times for women taking estrogen, especially when they take it for extended periods of time (five years or longer).‡

Katrina, fifty-seven, married twenty-seven years, a registered nurse who works in a women's health clinic, believes that many women who take estrogen for relief of their symptoms, in fact take it for psychological reasons. Menopause is a physical happening in a woman's life, it marks the end of her reproductive cycle. But it is a psychological and cultural turning point in her life as well. She explains:

In our society, menopause is the time when women more or less lose their function. At least in my generation, we were taught that our function in life was to produce and nurture children and when we were no longer able to do this, our function was gone. Also, we live in a society that literally worships youth, and when a woman has hot flashes she knows her youth is fleeing and she gets depressed, perhaps because she starts feeling worthless.

Many more women than need to are taking estrogen, mainly because they think it's going to relieve their depression. This depression is not physically caused by the hot flashes, except that the hot flashes may be exacerbated by the depression. The hot flashes are caused by lack of estrogen and the depression is caused by feeling that they no longer have a viable function in their families.

Most of the women we interviewed, perhaps because most have had interesting careers, satisfying marriages, or love relationships, were not unduly depressed during menopause. Aside from some lubrication difficulties and some lessening of desire, most women experienced no change in their sexuality after going through menopause. Jesse (sixty, divorced):

I never noticed any change sexually, not at all, as far as sexual need or activity is concerned either during menopause or after. I went

‡ Jick, Hershel, et. al. "Replacement Estrogens and Endometrial Cancer." *The New England Journal of Medicine.* Feb. 1, 1979. Pp. 218–22. Most physicians recommend low doses of estrogen in combination with progesterone for shorter periods of time for hot flashes and accompanying discomforts and the local use of estrogen creams, which is of lesser risk because of the low dosage, for vaginal atrophy. For long-term use, nonhormonal preparations have proven effective and injections of a noncarcinogenic progesterone derivative, has been effective for hot flashes. Also recommended is vitamin E—up to 1200 units per day.

through my menopause in my early forties. It was hard for my doctor to understand, but even at that time, I saw absolutely no interference or influence on my sexual activity because of my menopause.

In fact, many women who had reached menopause, like women who had undergone a hysterectomy, felt freer sexually because they no longer had to worry about becoming pregnant. Ann (fifty-nine, married thirty-six years):

The older I get, the freer I feel because I don't have to worry about contraception. I hated using the jelly and diaphragm. In my day it was called a pessary. I didn't want to use it, much less touch it. My husband would insert it—that's how much I didn't like it. So you see, I really enjoy not having to use a contraceptive. Sex has gotten better, more spontaneous, which I prefer. I still think, "Isn't it great that I don't have to worry about getting pregnant!"

Reduction of Energy

Age often brings illness and physical problems, which in turn may result in a decrease in physical strength. Not being as physically strong may mean that certain intercourse positions are more taxing than they had been in the past. This was by no means true for all the women we interviewed. Some felt that their lovemaking had not changed despite the years, but others felt some intercourse positions were too strenuous, so they developed others that were more comfortable. Bernice (sixty-seven, married forty-two years):

At this time I'm really not feeling as strong, so I can't be on top. Our best position is where we're both lying down. I'm on my back and my husband is lying on his side. He's at a right angle to me and I have one leg over him and one leg between his legs. At our age, it's a more restful position.

Miriam (ninety-one, widow):

At my age, people think you lose your sexual interest, but mine has always been very strong. It has always been easy for me to have orgasms. I've always been a very sexy lady! Since my husband died, it's become difficult for me to find a boy friend since so few men are alive to go around for all the women, and also because I was living with my daughter. Things changed though when I met George in Florida. He is younger than me and he only has eyes for me. He's eighty-nine, so don't tell him my age. George and I have a new way of doing it. First, we pile the bed with pillows and I lean back against the pillows with my hips down by the edge of the bed. I wouldn't want him lying on top of me with his big stomach. He would crush me! So he sits in a chair at the edge of the bed. Then he rubs his penis around my vagina and I have lots of orgasms this way. I don't like him to put it inside me because it hurts, so he just rubs it along the outside.

Some women found as they grew older they felt more tired, had less energy to devote to sex, and, consequently, felt satisfied with less sex than would have previously pleased them.

Jessica (sixty-seven, divorced):

Sex isn't as active physically now as it used to be. I'm satisfied with less physical activity, less thrusting, less gymnastics. I'm seeing a lovely gentleman now who is seventyish and our sex is less active because we're both getting older and we have less energy. I'm also satisfied with less. I enjoy our sex and our relationship and now I have someone to take me out whenever I want to go. We have a very good time and we're very nice to each other, but our sex is just not as active as it used to be.

Ann (fifty-nine, married thirty-six years) explains how less sex is not necessarily a negative thing. The sexual touching between her and her husband continues, it just doesn't lead to intercourse as often and their need for intercourse seems to be more mutual:

As we've gotten older, we're much more conscious of how good it is to just hug each other. We hug each other morning and night, and it's a new pleasure every time we do it. We don't get out of bed without hugging. There was a time when I was younger when I was almost afraid to get into that nice, warm intimacy because then Steve would want sex. In my mind, hugging led to intercourse. There would be times when I really didn't want intercourse, so I would be more cautious about hugging and cuddling.

And now, somehow it's okay. I guess we have a sense of our own limitations and our desire for sex is much more mutual so it's okay to do all the hugging we want. Before Steve was always ready. It seemed to me he spent his whole life being ready for sex. I didn't. If I didn't want sex, I would be quick to hug and turn over. Now I'll stay and hug and touch him until we're ready to go to sleep. Now we have an appreciation of how good it is to be together without sex.

Due to lessened energy, some women saved sex for those times when energy was highest. Ann continues:

We like to know that our time is all ours, so we make love on a night when we don't have to do anything in the morning. And then there's no question of how exhausted we're going to be the next morning. Steve can get up and play tennis if he feels like it, but I really have limited energy. I think it's because I'm getting older. So it's good for me to know that I don't have any responsibilities the next morning. Then we can have kind of ongoing continuous sex in the night and sometimes in the morning. Sex has always had the sense of a party feeling for us. Sometimes we say, "Listen, this Friday night . . ." and we anticipate it. We kind of set the time. And sometimes Steve wakes me up in the middle of the night because in the morning we'll have to rush out to do things. So when he wakes me up at three in the morning, it's always all right and I'm kind of tickled.

While loss of energy was typical, Charlotte (sixty-seven, divorced, retired) believes it is unnecessary to be satisfied with less:

Nothing will happen that you don't expect and if you think, that as a result of getting older, people have less energy, physically or mentally, then you'll expect to have less energy and you'll put out less energy in situations. Therefore, you'll get less back. You need to be on the lookout for that attitude; so you can overcome it; otherwise, you'll make it true.

Sexual Desire

Along with this slowing-down process, many of the women stated that they no longer felt as turned on sexually as they had in the past. They would still get turned on by specific physical stimulation, but they did not feel sexually aroused unless they were in the process of lovemaking and the appropriate touching was taking place. Betty (sixty-five):

Generally, I don't have a lot of sexual feelings like I used to when I was younger. I also don't seem to get turned on as easily. I can still have an orgasm at will. I can still masturbate successfully, but I don't feel turned on unless we're in the process of making love and my partner is doing something to me that starts to arouse me.

Janet (sixty-three) sees no change in her sexuality as she's gotten into her sixties, except that:

The urge to have sex is not as compelling as it used to be. However, when I am with my present partner, and we start to make love, it is just as good as it ever was. In fact, this week I really didn't think I was much interested, but I was. I had five or six orgasms that night, so that wasn't true. Sex is as good as ever.

Seventy-two-year-old Glenn also sees a change in her sexual drive, but attributes it to causes other than the aging process:

The only change I can see is that I don't feel as great of a sexual need. For instance, it used to be that if I wasn't having sex that often, it would have bothered me a great deal more. I can't say my change in feelings is due to my age. I think I've just adjusted to the fact that there aren't as many partners available. I think if there was a steady available sex partner, I would be just as interested in sex as I was when I was thirty.

Most of the women who felt less of an internal sexual need, for whatever reason, experienced a decline in sexual expression through masturbation. It was not that they could not masturbate, it was just that the same urge was not present. And since, with masturbation, there is no partner to begin the arousal process, many women seldom used masturbation. Bernice (sixty-seven, married forty-two years):

I don't masturbate anymore. I used to, years ago, when Alan would be out of town for a week or two on business. But now it just doesn't occur to me. I don't seem to have that sexual drive without any outside stimulation anymore.

Betty:

My masturbating has become very infrequent. I don't seem to need it as much. I use masturbation occasionally as a way to go to sleep if nothing else works. My life is so lacking in physical activity that I don't get tired enough and now and then sleeping becomes a problem, especially if my head is going on about something. I usually try just about anything else first. I take a hot bath, I read, but if nothing else works I use the massager because it's quick. I have a massager which I bought for my scalp and forehead. I used to always use my hands for masturbation, but that takes much longer and since masturbation for me is not so much something I do for the pleasure of it, but rather a way of going to sleep, it makes more sense to use the massager.

Even though Jesse's urge was not as great, she had more fun with sex and enjoyed orgasm more. Jesse (sixty, divorced):

I find my ongoing need for sexual experience seems to be less. I remember having a very strong need for an ongoing sexual experience when I was married, I'd say from age twenty-two through my forties. It was especially noticeable after each childbirth, when I really needed to make sexual contact again. Now I find that it's not that important. This might be merely the fact that I'm not married and it often becomes a matter of availability of partners. One thing I have realized is that masturbation is always an available outlet and, immediately after separation, I used masturbation a lot. This is no longer as necessary.

A few women mentioned that although they were still orgasmic, it was not as easy to come to orgasm as they remembered it being in the past. Some women found ways to deal with this change. Dolly (sixty-four, divorced) found it was easier if she waited a few days between having orgasms. She also developed a masturbation style that seemed to assist her in having orgasms:

It seems to me that it's not quite as easy to actually come to orgasm, perhaps because the urgency just isn't there. I use a lot more saliva on my fingers to continue to keep the area moist and sometimes it's been easier to masturbate in the bathtub, where it's already wet. Generally, I need more foreplay to give me the different kinds of stimulation that bring on an orgasm. Just using more pressure on the whole genital area helps. Sometimes when I'm not quite ready to do the genital masturbation, I caress myself by stimulating my breasts and other parts of my body or pressing on my whole genital area with my hand.

When I get to stimulating my genitals, I use my finger in a rotary way on my clitoris to masturbate. At the same time, I might insert my finger deep into my vagina and move it in and out.

MALE SEXUALITY AND THE AGING PROCESS

Older men, like older women, experience a slowing down of the arousal process. As a part of aging, men are slower to achieve an erection, slower to achieve orgasm. Actually, this change in sexual arousal and ejaculation pattern can often be an advantage. It means that lovemaking is slower, more relaxed. Foreplay and the whole lovemaking process can be longer and more pleasant, which is actually more compatible with the woman's arousal pattern.

Many of the women we interviewed said that men their own age were often impotent or seemed to have lost interest in sex. Many wondered why, and some had just accepted it as part of the aging process, as had many of their male acquaintances.

There seem to be several reasons why this experience might be so prevalent. One is the widespread belief that men lose the ability to achieve erection and ejaculation as they grow older. Since men, in this culture, have their masculinity intertwined with their sexuality, many men experience this slowing-down process as a sign of their termination as sexual beings. This, for many people, is a self-fulfilling prophecy. If you expect this to happen, when the natural aging process occurs you misread that for the beginning of your decline and react accordingly. Virginia (seventy-nine, recent widow, married fifty-two years) told us how this had happened in her marriage and how painful the loss of sexual intimacy was to her even though she and her husband continued to have a loving relationship:

My husband became impotent at about age sixty-five and we didn't have any sex for about ten years. I missed it terribly, but it didn't seem to bother him. We had been separated for three years as my husband was on a government mission. After he got back, he never quite had the same drive. Then we started to have some problems. He could have an erection, but he couldn't do anything. I mean he couldn't ejaculate. That was so painful for both of us. He would work so hard at it and not get anywhere. It was frustrating physically because I wouldn't get any relief and neither would he. It just wasn't fun.

I often thought that God made a mistake somewhere because men seem to want sex less and less as they get older and women want it more and more. That was certainly true for us. I didn't have to worry about pregnancy or using contraception anymore, so sex was easier and my desire went up. But, after that separation, my husband was never as good sexually.

What I finally did was to learn to masturbate. I was already past seventy and my husband had been impotent for a while. It was hard for me to do because I was taught that masturbation was a sin. But reading some books really helped me to change my feelings about masturbation. It was very pleasurable and satisfying. I'm just sad that I didn't know about that when I was younger. Also that my husband and I didn't try to get some help when he started having trouble. Maybe if we had known what to expect and what to do about it, it would have made a difference. It's not right to be so ignorant about these things.

Many of the women talked about ways they could help their partners maintain their erection. The most common ways were by giving him more prolonged and direct stimulation, particularly penile stimulation. Some talked about using lotion on his penis and manually stimulating him and others suggested more oral sex. Some of the women found that certain positions were helpful in aiding their partner in maintaining his erection. Gweneth (forty-four, married twenty-one years):

My husband is considerably older than me and sometimes has trouble maintaining an erection, so we use a position that makes it easier for him. We enjoy the position where I'm on top. He usually sits on a chair and I sit on top of him facing him. It's easier for him to maintain an erection if I'm on top.

BODY IMAGE

Evidence of the philosophy that you are as young or as old as you think you are was particularly noticeable when women described their feelings in regard to the normal physical changes their bodies had undergone over the previous years. Some women felt no change in their self-image, or even felt better about their bodies than they ever had in the past. These women tended to be very conscientious about taking care of themselves; they ate properly and exercised regularly.

Eileen, a sixty-three-year-old accountant, divorced and the mother of grown children, says:

I like my body. When I go swimming or I'm in the steam room, I think my body is just as attractive as girls in their twenties and thirties. I know when people find out my age, especially when I'm in a bathing suit or don't have any clothes on, they're really surprised. My body is very firm, probably because I swim half a mile every day. I feel more positive about my body than I did when I was little. When I was a teen-ager I was very self-conscious. If I walked down the hall in school and some guy looked at me, I would be sure that my slip was showing. Then I never felt relaxed in a bathing suit. When I look at pictures of myself as a teen-ager, I realize that I had a gorgeous figure and it makes me very sad because I was just so self-conscious then.

Jessica (age sixty-seven):

My self-image has not suffered as I've gotten older. I know I look good. I feel beautiful and I think I feel that way because of the compliments I get from men and because I keep myself in good shape. I watch my diet and don't get overweight. I have a lot of energy so I'm very physically active, even though I don't do formal exercises. I take good care of myself.

Other women felt very negative about the changes their bodies had been undergoing. Some of these women had never felt good about their bodies and their feelings during their later years were merely an extension of the self-image they had always had. Others had gained weight in recent years, which in turn made them feel badly about their bodies. In both cases, a woman's negative feelings about her body was definitely a factor which stood in the way of finding or maintaining a good sexual relationship with a partner. Betty, a sixty-five-year-old mental health professional with grown children, felt this way:

I've had six pregnancies and I got pretty big with some of those. I don't think my body has ever recovered. When I lose weight, my body actually looks worse because I get all wrinkly. It's been such a hang-up for me that I've even asked my doctor if he couldn't do some cosmetic surgery.

Actually, my feelings about my body aren't new and therefore aren't all due to the aging process. I've never felt good about my body. I was painfully thin until I was almost thirty, and I mean painfully thin— like about a hundred pounds. After that, the only time I really felt good about my body was when I was pregnant, because I was supposed to look that way. That might have something to do with why I had five kids, but we planned to have five from the beginning. The way I feel about my body has had more of an impact on my sexuality than anything else. I don't feel free to ever walk around nude or to fulfill any fantasy movements or positions, or to have the lights on, or to dance around with a partner, or any of the things I would do otherwise. If I thought I had a good body I'd be a wild creature! Because I don't, I keep myself very inhibited and closed in since my feelings not only place restrictions on whom I'll be seeing, but also on my movements. The negative feelings affect the entire sexual experience.

Dolly (age sixty-four):

My increased weight makes me feel less attractive. I have sometimes thought if I really had a chance for a good relationship with somebody, it might motivate me to do something about my weight. What I'm finally realizing is that I'm just going to have to do it for myself.

However, it was interesting that many women who had not exercised, who had gained weight, and who by objective standards had bodies in similar shape to the two women mentioned above, still liked their bodies. Also, they did not find that the changes their bodies had undergone were affecting their sexual relationships. Jesse (age sixty):

It's strange that there isn't more of a difference in my self-image as a sexual woman because from day to day I find I'm getting broader and broader around the waist. I'm very conscious of the loss of my youthful figure, but strangely enough, it doesn't seem to have interfered with my sexual relationships. That whole preoccupation has dropped now, the relationship is more important to me than how I look. Sometimes I think, "I wonder why I have not gotten to be uncomfortable about the way I look with no clothes on."

In day-to-day life, however, how I look is very important to me. I try to keep up with my exercises and to do something about my weight. However, I notice that if I'm relating to a man, it is the personal relationship that I'm concentrating on, and my bulging belly and pendulous breasts don't interfere. I forget them. Particularly if I'm with a partner who is sexually skilled and who is interested in me as a person. My bulging belly and pendulous breasts aren't important to him, so why should they be to me?

Charlotte (age sixty-seven):

I don't think your body has to change as a result of the aging process. Some things may sag and certainly do. There's no doubt that I have sagged in many places even though I still weigh almost the same as I did when I was married at the age of twenty-two. I had a real figure then, no question about it, and I don't anymore. But my skin is still soft and supple and except for my potbelly, I really haven't done too badly.

I went through a period, probably between fifty-five and sixty-five, when I sort of put myself on the shelf sexually and tried to face the fact that I no longer thought I could possibly attract or interest men. I felt vaguely defensive about it, but what has helped me overcome that negative attitude was meeting someone who was really supportive. I doubt if I could have changed my attitude and felt more attractive by myself even though I've always been interested in clothes and looking well. I've also been fortunate to inherit genes that will really prevent me from ever getting very gray for several more years, but I think the important thing I had to face was that I thought I couldn't look very good anymore to a man because of my saggy belly. I guess I needed a man to tell me I was still attrractive, and without that, I thought I was no longer attractive sexually because I was aging.

FINDING PARTNERS

A woman's feelings about her self-worth and attractiveness as a sexual woman seemed to influence her ability to find a partner. Some women still had qualms about the changes in their bodies over the years, but were able to forget about these feelings long enough or not let them interfere with attracting a partner, and attaining this relationship in turn enabled them to feel better about themselves and more desirable. As one woman confided: "When I'm in a loving relationship it's much easier to feel desirable and sexual."

The problem becomes how to find such a relationship. Even if a woman past sixty feels sexually attractive, she might have trouble finding a man in her age group whom she finds attractive as a sexual partner. Since women outlive men, in general, the number of men left to pick from is relatively scarce in later years.

Many of the women lacked partners because they were divorced or their husbands had died. All had had to face the prospect of a solitary life-style or decide to try to find a new partner. If they decided the latter, they faced the problem of how and where to find new lovers or new spouses. Everyone had different ideas about meeting men. Again, the attitudes the women had about themselves and what they considered appropriate behavior influenced their choice of solution.

One sixty-five-year-old divorced woman, for example, was very successful at meeting men. She had dozens of suggestions, all of which she had tried out at some time in the past. She had even married one of the men she met through an introduction agency. While the other methods had produced no long-term results, she enjoyed dating the men she had met. Her basic attitude was that there were men available if you were willing to be assertive and take some risks:

I seek out ways of meeting men like going through an introduction agency. An introduction agency is similar to a computer dating service. It's a place where you go and fill out an application indicating what sort of man you're interested in. Actually, my second husband was somebody I met through an introduction agency.

My friends discouraged me about doing that and said, "Only misfits go to these places," and I'd say, "Well, I'm not a misfit! And some other equally desirable person might be there too." The one I joined originally attracted people of a higher financial bracket. One of the men I met through that agency was the president of his own company, and interestingly enough, he was trying to reach me the weekend I was off marrying the man I met through the other agency.

I personally dislike indirect ways of meeting men, such as going to church, and maybe, just maybe, there'll be one or two unattached people there. I like to go right to the horse's mouth. I like to either go to an introduction agency or try some activities or clubs that are specifically set up for people who are looking for partners. I don't want to spend two or three years on some opera board that meets once every six months on the chance that I might meet someone. I want to go where it's already established that there are available men and they're in the age group that is suitable for me. I guess I want better odds.

Another thing I feel strongly about is telling friends that I want to meet someone. I saw a woman friend of mine recently and said, "I really wish somebody would call me up and say, 'Have I got a man for you.'" And one week later, that's what she said! Women have to put out a clear statement of what they want. If they go through life the way most of us do, thinking and feeling one thing and doing another, people will not know that what they really want is "A" when they're putting out "B."

Sixty-four-year-old Dolly, who is divorced, felt that the singles organization she actively participated in was important to her at the time:

For many years, I was active in a singles organization. I went to a number of their parties and they resulted in a number of one-night stands. Then I was happy to have a one-night stand, although I didn't think of it in those terms then. I guess I always had the feeling that it might turn into something else. I must say, though, that one affair lasted for about a year.

Glenn (seventy-two, divorced, retired) is an avid traveler and feels that traveling is a good way to meet men:

I have had more sexual encounters with men who became sexual partners when I traveled than when I was at home. Somehow, the farther I got away from home, the easier it was to just start talking to someone or to be receptive to someone approaching me—mainly just because we were both English-speaking people! When you're in foreign countries, you feel like you have an immediate bond with anyone who speaks English. If we also were attracted to each other and liked each other, we both seemed to feel that it was all right to have a casual sexual relationship even if the man might be married. It was simply something we both enjoyed and something that wasn't doing anyone any harm and that was that.

Meeting people right here in the small town that I live in presents problems. There are some women in my age bracket who have a boy friend over a long period of time and it seems to be accepted, but if I were suddenly to acquire a boy friend who lived in my house, the whole neighborhood would be up in arms. Not that it would make any difference, but nevertheless, there would be a lot of talk about it.

Janet, sixty-three, divorced, has been in a relationship for the past twenty years and has a well-established circle of friends. However, she tries to enlarge that circle whenever possible and has the following advice for women who are feeling isolated and looking to meet men:

I think what happens to many women my age is that they stop living when their husband dies or their romance ends and so they don't make any plans, they don't invite anybody in. I think older women say, "I can't be bothered with that." Frankly, if I didn't have enough friends, I would invite men and women over for dinner even if I didn't really know them. There's a home for senior citizens here, for example. Okay, you've got umpteen men and women; invite some of them for Thanksgiving dinner or for a meal. Even though they might be strangers, everyone could be old together. Or if you know somebody that's been recently widowed, invite him over. A friend of mine knows someone whose wife died recently and she's having him over to a party. I don't think it's all that hard meeting men unless you're really looking for a husband. And even that's not hard. I think any woman who wants to get married can find a husband if she's serious about getting married.

A variation on the party theme was mentioned by another woman. She and three or four single female friends of hers would plan dinner parties periodically. Each woman would invite an unattached male friend who they thought might be of interest to one of the other women. This provided a comfortable evening with friends and a safe way to meet new men.

Apparently, given the lack of available men, the difference between women who found partners and those who didn't had something to do with their flexibility and their motivation. When we are motivated to be in a relationship, we project our feelings nonverbally and attract people. Glenn (seventy-two, divorced) realizes that her attitude about sexual relationships might be unconventional, but believes that men pick up her openness and respond accordingly:

A lot of women my age are absolutely terrified at the idea of sex without marriage. That has not been my attitude at all. I think the fact that I am not unwilling to enter into a sexual relationship is apparent to members of the opposite sex. I am not more attractive than a lot of women my age; it's just that men realize that I have a slightly different attitude than most women my age, that I'm not going to jump down their throats if they make a pass at me and that in fact, I'll probably be interested.

She goes on to explain how her sexual philosophy may account for the fact that she has several sexual partners and has not found meeting men as much of a problem as her contemporaries:

I have met several people over the last ten years or so with whom I have been friendly and where there has also been a sexual relationship. There have been no strings attached. It was simply something that both of us enjoyed. We didn't make demands on each other. We knew there was not going to be anything more. I have always been with somebody that I liked. It did not have to be somebody that I have known a great many months nor did it have to go on for any expanded time. We just enjoyed it while it lasted and that was that.

Being Assertive

One of the major difficulties encountered by women over sixty who want to meet partners is the difficulty involved in initiating the contact. Women of this era were explicitly trained to be passive and to wait for the man to make the first move. Although the female role scripting in this country is changing and younger women are experimenting with being more assertive, most women over sixty still find it very difficult to overcome the many years of role scripting, which dictates that a nice woman does not make the first move. If she does, she is considered "cheap" or "forward." Also, many women, like Dolly, hesitate to let a potential partner know of their interest because of their fear of rejection:

Taking the initiative is a risk, and something I've never felt quite able to do. Part of it is being unwilling to risk the rejection. I've not been able to inure myself in advance to the hurt of rejection. That's probably the fear that's operating. I wish I could be like a friend of mine who explained that although you may get rejected nine times, there is always the possibility you may be accepted the tenth time.

I realize in my own life experience that I have found it difficult to ask and the result has been feeling that I am not given to sufficiently. Although I have had great difficulty in being able specifically to make requests, I appreciate it when other people do. For example, and this has nothing to do with sex, my youngest daughter was able to ask very directly for what she wanted and that made it a lot easier for me to give it to her.

Betty (sixty-five, divorced) has spent considerable energy overcoming what she now believes was negative training. She has even tried to teach other women in her age group the skills necessary for starting conversations with attractive strangers. In the following excerpt, Betty describes a spontaneous training session:

Women who can't find partners are women who don't take the initiative. They don't strike up a conversation with men they find attractive, perhaps because they don't have the skills. I'm able to say to a man, "I want to say something to you that's not easy to say, but I'm going to say it anyway." That kind of introduction gets his full attention. Then I say, "I'd like to get to know you better." My introductory phrase takes the edge off the aggressiveness of the second, and what can he do to me? The worst he can do is to freeze, look uninterested, squirm, and/or try to get out of it. Most of the time, whether he means to or not, he indicates an interest because it's so flattering, such a positive stroke. It certainly doesn't do any harm, but in order to do something like that, you have to feel pretty good about yourself. You have to have a pretty strong center of your own.

Let me give you an example: I was having lunch with two women and they were talking about how hard it is to approach someone, a stranger who seems interesting. So I explained my philosophy: "If you make something up that has no truth or energy behind it, it will probably fall on its face. Now, for instance, I've been observing a man sitting over there and all I've thought in my mind is that he has an interesting face." He was the right age for me. His beard was gray and he looked like he might be in his early sixties.

Anyway, I wouldn't go over to him and ask for a match when I don't smoke. That's so contrived that unless I were the greatest actress in the world, it would be too obvious and I'd be very uncomfortable saying that. So I told them, "I'm going to go over there and I'm going to tell him exactly what I was thinking—that he has an interesting face." So I passed by him to get a glass of water and as I came back, I stopped at his table and I said, "I've been sitting over there thinking that you had such an interesting face and I was also thinking that if I didn't share that with you, it wouldn't do *you* any good. So I wanted to tell you that." His response was what you'd normally get. He was flattered and surprised and said, "Oh, you've made my day." That was the end of the conversation and he didn't pick up at all on my comment about wanting to get to know him, so my conclusion was he's either married or he's got some woman somewhere and that's okay. Actually, what I did with him was the same sort of a thing I'd do with a woman. I've gone over to a woman and said, "You must be doing something right, your child is so charming and well behaved and I don't see much of that."

Jesse (sixty, divorced) has another outlook:

I've never gone out of my way to "meet men" and frankly I think this might be a dubious kind of undertaking. The partners I've had since I have gotten divorced have been people I have worked with or have known through my job and our relationship grew out of that. I think if you find people who are compatible, no matter what area of employment you're in, this is where you'll begin to develop a relationship that is very natural and where you will have interests in common. I think when you try so hard to establish something solely out of your own need, you risk the danger of building a close relationship on quicksand, or one that doesn't have the basis to lend itself to an ongoing relationship or even one or two very lovely experiences.

Expanding Options

In general, many of the women who had partners found that their willingness to be open to new ideas and go beyond cultural prejudices meant that they were able to consider more people as potential lovers—people whom earlier in life they might have rejected. The most common prejudices to put aside seemed to be race, age, gender, and religion. Charlotte (sixty-seven, divorced after a thirty-year marriage):

It's a tremendously difficult situation for an older woman to find partners, but I am very happy with my present partner. I was introduced to him on the telephone through a man that I had had an affair with years before. He told me that he had a very good friend in his seventies who was going into a slump because his companion, a lovely woman, had just died. So we got together for coffee and have had a loving, wonderful relationship ever since. He's black and I'm white, but since I was fortunate enough not to be brought up to be prejudiced against blacks, it has been absolutely no problem to me at all. And that attitude really enhances the availability of partners. In fact, my friend has offered to find some men for some of my friends who are my age, but they really cannot make the racial jump I made.

Many women not only saw younger men as acceptable sexual partners, but actually preferred them. Younger men were seen as more interesting, more open, more liberated, and, in short, pre-ferred partners for a relationship. The hardest block for the women seemed to be overcoming their own internal prohibition that the man should always be older, otherwise they would look foolish or people would think they were just desperate. Even though many women might easily accept the idea of a sixty-year-old man in a relationship with a forty-year-old woman, they had difficulty re-versing the scripting. The ones who were able to felt much freer and certainly had more partners to choose from. Jesse:

Actually, younger men always seemed to be interested in me, whereas the same thing didn't occur with men my own age. I really enjoy being around younger men more. They seem freer in many areas than men in my generation. For one thing, they aren't afraid of being looked upon as a bit feminine occasionally, which gives me a kind of added freedom to express any masculine aspects of myself without wor-rying about how they are going to feel about it.

I think younger men sense in me a young attitude, and by that I mean a freedom to be what I want to be, to dare to do what I desire. That is actually the way I live. I'm an artist and I think artists have to have a kind of youthful attitude, maybe because a great deal of art is play, and if you lose that quality of playfulness, you stand in danger of losing your creativity. This playful quality, too, can extend into sex, and really enhance it.

All of the sexual relationships I've had as I've been older have been with younger men. In fact, I've never had a sexual relationship with anyone over fifty-five. The typical age difference has been about fifteen years. My husband and I were the same age, but after I was separated, the partners I chose were much younger. To me, I'm much more interested in the person first, rather than his age. At my age, of course, I'm not interested in an ongoing relationship with a man. I think if I were, age would be more important because it would bring up all the problems of where he would fit in when I'm getting noticeably elderly.

Jessica (sixty-seven, divorced, retired):

It is so easy to meet men, so easy. What I did was to go to graduate school, even though I was much older. And as far as I'm concerned, it's just fine that the men are younger. In fact, sometimes I prefer younger men. I like intelligent, well-educated men, although sometimes the man doesn't have to be so well educated, but age or race really doesn't make any difference. Actually, the reason I think I don't have any problem meeting men has to do with how I feel about myself. I think I'm pretty and I've learned much more about men since my divorce. I've learned how to make them feel flattered and happy, so I'm not having a problem. I could have had any man I wanted in this retirement house and these are old men!

Sex in my marriage was just routine, not very exciting. I was forty-seven when my husband left me for a woman who was twenty-seven, and it was rough! For a while, I didn't like men very much. I was working then as office manager for a large firm in Philadelphia. I had four secretaries under me and was very involved in my work. These executives in the firm who were much younger than I was would come by and say, "Would you like to have a drink?" "Do you want to go to dinner?" and invariably I would say no. One night, a good friend said, "What's the matter with you?" And I said, "They're too young for me!" He said, "Well, all right, turn them down once or twice, but if they ask you the third time, go with them!" So I began accepting and I had a very good time. Then I began to have a very, very active affair with a black man who was the most beautiful man I'd ever seen. He was not yet thirty and I was in my fifties and he was teaching school in the public schools in Philadelphia. He graduated from the University of Pennsylvania, second highest in the class. Then I had an affair with another man who won an award for the finest musician in the country, and that one lasted for four years. It was from these experiences that I learned what sex was all about. I learned about having orgasms and I learned how to play with a man and let him play with me. That had never happened in my marriage. With my husband, there was no caressing; sex was just an act. Sex was intercourse. I had two children and I rarely had an orgasm. We just had sex regularly once a week, maybe twice a week at Christmas, and it was only intercourse, it was nothing else. It was usually over in minutes, seconds. In retrospect, I think I was terribly bored. But while it was occurring I never knew the difference. I think most of my friends were in the same situation.

Many women who had previously held firm convictions about having a spouse or partner of the same religious persuasion when they were younger were more flexible in their later years. It was not that they were necessarily less religious, but rather that the companionship and intimacy offered in a relationship were more important than belonging to the same religious group. Also, now that their children were grown, there was no struggle as to what religion their children would be raised with if their husbands practiced a different faith.

For many, the idea of nonmonogamous relationships had gained far greater acceptance than at earlier points in their lives. Not only did the women feel more independent than they had in their younger days and therefore in less of a need to rely on a man, but they were realistic about the number of men who were available. Hence, many women felt less possessive and more willing to share their partners.

Few of the women we talked with had considered the possibility of a female as an alternative due to the lack of males in their age group.* However, a couple of women were open to this possibility. They enjoyed women and although some had never had a female lover, they said they would consider experimenting in this direction, especially since there were so many more women than men to choose from. Jesse (sixty, divorced):

I found much to my surprise that I had a relationship with a woman when I was in my fifties and the way this came about was very strange. One night I dreamed of having sex with this very dear friend of mine whom I can openly say I love. My response to that dream was the thing that surprised me. Even in my dream I kept thinking, "I should be shocked. This is against everything I have been brought up to be-

* Kate Ludemean. *The Sexuality of the Older Postmarital Woman: A Phenomenological Inquiry.* Unpublished doctoral dissertation. Humanistic Psychology Institute, San Francisco. 1979.

lieve." But the acknowledgment that it felt right made me realize that it couldn't be that wrong. It was from that point on that the sexual relationship developed. The sexual relationship only lasted for a year, but in many ways it was just as gratifying as a relationship with a man.

Although I wouldn't categorize myself as a lesbian, I think this happened because my attitude was essentially toward the individual first and their sexual orientation second.

If none of the previous options were acceptable, masturbation continued to remain a viable alternative for many. Tricia, age sixty-seven, said:

The nice thing about being in your "autumn years" is that you don't have to lose your sexual feelings. If I'm in touch with my body and I feel a terrible desire, I find the time to be sexual. Actually, the way I can tell when I'm sexually frustrated is when I start looking at young kids and they look desirable, and I start fantasizing about them. Then I know it's time to use my vibrator. That way I can't get into any trouble.

However, for a few women, masturbation was not an option. For these women, the negative messages they received about masturbation while growing up persisted, eliminating the possibility that it could be used as a form of sexual gratification.

For many women the awareness of being in their twilight years sharpened their desire to have certain experiences, particularly sexual experiences, before they died. One attractive, energetic sixty-three-year-old widow had recently entered into an affair. Her husband had died the year before, and although they had had a long and loving relationship, their sex life had been disappointing to her. Her new lover placed a high premium on sexual fulfillment and had urged her to learn to masturbate. She did and had her first orgasm at age sixty-three! Then she attended a sexual education group to find out what she could do to have an orgasm with a partner. She said she didn't know how many years she had left, but she decided that she was going to do everything she could to be able to experience a really good sexual relationship. As she said, "I deserve it!"

Betty (sixty-five, divorced) recalled that for the first time in her life, at the age of sixty-two, she had been intimate with two men she was dating:

I never thought I would ever be able to sustain two sexual relationships simultaneously. I still much prefer one at a time, but there was a short period where I did that. My children were goading me into it, saying, "Ah, Mother, don't be like that," and I tried it and found that I didn't die. It happened about two or three years ago. I talked to my children about it and actually their encouragement helped. I started out saying, "Oh, I don't know how I'm going to handle this. Greg's coming back and I don't know how long he's going to stay." They said, "What's the problem?" I said, "Well, I certainly wasn't going to take the position with Gordon that every time Greg appeared, 'you're out and he's in,' and on the other hand, I can't imagine just not going to bed with him." And they said, "They're two separate relationships and you just make plans with them separately."

Seventy-five-year-old Virginia (a recent widow who had been married for fifty-two years) was contemplating having an affair with a man with whom she has had a deepening friendship for the past thirty years:

During the Second World War, my husband served in the Army overseas and was away for a total of three years. During that time I was alone with my children and I developed a close friendship with a neighbor, Philip. Our families spent a great deal of time together. It was during the time of gas rationing and we would often drive each other's families to activities. We became kind of one big family. I developed a great deal of affection for this person and in fact he did for me too. This affection turned into love, but neither of us considered having any physical expression of that love. We have to this day always kept family ties and I have often thought that if I were to marry anyone else, I would have married this man.

My husband just recently died and Philip, who is divorced, and I are very drawn to each other. This is not because I didn't love my husband or I didn't have a happy marriage, but rather that our love has brought us together again. So we have decided to start a relationship as lovers.

This is a monumental decision for me. My friends and maybe even my children will be shocked, but I think it would be too bad not to do it. After all, what's more wonderful than to be wanted and to know someone cares? Also, I think I missed a great deal sexually in my marriage. My husband was impotent for the last fifteen years of our marriage and our sex life was never that exciting. That was a shame and now I want to find out about what I missed while I still can.

So we see that our remaining two or three decades can be a time for adventure if we choose. Perhaps the most powerful general impression we are left with is that sex in our sixties and seventies and even later can be an important and rich part of our lives. The most important factors limiting this, not withstanding health and physical fitness, are the attitudes we hold. We need to be able to think of ourselves as sexual, attractive, desirable women throughout our lives. Sometimes this means challenging old myths about aging and sexuality. Sometimes this means working on ourselves, finding ways to relinquish the negative images that hold us back. We are limited only by the ways in which we define ourselves. We always have the power to choose—to choose to experience something or not to experience it. We never have to do things that we do not feel right about doing, and we can continue to be and feel sexual throughout our lives if we want to.

10

What to Make of It All

Sexuality is a growth process. It begins at birth and continues to evolve and develop throughout our lives. This process is similar to that of someone who graduated from school and is just beginning a business or a profession. At age twenty-three, we would expect this person to be still struggling with her new career. However, once into her thirties, we might expect her to be more comfortable with her job and her responsibilities. She would be less likely to be concerned with the survival of her career and more concerned with developing her interests and talents in other areas. Sexually, a woman in her early twenties might be gaining comfort and knowledge about her sexuality. In her thirties she might be involved in exploring her sexuality within an intimate relationship. In her forties, she might wish to broaden the variety and intensity of her sexual experiences with her partner and so forth. Another woman might reorder this process and begin with variety and experimentation, eventually settling down to a deeper and more emotional sexual experience. For many women, sex will be relegated to the back burner while they concentrate their energies on developing a career, or raising children. During this period they may experience little interest or growth in their sexuality, only to find their interest piqued again some years later as their focus changes and they concentrate more fully on their own personal and emotional needs. And for some women, sex will never be an important part of their lives. They would really be just as content never having sex, if it weren't from outside pressure from their partners and from the media.

At this point we would like to reemphasize that sex has many purposes beyond procreation. It can be a vehicle for expressing caring, affection, and/or love for another person or for yourself; a vehicle for release of tension, stress, or energy; or a playful interlude. The common denominator of all of the above is that the experiences are pleasurable and gratifying, whether on a physical, emotional, psychological, or spiritual level. If sex is not fulfilling, it may be important to reevaluate your sexual encounters and your sexual relationships with others to determine what is missing from these experiences.

Spend a moment to check out your attitude about your current situation. Do you feel it is hopeless? If so, you might look to see if you are possibly setting up a self-fulfilling prophecy. Perhaps by thinking that change is impossible, you do not expend the energy necessary to create change. Not working at it then results in no change, which only fulfills your expectations. However, would change occur if you were willing to put in the additional effort and to take the necessary risks involved? The major risk is that even after working to alter the situation you may be unsuccessful and have to face other alternatives. Some people would find the investment of energy, with no progress to show for it, more upsetting than making no effort at all. Others recognize that no matter what the results are, there is valuable experience and knowledge to be gained from trying something different. This new knowledge and understanding can then be applied to future situations if the current one should evolve unsuccessfully.

Of course, at the other end of the spectrum is the equally valid position that sexual pleasure need not be a priority in one's existence and that putting any effort in that direction at all produces nothing much of value. Often we feel that too much is made of sexuality in this culture so that one's sex life is blown out of proportion from other daily necessities and interests. Consequently, reading this book might just solidify your conviction that you are absolutely content with your sexual life and do not wish to make any changes in it whatsoever.

If you are not content with your sex life, there are a number of options that are available to you. You can do nothing and wait to see how it evolves over time. This does not mean that if you choose not to deal with the issue in the present that you never intend to deal with it. It might mean that your current life priorities utilize most of your available energy, but that you might foresee, in one year or five years or after you get married or find a close emotional relationship or whatever, expending energy in that direction. Or, you may decide that you have been living with a less than optimal or even an intolerable sexual situation and wish to focus on that issue as soon as possible.

Before making any changes in your sex life, it is very important to first very carefully evaluate the situation in its present state; to ascertain what you do and do not like about your current sexual experiences. Gaining this information better enables you to determine and to understand what you would like to experience more of and what you would prefer to eliminate.

You might want to begin by evaluating your relationship(s). If you had absolute freedom to choose any relationship style, what would you choose? Would you prefer to be perfectly free, having occasional sexual relationships as the mood hits you without any serious involvements? Would you choose to have a deep and committed relationship with one person? Would you prefer to have one committed relationship with the understanding that you can be sexual outside the relationship under certain specified conditions?

After you have given this question some thought, you might compare your current situation with your current ideal. Maybe your sexual dissatisfaction comes from not having a committed relationship or because you and your mate have for a long period of time been estranged while continuing to live under the same roof. If you are not in the relationship situation you would prefer, what are some concrete steps you might take to change it? Should you go out to parties or meetings, actively socializing as a way of meeting a partner with whom a permanent relationship might result? This might entail cutting back on the hours spent dating people who are not real possibilities in this direction. You might need to have a serious conversation with your current partner to more clearly define the future of your relationship. Sometimes it is easier to focus on the sexual dissatisfaction than to face some of the larger issues of which the sexual dissatisfaction is symptomatic. If this is the case, and you feel the situation is hopeless, you may want to discuss a possible separation or divorce from the person you are now living with.

The first important step to take is to separate a sexual problem from a relationship problem, often a complex distinction to make. For example, a woman who is never turned on to her husband, but walks around all day feeling sexually aroused and fantasizing about other men, obviously does not have a problem with sexual desire. She has plenty. Why then is she not turned on to her husband? Is it because she hates the way they make love and finds it very unsatisfying or is she so angry at him all the time that her sexual feelings toward him have become buried? If there are extensive nonsexual problems which overflow into the sexual area, you might want to see a therapist to help you straighten out the nonsexual problems and communication difficulties before addressing yourself to the sexual area of the relationship.

If you feel that the basic difficulties lie predominantly in the sexual relationship, we recommend the following process to determine exactly which changes would be most beneficial. To begin with, recollect a few particularly good sexual experiences. Then take each experience separately and imagine it from the beginning to the end. Don't try to rush the process. It may take five or ten minutes to recall the necessary details. First, whom are you interacting with sexually? How do you feel about this person? Go back over the hours preceding the sexual encounter. How did you feel about yourself during that period of time? What had you been doing? Had you been interacting with your partner over that period of time and if so, what kind of interaction had been taking place? When the actual lovemaking began, who initiated it? How did the initiation take place? Where were you at the time? What was the environment like? What kind of touching was taking place? Who was being assertive? Who was being passive? What kind of lovemaking activities transpired? Oral sex, anal sex? Which intercourse positions, fantasy, or sexual talking played a part in the sex? How did the experience end? What did you do afterward? How were you feeling about yourself and about your partner throughout the process?

Repeat the same process, imagining another good sexual experience. Then go through the process one more time with yet a third good sexual experience. What factors do the experiences have in common? Did you gain any better understanding of what facilitates a positive outcome in a sexual experience for you?

Now recollect three negative sexual experiences. Repeat the above process for these experiences to help determine what they have in common. Do you now better understand which factors interfere with creating a good sexual experience?

Once you have determined what you would like to have happen differently in your sex life, in terms of both adding the positive and eliminating the negative, the most difficult step is ahead of you—actually changing the situation. It is important, when trying to make changes, not to move too rapidly. Break the goal down into a number of small steps rather than trying one grand leap. In taking too large a step you are more likely to slip, to not quite make your mark. Then, as so often happens, you might give up the whole notion of change, deciding instead that you have already failed and that any further attempts would only continue to reinforce feelings of inadequacy, depression, and helplessness.

In contrast, taking small steps toward a goal enhances the possibility of experiencing success with each step along the way. This process requires a fair amount of time. It will not provide a total reversal of your sexual situation in a day; but after a number of weeks or months the changes you do make will be more solidly entrenched.

For example, let's say you have determined that sex just isn't as much fun as it used to be; it's too serious; there's too much pressure to perform. A huge step that might lead to failure would be to surprise your partner by arranging for the two of you to attend a group sex party without discussing it together first. Your partner might respond negatively. Or, if your partner responded too positively, you might become anxious, concerned about what you might have started. Either response might produce sufficient anxiety to keep you from enjoying the experience you engineered. It would be possible, however, to subdivide the process into a number of smaller steps. First you could talk to your partner about your desire to lighten up your sexual encounters. Your partner might have some useful suggestions as well, thereby adding to the likelihood of success, particularly since both of you will be working together toward the same goal.

Likewise, you could decide that you would like to try overtly to bring fantasy into your sex life. But since you have never tried this before, you are apt to be uncertain about how to begin. Again, you could begin slowly by talking with your partner about it. If talking to your partner is too difficult a first step, you could ask your partner to read certain portions of this book, possibly those portions you have underlined because of your interest in trying them. Then you might imagine acting out a particular fantasy by daydreaming about it ahead of time. After that, you or your partner could initiate a fantasy for a couple of minutes during your lovemaking. After this brief experiment you might feel more comfortable reverting to your more usual ways of making love, and extending the experiment at a later date.

But no matter which route you decide to take, the process of making changes in your sex life will entail taking a risk. It is impossible to change the status quo without risking. Doing something new always entails some uncertainty. You can never be assured of the outcome. Also, since you are attempting something new, something you have never tried before, you may find yourself being concerned about doing it right, anxious that it won't work according to plan, that it might backfire. You may also be worried about your partner's response—that he or she might be appalled and might not respect you afterward. Or, you might worry about what others would think if they knew—how your mother or father might respond to knowledge of your sexual fantasies or sexual activities.

Our sexual attitudes develop through contact with those who are close to us—our parents, partners, friends. These attitudes and beliefs govern our behavior. As long as our attitudes and activities coincide, we have no need for concern. Problems and discomfort arise only when one's attitudes conflict with one's sexual desires. Oftentimes, in these situations, the person who even allows herself to recognize her sexual fantasies when they contradict the attitudes she was raised with begins to feel bad or promiscuous. It is these feelings that interfere with enjoying sex, not the activities themselves. There is no difference between a sixty-five-year-old woman who is having an affair with a fifty-year-old man and a sixty-five-year-old woman who would never consider such a thing— except their attitudes. One woman is not inherently bad, the other good; one right and the other wrong; both are acting in accordance with their attitudes. Sexual attitudes pose no problems unless they interfere with obtaining the pleasure we seek. Obviously, we are not talking about intentionally hurting another person either physically or emotionally. We are saying that there is nothing wrong with wanting to explore your sexuality further. In the same vein, there is nothing wrong with being content with the way things currently are and desiring no change—even if lovemaking has followed the same pattern for fifty years. You may have followed that precise pattern because of the satisfaction and pleasure it has provided.

If you do feel that there is something you would genuinely like to do to expand your sexual relationship, but hesitate to do so for fear of what others might think, explore your attitudes further. Why would it be wrong? Why shouldn't you have such desires? Is there a voice and a face behind the words? Are these really the values of another—a religious figure, a parent, a friend—that you have internalized as your own? Now that you know who the words originally belonged to, do you wish to keep them? This situation is similar to a daughter who has grown up with her mother's attitude that it is not possible for a woman to become a medical doctor. Because of this attitude, she does not apply to medical school, but becomes a nurse instead. From this point on, she is constantly frustrated. She realizes that she is as intelligent as her physician counterparts, but does not have the same authority or status. Her attitude that women cannot be doctors held her back from getting the appropriate training. If she were able to change her thinking and decide that there was no reason that a woman could not be a doctor, she might free herself to attend medical school and begin the process of becoming a physician. It might be more difficult for her at this point, being a few years older than her medical student peers, but certainly not impossible. However, if she were to have the belief that it was too late, that her opportunity had passed, she might relegate her future to constant frustration and constant compromise, knowing full well that she was capable of much more.

It is never too late. As one sixty-seven-year-old woman told us, "I've recently entered into the most loving, exciting, and by the way, sexually fulfilling relationship I've ever had. And nothing would have happened if I hadn't changed some of my attitudes and been open to his advances." As with this woman, it is no one's choice except your own how you would like to lead your sexual life. You can change your attitudes at any point in your life. And no one, save your partner, need ever agree.

Bibliography

CHAPTERS 1, 2, 3

Blank, Joani. *Good Vibrations: The Complete Woman's Guide to Vibrators.* Burlingame, Calif.: Down There Press, 1976.

Comfort, Alex (ed.). *The Joy of Sex.* New York: Fireside, Simon and Schuster, 1971.

———. *More Joy.* New York: Crown, 1974.

Otto, Herbert, and Otto, Roberta. *Total Sex.* New York: Signet Books, 1972.

Rosenberg, Jack. *Total Orgasm.* New York: Random House, 1973.

CHAPTER 4

Barbach, Lonnie. *For Yourself: The Fulfillment of Female Sexuality.* New York: Doubleday, 1975.

Blank, Joani, and Cottrell, Honey Lee. *I Am My Lover.* Burlingame, Calif.: Down There Press, 1978.

Dodson, Betty. *Liberating Masturbation.* New York: Body Sex Designs, 1974.

Hite, Shere. *The Hite Report.* New York: Macmillan, 1976.

CHAPTER 5

Bach, George R., and Goldberg, Herb. *Creative Aggression: The Art of Assertive Living.* New York: Avon, 1975.

Bach, George R., and Wayden, Peter. *Intimate Enemy: How to Fight Fair in Love and Marriage.* New York: Avon, 1968.

Bach, George R., and Deutsch, Ronald. *Pairing.* New York: Avon, 1970 (paper).

McCarthy, Barry. *Sexual Awareness: A Practical Book.* San Francisco: Boyd and Fraser (copublished with Scrimshaw), 1975.

McDonald, Paula and Dick. *Loving Free.* New York: Ballantine, 1977.

Miller, Sherod et al. *Alive and Aware: Improving Communications in Relationships.* Minneapolis: Interpersonal Communication, 1975.

Satir, Virginia. *Peoplemaking.* Palo Alto, Calif.: Science and Behavior, 1972.

CHAPTER 6

Barbach, Lonnie. *For Yourself: The Fulfillment of Female Sexuality.* New York: Doubleday, 1975.

Becker, Elle. *Female Sexuality Following Spinal Cord Injury.* Bloomington, Ill.: Cheever Publishing, 1978.

Boston Women's Health Collective. *Our Bodies, Ourselves,* "Sex Lessons for an Easier Childbirth." Second ed., rev. New York: Simon and Schuster (Touchstone), 1976.

Brecher, Ruth, and Brecher, Edward (eds.). *An Analysis of Human Sexual Response.* New York: Signet, New American Library, 1966.

Kaplan, H. K. *The New Sex Therapy.* New York: Brunner/Mazel, 1974.

Lansom, Lucienne. *From Woman to Woman: A Gynecologist Answers Questions About You and Your Body.* New York: Knopf, 1975.

Masters, W. H., and Johnson, N. E. *Human Sexual Response.* Boston: Little, Brown, 1966.

Masters, W. H., and Johnson, N. E. *Human Sexual Inadequacy.* Boston: Little, Brown, 1970.

Ctto, Herbert A., and Otto, Roberta. *Total Sex.* New York: Signet, New American Library, 1972.

Scheingold, Lee, and Wagner, Nathaniel. *Sound Sex and the Aging Heart.* New York: Human Sciences Press, 1974.

Task Force on Concerns of Physically Disabled Women. *Toward Intimacy: Family Planning and Sexuality Concerns of Disabled Women.* New York: Human Sciences Press, 1978.

Zellergeld, Bernie. *Male Sexuality: A Guide to Sexual Fulfillment.* New York: Bantam, 1978 (paper).

CHAPTER 7

Bing, Elizabeth, and Colman, Libby. *Making Love During Pregnancy.* New York: Bantam Books, 1977.

Boston Women's Health Collective. *Our Bodies, Ourselves,* "Sex Lessons for an Easier Childbirth." Second ed., rev. New York· Simon and Schuster (Touchstone), 1976.

Lichtendorf, Susan, and Gillis, Phyllis. *The New Pregnancy.* New York: Random House, 1979.

Samuels, Mike, and Samuels, Nancy. *Seeing with the Mind's Eye.* New York: Random House, 1975.

CHAPTER 8

Andry, Andrew, and Schipp, Steven. *How Babies Are Made.* Alexandria, Virginia: Time-Life, 1968.

Bernstein, Ann. *The Flight of the Stork.* New York: Delacorte, 1978 (hard); New York: Dell, 1980 (paper).

Boston Women's Health Collective. *Ourselves and Our Children: A Book by and for Parents.* New York: Random House, 1978.

Gochrost, Jean. *What Do You Say After You Clear Your Throat?* Los Altos: Pacifica Publishing Company, 1979.

Gordon, Sol. *Let's Make Sex a Household Word: A Guide for Parents and Children.* New York: John Day, 1975.

Hamilton, Eleanor. *Sex with Love: A Guide for Young People.* Boston: Beacon Press, 1978.

Handman, Heidi. *The Sex Handbook: Information and Help for Minors.* New York: Putnam, 1974.

Loulan, JoAnn Gardner, Lopez, Bonnie and Quckenbush, Marcia. *Period.* Burlingame, Calif.: Down There Press, 1979.

McCary, James Leslie. *Sexual Myths and Fallacies.* New York: Schocken, 1971 (paper).

Pomeroy, Wardell B. *Your Child and Sex: A Guide for Parents.* New York: Delacorte, 1974.

Radl, Shirley. *Mother's Day Is Over.* New York: Charterhouse (imprint of McKay), 1973.

Selzer, Joae. *When Children Ask About Sex: A Guide for Parents.* Boston: Beacon Press, 1976.

Sheffield, Margaret, and Bewley, Shelia. *Where Do Babies Come From?* New York: Knopf, 1973.

Women's Educational Project. *High School Sexuality: A Teaching Guide.* Amazon Reality Collective, 1975. (P. O. Box 95, Eugene, Oregon 97401) $1.00.

CHAPTER 9

Butler, Dr. Norbert, and Myrna, Lewis. *Sex After Sixty.* Boston: G. K. Hall, 1977.

Comfort, Alex. *Good Age.* New York: Crown, 1976 (hardcover); New York: Fireside, 1978 (paper).

Kuhn, Margaret, and Hessel, D. *Maggie Kuhn on Aging.* Philadelphia: Westminster Press, 1977.

Ruben, Lillian. *Women of a Certain Age.* New York: Harper and Row, 1979.

Index

qualities of good sex and, 1, 2, 6, 20, 30
setting the scene and, 35, 39
unusual sexual experiences and, 95–96, 99
Cunnilingus, 14, 65, 66–68, 94
dislike of, 66
inhibitions about, 179–80
and simultaneous fellatio, 67–68
See also Oral sex
Curlers, 42
Current Population Reports, 299 n
Cystitis, 199

Death, the specter of, 304–5
Déjà vu experiences, 97–99
Delivery, 240–42
Cesarean, 250
yoga and, 241
Deodorants, 39
Diapers, 94–95
Diaper service, 245
Diaphragms, 195–97, 203
bladder infections and, 199
after childbirth, 250–51
use for masturbation, 123
use during menstruation, 95
vaginal infections and, 198
Dildos, 81, 82–83, 122–23
after childbirth, 247
vegetables used as, 83, 122
Divorce, sex after, 189–91
Douches, 39, 197–99
Drugs, 25, 49–50

Ears
kissing, 154, 161
tongue in, 140
Education, xv, xvi, 301
Ejaculation
fellatio and, 66, 67, 179
problems in, 192, 193, 194
Electric blankets, 55
Emanuelle (motion picture), 132
Episiotomies, 241–43, 246
self-healing after, 247–48
Erection problems, 192–94
aging, 307, 317–18
Erotica and Erotic Subjects,
books, 34, 37–38, 77, 78
films, 77–78, 83
magazines, 38, 77, 131–32
masturbation and, 128, 131–33
pictures, 37, 38, 131–32

self-created, 132
See also Pornography
Estrogens, 258, 309, 310–11
Eve's Garden, 53, 126 n
Exhibitionistic experiences, 99–105
Eye contact, 161

Fantasies, 5, 84–92, 339
acting out, 84, 85–86
alcoholic beverages and, 85
breast play and, 38
call-girl image, 86, 90
communication as, xix–xxi
culture and, 88–89
dominance and submissiveness, 87–91
feminists and, 88
Girl Scout, 86
group sex, 84
guilt feelings about, 84
marijuana and, 85
masturbation and, 90, 116, 128–31
music and, 54
oral sex and, 90
orgasm and, 111, 124, 129–30
of the penis, 131
pregnancy and, 222
rape, 88–89
re-creating a first meeting, 85
as secret turn-ons, 84
as a substitute for reality, 91
"tie and tease" games, 87–91
ground rules for, 90–91
travel, 86–87
verbal sharing of, 84, 86–87
Fantasy fuck, the, 12–13
Fears, 2, 216–17
of getting pregnant, 187, 203, 230, 235, 301
of hurting the baby during pregnancy, 220, 238
of rejection, 162–64, 165, 166
of stating sexual preferences, 139–42
Feather dusters for masturbation, 56
Fecal incontinence, 212–13
Fellatio, 65–68
controlling thrusting, 181
ejaculation and, 66, 67, 179
hairstyle and, 67
inhibitions about, 179–81
and simultaneous cunnilingus, 67–68
while watching pornographic films, 78